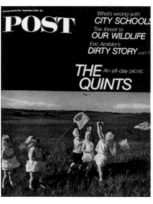

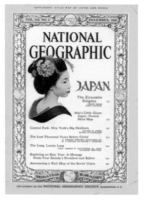

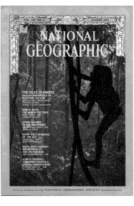

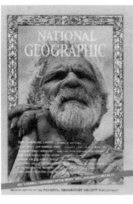

John Launois

COPYRIGHT © 2013 ESTATE OF JOHN LAUNOIS

ALL RIGHTS RESERVED.
PRINTED IN THE UNITED STATES OF AMERICA
FIRST EDITION

PUBLISHED BY PROSPECTA PRESS
P.O. BOX 3131
WESTPORT, CT 06880

COVER AND CONTENTS PAGE PHOTOS: RICHARD WOOD
PROLOGUE PHOTO: KOICHIRO KURITA
BACK COVER PHOTO: COLLECTION OF THE AUTHOR

HARDCOVER ISBN: 978-1-935212-62-1
FOR PUBLICITY / INFORMATION
CONTACT CHRIS PAN LAUNOIS
EMAIL: PANMAIL@AOL.COM
WWW.LAMERICAIN.COM
WWW.THEAMERICANBOOK.COM

BOOK PRODUCER
REGINA RYAN BOOKS
REGINARYAN@REGINARYANBOOKS.COM

EDITOR
ABIGAIL WILENTZ
ABW145@GMAIL.COM

DESIGN BY TIMOTHY HSU
HSU+ASSOCIATES

PRINTED AND BOUND IN CHINA
FIRST EDITION 2013

NO PORTION OF THIS BOOK MAY BE REPRODUCED IN ANY FASHION, PRINT, FACSIMILE, OR ELECTRONIC, OR BY
ANY METHOD YET TO BE DEVELOPED, WITHOUT THE EXPRESS WRITTEN PERMISSION OF THE PUBLISHER.

FOR INFORMATION ABOUT PERMISSION TO REPRODUCE SELECTIONS FROM THIS BOOK, WRITE TO:

PROSPECTA PRESS
WWW.PROSPECTAPRESS.COM

L'AMÉRICAIN

A PHOTOJOURNALIST'S LIFE

JOHN LAUNOIS

WITH

CHRIS PAN LAUNOIS

PROSPECTA PRESS

TABLE OF
CONTENTS

INTRODUCTION

DONALD S. CONNERY

The first American he ever saw fell out of the sky.

In 1943, John Launois was Jean René Launois, a rebellious, high-spirited 14-year-old, who lived with his working-class family in a town near Paris in Nazi-occupied France. World War II was the terrible reality of his childhood: nearly five hard years of hunger, deprivation, oppression, and national humiliation.

One day, the boy watched as the crew of a B-17 Flying Fortress bailed out after being struck by antiaircraft fire. A parachute "wrapped around itself and one young airman fell straight to earth," as John tells us in this book. He raced to the scene but the Germans had already removed the corpse. "Engraved in the soft grass was the imprint of a body."

Ashamed of his country for collaborating with Hitler, the schoolboy despised the autocratic, class-ridden society determined to stifle his chances for a better life and marveled that a faraway country—the United States of America—would send its youth across the ocean to save France.

"I wanted to know more, but all things American were banned. In my mind, I began to create a mythical America. I told so many tales, real and imaginary, that soon my nickname became *L'Américain*."

The youngster fantasized about going to the USA. He would shed his European skin and become one of the free and the brave. He would Americanize himself so completely that no one, not even his own family, would ever again think of him as anything but American.

He succeeded in this transformation far beyond his wildest dreams.

Before the ascendancy of television as the prime purveyor of images, *Life, Look, Paris Match* and the other great picture magazines in America and Europe captured world events for readers who numbered in the tens of millions. During the 1960s and 1970s, the final decades of the "golden age of photojournalism" that had begun in the 1930s, John Launois blossomed as one of the most resourceful, inventive, prolific, highly paid, and widely traveled of the elite corps of press correspondents and cameramen sent to the ends of the earth to record history in the making.

John made himself the master of the deeply researched photo essay and always clung to his independence, selling his pictures and photo essays through New

York's Black Star agency, with his published work appearing for over a quarter century in *Life*, the *Post*, *National Geographic*, *Fortune*, *Time*, *Newsweek*, *Look*, *Rolling Stone*, *Paris Match*, London's *Sunday Times*, and many other American, European, and Asian publications.

I was Time-Life's Tokyo bureau chief in 1960–1962, and before going on to Moscow to cover the Cuban Missile Crisis for Time Inc. and NBC, I worked with John soon after his emergence from poverty and obscurity. In the perilous Cold War summer of 1961, we teamed up for a month-long, round-the-world journalistic coup that propelled him to the top rank of his profession.

It was John—with typical initiative and cunning, his Gallic charm melting the frozen-faced Russian diplomats in Japan—who wheedled a way for us to do the seemingly impossible. Despite the ongoing Berlin Wall crisis that threatened to touch off World War III, we quietly entered the Soviet Union through its Far Eastern back door and rode the Trans-Siberian Railway 6,000 miles to Moscow.

At stops along the way, always under surveillance (and several times accused of being CIA spies), we recorded everyday life in cities and villages and on collective farms that had been closed to Western observers since the end of World War II.

Our editors expected the Trans-Siberian Railway, the world's longest, to be the centerpiece of our story, but as our journey began, the Soviets said it was out of bounds for security reasons. We were forbidden to take pictures "of the train, on the train, or from the train." As John explains in one chapter, we found ways to break the rules. Miraculously, considering the risks we took, we avoided arrest and flew away to Paris and New York with all of our film and notes intact.

That world scoop, told in a black-and-white spread in *Life* and in a lavish color section in *Time*, was promoted as "Two Yanks in Siberia." For John, being certified as an American—a Yank!—by the world's most powerful publishing company was fully as satisfying as his sudden new status as a top-gun photojournalist.

After Siberia, I could only keep track of him by reading the magazines that benefited from his workaholic ways. He seemed to be everywhere: from London with the Beatles, to Cairo with Malcolm X, to the jungles of the Phillipines with a lost Stone Age tribe.

With the passage of years, I found myself ever more fascinated by the makeover of the thin, ill-dressed, insecure, yet fiercely ambitious young man I had first met in Japan. The slight stoop of his nearly six feet, I later surmised, had been acquired as a boy hauling heavy sacks of potatoes for a grocer. His earnest hazel eyes, shaggy auburn hair, and his eagerness to get moving on a story gave him an aura of unstoppable purpose. He was more winsome than handsome. The longing and sadness of his expression—perhaps the result of his mother's taunts that he would never amount to anything—aroused the maternal instinct of female admirers.

As John's accent faded away, I came to think of him as "the un-Frenchman." He smoked filtered American cigarettes instead of the stronger Gauloise or Gitane of his native land. He preferred Scotch over wine, and in ample quantities. He made no great fuss about food. He was more of an American prude, putting women on pedestals, than an all-knowing French lover. Nonetheless, he always had a sympathetic ear. In Kyoto for a *Life* cover story on actress Shirley MacLaine dolled up as a geisha, I observed John's way of attracting the most intimate of confidences from new friends, as his look-alike, French actor Yves Montand, poured out to him his woes of romantic entanglements.

In the field, John wore the usual safari garb of his calling, but as success brought sophistication, his style of dress at home was strictly Ivy League. He was the life of any party, a convivial host, and the inevitable center of attention as he spoke of exotic lands that most people could only dream about. Yet his mood could shift in a week's time from elation about a job well done to a desperate need to get back into action.

In time, as the mass-circulation picture magazines died off one by one, John found no satisfaction in corporate assignments or "just taking pretty pictures." Always the photojournalist, believing in the power of images to expose, inspire, and help make a more humane world, he could not stomach being less a journalist and more a photographer.

At the turn of the century, John told me he was working on his autobiography. He would, of course, tell of his often perilous experiences as a globetrotting photojournalist, but uppermost in his mind was his unquenchable love affair with America.

As a self-described "American idealist," he was forever loyal to the land of his childhood imaginings despite endless disappointments. As I knew from his frequent late-night transatlantic calls, he took personally every lapse of moral leadership in Washington, every display of military arrogance, every sign of hypocrisy by political leaders ignoring social injustice, and every departure from his vision of America's destiny as the shining city on a hill.

I encouraged him to tell his story. The world should know him as a modern Horatio Alger—a striving, idealistic, romantic immigrant who was more American in his sensibilities than most native-born Americans.

As a freelancer who carried out demanding tasks for a wide spectrum of publications, John enjoyed maximum creative freedom, but it had come at a price. He was such a loner that he never became a celebrity. He did not benefit from the *Life* and *Look* practice of promoting their star staff photographers. Even so, editors recognized him as the consummate professional. On one occasion, *Fortune* advised its readers that pictures by John Launois, the "indefatigable and far-ranging freelancer," could be found in four stories on four different subjects in that single issue.

I told John that there was value in his account of a photojournalist's life in that demanding era before satellites, personal computers, digital cameras. and phones that now flood the world with instant images. Today's amateur photographers can transmit pictures in seconds to anyone anywhere on earth, while yesterday's crack photojournalists often found that getting exposed film shipped to the home office by mule or a military flight could be the most challenging part of the job.

What I did not anticipate in John's manuscript was the naked honesty of his personal story. He exposes the demons that clawed at his mind. He is ruthless in blaming himself and his blinding drive to excel for so often distancing himself from his loved ones.

John virtually invites readers to dissect him psychologically as he lays out his contradictions. "An impossible man," according to his son, he was intense, impulsive, generous, self-centered, compassionate, endearing, and infuriating.

John died at 73 in May 2002, his manuscript nearly finished.

Had I known then what I know now, reading his story, I would have told him not to be so hard on himself. He was cherished by those who knew him best. This book has reached publication only because of their devotion and their desire to see that his life as a good man as well as a vastly talented man be more widely recognized.

The dedication to John's memory demonstrated by his first wife Yukiko in New York and his widow Sigrid in Liechtenstein has been critical to this work. His son, Chris Pan Launois, a Manhattan-based musician and song writer, helped create the manuscript, working on its completion as his father's eyesight faded in the years before his heart stopped.

For all three, it has been a labor of love. ●

PROLOGUE

CHRIS PAN LAUNOIS

L'*Américain* is the story of my father, John Launois, an impossible man with a beautiful heart. For most of his life, my father was far away from me, either on assignment or living abroad, but he'd call often to stay connected, exchange perspectives, or simply to say, "I miss you. I love you." On my repeated visits to him in Europe, he'd recount stories of his life with the humor and gravity of a passionate adventurer who had followed his dreams and lived to tell the tale.

As a poor boy in France, he faced a childhood that could have been imagined by Dickens. He once cut off the leather straps of his mother's whips to stop her from using them on his younger brothers and sisters. She constantly told him he was worthless: "You'll never amount to anything."

World War II brought the worst of times. Poverty for the least privileged of the French during Nazi occupation became life threatening, and John's father feared that his children, even if they survived, would never be free. Oppression fueled John's rebellious nature: as he defied the Germans at every turn and listened to clandestine broadcasts about the approaching liberation by U.S.-led Allied forces, the boy fell in love with America.

When free-spirited GIs finally arrived, personifying a democratic society so different from his class-ridden homeland, John was already such an enthusiast for all things American that his friends called him *L'Américain*.

Soon he had developed a grand vision of his future. Idealizing the land of his dreams, he vowed to turn himself into a "Yank" and work for *Life*, the greatest of the picture magazines. With nothing but $50 and a borrowed camera, he crossed the Atlantic. In time, after working a series of menial jobs in California and learning photographic skills, he would cross the Pacific as well.

John finally gained his citizenship while serving as a U.S. Army soldier, then struggled through his "noodle years" of low-paying photographic tasks before advancing to the highest ranks of international photojournalism during its "golden age."

Freelancing for *Life*, *The Saturday Evening Post*, *National Geographic* and many other leading publications, he traveled to the ends of the earth—always enterprising, creative, and fearless in a risky profession.

He covered wars, riots, and natural disasters; mingled with the rich, famous, and powerful as well as the downtrodden; and always marveled that he had come so far from the lower depths.

John was the picture of the globetrotting adventurer—photographing conceptual essays around the world, interviewing presidents, befriending the Beatles and revolutionaries like Malcolm X.

Ultimately, John was a Romantic who loved, lost, and loved again. His two greatest loves—my Japanese mother and my Austrian stepmother—became close friends upon his death. The three of us, drawn together by our affection for such a passionate, contradictory man, had urged him on as he devoted himself to telling the story of his life.

For seven years, my father and I worked on his manuscript. Sometimes it flowed easily; often the task was challenging. He persevered because he felt he owed a debt to the nation that had liberated France and shared her liberty at home. Alongisde so many other brave hopefuls who dared to carve out a better destiny, his name is proudly engraved on Ellis Island.

He once promised a dear friend that he would write this book. It's a memoir of a rebel and adventurous man. To keep a promise, this is the story of *L'Américain*. ●

OCCUPATION

FRANCE AT WAR

MARLY-LE-ROI, FRANCE 1940–1944

I swore allegiance to the Constitution of the United States of America on June 11, 1954, at Camp Otsu, headquarters of the U.S. Army's Southwestern Command near Kyoto, the ancient capital of Japan.

The examiner's only question was, "What is the meaning of democracy?"

I asked, "Do you want the original Greek meaning?"

"Yes" he said.

"*Demo* means people," I said, "*cracy* means government, so essentially it means government of the people, for the people."

He said, "That's fine, you are now an American citizen," and he shook my hand.

Though the test for citizenship took only a few minutes, my American story began many years earlier when I was a boy growing up under the German-Nazi occupation of France in the late spring of 1940.

One morning in our small town, Marly-le-Roi, a few miles west of Paris, panic erupted as huge blankets of smoke spread over the suburbs. We could no longer see the city in the distance. By nine in the morning, all was dark. According to rumors, Paris and the Rouen harbor were burning, and Germans had bombed the oil storage tanks. Others thought the French Army had released smoke screens to prevent German bombers from destroying the city.

For weeks, the streets were filled with refugees in horsedrawn wagons, overloaded cars, trucks, bicycles, and pushcarts. People struggled with heavy suitcases, all going south. Germans were invading from the north and east, and on June 11, Italy's dictator Benito Mussolini declared war on France and sided with the Nazis.

Women and children were advised to go south. The poor at best had only public transportation, and railroad stations were overwhelmed. Wealthy Parisians and suburbanites had already left their homes. Workingmen were ordered to stay on the job, while ministries of the French government burned important documents and packed to leave without warning.

There were rumors of German paratrooper spies dropping over the city, but with so many stories, we knew absolutely nothing. Prime Minister Reynaud spoke on the radio from Tours, telling the French how "heroic the French Army is," as our northern and eastern fronts collapsed.

That night, our neighbor, a lovely woman terrified of the Germans, asked my parents if I could stay the night in her stately house. As I was a child, I had no fear: everything seemed exciting, but adults were afraid with good reason. I was happy to be sleeping in the same bed with *la belle Chantal*, the most beautiful

and elegant woman in our town. Her husband was an officer serving on the northern front and there was no news from him. As darkness fell, she kissed my forehead and we fell asleep.

Next morning at dawn, my father, who, because he

John's parents, Paul and Marguerite Launois.

was a workingman, had to remain behind, bid us goodbye. He told me I was now the man in charge, at 11 years old, and had to take care of my mother, brothers, and sisters. So without father, my family joined our beautiful neighbor in her car. The roads were overtaken by thousands fleeing on foot. Inching our way on the highway to Orléans, we joined the exodus of the poor.

By nightfall, we had traveled only 70 miles and were out of gas, so our neighbor tried to charm northbound officers for fuel; she begged them but they couldn't help. People on foot pushed our car to the roadside.

In a thunderstorm, I left the family in the car and walked across a wheat field to a farm in the distance. The farmer and his wife said we could stay in their barn. In the pouring rain, we all kissed our neighbor goodbye and I led my family across the field. In our haste we forgot all our family photos and documents in her car. Mother carried my 14-month-old brother Jacquot in her arms while three-and five-year-old Odette and Paulette clung to her skirt. Nine-year-old André and I carried the family's luggage and a heavy shopping bag loaded with bottles of boiled milk and a few tin cans of food. Soaking wet, everybody fell asleep on the straw. We never again saw *la belle Chantal.*

With thousands of others, we walked the next day to the Orléans train station. On the long road to the railroad, two Italian fighter planes swept down. Fascinated, I could almost see the pilots' faces. An old man violently yanked my ankle and threw me in the ditch as the staccato of machine guns ripped through the air. The old man yelled, "You crazy fool!" Shocked, I asked, "Why?" He said, "Every time you see a low-flying plane, dive into a ditch!" Only as we marched toward the station and saw the dead and wounded on the road, did I realize the old man had saved my life.

After a long struggle at the train yard, we were herded into a World War I freight car designed for "40 Men or 8 Horses." Sixty old men, women, and children filled our car. There was no food. Threatened by constant bomb alarms, our freight train, pulled by an old steam locomotive, moved so slowly that we could talk to people near stations offering food. We jumped out of the train to gather water, milk, bread, cheese, and sometimes salami. Some people refused my money, while others charged outrageous prices we couldn't afford.

After two days, we arrived in Vierzon in the early morning. We settled in a very small house with mattresses on the floor. Demoralized French soldiers, believing the fight was over, knocked on the door asking for civilian clothes, hoping to escape German military prison camps.

In the late afternoon my brother and I went out looking for something to eat. We climbed a tree blooming with beautiful, juicy cherries. We were so hungry we ate till we were almost sick. Lying back, high up on branches, we suddenly saw a German motorcycle and sidecar with submachine guns approaching the edge of town. Frightened, we ran back to the little house and told mother who locked the door. After several hours, a man in the street began banging on his drum until he saw doors and windows open. "Paris and Vierzon are now under German control," he announced. "The High Command has assured us you may come out of your homes. You have nothing to fear."

We discovered the Germans would not cut off our ears as we had feared. A stranger was kind enough to drive us back to Marly. Again we ran out of gas. To our surprise, we were given fuel by an enlisted man in the German Army.

We returned to our home on June 16 and learned that two days earlier, the Germans had paraded with horses and mechanized forces down the Champs Elysées. The Nazi swastika now waved from the Eiffel Tower and Arc de Triomphe.

Father had a wound on his back but he never said what had happened. In his day, parents were supposed to give children a strong sense of morality and a good work ethic, and they never discussed their problems. However, because he had lived through the horrors of World War I and I was the eldest, he decided to try to prepare me for what we might confront.

On June 18, he took me alone to the kitchen, closed the wooden shutters, and turned on the radio. After a lot of static, we heard a voice from the BBC announcing: "I, General de Gaulle, presently in London, invite the officers and the French soldiers on British territory...with or without weapons...to get in contact with me...Whatever happens, the flame of the French Resistance must never go out and will not go out." Turning to father, I asked, "Who is General de Gaulle?" He said, "I don't know."

By that point, Hitler had taken Czechoslovakia, Poland, Denmark, Norway, Holland, Belgium, as well as France. England was thought to be next. "If England doesn't hold," father said, "I'm not sure you will ever be a free man."

I returned to primary school. Those of us with high scores were placed near the front, which had certain rewards. Our teacher was gorgeous, and by dropping your ruler, you could bend down and look up her skirt. She must have known what we were doing because only the boys in the front would drop their rulers.

In 1940s France, there was no opportunity for the son of a worker to enter higher schooling. The high school lycées and universities were the preserve of the wealthy ruling class. Even the exceptionally gifted could only further their education to the level of an elementary school teacher.

Because of my high grades, I could graduate immediately, a year early. My teacher came to my home and urged my parents to continue my education so I could become a teacher, saying I'd succeed in anything I chose. While my father was proud and enthusiastic, my mother yelled at him, "You don't even make enough to feed us and the five children, let alone the one I'm carrying! Jean must work. He has to work!" Father valued education, but mother had worked since she was 12 and couldn't see why I shouldn't as well. My teacher was sorry but understood mother's fears. I walked my teacher to the door and said goodbye, saddened but aware of my duty.

The economy slowed to a crawl. No jobs were listed. In the Paris region, half a million were unemployed. Factories shut down. Posters went up everywhere with curfew hours, restrictions, and rules of occupation. Most of the first harvest was requisitioned and shipped to Germany as were most goods and resources. Everyone had ration cards. Only parents with infants got milk, while coffee and chocolate disappeared completely. Though gasoline was reserved for only the privileged and emergency services, the rich could buy anything on the black market.

Eve, Lido, Folies-Bergère, and famous nude cabarets in the capital played to German armed forces and were packed every night. Some 40 whorehouses were reserved exclusively for the German infantry. Movies, theaters, and operas remained open. Champagne flowed endlessly. For the Germans the spectacle went on as though nothing had happened, but for the French there was an eleven o'clock curfew.

On July 3, after the commander of the French Navy refused to allow the fleet to join England or sail to America to keep ships from falling into German hands, the British Navy, following a six-hour ultimatum, destroyed much of the French fleet anchored in Mers el-Kebir, Algeria. Twelve hundred French sailors lost their lives.

In the wake of the tragedy, many who were sympathetic to the British felt betrayed. Newspapers, advocating collaboration with Germany, used Mers el-Kebir to reignite anti-British sentiment as readers were urged to join Hitler's European New World Order. My father told me to read between the lines.

In Vichy, where the new government of France had settled, the former World War I hero of Verdun Marshal Philippe Pétain assumed supreme power on July 11, 1940. Five days later, his regime stripped naturalized Jews of their citizenship. Then the Vichy military tribunal of Clermont-Ferrand sentenced General de Gaulle to death in absentia. DeGaulle was still in England and officially recognized by the British government as leader of the Free French.

My father had trusted Marshal Pétain, but on October 24, when Pétain shook hands with Hitler in Montoire-sur-le-Loir, my father's faith in the old hero was shaken. He wondered if Pétain had lost his senses. Father, prolabor, was shocked again when Vichy's government on November 9 banned all trade unions. Even so, those momentous and outrageous events did not address our basic fears.

Our main worry was finding enough to eat. With daily long lines for food, ration tickets were useless when supplies ran out. By the spring of 1941, father decided to turn our yard into a vegetable garden, and he began raising chickens and rabbits. My first job was to go to the countryside to buy grain for chickens and gather grass for rabbits.

Because the only groceries always available on the market were rutabagas, a bulbous root normally used to feed livestock, mother bought as much as we could carry. Almost every day she cooked them in a different sauce, but nobody asked for seconds. We'd share them with the rabbits. When we ate rutabagas, we talked about how few potatoes we had.

For a poor family, a potato was more precious than money. Near the outskirts of town at Mr. and Mrs. Jeanret's house, a long line of women was always waiting to exchange ration tickets for chickens, butter, and potatoes. It was here that I finally got a job: I stacked 120-pound potato sacks, served customers, and plowed the garden. I'd also cut wood blocks into tiny pieces to feed the wood-burning furnace that replaced their truck's gas tank. An average working day was never less than 12 hours.

It always seemed to me that Mr. Jeanret's body was short-circuiting. A wiry man, he never made a normal move. Instead, he jumped: When I handed him potatoes, he'd jump to the scale, jump to the customer, and jump to the cash register. The whole morning was a series of jumps. As women in line heard him shouting orders and saw me stacking potatoes, they'd shout, "How can you let a small boy lift such heavy sacks?" The boss could never identify a single voice, so he ignored them.

Whenever the potatoes sold out, Mrs. Jeanret sent me to Paris to pick up 60 pounds of butter to sell in her living room. She was so fat, I thought she needed two chairs to sit on, one for each cheek.

I stayed at this exhausting job only because I was paid in potatoes. It meant, for two days a week, my family didn't have to eat rutabagas. One afternoon, I was given a raise of two potatoes a day and was told by the boss that I had a great future in the chicken and potato business.

Every night, going home from work, I faced climbing a steep hill. In my imagination, the incline symbolized both my wiry old employer and the prospect of surrendering my life to the potato business. So I got up the hill riding my bicycle, furiously zigzagging: I never let the hill beat me. Had I walked it, Jeanret and that future would have won.

Meanwhile, Vichy crushed workers' rights. Harsh law and order ruled as France became a police state. The Catholic Church led the moral order as separation of church and state once again blurred.

Sunday was a day off except for church. At mass, I'd confess to cursing at my mother because after working 12 hours, she'd tell me to pick up more grass for the rabbits. For atonement, I recited several "Ave-Maria's," but in truth, I didn't feel guilty.

I was tired of being told what to do six days a week by mother, Jeanret, and the French and German street patrols. By Sunday, I couldn't listen to any more sermons. I didn't need or want moral guidance. On the Sunday before my first communion, as I received the wafer, I stood up suddenly before the full congregation and tore up my catechism page by page as I walked backwards to the church exit. I ended up throwing the half-empty book toward the altar and slammed the huge door of the church shut.

The congregation was shocked. After my first act of defiance, I walked home carefree and happy. Later our parish priest knocked on our door—Father had invited him to lunch. Father, who ran a small construction firm, made repairs at the priest's rectory, and the two of them were drinking buddies. The priest described my shameful act to my parents. Father took a swing to my face with the back of his hand but barely touched me. It was like a movie stunt. Alarmed, the priest said, "Paul, Not so hard!" That calmed my father, and I was sent to my room without my lunch, which wasn't much anyway.

Father was actually very secular and never trusted the Catholic hierarchy. He suspected the Vatican of collaborating with the Nazis, yet he wanted a Christian education for his children. He was more comfortable with our parish priest who shared his Christian humanistic values. One day in midoccupation, a great storm swept through town, damaging roofs and ripping the cross from our church steeple. The priest called on father in the middle of night. When the winds subsided, father climbed the high steeple and reset the cross. At dawn, they shared a bottle of the priest's communion wine.

On June 22, 1941, Germany, Italy, and Romania declared war on the USSR. Young Frenchmen were encouraged to join The Legion of French Volunteers to Fight Bolshevism. Thousands joined and were prepared for the Russian front by Germans who trained them and outfitted them in German uniforms.

Propaganda flowed. On July 18, the French Volunteers held a huge rally at the Vélodrome d'Hiver, and Marshal Pétain gave the new legion his blessing. Father was disgusted and wondered, "How could they?"

A year later, from the same site at Vélodrome d'Hiver, French authorities organized the first mass deportation of 13,000 Jews, who were sent to a prison camp at Drancy and then to death camps in the east.

Acts of sabotage and assassination against Germans and high French officials were on the rise. It was heavily publicized that for every German killed in France, 50 French hostages were to be shot. At first, they executed Communist and common-law prisoners, and by late October 1941, more than a hundred had been put to death.

For me, nothing changed. I was stacking potatoes and listening to Jeanret ranting, "Work faster! Quickly! Quickly!" Food was becoming scarcer, but there was no shortage of propaganda about German victories on the Russian front. The siege of Leningrad had begun, then Kiev and Odessa fell. From day to day, there seemed to be no hope.

Then on December 7, 1941, the Japanese bombed Pearl Harbor, and four days later, Hitler and Mussolini declared war on the U.S. Father was optimistic for the first time, believing that with America involved, the war would be won against the Nazis. From the BBC, we learned that on December 20 the German Army had been forced to retreat from Moscow. We secretly rejoiced every time the Germans lost a battle, but father repeatedly warned me not to tell anyone we were listening to British radio. If German or French authorities discovered we listened to the *French Speak to the French* daily broadcast, father could have been heavily fined and sent to jail for up to six months. Anonymous denunciations were widespread, often unwarranted, and to be feared. The occupation brought out the worst in people—as their manners were dictated by fear, generosity and principles often fell by the wayside.

Just east of Marly, in March 1942, Britain's Royal Air Force heavily bombed the Renault factories producing tanks and trucks for the German war effort, but civilian homes were destroyed as well. With 623 people killed, rescue teams were formed to dig out bodies from the rubble, and my friends and I were drafted for civil labor to help survivors. When we arrived at dawn at Boulogne-Billancourt, we saw more than a hundred corpses covered with white sheets.

We were assigned to an old lady who was hysterically screaming, "All my savings are under there!" When she calmed down, she told us that there was a box of gold coins buried under her collapsed house. Crawling on our bellies through debris, we found a metal box and many unbroken bottles of cognac. As we emerged from the wreckage, we held up the box and shook it so she could hear the coins. In tears, she hugged and kissed us over and over. Once she quieted down, we handed her the bottles of cognac. "No, no, no," she insisted. "You keep them."

None of us had ever tasted a drop of alcohol, so at the end of the day, we looked at each other and opened a bottle. Covered with dust and plaster, we laughed and passed the bottle back and forth till it was finished, then fell asleep, drunk, in the rubble. Our group leader had a hard time waking us, but we finally managed to walk home, in a daze.

In the occupied zone of France, as in the rest of Hitler's Europe, the Jews were required to sew a yellow star on their breast pockets after May 28, 1942. The only country that defied the order was Denmark, whose king asked all his loyal subjects to wear the yellow stars, Christians and Jews alike.

In July, rations were again reduced, and prices on the black market shot up. A working man like father made less than 900 francs a week, but a liter of cooking oil cost 1,000 francs on the black market.

The only good news came with the first assault on Hitler's Atlantic Wall at Dieppe, Normandy, on August 19 by British, Canadian, American, and Free French forces. For a brief time, we were euphoric, but the attack failed, and the French press emphasized the defeat of "the enemy."

The unoccupied southern half of France was taken over by German and Italian forces on November 11. The French fleet was still anchored in the naval base at Toulon, because French commanders, in 1940, refused to join England or sail for neutral America. As German Panzer tanks approached Toulon, French sailors scuttled their fleet to prevent Germans from taking it.

The grim year of 1943 marked the beginning of Germany's forced labor conscription. On January 6, one of the first shipments of drafted French workers, ages 21 to 29, filed into trains bound for German factories. At the station in Montluçon, an angry mob formed to protest the draft, and mothers laid themselves across tracks, stopping the trains. Most young workers escaped, and the trains were left almost empty.

On January 30, the British Royal Air Force bombed Berlin, and the following day, the Germans surrendered at Stalingrad. Only the BBC kept us informed of such momentous events—the French press had lost its credibility long ago.

The drive to recruit French forced labor intensified, and a quarter million young Frenchmen were ordered to go to Germany. Touching all professions, the order created national outrage and the end of apathy in France. Risking up to five years in prison or a hundred-thousand-franc fine, many young draftees refused to comply. They escaped into forests and mountains to join scattered groups of the Resistance.

The mood was changing. Any mention of de Gaulle's Free French could provoke arrest by French and German police, but when another trainload of workers were shipped from Paris's Gare de l'Est, the young men began to shout, "Long live de Gaulle," followed by the singing of "La Marseillaise," our national anthem.

In North Africa and Italy, Allies were scoring victories. The British by night and Americans by day were bombing Germany's industrial heartland. Our own skies were full of black silhouettes of B-17 bombers tracked by thousands of exploding anti-aircraft shells. Wherever we looked at the sky, there were planes—we'd never seen such an awesome display of power, the entire sky filled with "Flying Fortresses."

One day, an American plane was hit and fell out of formation, twisting out of control. In rapid succession, the crew members bailed out, but one parachute wrapped around itself and a young airman fell straight to the earth. We ran into the forest. The Germans had already removed the corpse. Engraved in the soft grass was the imprint of a body. Suddenly it seemed it was not just an imprint of a body but a man, and we began to wonder why these young Americans had flown so far from home, all the way across the Atlantic.

We ran into town for flowers, telling people about the fallen young American. Although we had never seen him, we gave him a face. It seemed everyone wanted to offer flowers to place in his imprint. We ran back to the soft grass by the lake and gently laid the flowers in the outline of his body. The Germans chased us away, but they didn't remove the flowers.

Later that evening, my thoughts drifted to a continent unknown to me, across the Atlantic, and the thousands of young Americans who crossed that ocean. We knew they were fighting battles in North Africa and Italy and were training in England for the day they would land on our shores. I wanted to know more but all things American were banned. My knowledge of America was limited to what I learned about France's participation in the Revolutionary War; the Rochambeau Army's long march to join Americans on the Hudson; General Lafayette's alliance and friendship with George Washington; and Britain's 1781 surrender at Yorktown. Otherwise all I knew were American movies and the big skies of American westerns.

In my mind, I began to create a mythical America. I imagined crossing the continent from coast to coast, completely free, not seeing a single armed patrol checking my identification, and not being bodily searched for 3,000 miles. The hungrier I became, the more I fantasized. To friends, I reported Allied victories heard on the BBC, often exaggerating German losses and American heroism. I tried to convince my closest friends that we should all leave for the USA when the war ended. I told so many tales, real and imaginary, that soon my nickname became *L'Américain.* Daily, I was asked, "Hey *l'Américain!* What's going on?" The name stayed with me long after the war.

In the summer of '43, Mr. Jeanret could no longer acquire enough to serve customers as I warned my parents I'd soon lose my job. For months, I watched supplies dwindle and eventually, Jeanret could handle the few potatoes he had by himself. After paying me my last potatoes, we said goodbye.

Out of a job, I was thrilled to play again with friends in the forest of Marly. Our favorite game was Cowboys and Indians. Divided into two camps, we played hide and seek, using ropes to tie our prisoners to tree trunks. The games ended when darkness fell, but one evening, as we roamed large areas of the forest, we forgot one of the kids tied to a tree, only remembering him by the time we reached town. Afraid to go back into the black forest, we found Mr. Depuis, the forest guard. Ashamed, we explained we had left a prisoner tied to a tree, but the worst was that we couldn't remember exactly where we left him. With a flashlight, we walked and walked, shouting his name—it seemed like an endless search. Finally we heard him screaming, "I'm here, here, here!" We freed our friend to great relief and walked back to town laughing.

In the same forest, we met a man who claimed to be with the Resistance. He told us, "If you find lead anywhere, bring it to me. We can make bullets out of it." We had never met anyone from the Resistance, so we asked him, "If we find lead, how do we find you?" He answered, "You won't find me, I'll find you."

By mid-1943, acts of resistance were rising. French railroad workers sabotaged locomotives and rail switches, derailing German supply trains. The Resistance blew up bridges, robbed ration tickets, and blank IDs from town halls. The BBC's French Radio broadcasted coded messages identifying British airdrops of ammunition and supplies, and the German military was short of labor everywhere.

Near Marly, they were recruiting at Fort "Trou d'Enfer," (Hell's Hole) where I was hired as a supply clerk to handle nails, screws, bolts, and lead bars. While stacking supplies, I thought of the man who spoke to us in the forest. From the first day, I began stealing pencil-thin lead bars by tying them to both legs, hiding them under my trousers and walking stiffly past the guard who'd check my pockets and lunch pail before waving me on.

For two weeks, I kept this game up and naively thought I was heroic for contributing to the Resistance. Each day I got bolder, tying more lead bars to my legs, until my last day, carrying about four pounds of lead, I limped so badly as I dragged my feet that the old sentry stopped me. He felt my right leg and found four bars of lead. Shouting at me in German, he led me to the guardhouse where I spent the night. When my father came to pick me up the next morning, an interpreter reprimanded us but let me go because I was so young. For some reason, the sentry never searched my left leg, also loaded with lead bars. As father took my hand, I whispered to him, "Not so fast, my left leg is heavy."

For father, stealing in any form was unforgivable. I told him about the man in the forest but it made no difference to him because stealing was stealing. I knew he understood what he called "my foolish act," but he knew the Germans were becoming more ruthless and so he locked up all the bars I had collected. In the end I couldn't help the Resistance. Months later, we learned the man in the forest and several others were shot while picking up a British airdrop.

At the end of summer, my fights with mother about gathering grass for rabbits resumed. Because I no longer had a job, she could again scream to the world that her son was the laziest human being on earth. Daily she'd insult me, and disgusted, I'd slam the door, run to the end of the garden, and to get even with her, ring the bell at the gate till she came out screaming. Waving a stick, she'd charge the gate, and when she got close enough to hit me, I'd run. Angry and frustrated, she'd yell, "Wait till I tell your father!" and I'd reply, "Go ahead. Tell him!" Father would always say the same thing, "You have to respect your mother." After a while, mother stopped telling father as it was obviously a waste of time.

When I was young, mother would punish us by whipping the backs of our knees with a whip. She gave up on this after I cut all the leather straps from her whips, leaving her with just the handles.

In her strange way, mother believed all her insults were challenging and building my character. When she told me I would "never amount to anything," I didn't believe it. But in the end, she did build my character: She and the war created a rebel.

By the late summer of 1943, I was living in rebellion against the ruling Vichy elite, the Catholic Church, the Bourgeoisie's contempt for the working class, and the overzealous French police, as well as the German occupiers marching down my street. There was very little not to rebel against.

In the fourth year of the occupation, more and more food and supplies were sent to Germany. Day after day, I traveled to the countryside, begging farmers to sell me potatoes, but each day I returned empty handed. At the same time, we were convinced that at any moment, the Americans would land, until finally, on September 8, 1943, Italy signed an armistice with the Allies. Rejoicing, we dared to believe the end of the war was near.

But Italy's collapse changed nothing. Mother was again cooking the hated rutabagas. Father often returned from his Sunday game of cards with a case of *vin triste,* or "sad wine." One evening, I heard father talking to himself in the kitchen, "Where do we get food now? Where?" I never let him know that I heard him crying.

The next day, I suggested to father that my daily trips to the country were useless, and that I should go much further and not return till I actually found food. I convinced him that my best friend Claude and I could survive on the road and sleep in barns.

My bicycle was hardly in shape to make a long trip, so I covered each of my tires with a second one to cover the holes of the inner tire. It worked, and my bike lasted till the end of the war. Claude, on the other hand, had a racing bike with very thin tires, and there was no way to reinforce them, so we simply had to take our chances.

Mother gave me money to buy about a hundred pounds of potatoes. Though it was illegal for us to buy anything directly from farmers, we hoped they'd be generous and overlook the laws. At dawn, Claude and I set off for the outer limits of l'Île de France.

On the first day, we traveled a hundred miles across numerous farms. Each time we were told that acre after acre, the endless fields of potatoes were requisitioned for the Germans. At the end of the day, a boy our age whose parents had just refused to sell us potatoes came to us and said, "Don't go away, you can sleep here in our barn." He brought us a large loaf of bread, a big piece of cheese, a pitcher of fresh milk, two glasses, and a knife. We thanked him and ate, then fell asleep, exhausted, on the hay.

Next morning we set off again, thinking that further west, away from main roads, we might find a farmer less afraid to sell us some potatoes, but all we could buy was enough bread and cheese to feed ourselves. By the third day, we began to have serious doubts that anyone would sell us even a small amount.

Day after day, we passed miles and miles of potato fields, and still we had not a single potato in our sacks. By the fifth day, we called upon one last farm, angry and dejected. We explained we had been bicycling for days, but received the same answer: Their harvest was requisitioned. Claude and I looked at each other, resigned. With night falling, we headed home disgusted, surrounded by fields of potatoes.

As the farm house fell out of sight, Claude waved his arm and said, "Look at all these potatoes." By a small cluster of trees, we stopped to eat our bread and cheese, cursing the farmers. As we sat chewing on our last piece of stale bread a mere three feet away from the green stems of potatoes, it suddenly seemed obvious what we had to do.

"Only take the big ones!" I said as Claude and I pulled at the green stems and dug out the biggest potatoes. Soon our hundred-pound bags were filled and loaded on our bikes. We knew we couldn't make it home before curfew, so our biggest challenge was to avoid main roads, roadblocks, and German patrols.

Covered by darkness, our bicycle headlights off, we rode dirt roads through the fields. It was a beautiful night, and though we were scared, we were happy. Our immediate need was to find a place to hide; hours later, we discovered at last another cluster of trees where we hid and slept uneasily through the night.

The next morning, we followed the most secluded roads possible. When the path led into a small village, one of us would walk ahead to see if there were any checkpoints or roadblocks. Instinctively, we trusted women more than men. If we saw a face we trusted, we would ask her if the road was clear.

Claude's racing bicycle was not made to carry a hundred pounds of potatoes. Every few miles his front tire would puncture, forcing us to remove the thin stitching, patch the inner tube, and re-stitch the inner lips of his tire. Slowed down by avoiding checkpoints and needing to constantly fix Claude's tire, we found ourselves again passing curfew.

Finally, we reached the forest of Marly, which we knew like the back of our hands. In the bright moonlit night, we could just see the trail leading into our town. Suddenly Claude's wheel hit a dirt hole, catapulting him into the air. Landing on the forest floor, he looked at his wheel, crushed like an accordion, and began to cry.

I said, "Claude, c'mon we'll figure something out." After Claude stopped crying, we broke into nervous laughter. Only two miles from home, we couldn't abandon his bicycle and potatoes. We thought for a while before I said, "My bike can take it. We'll load your sack on my rear-baggage rack, and you carry your bike on your shoulder."

After pumping more air into my rear tire, we loaded the potatoes and walked to the edge of the forest. We decided to go to Claude's house to bypass the center of town. Yet if we walked our bikes to his neighborhood, it would take an hour, and we'd be caught and thrown in jail.

"It's all downhill from here," I said. "We'll chance it." With a hundred pounds of potatoes in front and a hundred pounds in back, Claude sat side-saddle on the cross bar of my bicycle frame. His one hand on my handlebar, his other holding up his bike, letting the rear wheel roll, Claude balanced between my arms as I steered.

I couldn't control the speed. The brakes were fully drawn to the handlebars, but there was too much weight. At high speed, out of control, unable to stop, we rode through the dark town not speaking a word. As I tried to slow my rear wheel with my heel, we sped past the silent shuttered houses. Nothing could've stopped us, not even a patrol, unless they shot us. At the bottom of the hill, the thought struck me that if the railway-crossing bar was down, we'd be dead. We hit the tracks hard but the front wheel held.

Finally reaching flat road, we slowed to the front of Claude's house. As we rolled the bikes through his small garden, it dawned on us that we'd have to explain the potatoes. We feared our fathers more than all the obstacles we encountered on our five-day journey. Hearing us arrive, Claude's parents came to the front door and welcomed us in, exclaiming, "We were so worried!" When they saw the potatoes and Claude's crushed wheel, they couldn't believe we had ridden with all that weight.

Four hours after curfew, they realized how lucky we were. Claude's mother made us chicory coffee with biscuits. Answering their countless questions about our trip, we told them the truth except regarding the day we stole the potatoes. Uncomfortably we said, "On the last day, a farmer took pity on us and sold us two hundred pounds." I was sure our lies were written across our faces, but they didn't say anything. Claude's mother made an extra bed for me, and we slept into the afternoon.

In late 1943, potatoes were a luxury for a poor family. When I arrived home, mother was pleased. Father had been worried we'd been arrested so was happy to see me and hugged me. When I told him the whole story, he thought we were crazy, but I felt terrible having to lie to him about the stolen potatoes.

The potatoes were my third and last theft. When I was seven years old, I stole a toy car from a store in the next town. When my father saw me playing with it, he asked where I got it. As I answered, "A friend gave it to me," my face turned red, so he knew I was lying. The next morning, he angrily took me by the hand, and in giant steps walked me three miles back to the store, dragging me along—I practically had to run to keep up with him.

Calling the manager of the store, my father said, "Tell the gentleman what you've done." Ashamed, I described how I stole the car while no one was looking. My father said to the manager, "Do you think we should send him to prison?" to which the manager answered very seriously, "Well maybe." Father said, "Now that you have the thief, you should call the police." The manager scratched his head and said, "Maybe. But he's so young." He turned to me and said, "My little one, if you promise me never, never to steal again, I will let you go this time." Thanking him, my father said to me, "You're lucky the manager is a generous man." I thought I was lucky too as we walked out of the store, and father never said another word about it.

My second theft was trying to be heroic by stealing lead bars for the Resistance. I was arrested and again lucky to be released. My last theft was the only one I got away with.

Yet 37 years later, when my father was an old man of 75, I had the chance to tell him the truth about the potatoes. He sternly looked at me and said, "Son, you lied to me."

November 23, 1943, was my 15th birthday. My mother cooked two rabbits, letting them simmer in white wine, and the whole house smelled good. She also saved eggs laid by our four hens and made a soufflé. With a good meal, morale went up. Every time she cooked a rabbit, it would ease my anger about gathering grass for them because it tasted so good.

Even father had his share of gathering grass. Because cigarettes were completely scarce, he'd often collect grass from fields, dry it, roll it in paper, and smoke it like a cigarette. He longed for the war's end when he could once again buy his good tobacco.

With winter approaching, we gathered as much dead wood as possible to heat the house and wood-burning cooking stove. The only coal we could find for the stove were chunks falling from coal trucks. Running after them, we'd pick up the few pieces that fell.

All the chestnuts had been gathered and stored, and fruits and wild mushrooms were preserved and sealed in glass jars. Since our wooden galoshes were worn out from our summer adventures, father cut strips from old bicycle tires, nailed them to the soles, and hoped they'd last till spring.

In winter, there was no grass to gather and nothing to do except stand in ration lines for mother. Since there were no jobs, my friends and I amused ourselves. On the coldest days, our favorite diversion was to run and jump on ice in the gutter, skating downhill in galoshes.

On warmer days, we built go-carts using old steel ball bearings for wheels. Racing down streets at high speeds, our metal wheels made incredible noise. Daring each other, we steered head on into an old bus that climbed the hill daily. Riding head first underneath the bus, there was plenty of clearance, but it drove the bus driver crazy and eventually our "ball bearing chariots" were banned.

As winter dragged on and we entered the New Year, it was possible to be optimistic. On January 19, 1944, the Soviet Army broke the German siege lines at Leningrad. Three days later, British and American troops stormed ashore at Anzio, 30 miles south of Rome.

Though hopeful, we didn't know how far we could stretch the food we preserved and what supplies we'd acquire in the future. With nothing to do, hours passed slowly, and hunger and fear tempered our optimism.

Listening to the BBC, father explained how the Americans had tipped the balance of power in World War I and helped save France. Waiting for something for so long, we began to believe the Allies would land any day. I tried to imagine the face of freedom but I couldn't remember ever being free.

There were already over a million drafted Frenchmen working in German factories, which were under constant attack by Allied bombings. On February 2, 1944, Germany's forced labor conscription was extended to include all Frenchmen from ages 16 to 60, with exceptions only for heads of families with children. I'd be 16 in November, and father worried that I'd be sent to Germany, so he managed to obtain a new ID card for me: Suddenly I was 13. For weeks, father asked me constantly, "What year were you born?"

Identification checks increased as tensions rose in the German ranks, and raids on public places and cafés by the French police multiplied. Some 45,000 French fascist fanatics volunteered to join vigilante militias to help defend their ideal of law and order, primarily aimed at crushing the Resistance. Armed by Vichy, they terrorized real and imagined enemies in their Basque berets and uniforms. In their twisted ideology, they were determined to "fight bourgeois egoism, capitalism, and Marxism" all at once, and abused their newly acquired power like cowards with special police status.

On April 20 and 21, the Allies heavily bombed an industrial zone in Paris, killing over 600 civilians, giving the Vichy government an opportunity to circulate heavy anti-British and anti-American propaganda.

Allied bombings intensified over German-controlled factories in France. Every night, sirens went off, and entire families spent hours in cellars converted to bomb shelters. Children cried, tempers were short, and old women moaned, "When will it all end?"

On the BBC, we heard strange messages like, "We will force feed the ducks. My wife has a sharp eye. The chimney sweeper has taken a bath. The long sobs of the violin." In time we realized "sobs of the violin" was code for the Resistance in Brittany and Normandy to blow up railroad lines.

On June 4, Rome fell to Allied forces led by American General Mark Clark. When we heard the news, we thought Paris had to be next, but two days later, the American, British, and Canadian forces—the largest military armada in the history of warfare—landed on the shores of Normandy.

The news sparked incredible euphoria, but it was difficult to be certain of the truth. The collaborative French press, still propagandizing German invincibility, published headlines claiming, "The Invaders Will Be Pushed Back To Sea." We refused to believe the newspapers and wondered how long it would take the Allies to reach Paris.

With increasing pressure from the landings and the Resistance, German reprisals intensified. As a reaction to the killing of one of their officers, SS troops obliterated the village of Oradour-sur-Glane, 16 miles from Limoges: all the men were executed, women and children were burned alive in their church, and women trying to escape through windows were shot. Only seven survived. After all this senseless murder, a local commander admitted that they had mistakenly punished the wrong village.

In Marly, we didn't experience such atrocities but could see the Germans were tense. During the first year of occupation, they had shown courtesy to civilians, but by 1944, the policy of good manners eroded into sheer hostility. The Resistance had ambushed and killed too many of the enemy, Germans had shot too many hostages, and the urban population was close to starvation.

Our little garden was not producing enough food for the family, and our winter preserves were long gone. With the Allies advancing in Normandy, I convinced father that the farmers might be willing to sell us some food.

Though father told me not to go too far into Normandy, my secret, naive plan was to reach the battle lines. The British and Americans were my heroes, and I wanted to be among them, to welcome them to France, and to thank them.

Claude replaced his broken bicycle wheel and we set off for Normandy. We traveled westward for hours on back roads, while in the distance, we could see endless columns of German tanks, armored vehicles, and trucks towing artillery to reinforce German lines.

Suddenly squadrons of "double tail" American P-38s dove down one by one, strafing the columns with machine gun fire. Each time one hit an ammunition truck, it would explode in a huge ball of fire. The German convoy, stretching for miles over the main road, was burning, and columns of black smoke rose above the wreckage.

We watched in fascination, and after the explosions quieted, we biked close enough to see charred vehicles and the horror of burnt bodies trapped in their trucks or scattered along the road. From a distance, we admired the grace of American planes with white stars under their wings and the spectacle of the convoy going up in flames, but at close range, we felt sick. As we bicycled away in silence, war had lost its adventurous appeal.

In Normandy, we were close enough to hear shelling but far enough to be safe. Riding on, we saw cows in the fields but all farmers were gone. Finally we found a family of farmers packing to escape the war. When we asked if they could spare some food, they replied, "Anything you can carry, you can have." In awe, we filled our bags with lard, butter, cheese, and potatoes—we'd never seen people so generous.

With 20 pounds of butter each, we had almost more butter than our ration tickets had provided us over the last three years. The idea of soft lard spread across a slice of bread made my mouth water. With hunger setting in, we spread the soft white fat on our bread for dinner on the side of a small road and forgot about joining the British-American lines—we could hardly go to the front with such a heavy, precious load.

Returning home after dark, my parents were still awake, waiting up for me. As we displayed all the food on the table, they stared in disbelief. Father smelled the cheeses while mother waved flies away from the butter, saying, "To keep this much, I'm going to have to salt it." Sampling some cheese, father asked what I saw in Normandy. I told him about the burning convoy and how farmers were in such a hurry to escape the war zone, they were giving food away. In the excitement we suddenly realized our bread rations were so small, we'd have little to spread our precious goods on, but at least we could sweeten rutabagas with butter and spread lard over baked potatoes for a great feast.

By late July 1944, German forces with military bands were still parading down the Champs Elysées, while in Normandy, the Americans smashed through German lines in St. Lo, capturing rear artillery positions of the enemy on their way to liberate Brittany. The British and Canadians seized the bombed ruins of Caen and were racing southeast.

In the August heat, German behavior became unpredictable, and increasingly the Germans ransacked and pillaged shops and farmhouses at random. In Marly, SS troops robbed our Café Tobacco store at gunpoint: lining us against the wall, they emptied the cash register and stole what little tobacco there was.

With the Allies so close, my friends and I began to get cocky, often mocking the Germans. In the café where we played billiards, I taunted a German soldier by placing my wrists together as if handcuffed, telling him, "Soon you'll be a prisoner of the Americans." With the back of his hand, he angrily hit me and sent me sprawling to the floor, then left, slamming the door behind him. Laughing uneasily, I got up and rubbed my cheek.

In some ways we hated the French police more than the Germans, because they had done the occupiers' dirty work and behaved like the enemy. In those August days, we could defy them at last. Once as we came out of a movie, they were checking our ID cards as usual when I said to the French plainclothes officer, "Soon the Americans will be checking yours." He grabbed me, took me to the police station, and booked me for "insulting an officer of the law." I assured him, "Soon your days of collaboration will be over, and you'll have to answer for your actions." He slapped me to the floor, and I repeated, "You'll have to answer." He slapped me down again, but I got up and said, "The war is ending! You will have to answer." He hit me again—this time I went down and stayed down.

The next morning, my father came to pick me up. Seeing me bruised and with black eyes, he glared at the duty officer, demanding, "Who did that to him?" He won't get away with it!" But with France still a police state, he did get away with it. Meekly, the duty officer replied, "I don't know anything. I wasn't on duty." He read my father the charges held against me and I was released, and we never heard from them again.

On August 15, a massive allied force landed on a hundred-mile coastal strip from Nice to Marseilles. For the first time, the Free French Army was participating in the invasion. While the U.S. Seventh Army was fighting in the streets of Cannes, the Resistance took over several Savoy villages, and in Paris, "La Marseillaise" was sung in the streets.

For the first time, we saw occupying forces in and around Marly retreating eastward in military vehicles, horsedrawn carts, loaded bicycles, and anything with wheels they could steal. From a distance, we watched humiliated Germans falling back through narrow streets of Marly, joining the exodus of August 1944. Seeing a break in their long procession line gave me an idea.

For four years, the Germans had posted road signs in their own language. As the Germans methodically relied on their own signs, it dawned on me that we could easily create confusion for retreating forces.

During occupation, it was not permitted to publicly assemble in groups larger than three, so in three groups of three, we set out to the outskirts of town. Each group had a lookout and a hammer. As signs were placed high up on telephone poles, we quickly climbed our friends' shoulders, yanked out the signs, turned them around, and hammered them back in so that at each intersection, the retreating Germans would go left instead of straight.

Later, again in groups of three, we stood waiting in the upper part of town to see if the Germans faithfully followed their signs. I said, "If this works, everything will stop." Within a few hours, the head column met the tail. Nothing moved: as far as the eye could see, roads were jammed with German cars, bicycles, and horsedrawn carts in a fantastic standstill. As the German soldiers craned their necks trying to see what was blocking their retreat, my friends and I, immensely enjoying ourselves, slapped each other on the back, saying, "Not bad."

Watching the Germans flee, we thought the Americans couldn't be far. From the BBC, we heard the Allies were advancing fast, and there were reports that some German units were surrendering at the first sight of an Allied plane. When a fighter-bomber came upon a convoy of tanks, some crews fled, leaving behind white flags in their vehicles.

Again Claude and I wanted to join the American and British lines, so Claude's mother sewed us a huge American flag with 53 stars, not realizing that America had only 48 states at the time.

On our bicycles, we set off westward, with our American flag flying high. Nobody knew where the Allies were, but people told us, "Be careful, there still might be some Germans around." Seeing the American banner, they said, "It's a little early for that. You might get shot."

We weren't shot. There were no Germans, but after traveling for miles and miles, there were no Allies either. Unable to find a single British or American soldier, we returned home dejected.

On August 22, Allied forces in Italy took Florence and the next day took Marseilles and Grenoble. Since Marly wasn't on any of the main arteries to the capital, we knew any action would be in Paris.

General George Patton's American Third Army swept through Orléans, Chartres, and Dreux to link with the British advancing on Rouen, while the Germans pulled back across the Seine. In Paris, street fighting broke out as the police went on strike and seized Ile de la Cité on the Seine. Eisenhower then took action, contacting the Resistance to overtake the Préfecture while sending orders for General Leclerc's French Second Armored Division to enter Paris.

On August 25, French tanks led the Allies into Paris. While Hitler questioned the German command, "Is Paris burning?" General Von Choltitz surrendered to Leclerc and ordered a ceasefire: he had defied Hitler's order to destroy Paris before accepting defeat.

Four years of occupation suddenly ended—we had waited so long. The Nazi swastika was torn down from the Eiffel Tower, and the Americans, British, and Canadians began celebrating the liberation of Paris to the cheers of millions.

It seemed as if the whole population of Paris was in the streets. People danced, girls, women, and children kissed, grandmothers hugged the Allies with tears in their eyes, and a tide of joy swept the streets. With our 53-star American flag, we cheered the tanks, half-tracks, and friendly-looking American Jeeps.

Singing and laughing, people climbed on top of Jeeps and trucks parading through Paris. In an endless flow of wine, elated Parisians thanked and welcomed the Allies with filled glasses and embraces. Hidden bottles of vintage cognac and champagne had been saved for that very day. Back on April 26, 1944, Marshal Pétain, the leader and symbol of French collaboration, was cheered by thousands at the Hôtel de Ville in Paris. From that same place, four months later on August 25, General de Gaulle delivered his liberation speech, before the joyful masses.

De Gaulle began his emotional speech:"...Paris standing up to liberate itself, by its own hands...Paris outraged...But Paris liberated by itself, liberated by its people with the participation of the Armies of France, with the support and participation of the whole nation, the fighting France, the only France, the true France, of the eternal France..."

The huge crowds cheered, and so did we, but we felt outraged. De Gaulle, "the man who saved France's honor," did not even mention the great sacrifices of the British, Americans, and Canadians who made the liberation possible.

Others noticed the omission too: four days later, in a radio address, the General said, "France renders equal homage to the brave and good Allied Armies and their leaders whose unstoppable offensive made the liberation of Paris possible."

The French Revolution of 1789 had initiated a sad tradition of anonymous denunciations, which reemerged during German occupation and again at the liberation of France. Though many Resistance groups participated heroically in winning our freedom from Nazi rule, the last days of August produced a new breed of overnight patriots who acted on anonymous accusations to punish the "Collabos" with summary justice. Those unappointed judges persecuted young women suspected of sleeping with Germans by shaving their heads and parading them down our streets to be jeered by crowds. The loud men leading the parades had never encountered the dangers, arrests, tortures, and firing squads endured by the Resistance. They were a long way away from the quiet hero I met in the forest during the dark days of German occupation.

The Germans had marched into my life, goose-stepping in their steel-studded boots, waking us every morning with the din of regimented heels. But when the Americans arrived, we were amazed by the soft-stepping sound of their rubber combat boots. They behaved and moved like free men, not as marching machines.

At last, one morning, Claude and I met our first American in Marly. When we discovered him, kids had already surrounded his Dodge military pickup truck. He didn't speak French and none of us spoke English, but he gave us "K-Ration" packages containing spam, hard chocolate, instant coffee, milk, and cigarettes. He grimaced at the American K-Rations and puzzled us by making drawings of peaches, apples, and pears. Suddenly we understood that "Bill of Charlotte, North Carolina" was looking for fresh food.

So we jumped in the passenger seat and pointed to the open country where farmers might be generous to our newfound friend. In the orchards, few people had seen our liberators, and they greeted Bill as a one-man army, filling his truck with all the fruits and vegetables of the season. At each orchard, farmers toasted him with champagne and vintage wines, and placed prewar bottles of *Eau de Vie*, (Water of Life), 25 percent alcohol or 50 proof, into Bill's crates of vegetables.

After all the kisses from women, girls, children, grandmothers, and all the hugs from old men, "Bill of Carolina" drove back to his camp in the forest of Marly, less than a mile from "Trou d'Enfer." There he received his second hero's welcome, cheered by the men and officers in his platoon. We didn't understand much, but it was obvious that Bill explained we had led him to fresh food. All of them shook our hands and slapped our backs.

We were surprised at the ease of manners between enlisted men and the officers with silver or gold bars, or other signs of rank on their shoulders. American soldiers were different from the French and German soldiers we encountered. The French were more rank conscious and contentious, and the Germans had the discipline of robots, while the Americans seemed less regimented and more egalitarian.

In following days, we brought Bill of Carolina and some of his friends home for dinner. We thought they'd be pleased to eat rabbit cooked in white wine, but when I drew a picture of a rabbit with two long ears, there was an uneasy lull.

It was inconceivable to father that anyone would be reluctant to eat the family's rabbit, so he brought from the cellar two bottles of Pommard wine saved since the war began and proudly displayed the label, having everyone smell the aroma.

Pouring the wine, we toasted the Americans. I never drank wine—I drank lemonade—but for that day, father gave me half a glass. To soften the taste, I thinned my wine with water as father yelled in despair, "How can you put water in my Pommard?" The soldiers laughed, and I went back to my lemonade.

As the evening went on, father brought out his homemade 50 proof Eau de Vie and plum schnapps, and they drank happily. Mother served her traditional meal, and the soldiers tasted the rabbit reluctantly, but after the first bite, they enjoyed it. Rabbit was our luxury meal, but for our next American guests, we'd say it was chicken.

After enjoying the exuberance of the Americans, their dances, music, and optimism of Glenn Miller's "In the Mood," I fell into a kind of post-liberation blues as the euphoria of liberation faded. American forces offered many jobs but to English-speaking French personnel only. Following long, fruitless daily searches for jobs in Paris, my fights with mother resumed as I went on gathering grass for the rabbits. Without a paycheck to bring home, I felt deeply troubled that I wasn't earning my keep—the fact of which mother continually reminded me.

I began to feel like a parasite, guilty for consuming even the most meager meals at the family table, so I often refused to eat lunch and dinner, claiming I was going to visit Pierre, an older friend, whose family often invited me to their home.

Instead I'd escape to my "dear mysterious forest," to a soft moss-covered hole where I could write poetry until nightfall.

In my poems, I wrote of following the sun to its destination as it set through the birches, oaks, and chestnut trees. On overcast days, I wrote of birds I'd never seen that could fly above the highest clouds and ride the wind. Always I wrote of rebellion and freedom from injustice.

My oldest sister Paulette, who was 10 years old, often came at dusk with a sandwich and instructions from Papa saying I would not be punished if I came home with her, but I never did. I'd ask my sister if she was afraid of the dark forest and she'd answer, "No! You are here." After escorting her to the road leading home, I'd return to my refuge.

When I slept there, it was cold and damp, but the morning brought visits from squirrels, and I shared with them a few crumbs of bread. One clear night, a wild boar family ran Indian file along a hunter's trail a few yards away, their feet crunching the dead leaves. Another time I heard the rustling of light footsteps and saw a deer looking at me inquisitively, unafraid.

Though I loved my forest and my town, I knew I could not stay. It was in that hole in the forest I reviewed the last four years of my life and decided to leave France.

France was liberated but not free. The privileged elite of the governing class were in France to stay, blocking my way to a better future, and there was no way I would spend the rest of my life under their control.

REBELLION

FILLES DE JOIE AND AN AMERICAN JEEP

FRANCE 1944–1950

Though father, an expert steeple builder, enjoyed a degree of respect as an artisan, I had too often felt the contempt of some classmates. I heard them ask friends who were better off than me, "How can you play with a son of a worker?" It was the ultimate insult.

"No one, ever, at birth, whether worker, bourgeois, or aristocrat, is better than you are," father told me in his great republican belief inspired by the Age of Enlightenment when French philosophers in 1789 had written *Les Droits de l'Homme et du Citoyen* (The Declaration of the Rights of Man and of the Citizen).

In September 1944, I was almost 16 but had never known a democratic France. I perceived the state of strife experienced in the past four years as fundamental and permanent. The occupiers had been removed but in my mind, the shackles of French society would remain. The only wealthy family I knew that didn't follow antiquated rules of the ruling class was that of my friend Pierre. His family was well off, liberal, and deeply influenced by America; they had the openness of America and were the only ones who supported my dream of going to that faraway land.

Pierre's mother loved me and treated me like a younger son, referring to me as *"mon petit Jean."* Her daughter had a crush on me, and Pierre let me drive his Citroën Classic.

While the only books in my house were prizes I had received from school, Pierre's house had a vast library, and they let me read whatever I wanted. The last book they gave me was *A History of America*.

In that book, I learned about Jefferson's Declaration of Independence, the idea of "life, liberty, and the pursuit of happiness," the U.S. Constitution, and the Amendments in the Bill of Rights. I was attracted to the first great right, guaranteeing freedom of speech, freedom of the press, and the right to assemble, as well as the fourth right in which: "The right of the people to be secure in their persons, houses, papers, and effects, against unreasonable searches and seizures, shall not be violated." This appealed to me because I had been checked and searched countless times during the past four years.

I was also impressed by Abraham Lincoln's humble origins, his birth in a Kentucky log cabin as the son of a typical pioneer family, and his leadership in the Civil War, which abolished slavery and freed four million slaves. Later I read about America's Great Depression and identified with the people's hunger and joblessness as well.

Finally, in October of '44, I found a job with a parcel-delivery service, bicycling all day in Paris, pulling a large heavy trailer. It was backbreaking work, but at least I was earning a weekly paycheck to give mother. She gave me 20 percent as a weekly allowance.

On November 23, I turned 16—no longer in danger of forced labor, I burned my fake ID card. To celebrate my birthday, my friends thought we were old enough to make a trip to Paris's Rue Taitbout and visit *les filles de joie*, literally the "girls of joy."

Though we behaved like children, we bragged about becoming men. We set off, full of bravado, talking about women, but we knew nothing about women at all. The only beautiful thighs I had furtively seen belonged to my grade school teacher.

Before heading out on our sexual adventure, we each had a shot of cognac. It was a challenge: "Either we all go or nothing." Hoping to boost our confidence, we told each other, "Guys c'mon, let's go already."

Together we walked along Rue Taitbout eyeing the street women. The way we hesitated, they knew it was our first time; they called out, "Are you going upstairs?" Large Rubenesque females overly made-up, they showed their wares in tight dresses draped over mighty breasts. These huge older women resembled seventeenth-century prostitutes, but they were all we could afford. They were like mastodons, especially compared to us—I found it frightening.

Eventually, they enticed us. After paying in advance for "30 minutes" and paying someone else for the room, each of us went upstairs with his own woman. I found myself in a tiny room with a bathtub and bed, used and filthy: nothing seemed clean.

My *fille de joie* told me, "Wash your zizi," then began removing her clothes. I froze as I saw her fat derrière, thighs, and hanging breasts. "No thank you," I said, "another time," but she put her hand on my hand before I could turn the doorknob.

"Nobody's going to believe you if you go down now," she declared. "Better wait 10 minutes, otherwise your friends will know you didn't make it."

So I waited. She told me, "Don't worry, it happens all the time. Many young men are shy." She reassured me, "One day, you'll discover the pleasures of love," but I just wanted to get out of there.

The strange thing was, my friends and I all came out at the same time. At a café, we asked each other, "How was it?" Avoiding each others' eyes, we all said, "Great, great." Since then, I never went back to Rue Taitbout, and though we never spoke of it again, I was convinced we had all remained virgins that day.

In December 1944, as the Allies pushed German forces back to Berlin, the *New York Herald Tribune* was again available in Paris. For five hard-earned francs, I'd buy the paper and read it with a French dictionary. I went to American movies to watch and listen to Gary Cooper, Rita Hayworth, Humphrey Bogart, and other Hollywood stars, while learning English reading subtitles.

April 12, 1945, less than one month before the end of the war in Europe, President Roosevelt died, and Vice President Harry S. Truman was sworn in as America's 32nd president.

Father thought it was sad that Roosevelt had not lived to see the end of the war. He greatly admired Roosevelt for standing up for "the little guy" while lifting America out of the Great Depression and leading the U.S. war effort. My father was not alone in his admiration: eventually a metro station on the Champs Elysées was named in Roosevelt's honor.

Meanwhile, in Paris, the Vichy police chief was sentenced to death. Marshal Pétain was arrested on the Swiss border, and in Italy, a cowering Mussolini and his mistress were executed by partisans and strung up by their heels in Milan's Piazza Loretto.

On April 30, 1945, Hitler, the self-proclaimed leader of Germany's "master race," brought to power by industrialists, army generals, junker landowners, and millions of ordinary Germans, shot himself in the head in his Berlin bunker.

Soviet forces and Western commanders accepted Germany's total surrender on May 8, marking the end of the Nazi's 1,000-year Reich and evil campaign. In my mind, both Germany and Nazism were one and the same. On the Champs Elysées, we sang, marched, and drank, but after the celebrations, I resumed pulling my bicycle trailer, delivering packages in Paris.

In July, trials for murder and the betrayal of France against Pétain, his deputy Pierre Laval, and other collaborators began. Though the defense claimed Pétain had helped save France, he was sentenced to death, but because Pétain was 89 years old, his sentence was commuted. Laval, however, was shot.

Still, in speaking to the men on my delivery routes, I began to understand that many who had served the Vichy government would never have to answer for themselves and would remain in power. As long as enough wine flowed and starvation was avoided, the bureaucracy would hardly change. By 1945 the occupation had exhausted the people of France and they would no longer take to the streets—there would be no people's revolution seeking a more just society. Celebrations were over: I had lost faith and felt I no longer belonged in my own country.

On August 6, Japan's Hiroshima was completely destroyed by America's atomic bomb, and the obliteration of Nagasaki followed soon afterward. That horrible new weapon put an end to the war with Japan's unconditional surrender on August 14.

These monumental events all took place very far away, while in Paris, little had changed since liberation. Through a friend, I got a job at the Chapuis Brothers' Bicycle Factory. They treated me decently and paid me a technician's salary, but I continued to talk about the United States. My dream was to drive across America and write poetry, and after nine months and several raises, I finally saved enough money to get my driver's license on Christmas Eve in 1946—it would be "my license to freedom."

In Marly, early 1947, I heard about an American photographer, Joe Pazen, who had a temporary job offer for an assistant who could drive, help carry equipment, and make rough translations. Pazen was a photojournalist for the Black Star photo agency in New York and a regular contributor to Life magazine's Paris Bureau. The idea of driving Joe Pazen's American Jeep was irresistible.

When I told mother I was quitting my job at the Chapuis Brothers for a two-month assignment with an American photojournalist, she said, "How can you possibly quit a secure job to work for an American for just two months?" She thought I was a fool, as did the Brothers Chapuis, but they promised to make me a director in a few years if I came back. But I never did go back.

Joe Pazen told me to call him by his first name, which was unheard of in France. It took me a while to get used to calling him Joe, so for a long time I called him, "Monsieur Joe."

Slightly heavy, Joe would often go on a diet, but he loved good food and whiskey. Twice a week he played poker with other American journalists. In one night, he'd win or lose as much as my father made in a year.

There was a great love affair at that time between the French common man and the Americans, the most generous, egalitarian people I had ever met. Joe was always welcome in my home.

He took me to restaurants where we discussed assignments, then every night, he let me take the Jeep home. To protect it from thieves, I'd park it in my father's garden, chain the steering wheel to the clutch, and remove the rotor from the distributor to cut off the distribution system.

Looking at the great holes I made in our vegetable plot, father complained, "You're crushing my vegetables!" But he admitted France was so poor that thieves would steal anything, and we couldn't let that happen to our American Jeep.

Under the windshield were the huge letters, "U.S. PRESS." With that identification, you could virtually do anything. The American Jeep was the most popular vehicle in postwar France, and driving it made me a hero with my friends. "Johnny what's happening?" they'd ask as I drove into Marly where there were practically no other cars. Though I was always speeding, I never got a ticket, because in that American Jeep, you could do no wrong—you were king of the road.

Two months quickly passed, and Joe hired me for two more years. Through Joe I met Kurt Kornfeld, vice president and one of the original founders of Black Star, on Kurt's first postwar visit to Paris in 1947. Kurt had not seen Paris since 1936, after escaping Hitler's Germany, before immigrating to New York.

Kurt was an ebullient man who called everyone "friend." Perhaps because Kurt lost a son, a *Time*-magazine correspondent, killed in a jeep accident on his way to cover the Nuremberg trials the previous year, he insisted I walk him all over Paris "to breathe the free air on foot and not from a jeep." Kurt was a fatherly man, generous with his advice, who assured me, "Photojournalism is a great calling."

Joe Pazen became my mentor who taught me the first steps of the profession. As he believed my ambition to drive a truck across the USA to write poetry at night "wasn't realistic," Joe gave me a year's worth of *Life* issues and told me to read Henry Luce's definition of the greatest picture magazine in the world.

It read: "To see life; to see the world; to eyewitness great events...to see strange things—machines, armies, multitudes, shadows in the jungle and on the moon; to see man's work...and discoveries; to see things thousands of miles away...things dangerous to come to...to see and be amazed..." Henry Luce had put into words exactly what I wanted to do and what I would do.

Joe, who met and married a beautiful woman in England, eventually brought me to that island nation at the end of 1947—I loved England, for helping to liberate France.

From London, we produced one story a week, and I was popular in the new milieu of British journalism. A waitress on Fleet Street, the press district, regularly called me "dear," and because I was so thin, she saved me steaks even during those rationed postwar days. It was a wonderful time.

Joe's wife, "Paddy," was tall, blond, blue-eyed, and beautiful with full lips and high cheekbones. Long-legged in a bathing suit, she looked like pinups of Californian women I'd seen in Joe's copies of *Yank* magazine, yet with her satin-white complexion, she was clearly English.

In a confused way, I was in love with her, but she never knew. Like the English, people in Marly and Paris stared as she walked by in her elegant clothes. During subway rush hours in Paris, I often found myself squeezed against her, and embarrassed, felt erotic desires. Still a virgin, I was troubled and afraid to look at her when we got off the train, but never said a word. However, one day she explained she needed an "escort" because so many Frenchmen in the subways would pinch her behind, so one of my jobs became to stand behind her to ward off my pinching countrymen. She treated me like a brother, and I was happy.

In the spring of 1949, Joe went back to California and said I could join him there. Because I had no cameras of my own, Paddy lent me her Rolleicord, saying, "You can return it when you reach the west coast."

Joe paid my last six months' wages in American dollars so I could avoid the long wait of changing francs to dollars. Soon I knew I'd be going to California, with its Hollywood, Golden Gate Bridge, Death Valley, and Pacific Ocean.

All my friends in Marly learned of my imminent departure, but they didn't share my enthusiasm. In a daze of excitement, I made preparations: for seven years I'd been waiting for this day. Meanwhile, Pepi, Time-Life's bureau manager in Paris, made my reservation for third-class passage on the *Liberté* ocean liner.

Joe signed and mailed my sponsorship papers to the American Consulate in Paris. All I had to do was produce a valid passport with a "Certificate of Military Position" from French military authorities and my visa would be issued immediately. I rushed to the French National Service Bureau for the missing certificate, where, to my horror, I was handed an immediate draft order into the French Army.

It was one of the saddest days of my life. I suddenly had military instructions to report to Thionville, east of France, within 48 hours. Waiting at a café at the Gare de l'Est train station in Paris, I met a beautiful Flemish girl and told her my story. Speaking a mixture of Dutch and English, she took my hand and held it to

her face, which had become as sad as mine. When my train came, we wiped each other's tears, hugged, and kissed passionately. As the steam engine pulled out of the station, she waved goodbye to me, running after the train. We never saw each other again.

Thionville was the most dreadful, dreary, depressing military town I'd ever seen. As I arrived at the garrison, all I could see was a lonely soldier walking with a rifle.

When I reported on May 17, 1949, to the Registering Office, an officer looked at my papers and said, "You don't have to serve—you're a resident of London." It was incredible news, but it would take a year to process the paperwork. Though I kept asking to be relieved of duty, nobody did a thing. In the end, I had to serve for a year.

The next day, I was issued my uniform: all used clothing and boots. In fact, everything I received was used including a filthy, beat-up, metal wine cup. France was so poor in those years that our uniforms looked as if they were made of carpet felt.

Basic training had already started by the time I arrived, and I was quickly thrown into rifle drills, saluting, marching left and right, roll calls, inspections, and lines to the canteen. Everyone in my platoon, company, and regiment knew I had been drafted while about to embark for California, and they all sympathized and shared my disgust.

Assigned as a crewmember for the "Long Tom," a 155-millimeter American long-range cannon, I met a painter named Lulu. A private from Paris who always spoke of his Russian ancestors, he sprinkled his conversations with Russian words. He was upset that his work in "postwar expressionism" was suddenly interrupted by the draft. I agreed with his sentiment; artists had no place in the Army.

During breaks, Lulu spoke of Venice, Verona, Florence and lectured our gun crew about the architectural Renaissance in Italy. In midstream he'd switch subjects to his Russian grandfather's odyssey to France after the Bolshevik revolution.

Losing the crew's interest, he'd regain a full audience by objecting to the low quality of food we were fed daily, particularly the disgusting beef stew. We all agreed it was not fit for humans.

My first meal in the Army, beef stew, was so hard to chew that soldiers joked it was made of leather soles from discarded boots. It was followed by an inedible green salad.

Lulu told me, "If you don't like the food and you have some money, it's easy to jump the wall and find a restaurant." He knew all the tricks about leaving the garrison without getting caught. Sneaking out to the city with Lulu, I treated him to dinner because most draftees in the French Army had no money. Full of wine, we came back pretty merry even though we knew we had missed roll call.

We crept to the low part of the wall where you could jump in and out easily. Scrambling over the wall, we fell right into the arms of the warrant officer.

So, on my first night in the French Army, I was taken to jail. We were each given a quarter loaf of bread and bottle of water. Lulu, having already been to jail for the same reason, told me, "You better wrap your bread with a towel and hang it from the wall or rats will eat it." With just a blanket, we slept on wooden planks. After sleeping badly, we discovered that the rats had devoured our bread.

For our hearing, we were called in front of three officers. In five minutes, we were found guilty, sentenced to two weeks in jail and the immediate shaving of our heads. As we walked out of headquarters, a clerk from the window upstairs shouted to the guards leading us to the military barber, "Hold on! Launois got a suspended sentence!" Lulu was taken to the barber, but I was released because it was my first offense.

The Army didn't know what to do with an artist. So one day they asked Lulu to think of a motif and paint the officers' recreation room, reflecting France's honor with great glorious battle scenes. He told me he was going to paint nude women in the Pacific. I learned later they caught him before his sketches became murals. I never found out what happened to Lulu.

During the first few months of service, I met another character named Lulu, a soldier from the rugged mountains of Auvergne. He was huge. He became kind of a bodyguard for me. Assigned to Germany for military maneuvers, we refused to ride the freight car made for eight horses or 40 men, so we got permission to ride the flatbed car where our artillery pieces were anchored.

Lulu had a fever from a bronchial infection and began coughing. When it started to rain heavily, I took my poncho off and wrapped him up in it. He never forgot that gesture.

Later, when an Alsatian sergeant, speaking French, gave me orders in a heavy German accent, I responded, "Four years of German orders are enough! I'm not going to take any orders from you." As the sergeant reached over to grab me, big Lulu stepped between us. "You touch him," he said, "you touch one hair on his head, and you're finished." The sergeant stepped back and never bothered me again.

In 1949 France, it was your national duty to serve your country, but the majority of draftees felt they owed little to France—certainly not their liberation, which they credited to the British and Americans.

The nation was poor and its conscript wages were so low you couldn't buy necessities let alone a decent meal. As compensation, the Army issued its troops awful cigarettes made of the cheapest black tobacco. Most of my squad spent their weekends in barracks playing cards and drinking cheap wine. Everyone spoke of civilian life, symbolized by a "skittle," a bowling pin, raised each day to the rafters like a flag.

After basic training, Lulu from Auvergne became the regiment's head cook. He set us a separate table from the rest of the enlisted men, which meant we had the best cuts of meat. Lulu was a good friend, but he was upset about my plan to go to America. He had seen too many Hollywood films about Indians massacring white people.

When I was transferred from Thionville to Fort Romainville near Paris, Lulu made a basket of food that would last me a week. Walking me to the gate, he wept inconsolably, saying, "If you go to America, you'll get killed by the Indians and I'll never see you again." We hugged goodbye and I never saw him again.

After six months, I was promoted to "brigadier chief," an NCO, noncommissioned officer, putting me in charge of about a dozen men. At roll call and when assigned various duties, they obeyed without enthusiasm except for standing smartly at attention each morning to solemnly salute the "rising pin."

Everyone dreamed of civilian life. At daily dismissal, one man would cross out another day on the barrack's wall calendar. All the men cheered and shouted, "One less day!" Being an NCO put an end to my awful cigarettes and hard soap from Marseilles. No longer eating with enlisted men, I dined at the officers' mess hall where the quality of food was much higher and wine was served in glasses instead of battered cups.

One day I was shocked noticing the steaks for officers were twice the size of steaks for NCOs. Angry, I convinced all the NCOs not to touch their plates until we were served steaks of equal size. All agreed, and they followed me out of the mess hall. Our food was left untouched on the table.

To my colonel, the commanding officer, I was immediately reported as the instigator. He was enraged. "I have no choice but to court-martial you for mutiny." I was scared because I knew what mutiny meant.

Even so, the colonel liked me because I often translated for him and photographed the regiment, making big prints for him, courtesy of *Life*. "What do you have to say for yourself?" he asked. "This incident was not an isolated event," I said. "It was unfair and we shouldn't be treated as inferiors."

The lieutenant and captain, my immediate superiors, pled my case, saying I had "shown great initiative and leadership qualities." After their pleas, I reported back to the colonel. He said, "I'll make an exception for you but never put yourself in this position again. Next time, put your complaints in writing through the chain of command and don't act like a revolutionary."

So I went on photographing the regiment, developing my film at *Life*'s office in Paris. Making prints for the great *Life* photographer Dimitri Kessel and others, I earned $10 a night, almost more than I made in a month from the French Army.

Joe Pazen was kind enough to give me his American war correspondent's uniform, which I recut to fit me. So in the French Army, I was dressed in an American officer's uniform. Nobody complained.

Two months before my military discharge, I was assigned to make a pickup at Fort Vincennes. I brought with me four or five guys dressed in fatigues, the Army's work uniform. Hungry, we parked my Dodge pickup by a sidewalk café. Just as we were dipping some croissants in our coffee, a Peugeot came to a screeching halt. A full colonel got out and shouted, "Who's in charge here?" I said, "Moi, mon colonel." Yelling, he said, "How can you let your men possibly have coffee in a public place in fatigues?" I explained, "They had no breakfast when we left. The men were hungry."

Ordered to report to his office, I stood at attention as the colonel snarled, "Your conduct was inexcusable and you put the Army to shame. I'm recommending a four-week sentence in jail!"

He dismissed me and I saluted in disbelief. It was late spring and less than a month away from my discharge. The charges meant my class would be released from duty while I'd stay behind in jail.

Upon receiving formal charges, my colonel, captain, and lieutenant made an impassioned plea for a suspended sentence in view of my "exemplary leadership qualities, photographic work, and for being a good example to my men."

The colonel in Vincennes reluctantly agreed to suspend my sentence. The problem was that I already had one suspended sentence from jumping the wall in Thionville. With both sentences combined, I'd have to spend six weeks in jail.

I must've had a friend in the records department, as somehow my first suspended sentence disappeared from the books, or perhaps my commanding officer just ignored it. I'm sure they thought being thrown in jail for taking my men in fatigues to a café was absurd.

After one long year, on May 17, 1950, several of us dressed in civilian clothes made bundles of our uniforms and boots and returned them to the quartermaster's supply store for the next class of conscripts. The men I had authorized to have coffee and croissants in Vincennes invited me for a round of cognac as soon as we were out of Fort Romainville. We toasted our newly won freedom late into the evening. The colonel from Vincennes was cursed profusely while my ex-commanding officer was praised for permanently suspending my sentence.

With my discharge papers finally in hand in May 1950, I obtained my "Certificate of Military Position" at last and went to the American Embassy in Paris to obtain my Visa while Time-Life's general assistant, Pepi, again reserved my third-class space on the *Liberté* liner. When I went to American Express to buy my ticket, I discovered the $300 Joe Pazen had paid me were all counterfeit. I figured he must have won the phoney money in a poker game.

Once again, Pepi had to cancel my reservation to America. I was devastated and had to find work. Fortunately, Time-Life's bureau chief, Elmer Lower, found me a well-paid job as a photographic technician in Paris at the Marshall Plan headquarters.

By the fall of 1950, I had finally saved enough to buy a ticket on the *Liberté* liner to New York, with $50 left in my pocket. Mother seemed to look forward to my departure, perhaps annoyed I had kept most of my wages to buy the boat fare. "When will you leave?" she kept repeating, and I'd answer, "One day soon, and you may never see me again."

My last month in France was a lonely time. Pierre's family was still supportive, but most of my friends thought I was an "idealistic fool," asking, "What can you find in America that you can't find in France?" I replied, "Freedom, opportunity, and open roads." It was all beyond their imagination.

My father could climb a steeple, but he could not cross an ocean, and he imagined the American continent fraught with dangers. Remembering our American GI guests, he said, "They don't even appreciate good wines over there." But he knew I didn't drink much wine.

DEPARTURE

A JOB IN CALIFORNIA

SAN FERNANDO VALLEY, CA 1950

On November 4, 1950, my day of departure finally arrived. My brothers and sisters all stood around, hugging and kissing me. Mother remained upstairs, crossing her arms, resting her elbows on a window bar, watching me cross the garden for the last time. She didn't say a word, not even goodbye. It hurt. I never knew what she felt. As she looked down from her window, I said, "Mother, you wanted me to get out, so I am getting out, and I'm not coming back till my name is in *Life* magazine!"

Father tried to hand me an envelope with the family's small savings, but I refused it. He walked me down the long driveway and hugged me, saying, "You do understand why I can't go to the station with you." Tears were streaming down his face. So we said goodbye and I walked to the station with my cardboard suitcase and brown hand-me-down suit.

All my friends from Marly and my oldest sister, Paulette, with tears in her eyes, came down to Gare St. Lazare in Paris to the boat train for Le Havre. Girls kissed me, guys hugged me, and all wished, "Bonne chance!" and "Bon voyage!" I later heard that my friends thought I was crazy, making comments and predictions like "Where the hell is Jean going?" and "He'll be back soon." Soon would be 10 years.

Boarding the *Liberté* on November 5, I was finally on my way with no regrets, but my stomach was in excruciating pain. A strange feeling overcame me when the ship left the shore of France, and the *Liberté* whistle blew.

I shared a two-bunk cabin with Jonathan, a young American student. He gave me a pamphlet about the Statue of Liberty. French artist, Frédéric Auguste Bartholdi, created the statue, a monument to liberty, and dedicated it to America on October 28, 1886. Frenchmen like Bartholdi, long before I was born, crossed the Atlantic to express a longing for freedom. For me, it was symbolic: like them, I was leaving France to find liberty in America.

From the booklet, I learned "Lady Liberty" was 151 feet high and over 300 feet with the pedestal. I read Emma Lazarus's poem, "The New Colossus," inscribed on the pedestal. My tears flowed as a I read, "Give me your tired, your poor, your huddled masses yearning to be free." I wasn't tired, just poor.

But "the wretched refuse of your teeming shore" angered me. "Damn it," I thought, "I am not wretched refuse." I was again moved reading, "Send these, the homeless, tempest-tossed, to me." I was not homeless but my soul was certainly tempest-tossed.

After five days, the *Liberté* sailed into New York Harbor. The crew woke everyone to see the Statue of Liberty. When I saw her, I remembered, "I lift my lamp beside the golden door."

Approaching Manhattan, I was amazed by the endless array of big yellow cabs cruising silently by, flanked by massive skyscrapers.

After docking, we went through customs. I had two expensive bottles of Chanel No. 5 perfume for Joe's wife, Paddy, but only one bottle was duty-free, so I left the other with customs.

Standing in a huge crowd was good old Kurt Kornfeld of the Black Star picture agency waving to me. Years ago, I gave Kurt a tour of the liberated streets of Paris. Welcoming me to America, he hugged me and took me on my first cab ride through the avenues of Manhattan.

Handing me a dollar bill, he said, "Keep this as your first symbolic American dollar." He took me straight to Saks Fifth Avenue, saying, "I want to be the one who buys you your first American necktie."

I thanked Kurt, and we shook hands. I put on my new necktie, walked to Grand Central station where I had left my cardboard suitcase in a locker, and took a bus to upper Manhattan's YMCA hostel. It almost seemed as far away from Saks Fifth Avenue as America seemed from across the ocean.

I checked in, paid for the first night, flopped on the bed, and felt such painful cramps, I thought I had appendicitis, or worse, peritonitis. I broke into a heavy sweat and fell asleep.

Waking at daylight, I touched my belly, felt no pain, and had breakfast. Somehow the anxiety had passed. I decided to walk all the way to the Black Star agency in the Graybar Building at 420 Lexington.

Kurt Kornfeld, one of the three founders of Black Star.

Walking downtown, again fascinated with the yellow cabs, towering buildings, and people in the streets, I talked to myself out loud, "I am in the new world!" I kept repeating in French, "*le nouveau monde*" and then in English, "the new world." As people heard me, some waved, others said nothing, yet many smiled. No one was surprised. By the time I got to Black Star I was elated.

When I reached the office, I told Kurt Kornfeld about my talking to myself. He understood immediately—he had left Nazi Germany many years earlier.

"Yes, this is the new world," he assured me.

Kurt took me around the office, introducing me to Kurt Safranski and Ernest Mayer, two key figures who introduced photojournalism to America, the men who helped *Life* magazine get started in 1936, the same men who eventually lost their best photojournalists to *Life*'s generous salaries.

In Mayer's office, I could see he and Kornfeld were anxious to give me some good news. The agency had sold my picture story on an American girl who opened a riverboat bar on the Seine in Paris.

Black Star had sold it for $100. Since I'd get $50, I wouldn't have to borrow from my mentor, Joe Pazen. I could buy a one-way ticket to Burbank, California, and start life in the new world without debt.

Black Star reserved me a seat on American Airlines. To me in 1950, all airlines were American. It was late November, somewhat cold. On my last day in Manhattan, I checked out of the YMCA.

After putting my suitcase in a midtown bus terminal locker, I walked to Central Park. Falling leaves had turned yellow and brown. Soon the trees would be bare. I sat on a bench by a pond and fell into a reverie, musing about seasons, other autumns and winters far away.

No one informed me whether American Airlines would serve food on the 16-hour journey to California, so I went downtown to an Automat, the strangest restaurant I'd ever seen. With rows of glass boxes filled with food and snacks, it was the ultimate in self-service. I got three sandwiches and a Coke to last me halfway across the country. After that, I could eat at numerous stops scheduled on the California flight.

In the Automat, I noticed a very old lady sitting at the next table with a single cup of coffee. Watching her discreetly, I saw that before each sip, she'd put several spoons of sugar in her cup. She repeated the ritual until her cup was empty. Then she used the spoon to finish the sugar at the bottom of her cup. Looking at her drawn features and shabby overcoat, I realized she was hungry and poor, and that she was consuming the sugar for energy.

She was the first poor person I had seen in America. Poverty in the U.S. made no sense to me. So as she left carrying her two heavy black bags made of oily cloth, I ran after her. "Excuse me, this dollar dropped from your bag." She turned and said sternly, "Young man, all I own is in these two bags, and I can assure you there wasn't any money in my bags." I said, "Maybe someone dropped a dollar into one of your bags. That would explain why it fell out."

At that moment, I kept remembering the GIs in France giving chocolate, C-rations, and cigarettes to people lining their routes. Reluctantly, the old lady took my dollar. She said, "Thank you, young man," and left the Automat.

With hours to spare, I left the Automat and walked south to the Lower East Side. I found myself in blocks of tenements, hearing languages I'd never heard. They were not English, French, or German, but I was sure they were European. By late afternoon, I returned to the bus terminal, retrieved my suitcase from the locker, and boarded a bus for LaGuardia.

LaGuardia Airport in 1950 had an easygoing atmosphere. Flights were not posted. A friendly woman at American Airlines told me, "We'll announce your flight over the loudspeakers. Since you've already checked in, we'll find you. Relax."

I couldn't possibly relax, but finally my flight to Burbank, California, was announced. In small groups, we were herded into the airplane, a Douglas DC-4 carrying about only 30 passengers. We'd fly across the United States at an average speed of 220 miles an hour at an altitude of 14,000 feet. We made four or five refueling stops as we crossed Pennsylvania, Ohio, Indiana, Illinois, Kansas, and Arizona.

It was a smooth flight until I thought our right engines were on fire. I pointed out the burning engines to the stewardess. She reassured me, "Those flames are just from the exhaust pipes. Relax."

After about 15 hours of flight during the night, I had seen nothing. Daylight broke somewhere between Kansas and New Mexico. Even at 14,000 feet, the deserts of New Mexico and Arizona looked beautiful.

At all stops, the airports looked the same. Coffee tasted the same, cherry pies tasted great, and I loved them. I expected my journey to California from New York to take 16 hours, but it actually took 21. Thinking that flying robbed my sense of travel, I vowed to one day cross America on land.

Our plane touched down at Burbank Airport around noon Pacific Time, November 14, 1950, nine days short of my 22nd birthday. As our aircraft taxied to the terminal, I didn't recognize any of the passengers who had boarded with me at LaGuardia. Most had left during night stops.

Looking out my porthole, I could see Joe, Paddy, and their two-year-old son Mark, standing behind a wire fence 20 feet from the plane. The Burbank terminal had an even more casual setting than LaGuardia. After stairs had been rolled to the door of the DC-4, Joe, Paddy and Mark came to the foot of the stairs. I hugged Paddy first, then Joe, and kissed little Mark on both cheeks.

Suddenly the heat overwhelmed me in my heavy, hand-me-down brown suit. Everybody else was in short sleeves. It must have been 25 degrees Celsius (77 degrees Fahrenheit). It was hot.

Paddy wore a light blouse and shorts, revealing her nice legs, no longer English ivory but California tan, while Joe was in khakis and short sleeves. It was southern California.

Joe and Paddy were full of questions about my trip, about Marly, which they loved, and about how my parents felt about my coming to America. Our conversations overlapped.

We walked to Joe's 1949 Chevrolet station wagon with sidewood panels and took off for Van Nuys in the San Fernando Valley. Seeing me sweat profusely in the front seat, Joe decided then and there to take me to a sports clothing store.

Within 45 minutes, I too wore khakis and short sleeves, and I threw away the hated brown suit. All I had left was Kurt Kornfeld's symbolic dollar and some loose change, but Joe said, "Don't worry Johnny, I'll deduct it from your pay."

As we drove westward on Vanowen, I remarked that everything seemed to have been built overnight. "In a European sense it was," Joe said. "Don't look for medieval cathedrals or castles here. We don't have any. Thank God America doesn't have a medieval past. We've had enough troubles in our 170-year history to last us a long while."

After we had driven miles along Vanowen, I couldn't believe we were still on the same street. Keeping track of house numbers, I was amazed to see number 10,000. At 14,000, Joe turned south toward Van Nuys Boulevard. The longest street I had ever walked on in 1941 Paris was Rue de Vaugirard with 407 numbers. I imagined no country in Europe with a medieval past could ever have built a straight street with over 14,000 numbers. The last time I checked a map of the San Fernando Valley in 1996, Vanowen had 24,000 numbers.

Paddy spoke from the rear seat, "Let's take Johnny to Van Nuys and show him Main Street and the center of town." I looked at all the movie houses, coffee shops, parking meters, the Bank of America, the hardware store, drug stores with soda fountains, the Veterans of Foreign Wars building, the vacuum cleaner store, and the U.S. Army Recruiting Office.

Joe pointed out the post office, the photo shop where he bought supplies, and the Western Union Office where he said I'd often go. Paddy teased my hair and said, "Johnny, that's Main Street Van Nuys, but it could just as well be Main Street in San Fernando Valley. They all look the same." I realized later that there was a note of nostalgia for old England in Paddy's voice.

As we drove through the residential area of Van Nuys to Joe and Paddy's house, I immediately noticed there were no fences or walls around the houses. The San Fernando Valley in 1950 looked prosperous, open, optimistic, and if nothing else, disturbingly uniform.

Joe and Paddy's ranch house was a couple of miles from Van Nuys Boulevard. When Joe rolled into his driveway, I saw a pleasant house with a green lawn and a red, tile-covered roof. They gave me a tour of their three bedrooms, two bathrooms, kitchen, dining, and living room. In the back, there was a garden with a huge walnut tree and double-car garage, which Joe turned into a photographic lab, where I'd spend many nights processing color films.

In the living room, I gave Paddy her bottle of Chanel, and in return, got two kisses. I gave Joe a bottle of father's Pommard, which father had wrapped in my sweater with rubber bands, and Joe asked me to write him a thank you note. But for little Mark, I had nothing. He had been an infant when I last saw him and I had forgotten to get him a gift, but eventually I made it up to him.

I returned Paddy's Rolleicord that I had used to produce my first story sold in America. Paddy wanted to know about my days in the French Army. As I narrated my adventures, she laughed and hugged me a couple times.

Joe wanted to know about the counterfeit $300 he had paid me. He remembered the luxurious hotel in Paris that had exchanged his traveler's checks. I had taken the phony dollars to the same hotel but they denied any wrongdoing, confiscated the counterfeits, and gave me a receipt. When I translated the contents of the receipt to Joe, he blew up and said, "I'll sue them!" But we had no proof.

Joe's sense of outrage eased after calling the hotel's cashier a "bastard" one last time. "Johnny, let's celebrate your coming to California," he said. Paddy talked me into trying a Bourbon Seven Up. Joe went to the kitchen to prepare drinks, calling out, "Two Bourbon Seven Ups for Johnny and Paddy, one Coke for Mark, and one Jack Daniels on the rocks for his daddy."

Then we all toasted my arrival in California with my very first whiskey. I basked in the warmth of our reunion, pleased Paddy and Joe seemed so genuinely happy to see me.

Strangely, I had no sense of place. On the road to Van Nuys, I noticed hundreds of shining American automobiles rolling along or displayed in new and used car lots. I saw hundreds of palm trees and one-story houses, yet I kept asking myself, "Where is California?"

In New York City, I felt excitement running through my veins, heart, and head—it was exhilarating. I immediately felt creative there, thinking of poems I might write. But here in the San Fernando Valley, I felt adrift without an anchor. Something was missing. I attributed my sense of loss to exhaustion.

I asked Joe if greater Los Angeles had a center somewhere. "Los Angeles has a downtown," Joe said. "I'll take you there, but you wouldn't want to live there."

In the evening, he lit a torch light by a huge walnut tree in the back garden as we continued our conversations under the nearly leafless branches. Sitting under the tree felt reassuring, and my brooding eased. I asked Joe for a second Whiskey Seven Up and felt mellow.

Soon after, we ate Paddy's meat loaf and salad. Then my hosts walked me to my bedroom and told me to sleep as long as I wanted. I fell asleep almost immediately, still thinking, "Where is California?"

After sleeping 14 hours, I woke to find Paddy had already prepared bacon and eggs with toast. Joe walked in through the kitchen's back door and said, "Paddy and I talked about you last night because we saw you so forlorn, so I want you to know that even though you're working for me, you're family to us." Then Paddy showed me the kitchen "where all the goodies are," cookies, chocolates, and candies.

In France and England, Joe and Paddy never treated me as an employee. Joe had always been a leader, teacher, and mentor. Paddy had always been a confidante, an abstract love in my life. She treated me like a little brother, even though she was not much older than I was.

After breakfast, Joe and I talked business. He said a large part of his work involved photographing movie stars for covers of Sunday newspaper supplements. He also filled me in on his latest purchase of stroboscopic lights, the largest on the market, which made it possible to photograph a jet taking off at night in multi-exposures, or a man flying out of a circus cannon, or the trajectory of a baseball thrown by a pitcher.

He said, "In London with me, you learned more about strobes than nearly anyone in the business, so your experience will help us with my new ideas." It all sounded exciting—movie stars, jets in the night—but I didn't know what a curved baseball was.

Joe proposed a salary of $20 a week, plus room and board. For that, I'd assist him on all assignments while having the right to use his equipment to shoot my own stories for Black Star. I'd have to process all color films overnight in his new air-conditioned lab.

I could also go to San Fernando College at night as long as I processed our previous day's shoot, and I could use the station wagon to drive to college until I could buy a car of my own. Twenty dollars a week wasn't much in 1950 California, but I'd learn and be paid. Money was profoundly academic to me. Elated, I shook hands with Joe.

While Joe was between assignments, he wanted me to immediately familiarize myself with his new strobes. I'd never seen such monstrously huge equipment. They had to be rolled on a dolly strong enough to carry a grand piano. Each condenser box was 8 inches high, 8 inches wide, 2½ feet long, and each weighed nearly a hundred pounds.

The four condenser boxes had to be connected by cables thicker than my thumb. Each condenser stored thousands of volts, which when released into a gas tube, sounded like a cork exploding from a bottle of champagne. All this energy was released when you squeezed a camera shutter connected to the "monsters," as I came to call them, by a straw-thin wire synchronizing their light energy with the opening of the lens aperture.

I once calculated that in a 30-foot radius, Joe's monsters were four times more powerful than the California sun at high noon. With so many technological advances in the early twenty-first century, it might be hard to understand how technically complicated color photography was in 1950. Film emulsions could not be trusted for accuracy: they had to be tested and corrected with Kodak CC color correction filters.

Photographers in the 1950s who could master color were paid twice the normal day or page rate. In that day and age, Joe Pazen commanded a leading edge and could take any assignment in color. We had enough strobes to light a stadium at night in color. It was a technical skill and advantage but not really a creative innovation.

Trying to recoup his expensive investment, Joe rented out his "monsters" with the station wagon and his technician, me. I became part of a package deal: technician, station wagon, and strobes.

I made several trips with the strobes. Once I drove to Phoenix, Arizona, for a photographer shooting a Ford Motor Company's double-page, print advertising campaign. The idea was to show a Ford running over a railroad track to demonstrate the great performance of the shock absorbers. We had to capture one picture, shot at night with multiple exposures to show the operation of the wheels on the track. I set up the shot at dusk, tested a release for five exposures, and it worked. Then the photographer, his assistant, and I waited for deep night in the desert of Arizona to shoot the final photographs of a Ford sedan gliding gracefully over a railroad track.

When total darkness came, I gave the "go" signal to the photographer. The Ford drove over the track, touched my first four electric contacts perfectly, then a condenser blew up before the fifth exposure. Suddenly I had the photographer, art director, account executive, Ford executive, and all the assistants on my back screaming about the thousands of dollars that the project cost.

I felt ashamed, not about the thousands lost but because I was the one who had prepared all of "Joe's monsters." I turned to the photographer and said, "If you can open up a quarter of a stop on your shutter, I think I can bypass the burnt-out condenser unit," which was still smoking. He said, "Alright."

The manual indicated, "To discharge a condenser: Touch the positive and negative poles simultaneously with a safely insulated instrument. Caution: A disabled condenser can still store a very high amount of voltage." So I wrapped the plastic handle of a huge screwdriver with cloth and used it to cross the negative and positive poles. Sparks flew out and the screwdriver melted. I had bypassed the burnt-out condenser, giving us another chance at the shot. The Ford ran over the track again, and all five exposures worked.

The next day, the photographer called my motel very early in the morning. "You were heroic," he said. "The ad agency people are enthusiastic. The picture looks great. Look for it as a double page!" He also called Joe. Driving back from Phoenix to Van Nuys took about 12 hours including stops to eat where I could keep my eye on the heavily loaded station wagon. Those advertising people screaming about "thousands of dollars lost" left me unnerved. Hell, I thought, I made it work, all that on my $20-a-week salary.

Joe congratulated me upon my return and made me a Bourbon Seven Up. I wanted to tell him I didn't like being packaged with his strobes. Advertising was not what I wanted to do, but I said nothing. He was my mentor, and after my initial anger, I still admired him and was learning.

For my 22nd birthday on November 23, 1950, Joe and Paddy gave me a short-sleeved shirt. During my war years, my parents only celebrated the children's birthdays when there was enough food. In California, Paddy had prepared so much, we had leftovers for days.

When I blew out 22 candles, I felt I was running out of time. I was an old man. I had already worked 10 years, never had time to be a teenager, and was nowhere. I wasn't a photojournalist yet, and all my photographs were based on what Joe wanted.

Later that afternoon, doing errands in Van Nuys, I was enticed into a drag race by seniors from the local high school. I didn't understand their hand signals and roaring engines, and was squeezed into the right lane, endangering Joe's wood-paneled station wagon, so I pulled onto a curb.

Seconds later, the students came back, calling me, "chicken." In French slang, "chicken" meant "police." I had been terrorized by French police checks during war years in France, so I reacted by instinct, expecting police cruisers, but there were no police in sight. Puzzled, I finished my errands and drove back to Joe and Paddy's place.

I related the story to Joe. Laughing, Joe told me, "Johnny, 'chicken' in America also means coward, but I'm glad you didn't understand, because my station wagon isn't made to drag race against souped-up cars."

My American education was underway. Joe taught me about drag races, souped-up cars, hot rods, and the double meaning of chicken. By midnight, I thought again of the students from Van Nuys High, driving to school, tinkering with their engines and turning their cars into hot rods. They were not yet 18, and they belonged to a golden age in a country that seemed to worship its youth. Still, I felt no envy.

When I spoke to Joe about the easy life of California students, he said, "Their parents became adults during the Great Depression, a time essentially left behind after World War II when America emerged as the only wealthy nation on earth. So most parents of the kids who challenged you today wanted to give their children what they never had."

He elaborated, "America is a story of booms and busts. Right now we're experiencing the biggest boom we've ever had. From 1930 to 1941, there were bread lines and soup lines across the country. You only know the generous GIs liberating France from when you were a kid. When you go to night college next year, you should concentrate on American literature and American history." Nearly half a century later, I came to think that the generation of the Great Depression was exceptionally generous and humanistic.

Shortly after my birthday, I learned from Joe's newspapers that the Chinese had entered the Korean War. American forces were said to be retreating in disarray under a huge assault by the Chinese. The U.S. Eighth Army was outflanked, while Marines, trapped at the frozen Chang Min reservoir, south of the Yalu River, were fighting their way to the Sea of Japan.

In my mythical America, U.S. forces never retreated. I imagined they always turned things around as they had in Europe and the Pacific, but on December 16, 1950, President Harry Truman declared a national state of emergency as "U.S. and U.N. forces suffered further setbacks in Korea."

My war years and service in the French Army were events of the past, best forgotten. The Korean War was an abstraction. In 1949, my father, an idealistic French liberal, warned me about the dangers of international communism and Mao's victory in China. He showed me an old world map, outlining the territorial gains of the Soviet Union and China, and told me, "The Communists intend to rule the world. They are as ruthless as the Nazis were."

Discharged from the French Army, I was put on "active reserve," but by leaving France, I was classified as "unavailable." In America, I was a French citizen, so it never occurred to me that I could be drafted into the Korean War.

That Christmas, 1950, I helped Paddy put colored lights on the walnut tree. Unlike France, where Christmas Eve was celebrated after midnight, we ate turkey late in the afternoon on Christmas Day.

All of us were in short sleeves in the balmy weather—it felt more like we were celebrating the summer solstice than Christmas. Always shining, the sun seemed to be going nowhere anytime soon. I missed the Paris winters, but I did not miss France.

For New Year's Eve, Joe and Paddy invited a few friends, and we all toasted 1951 with champagne. I shook hands with men and kissed women on both cheeks. Paddy teased me, saying I kissed the prettiest women twice, but I pointed out that it was the women who came to me for a second kiss. Paddy laughed, so I kissed her cheeks again. She said, "Johnny, you're a cheeky boy."

I was not a social drinker, and being sober in a very merry crowd was somewhat depressing, so I asked Joe for the keys to the Chevy. Heading south, I drove to the crest of the Santa Monica mountains on Mulholland Drive where the view of Hollywood and Los Angeles revealed a magical sight: endless miles of still and moving lights. I was reminded, that first day of 1951, of the great contrast to my home—how dark Paris, "the city of light," had been during the war, and how we had come to call the darkened Eiffel Tower, "the Black Widow."

Seen from above, great boulevards sliced through darkness in straight illuminated miles. I was mesmerized by the sight and returned often to those mountains.

From there I drove down into Hollywood and cruised aimlessly up and down the Sunset, Santa Monica, and Hollywood boulevards, joining other cars. Everyone was shouting, singing, and honking horns in the first hours of 1951. In Santa Monica, I walked barefoot on the beach and encountered revelers in funny hats, blowing noisemakers and wishing Happy New Year to the Pacific Ocean.

On the other side of the Pacific, four days after the New Year, Seoul, Korea, fell again to the Communists. While some World War II veterans on reserve status were shipped to fight in the new war, many of the new draftees were younger brothers of the men who had liberated me in France in 1944. As Joe was over 30, he escaped being recalled into service.

Each week as the war escalated, I was thrilled by *Life* magazine's photographic coverage. I studied photographs by top professionals like John Dominis, David Douglas Duncan, and Hank Walker. I had no way of foreseeing my future—that in a few years I'd work with Dominis in the Far East; then in the early '60s in the south of France, I'd discuss Dave Duncan's book on the Korean War, *This is War*, with the author himself; and in 1962, I'd meet Hank Walker in Vietnam in an encounter that would change my professional life.

In 1947, I met Robert Capa, the legendary war photographer in Paris. I'd been impressed by his pictures of the landings in Normandy, published in *Life* and other publications. His work seemed glamorous and dangerous—the sheer drama of recording war and its horrors at once attractive and repulsive. Seeing the Korean War in the pages of *Life,* I felt the same attraction to the danger and action but was repelled by the idea of men killing one another.

As Joe's assistant, I was introduced to the glamour of Hollywood. My job was to help Joe while he shot cover stories on Fred Astaire, Ginger Rogers, Cyd Charisse, Anne Miller, and many other film stars.

In London, I'd been surprised when a waitress called me "dear," but in Hollywood, I was dumbfounded when several stars called me "darling" as they asked me to do minor things during a shoot.

The first time a gorgeous star called me "darling" on the set, I blushed. On the way home, I couldn't wait to tell Joe. He laughed and said, "Johnny, I don't want to destroy your dreams but didn't you notice that all the women stars call everybody 'darling'—the director, assistants, gaffers, electricians, makeup men, the parking attendant?" All I could say was, "You're putting me on."

On the next shoot, I paid attention and Joe was right. More than 20 years later, when I met Ginger Rogers again after one of her last performances in Las Vegas, I told her the story. "That's very dear of you," she said, and gave me a kiss.

Joe and I were once assigned to photograph Gene Kelly. When I saw his film, *An American in Paris,* I felt no nostalgia for Paris. I had entered my "Americanization" phase and was trying hard to forget France. Although women found my French accent charming, I was trying hard to erase it by imitating American voices I heard on the radio.

Early 1951, I started night school at Van Nuys Junior College, limiting courses to American history and literature. For me, the opportunity was invigorating—in 1940 France, high school was a privilege only for the wealthy, where in California, higher education was open to all.

All my notebooks from those years have been lost or destroyed except for one containing quotations from Thomas Jefferson, Abraham Lincoln, and Franklin D. Roosevelt.

One passage I particularly related to was from Jefferson's January 16, 1787, letter to Colonel Edward Carrington: "Experience declares that man is the only animal which devours his own kind; for I can apply no milder term to the governments of Europe, and to the general prey of the rich on the poor." Although Jefferson's letter had been written two and a half years before the French Revolution of 1789, I felt it described the French government and society I had just left.

From Lincoln, I saved a passage from his March 17, 1865, address to a regiment in Indiana: "I have always thought that all men should be free; but if any should be slaves, it should be first those who desire it for themselves and secondly those who desire it for others. Whenever I hear anyone arguing for slavery, I feel a strong impulse to see it tried on him personally."

Except for historical dates, I knew almost nothing about the history of slavery in America. Imagining such abominations, all I could think about was the brutality of the German-Nazi occupation of France and harsh treatment even from my own people, such as Monsieur Jeanret working me 12 hours a day at age 12, stacking 120-pound sacks of potatoes. That felt like slavery to me, yet it technically was not. What I experienced was brutal oppression and shameless exploitation, but slavery was a far greater crime. It would be many years into my "Americanization" before I learned more about this great American shame.

In my notebook, I saved a passage from Franklin Delano Roosevelt's June 27, 1936, speech accepting his renomination: "Out of this modern civilization, economic royalists carved new dynasties...The royalists of the economic order have conceded that political freedom was the business of the government, but they have maintained that economic slavery was nobody's business."

All three quotations inspired me because they reflected conditions in France that I had known between 1940 and 1950. Interestingly, those words were not written by Frenchmen but by three American statesmen in three different centuries.

By May 1951, while in college, I had saved enough from my $20 weekly salary to buy my first automobile. It had been on sale for several months at Palmer's Texaco gas station where we serviced Joe's Chevrolet.

It was a 1936 black Chrysler Coupe with an asking price of $75. I had looked at it several times, and Palmer said he would give me a fair price, so one fine morning, we haggled over the price and finally settled on $60. I paid cash, Palmer took care of the registration, and I drove home to Paddy and Joe who congratulated me.

The car's black paint was somewhat faded. There were traces of rust on the bumper but no holes in the body, and the tires were okay. The hood was incredibly long, and the interior included a single-bench seat, a floor shift, oil pressure, water gauges, and not much else.

I immediately washed the old Chrysler. As I removed the ashtray to clean it, I found an envelope containing $60, exactly what I had paid for the car. So I drove back to Palmer and played a guessing game with him, "Guess what I found in the ash tray?" He answered, "Cigar butts." Then I showed him the envelope with the money. He had completely forgotten that he used the ashtray to hide his horsetrack betting money from his wife.

Palmer was so impressed I had returned his money that he gave me a bear hug. He said, "Johnny thank you. That's so nice of you. Listen, if you ever need a credit rating in the future, I'll gladly give you one."

He did a year later when I needed a loan from Bank of America to buy a newer Pontiac for $400. While approving my loan, the officer said, "This is the most glowing credit report I've ever seen!" It was my first credit rating report in America.

Palmer had warned that my Chrysler was a "gas guzzler" and advised me to check the oil constantly. He was right: I got an average of seven miles per gallon on highways and less in the city. It burned one quart of oil per hundred miles. For long trips, extra cans of oil were in the trunk. But I never had any real problems with it. My Chrysler had over 200,000 miles on it when I exchanged it for a 1938 Buick with spare wheels on the front fender.

Having my own car gave me a degree of independence. I had often gone on long walks rather than ask for Joe's car, but southern California was designed for automobiles. During one of my walks on Vanowen, the State Police stopped to ask if I needed help. "It's okay," I said, "I'm just walking." But they gave me a ride home, saying, "The main drags aren't made for walking. You might get hit since there's no sidewalk."

My earliest encounter with the police occurred when I arrived in California and was driving while Joe slept. A strange car with flashing lights appeared behind us. I thought someone was trying to run us off the road, so defiantly, I wouldn't let them pass. Suddenly, sirens blared and Joe woke up saying, "Jesus! What are you doing? Pull over!" He had to explain that I had just arrived from France and didn't know they were police. After looking at my French driver's license, they let us go.

I hadn't been in California long and was already working on my own during my free days. I had bought a car and had the means to move. Moving, it seemed, was my way of life.

I assisted Joe photographing some of the greatest stars in Hollywood, walked in the Pacific Ocean, and looked at the stars in the desert sky, yet I kept asking myself, "Where is California?"

Shortly after my arrival, I already felt a sense of the restlessness of California. Unconsciously, I knew I had to move in order to survive.

YANK

DRAFTED

SAN FERNANDO VALLEY, CA 1951–1953

never discovered southern California's "golden dream." I found the sun, Pacific Ocean, Mojave Desert, mountain ranges, and new friends—my "early American architects," as I came to call them, who would mold me into the American I would become. But that's all I ever found. Perhaps southern California was where America's restlessness overflowed and never came to rest.

In the spring of '51, I was informed by Selective Service that I would be heading westward, toward Asia. With my U.S. draft number, 4-83-28-727, I was classified "1-A" and immediately eligible to fight in the Korean War.

Joe was shocked and said, "How can the U.S. draft you? You are a French citizen, damn it! You survived four years of war. Then you were drafted by the French Army. France is an ally. They can't draft you!"

But Joe was wrong. I had a permanent resident's visa and under U.S. law, I could be drafted. My night college courses wouldn't delay my "call to duty," but joining the National Guard might, unless my unit was called into federal duty.

So on June 15, 1951, I joined the California Air National Guard's 146th Fighter Squadron Air Group based in Van Nuys. Major Douglas Parker, the squadron commander, swore me in. Issued the light blue uniform of the U.S. Air Force, I became Airman Jean René Launois, U.S. 281-934-55. Eventually I grew tired of being called "Gene," as the Americans pronounced my first name, so I translated it into Johnny, and later into John.

Major Parker immediately assigned me to the squadron's photographic unit, which had a laboratory, a couple four-by-five Speed Graphics, and a K-20 for

air-to-ground photography. We generally served one day every other weekend. I found myself with a group of World War II heroes who had flown missions in Europe and the Pacific. The squadron was made up of P-51 Mustangs, the fastest aircraft in World War II.

With these pilots, I broke out of the isolation I felt. Soon I was flying missions in a T-6 trainer with First Lieutenant Bob Boal, a veteran of the Pacific and our public relations officer.

Teaching myself air-to-air photography, I composed photographs at 12,000 feet, carefully placing several Mustangs in my camera frame as we all flew at high speed over California mountain ranges. Half the veteran pilots in my photos had flown missions over my head, escorting B-17 bombers on their way to bomb Germany, when I was a kid.

Looking for new ideas, I decided to photograph an F-51 Mustang taking off directly overhead. Major Parker had to be persuaded. He resisted, argued safety, then relented. We rehearsed the shot a number of times, then finally, on a stormy day in California's rainy February season, First Lieutenant Erfkamp's Mustang took off. As I lay supine in the middle of the runway, looking at the great sky, the Mustang roared above just 12 feet over my head. I caught the graceful airplane on film with its gears retracting against a darkened sky and mountain range. My photograph, published locally and nationally, was an instant hit. All the pilots wanted enlargements—so did the men in the squadron.

Overnight I became the pilots' photographer. I spent many weekend evenings at the Officers' Club even though I was merely an enlisted man. In the early 1990s when I asked Major Parker, who had retired as Colonel Parker, why the pilots had ignored the Air Force rules of fraternization between officers and enlisted men, he simply said, "John, you had a special rank among us. You were our photographer and we were weekend warriors."

So for a while, I delayed my draft into the Korean War and had new friends among the pilots and crewmen. Meanwhile, when not on assignment with Joe, I began shooting my own stories.

At Grauman's Chinese Theater entrance on Hollywood Boulevard, I became fascinated watching people trying to fit their own hands and feet in the prints of celebrities set in concrete. But as soon as people saw me with a camera, they shied away, so I decided to photograph them from a rooftop with a telephoto lens.

I got permission from the director of Grauman's Theater to climb the straight-iron ladder leading to the roof. The ladder anchored to the outer wall of the building had no safety guides, and the first time I climbed, the ladder's anchors came partially out of the wall. My section of the ladder no longer matched the section above me. At some 300 feet above the ground and just inches from the wall, holding a four-by-five Graflex and a tripod, I was unable to reach the upper section. So I bumped my chest against the ladder to drive the anchors back into the wall until inch by inch, the anchors went in, and I reached the upper section to the roof.

Unseen, I photographed people trying to match their hands and footprints to the great stars of Hollywood. It took several days to take enough photographs for an essay. Each day, I looked at the thickness of the anchors, trying to figure out if they would come out of the wall, and each day, I had to bump my chest against the ladder, driving the anchors back in. Thankfully, the ladder held until my essay was finished.

Black Star sold the essay to a Sunday newspaper supplement and my name was bylined. It was also sold in Europe and made $700. With my full agreement, all money for that and other assignments I did for *Ebony* magazine were credited to Joe's account at Black Star. I saw none of the money. Eventually, Joe couldn't even pay me my $20 weekly guarantee.

I knew Joe had financial troubles but never understood why. He began telling me, "I can't pay you now but, instead, I'm giving you part of the laboratory." That was not much of a consolation—I didn't even have cash to go to the movies.

Soon I owned part of the lab. One day, when I was again rented out with Joe's strobes, we had technical problems. When Joe suggested the problem was my fault for failing to check the strobes, I blew up. Enraged, I ripped the air conditioner from the window of the photo lab and threw it to the floor. Then I drove to the edge of a cliff by the ocean near Malibu. Near tears, staring at the Pacific in the night, I knew my time had come to move on.

A few weeks earlier, I had been offered a photographer's position by the State of California to cover the Air National Guard's 146th Fighter Air Group. I told Major Parker that I'd take the offer. It may not have been photojournalism, strictly speaking, but at least I'd earn a decent salary and be able to continue college courses.

By late 1951, I had a few dollars in a savings account but not enough to buy a Leica or Rolleiflex. Palmer, the man at the Texaco station, found me a small studio shack to rent in Vanowen. It wasn't much of a place, but it had a shower, toilet, and a room with two beds and a kitchen.

I packed my cardboard suitcase from Paris, threw it in the trunk of my 1938 Buick, and moved to a place of my own about 20 blocks from Joe. Leaving wasn't easy. I kissed Paddy, little Mark, and hugged Joe goodbye. "Johnny," he said, "this is a passage of time in your life. We will miss you. Don't be sad. You are a very talented young man. You will make it and part of the lab is yours."

I said, "Joe, forget all that stuff about the lab. You owe me nothing. I owe you all I know in photojournalism." Joe Pazen was my first mentor and the first of my "American architects," the men I encountered in my early years on the road to becoming an American.

During that time, I kept in touch with Claude, my childhood friend from France. In Paris, he became an excellent pastry cook and chef, and by February 1952, he had saved enough to come to California.

His arrival was exciting. Within two weeks, Claude found a chef's position at the Beverly Hills restaurant, Jean's Blue Room. Pay was good and the restaurant's credit rating got him an immediate loan on a 1946 Chevrolet coupe.

To a World War II boy from France, arriving in California as a young adult, quickly acquiring a job as a chef and a car of his own within weeks, California was indeed the "golden state."

Claude and I began sharing rent for our room. We updated each other on our lives. When he heard about my leaving Joe and Paddy, Claude prepared a gourmet meal for them in our "shack." It was a feast. Claude even found good French wines for the occasion, and Joe and Paddy thought Claude had brought over a little bit of France to California.

On Claude's nights off, we'd drive to Santa Barbara, often racing each other, breaking the 65-mile-an-hour speed limit. Since my '38 Buick was older than his '46 Chevy, it was a point of pride to win the race, and I easily did. But one night I overdid it. After passing Claude, I was pulled over by a state patrolman and issued my third speeding ticket in less than three months. A month before, the judge warned me, "One more ticket and I'll send you to jail for one week to slow you down."

I dreaded appearing before the same judge. Though I normally didn't wear it during the week, I showed up for my court appearance in my Reserve Air Force uniform. It worked. The judge fined me $20 and said, "Young man, if you were not serving your country, I would have sent you to jail for two weeks."

For the 146th Fighter Squadron, my job proved to be far more technical than anticipated. I'd photograph defective engine and aircraft parts for documentation as well as make calculations for air-to-ground photography.

In the summer of '52, the 146th Squadron was shipped to Boise, Idaho, for a two-week training mission. General Dwight Eisenhower paid us a visit, gathering votes for his presidential campaign, and I was happy to photograph the great hero of my adolescence.

Having no political views of my own and still a French citizen in America, I thought Eisenhower, like Presidents Roosevelt and Truman before him, was a Democrat. To me, all Americans were Democrats. America was the world's oldest democracy.

But in Boise, Idaho, First Lieutenant Bob Boal, a Republican, began my American political education. Almost half a century later, my dear friend, Bob, from conservative Orange County California, would still be trying to convince me that all good Americans were Republicans.

I liked Eisenhower's speeches about ending the war in Korea. The idea of one more war in my life was sickening. His promise was still in my mind when I was drafted out of the Air National Guard into the U.S. Army Infantry and ordered to report to Fort Ord, California, on March 10, 1953.

The war in Korea was claiming daily casualties. In November, I'd be 25 years old. I wondered why I should fight North Koreans and Chinese when I had yet to begin my life.

It was a moral dilemma. I was a French citizen yet emotionally American. The Americans had saved me, my country, and Western Europe. In my head, going back to France would have been an act of cowardice, so I reported for war duty as ordered.

Driving north to Fort Ord, near Monterey and Big Sur, I reflected on what it was like to be an infantry grunt. *Life* magazine's war coverage looked grim and miserable.

Drifting in my thoughts was Patricia's beautiful face, my first American love. She was a student psychologist at the University of California. A few weeks earlier, on the delightful Santa Barbara campus, she told me she was pregnant and needed $300 to help pay for an abortion.

On our last trip to her parents' home at a naval research base in the Mojave Desert, she spoke of her need for post graduate work. As a psychologist, she was sure I could not be in love with her. "I am the mirror of your idealistic America," she said. "I am the California girl, the golden dream, the marshmellows roasted on the beach of Santa Barbara. But you cannot love me, and you must not love me. I don't want a child."

My generation was rather naive about sexual matters, or at least I was. But I was always careful not to make her pregnant. Patricia insisted it was an accident and I believed her. I was just able to raise the money she wanted. It wiped out my savings, and I had to take out a loan from Black Star, which would take a long time to repay.

I was stunned as we departed in the cool night of the Mojave Desert. I drove back to the San Fernando Valley in a kind of infinite sadness that lovers know. The next day in the 146th Fighter Squadron's lab showroom, I tore up all her 16-by-20-inch pictures displayed among the Mustang airplanes.

Back in basic training, I was exhausted and slept the few hours the Army allowed. I was comforted by a photograph of the luscious young Hollywood starlet who tried to console me before "my going to war."

Patricia eventually receded from my mind, so I was surprised in the early 1990s to receive a letter from her University of California roommate. "I tried to reach you for decades," she wrote, "but I had no idea where you were. Last week I saw your name, and your agency gave me your address. What I wanted to tell you is that you were right in questioning your paternity with Patricia decades ago. Patricia became pregnant by a South American playboy who disappeared after he had an affair with her while you were in the San Fernando Valley. She told me that herself. She told me she felt bad you were going to war but she was desperate. My conscience bothered me for all these years. I'm glad I finally found you."

Stunned by the letter, I telephoned Patricia's ex-roommate in Ventura, California. All she told me was that Patricia had a talk show on television "somewhere," giving advice as a psychologist. On the phone, in the background, I heard her husband say, "You've cleared your conscience! Now drop it!" I dropped it too. If indeed Patricia had been my California "golden dream," then it certainly was a tarnished one.

Back in basic training, the American Army was physically demanding and emotionally crude, designed to turn 18-year-olds into disciplined fighting machines. After four months of running in deep sand and enduring punishing exercise, I felt more physically fit than at any other time in my life.

Our first sergeant had just returned from a tour of duty in Korea. He described the "gooks" storming his entrenched position. "All we can do here," he said, "is give you the best training in the world and that won't be enough. You will train day and night, sleep some, and when you are exhausted, ready to fall, you will have to go again until you really fall."

The military, as it prepared us for the stresses and dangers of warfare, wanted us to learn to depend on each other. But because one of our men had gone AWOL, "absent without leave," my platoon became known as the "Goon Platoon." Our sergeant, saying a man of such low character would endanger our entire platoon in combat, suggested that all of us, some 60 boys and a few men, should "teach him an everlasting lesson and make the third platoon proud again."

We all understood "the lesson" meant a beating, but I didn't think anyone would follow the suggestion. When the soldier came back from yet another absence without leave, a dozen of his buddies, dressed in fatigues and combat boots, waited until he entered the darkened first floor of the barracks. Switching on the lights, they jumped him.

The soldiers began beating him with fists and kicking him with combat boots. When I heard the screams, I ran downstairs barefoot to the first floor. I couldn't believe the savagery. I tried to calm the mob saying, "He should be judged by a military court." One guy crushed my toes with his right boot and told me to "Shut up."

After the incident, suffering a black toe for my interference, I limped for days. But the badly beaten soldier "shaped up" and never again went AWOL for the remainder of basic training. The third platoon was no longer the "Goon Platoon."

We went through extensive rifle practice, grenade throwing, undergoing the infiltration course under live-ammunition fire, marching with heavy packs day and night, compass training, night navigation, and other challenges to mind and body.

Though I had no thought of killing while firing my M-1 rifle on the range or thrusting my bayonet into a dummy while screaming for psychological effect, I was reminded that soon I might have to kill other men. During our short hours of sleep, I'd dream the dummy was a faceless, screaming man charging me.

My platoon sergeant continued to incorrectly pronounce my name, Launois, as "Illinois" instead of "Lawn-wah." Exasperated after two months of training, I refused to respond at roll calls until the sergeant said my name correctly. He finally did but my defiance cost me an extra day of kitchen-police duty.

All our instructors had seen combat, and they pushed us mercilessly through training using foul and vulgar language I had never heard before. When they spoke to us directly, they shouted orders two inches away from our faces and spat the words.

Using obscene language during basic training in the U.S. Army was common practice in 1953. Younger recruits in my platoon saw it simply as "bullshit," which would end with our graduation from basic training. But as the oldest man in our platoon, I found the humiliation difficult to take. It reminded me of the abusive language the French and German police used during the occupation of France.

When we were first indoctrinated, we were read our military Bill of Rights, and I vaguely remembered that a soldier could not be abused verbally or otherwise. I didn't know how and when to exercise my rights, but I assumed, as a French citizen in the U.S. Army, I had the same rights as my American buddies.

One day late in the fourth month of basic training, we had to ready ourselves for the Inspector General's official inspection. All squads spent the entire morning cleaning, dusting, and checking the special folds on our double bunks in preparation for inspection. In my squad, our clothing lockers, footlockers, everything, including our feet, stood in perfect lines. None of us understood what authority an "I.G." actually had. I knew vaguely that he had investigative powers.

The officer, a full colonel, arrived to look us over. We stood at stiff attention. From head to toe, he inspected the barrack floors, windows, bunks and lockers, or so I assumed. Standing at attention with my eyes looking straight, I couldn't see what he was actually looking at.

Then he nodded to our platoon sergeant who gave the order, "At ease, men." Addressing our two squads, the colonel told us, "I'm here to listen to any complaints you men might have, any mistreatment..."

Nobody said a word. Sensing our discomfort in front of our sergeant, the colonel asked to be left alone with us. Still no one said a word. Realizing it might be my last chance, I stood again at attention, introduced myself as Private Launois, and blurted out that I resented and was disgusted by all the foul language and obscene names we had been called during the last several months.

There was a long silence. I felt absolutely alone. Suddenly, more than 30 voices shouted in anger, "He's right sir. He's right!" The colonel ordered me, "At ease." He asked the men to gather around. Everyone confirmed what I had just said. One soldier added, "If we are men enough to go kill or get killed, then we shouldn't be called the scum of the earth."

When I was standing alone reciting my grievances, it occurred to me that my young buddies in the third and fourth squads might have thought I was a wimp to make an issue of obscene language since they had dismissed foul language as "bootcamp bullshit." But their dignity had been hurt too. Some who had called me "Frenchy" in the past said, "Thanks for speaking up." Others began to call me the "French Revolution."

The colonel assured us he would look into our complaints. He did. The next day, the obscene language ended.

After basic training, all the men in K-company expected to ship out to Korea. In retrospect, we had been superbly trained both physically and psychologically. The graduation ceremony was moving: not only had the U.S. Army made us fighting men, it had made us American patriots. When we were ordered, "Eyes right," we saluted and looked at the reviewing stand with its officers wearing their stars and eagles, brass band playing, and the stars and stripes flying in the Monterey wind.

We thought of ourselves as the proudest Americans Fort Ord had ever seen.

We were going to fight for freedom against the "Commies" in Korea. I thought of my father and how he had told me that, "Communism was a noble idea in the nineteenth century, born out of a reaction to excesses of capitalism, but it became a monstrous experiment in the 1930s." He said its fraudulence was confirmed by Stalin jumping into Hitler's bed when the two dictators signed their nonaggression pact in 1939.

So there I was in mid-July of 1953, an American patriot in U.S. uniform with an "alien registration card" in my pocket, ready to fight for America as a French citizen, because I knew America had saved me and Western Europe during World War II. Now, in the Far East, America was needed again. At that time, things seemed just that simple.

After graduation, we were given a pep talk. The sergeant read the names of the few who were assigned "stateside." A week earlier, the colonel who ran Fort Ord's photographic activities told me he was impressed with my experience, so I suspected I would be among the lucky few. I was and soon found myself working in the colonel's Photographic and Public Relations Department.

Then, on July 27, 1953, less than two weeks after our basic training ended, an armistice was signed in Panmunjon, Korea, leading to the division of the Korean peninsula.

Beginning my new assignment, I learned the 7:00 A.M. roll call was made by a "professional private" who had been in the Army for years and had gone back and forth between private first class to plain private time and again because he picked a fight with every newcomer.

He was from Poland and insisted on being called "Polack." From his last fight, he had an infection from being bitten by his adversary. His right hand was still bandaged. Because he was a regular Army volunteer and I was a draftee, Polack predictably picked a fight saying, "You were the last one to fall out!" even though it was not true.

On the way to mess hall, he grabbed me. I turned around, held his collar, and asked him, "Do you have a car?" "No," he answered. So I said, "Polack, because of your last fight, you're a one-armed fighter. So tonight, you and I will drive to the beach in Monterey in my car, and I will beat the hell out of you. But don't expect me to bring you back."

Before finishing breakfast, Polack came to my table and told me what I had said made sense. With his left hand, he shook my hand and never bothered me again.

Because of the armistice, all my bootcamp buddies and I had escaped war in Korea. Most told me I was lucky to remain stateside, but my photographic assignments at Fort Ord were rather dull. With the war over, there was little satisfaction in photographing medals being pinned, VIP handshakes, and fresh recruits being trained. During basic training, I had seen the seriousness in my comrades' faces, but after the armistice, the looks of new trainees had none of that anxiety or sense of urgency.

For something new, I asked permission to photograph the faces of trainees in infiltration courses as they crawled through a barrage of live ammunition. My request was considered for a while but ultimately rejected as unsafe for the photographer and planners of the course. My ambition of course was to have my work published in a national magazine and bylined, "J. Launois, U.S. Army."

Knowing I was unhappy that my request was rejected, my colonel tried to cheer me up, saying, "Launois, you're our best photographer and I promise you'll get the best assignments. I want to keep you satisfied. Think of all your buddies in Korea while here at Fort Ord you have everything, Monterey, Carmel, Big Sur. As soon as regulations permit, I'll promote you to private first class."

But by that point, I was psychologically prepared for Korea. It sounded exciting and exotic—I wanted to see and photograph people of "the land of the morning calm" and capture images of "Heartbreak Ridge" where so many Americans fought and died.

The colonel was shocked when I requested a transfer to the Far East, to Korea or Japan. Instead of forwarding my request, he gave me another enthusiastic talk about my advantages at Fort Ord.

I submitted my request again, and again he didn't forward it. His attractive blond secretary told me, "Your request is still on his desk. The old man said you're a nitwit to want a transfer from California to Korea." Even so, she liked me enough to reveal an address where I could request a transfer directly and bypass my colonel.

From the French Army, I inherited the military tradition of referring to the colonel as "my" colonel even though an officer is not "yours" at all: you are at his command. I didn't want my ambitions to be compromised by my colonel. With his secretary's help, I submitted a direct request for transfer, and in late November 1953, I received orders for a Far East assignment.

I decided to make one last trip south to sell my car and see my old friend Claude in Van Nuys. Goaded by friends in the car, I pushed my '46 Pontiac too fast and blew out my engine. The car was sold as scrap for $10.

Returning to Fort Ord by Greyhound bus, I wrote a goodbye note to Claude, packed my duffel bag, and headed north to a briefing area for processing. There I endured lectures on Japanese and Korean cultures and the dangers of sexual promiscuity in the Far East.

We soldiers were reminded that Japan and America had signed a peace treaty the year before and we were to behave as guests in a "host country." They told us, "As ambassadors of good will, your conduct in Japan and Korea is to be exemplary. You are expected to respect cultures you do not understand and learn from them."

The lectures reminded me of post-World War II days in Germany and how disturbed I was when Americans treated the defeated Germans as friends. "The French and Germans have been killing each other since 1870," my father had said. "Millions of the dead speak to us today. These two enemies must share their destiny." Father had been a pro-European advocate long before the Treaty of Rome was signed. Now America was demonstrating exactly the same spirit of magnanimity toward Japan.

I wondered how a man with only a primary school education could be so wise. Though his family had lost everything in the First World War, father could still tell me why "enemies must seek reason."

After the briefing lectures, we had to watch films about sexual diseases in Asia. They described diseases I'd never heard of; the corrosive effects of syphilis were illustrated by men on the screen with faces, noses, and lips falling off.

As a romantic I couldn't completely believe in all the horrors in the film. I suspected many of the men we saw were afflicted with leprosy. But the Far East had its share of deadly venereal diseases, and the U.S. Army made it clear that a prudent soldier will restrain himself, abstain from sex, and contain his lust until returning home to the U.S.

I decided my own sexual energy could be eased by working very long hours. Thus far I had experienced love making with Patricia and the young Hollywood starlet doing her "patriotic duty" to comfort me before I went off to war, but such encounters pretty much summed up my sexual experience.

Shortly after my 25th birthday, I boarded the troopship *Saint Patrick* in San Francisco. I couldn't help thinking, "When I get out of this, I'll be going on 27, and my chances of making it with *Life* magazine will be close to zero."

My orders didn't say where I was going, but all 5,000 of us soldiers were convinced we were headed for Korea. The multileveled bunks in the ship were stacked one on top of the other. I made the mistake of choosing an upper bunk where the smells and heat of the ship rose till it was difficult to breath, and the problems of seasickness were more distinct. I ended up sleeping on the deck.

By midmorning, we sailed under the Golden Gate Bridge, and all of us were on the rails of the *Saint Patrick* to gaze at the magnificent structure. For me, the "Golden Gate" held special meaning, symbolizing the search for another land. I had always gone westward, from France to New York, to California, and now to the Far East. Once again, I sensed something ending and something beginning.

The difference between the relative calm of San Francisco Bay and the vast rolling waves of the Pacific Ocean initially made almost everyone sick. In the first hours, then days, many of us never made it to the dreaded "chow calls."

I learned if I could stay up on deck, let the Pacific wind and saltwater spray my face, I could make breakfast, lunch, and dinner without throwing up. But watching others be sick required reminding myself that food was energy and therefore essential. I made a habit of waiting till "last call" for dinner, so I could see more of the last light of day from the deck.

After the first few miserable days of crossing the Pacific, I began to feel a stirring of unknown emotions. I was going to where the sun sets, fulfilling some early personal yearning.

Thousands of us were going to Korea, but Japan was considered the ideal assignment. A short list of names was posted for the few men disembarking in Yokohama; though I'd expected to go to Korea, I was delighted to find my name on the list for Japan.

RISING SUN

AMERICAN GI IN JAPAN

TOKYO 1954

The seagulls that followed our ship for a short while from San Francisco were long gone. New seagulls swirled about the ship as we entered Yokohama harbor on our 14th day at sea.

I had mixed feelings about being one of the "lucky few" who watched the *Saint Patrick* sail on to Korea. My head was full of negative images about Japan, "the imperial power" that had joined the "Axis powers" after the 1941 attack on Pearl Harbor. The collaborative French press of my childhood had praised Japan's alliance with Germany, while the BBC denounced it. My father and I trusted the BBC.

Despite Army briefings about our role as "ambassadors to Japan," I felt no desire to be friendly as we waited to board buses headed for Camp Drake in Tokyo. I found it annoying when dockworkers responded with "Hi, hi"—"Yes, yes"—to every question I asked.

Japan had not yet recovered from damages of war. Riding through Tokyo among scarred buildings, I saw people rushing in all directions. Mothers carried babies strapped to their bodies, and men and women were so loaded down with heavy bundles, it seemed they were carrying the whole city on their backs.

Many women had hunched backs from years of working rice paddy fields where they planted delicate green shoots of rice. The Japanese carried even heavier loads than the potato sacks I had lifted in childhood. As I watched on from my comfortable bus seat, whatever hostility I had felt toward the Japanese soon vanished.

As the bus continued on, I noticed small, three-wheeled trucks weaving in and out of traffic with huge loads as well as pre-World War II taxis called Datsuns that were too small for Americans to ride with any comfort. At Camp Drake, I was briefed by a sergeant major. "You're assigned to Southwestern Headquarters at Camp Otsu on Lake Biwa. That's near Kyoto, the ancient capital of Japan. Your assignments will include coverage of Nagoya, Kobe, and Osaka. It's just about the best Army job in all of Japan."

At Tokyo's Grand Central station, I boarded a train pulled by a steam-engine locomotive. Lined up on boarding platforms were vendors selling *obento*, rice wrapped in seaweed and dried fish in wooden boxes.

American GIs and some Japanese commuted in first-class carriages, but most Japanese traveled in second class. After a few hours, carriage floors were covered with empty food boxes and discarded wrappers, and a cleaner would sweep aisles of trash at each stop.

The garbage in the train surprised me, because I had read in one briefing that the Japanese were "the cleanest people in the world." It took me a long time to understand how, in a highly disciplined society with rules of etiquette and behavior for each move from birth to death, the endless rules did not cover disposal of trash on a crowded train. That was Japan in the 1950s.

On the train, sounds of the Japanese language were so foreign, I couldn't understand the conductor as he announced stations. During the entire trip, the only two words I understood were Gifu and Nagoya, so I missed Otsu altogether.

Two other American soldiers also missed Otsu, so we all got off in Kyoto. Unable to find a military bus, the three of us shared a Datsun to Camp Otsu. Heading east toward Mount Hiei and Lake Biwa, the little car loaded with three GIs and three duffel bags stalled. So we got out, pushed the taxi over the hill, and jumped back in as the driver clutched into second gear, and "the little box" started again.

Driving through Kyoto, once the ancient capital city of Japan and residence of the imperial family for nearly 11 centuries from 794 to 1868, I saw an enchanted world of Buddhist temples, Shinto shrines, and simple people living in ways totally foreign to Western experience. I smelled aromas I had never known.

The little taxi made it to camp, and the military police led us in at the gate. After reporting for duty, I was assigned to a 10-man room in barracks identical to California's—it was like being back in Fort Ord. In military culture, you never got away from regulation barracks. I was foolish to even imagine barracks in Japan shaped like pagodas.

On the bright side, it was good to know the U.S. Army took better care of its soldiers than the French Army. We were actually paid a small but decent wage, and as Camp Otsu's processing sergeant told me, I could participate in the "caretaker program," in which a Japanese man would make our beds, shine our brass, and take care of all our cleaning duties. I gladly joined. We also had a PX post exchange where goods were tax-free. In 1954, a pack of cigarettes was 10¢.

I constantly compared the French and American armies. Though drafted into both, I went into the French Army respecting the laws of France, and the American Army respecting my own set of values. With the U.S. forces, I felt a sense of duty and a need to repay an emotional debt.

But when I checked into Camp Otsu as a French citizen, the guns of war in Korea had been silenced. Since the fighting was over, I wondered why most of my fellow draftees and I still had to serve 14 more months of active duty. As a 25-year-old unknown photojournalist who didn't even own his own 35-mm camera, my genuine fear was that after being discharged from the Army, I'd be too old to make it in photojournalism.

My anxiety eased somewhat after a briefing from officers of the photographic section of the Signal Corps and Headquarter's Public and Press Section. I learned my new assignments would be far more diverse than Fort Ord's. Beyond covering Army activities, I'd photograph events for military publications, press releases for Japanese press, and with luck, special features for the Stars and Stripes newspaper. I'd also cover two other camps, one in Kobe and the other in the Gifu-Nagoya area.

Most of my work would be unsupervised, meaning: "Do a good job and you will have a great deal of freedom." Also I'd often be put on TDY or "Traveling Detached Duty," meaning an extra $15 pay per diem when military facilities were not available. In 1954, Japanese inns and restaurants were inexpensive, and the dollar was almighty, so $15 went a long way. I often saved half of it when traveling outside military areas.

As a rule, I tried to travel with another photographer. I teamed up with Private Timothy Asch, who studied anthropology at Harvard. As a private first class, I was put in charge of our team.

Though neither of us knew we'd be assigned to Japan, Tim prepared himself well for Japan's complex society. He brought books by nineteenth-century, Greek-born American author, Lafcadio Hearn, who had written at length on Japan. Tim's most informative book was *The Chrysanthemum and the Sword* by Ruth Benedict. A professor of anthropology at Columbia University, she had been given the formidable assignment by the Office of War Information to explain Japanese culture to leaders of American occupying forces in Japan. First published in 1946, her book became recognized as a classic.

L'AMÉRICAIN

Tim had a scholarly anthropological approach to Japan, while mine was instinctive and reactive to sights and sounds of the country, so the two of us made a good team. Covering three camps and diverse subjects outside the military world kept us permanently busy. When not at headquarters, we'd often shoot pictures the entire day, then process film and write captions until two in the morning. On "Detached Duty" in Camp Kobe, we had a private room in one of the barracks and made our own schedule until a platoon sergeant at Kobe insisted we appear for all calls, including the 6:00 A.M. roll call.

As I was on my way to Camp Gifu, Tim was left alone to debate with the sergeant. When I got back, Tim was restricted to camp. I began working on regaining Tim's freedom, but things moved slowly in the Army's bureaucracy.

A few days later, the new commander of Camp Kobe, a full colonel and a "West Pointer," called for a full inspection of camp including our photographic facility. The night before inspection, Tim and I prepared our official production reports, illustrating the variety of our assignments and documenting our long hours of overtime through the week and weekends.

When our unreasonable sergeant and the new colonel arrived for inspection and reviewed our reports, I said, "I'd like to bring up a serious disagreement we have with the sergeant here present, sir!" I continued, "How can we be expected to make the 6:00 A.M. roll call when we often don't finish our work till 2:00 A.M., notwithstanding the technical work we do for the Criminal Investigation Division, which is highly classified and cannot be given to our Japanese technician, sir?" The colonel paused, turned to the sergeant, and said, "Sergeant, lift Private Asch from camp restriction immediately." So once again we were in charge of our time.

On one assignment, we went to a Japanese hospital and photographed a pale little boy, barely breathing. His mother was beside him, imploring us to do something to save his life. Neither the parents nor hospital could find in Japan the iron lung the boy needed to survive, nor could they afford to have one flown in from the United States. An English-speaking Japanese doctor told us it was a matter of days before the boy died.

Without permission, Tim and I printed our photographs and released them to the Japanese press along with the plea from the mother. By the time we got back to headquarters, the story was all over the papers.

The major in charge of public relations was angry with us for not checking with him before making the release. Our story had obliged the military public relations machine to react. The U.S. Air Force flew in an iron lung to Japan, saving the boy's life, at least for a while.

Other assignments involved finding rest-and-recreation locations and resorts for GIs arriving from Korea. We thoroughly covered the more exotic and typically Japanese inns that were available. Happily testing everything R&R soldiers would experience, we covered Japanese cuisine, consumed rice wine served warm, and immersed ourselves in hot baths. At 110 degrees Fahrenheit, the baths had to be taken only after thorough scrubbing and washing outside of the tub while seated on a small stool. The point of the Japanese bath was not to get clean but to give your body pleasure.

Because inn owners knew we were doing them a favor by featuring their establishments, sake flowed freely, and often drinks were not charged. If we protested, they patiently explained Japanese culture: *Giri* meant they must return our favor to keep their reputation intact. *Giri* was part of a very complex ethical code, difficult for foreigners to understand, so we honored their code and often drank too much sake.

After long trips to resorts in the countryside, we'd sometimes long for American comfort and return to headquarters. There we'd rent a small boat and sail across beautiful Lake Biwa to the Officers' Club on the opposite shore. Though enlisted men were not allowed in the club, being photographers in civilian clothes gave us certain privileges. We made friends with the bartender, and for 25¢ I had my first dry martini.

Time passed quickly. We explored Kyoto, Nara, and photographed the most famous temples and shrines. By April 1954, I began taking weekend trips to Tokyo, proposing story ideas from our southwestern command to editors at *Stars and Stripes* and the English editions of Japanese newspapers.

Unfortunately, not many editors were interested in my ideas: their eyes were on the fierce battle in Indochina where Dien Bien Phu had been besieged for weeks. There was talk about the heroic efforts of French Legionnaires and paratroopers holding the fortification, but after 55 days, Dien Bien Phu fell to Vietminh forces on May 8, 1954. All 16,000 men, including 3,000 paratroopers, had been captured or killed.

Discussing the loss with other GIs, I recounted what little I knew of France's colonial history in Indochina. Thinking of all the dead, we all asked, "Why?" We agreed Eisenhower was right in ending the war in Korea and hoped he would keep us out of Indochina. Although Dien Bien Phu signaled the end of French colonialism in Indochina, the war continued to claim casualties, including the legendary photojournalist, Robert Capa. Born in Budapest as Andrei Friedmann, Capa was an American who was one of the founders of the Magnum Agency. He was on assignment for *Life* when he reportedly stepped on a land mine and died on May 25, 1954, not far from Hanoi, at the age of 40.

Capa was the supreme photographic recorder of the horrors of war. I met him a couple of times and, like all aspiring photojournalists, greatly admired his work on the Spanish Civil War, his coverage of the Normandy landings, and other great engagements of World War II.

With Capa's untimely death, the world lost its greatest war photographer. Like others at *Life* magazine, he had mastered the use of 35-mm cameras, particularly Leicas. I had used the Army's 35-mm camera, but its lens was not much better than the bottom of a Coke bottle. Finally, with great enthusiasm, I ordered my first Leica F-2 with a 50-mm Summicron lens from Camp Otsu's PX.

While waiting for the camera to arrive, I was notified that I could take my American citizenship examination. Feeling emotionally American since my youth, I felt it was time to make my attachment to the U.S. legal.

Tim Asch gave me encouragement. He genuinely wanted me to become a citizen, so for days, he tested me on American history, the Constitution, Bill of Rights, Civil War, and Federalist Papers urging the Constitution's ratification, with essays by Alexander Hamilton, James Madison, and John Jay.

I felt ready for the exam, though I was worried my knowledge of the Federalist Papers was vague and hoped I wouldn't be questioned extensively on it. On the day of the exam, I ran into a young Marine crying on his way out of the testing building. He blurted out that he had failed his test and would have to take it again in a few months. I was sure that questions on the Federalist Papers made him fail.

For my exam, the first and only question was, "What is the meaning of democracy?" I said, "*Demo* means people and *cracy* means government, so essentially it means government of the people, for the people." The examiner said, "That's fine, you are now an American citizen."

I held up my right hand, and on June 11, 1954, in Camp Otsu, Japan, on the shores of Lake Biwa, I pledged the oath of allegiance to the Constitution of the United States of America. The examiner then asked if I wanted to change my family name, which surprised me, and I answered, "No." We shook hands, and he congratulated me. After all the studying I had done, passing the exam felt anticlimactic.

Friends at the photographic section prepared a small party for me. "To our new American," they toasted. Later, Tim and I went to dinner and talked about our future. He had hopes of getting a grant to study Aborigines in Australia, while I had written and asked Kurt Kornfeld of Black Star to send an introduction for me to their press agency in Tokyo, Pan Asia.

Black Star did not have a permanent correspondent in Japan. I knew Ernest Mayer and Kurt Kornfeld, the Black Star bosses, were European-oriented and not very interested in Japan, so cautiously and gradually, I began constructing arguments why I should be their correspondent in Japan and the Far East. From my own observations and from conversations with journalists, it became obvious that Japan in the summer of 1954 was not only recovering from war but was on its way to becoming an industrial power with America's approval and assistance.

A reservist major who was recalled for the Korean War told me, "The Korean War was the turning point. Soon Japan will become America's greatest ally in the Far East." Unfortunately, my credentials at Black Star were extremely limited. Unless I came up with at least two good essays on Japan, my chances with the agency were slight, so during weekends, I planned two essays.

For one, I'd photograph the interplay of shadows I often observed through paper screens of geisha houses in Ponto-cho and Gion. I had a title: "The Shadows of Kyoto." The second essay focused on the Kyoto-Tokyo Express, a wonder of railroad history. The first essay would have a sense of mystery while the second would be harshly realistic.

Throughout the early years of trying to break through as a photojournalist, I kept in touch with my family through letters. It had been nearly four years since I had seen them, but I never mentioned how difficult life had been.

Because father thought it was mother's duty to write, most mail I received came from her. Her letters always began with, "I am glad you are in good health," even though I never mentioned my health at all.

After writing to my father about becoming an American citizen, he wrote back, asking, "What's wrong with being French?" His letter seemed sad but not critical. "In my heart," he wrote, "you will always be French, but as you know, I have nothing against America."

His letter made me feel lonely, and I would not see him for many years to come. I could not tell him that my plan, after returning to America, was to return to Japan, for I had no thoughts of returning to France.

I began photographing shadows of Kyoto and the Kyoto-Tokyo Express. On the train I again saw the Japanese struggling with their heavy loads. They never complained; they accepted the struggle—I had never seen such stoicism before.

Searching for pictures, I spent long hours on the train. One day, through my Leica viewfinder, I saw a young woman in a sleeveless summer dress making sketches of the countryside from her seat. Discreetly, I watched her; through my camera, she looked like a whisper in the chattering crowd of passengers.

I gazed at her full lips, the hollow above her upper lip, her thin nose, slender bare arms, long elegant fingers, short haircut, narrow waist, gentle breasts. As I photographed her, I focused on her almond-shaped eyes.

I was just a few feet away. She never looked up though I knew she had seen me. After hours on the train, I finally worked up the nerve to talk to her, struggling to speak in Japanese, and she responded in fluent English. Her name was Keiko.

She told me she was a student at Sofia University in Tokyo and would soon graduate. For a woman in 1954 Japan's patriarchal society, that was extraordinary. I told her that in my camera, she looked like a single white flower in a sea of dark pebbles. She smiled shyly and said, "I've been watching you ever since you entered our car."

I raised my right hand and slowly spread my fingers apart. One by one, starting with my little finger, she matched her fingers with mine. When she touched my thumb, she pressed slightly. Without words, we looked at each other and understood something was beginning.

As the train headed for Tokyo, we spoke about our lives. Since I was based by Lake Biwa, she said we could see each other soon because she had friends near Otsu where she could spend part of her summer vacation. In Tokyo, she changed trains for Fujisawa, but we promised to see each other again. Since long-distance telephone service was primitive in Japan, we'd keep in touch by mail.

Spending a few days in Tokyo, I met with John Taji, director of Pan Asia news, to discuss setting up a Black Star-Pan Asia office once I was out of the Army and able to return to Japan. I needed to know what Pan Asia would expect as a percentage.

I was cautious because no one at Black Star had shown any interest in my returning to Japan. The agency's president thought I should take advantage of the GI Bill and go to college. My abstract plans for the future seemed difficult but not impossible.

I received a letter from Keiko telling me she was going to Kyoto for two weeks and hoped we could see each other. We managed to meet almost every evening.

Day by day, we found ourselves falling in love, but in Japanese culture, expressing your feelings physically in public was forbidden. Instead, we exchanged poems daily. Only once had our fingers touched, when we first met on the train. On the shores of Lake Biwa, we could never hold hands, and walking the streets of ancient Kyoto, we could only express our affection with words.

She explained the taboos of her culture. A public display of emotion was a shameful act. Though it was painful, I accepted Japan's subtle language of love. To a Western mind, it didn't make much sense, but poetically, it awakened me. What I could not say with a kiss or a touch, I could try to write in daily poems.

By the end of July, she returned to her family's summerhouse and soon invited me to come for the weekend. Keiko picked me up at the Fujisawa railroad station, and we walked to her house.

In their perfectly manicured garden, the gardener dropped pine needles on the paths to make it look as though needles had just fallen from the trees. The green of the garden flowed into the architecture of the main house in perfect harmony. It was a classical Japanese design.

I met Keiko's parents and her brother. They all spoke fluent English except for the mother for whom Keiko translated our conversations. Bowing servants served a delicious Japanese dinner.

Keiko's father wanted to know about France during the war, so I told him what I knew. Keiko's older brother Kenji asked what I wanted to do when I returned to America, so I told him I wanted to work with Black Star but didn't mention my plan to return to Japan after the Army.

Keiko's father was erudite in matters concerning Europe. Receiving his business card, I discovered he was an executive for a major oil company based in Europe. During my visit, Keiko and I were so reserved, no one in her family suspected we had fallen in love. Late in the evening, I was escorted to the guesthouse, which was actually a teahouse where the Japanese tea ceremony was performed. Again I noticed how designs of the garden flowed in harmony with the architecture.

When I lay back on the guesthouse's futon, I felt as though I had entered an enchanted world. The lights went off in the main house, and my senses were overwhelmed.

Drifting to sleep, I saw Keiko in a white nightgown running through the garden. She opened my shoji screen and joined me on the bed; with me under the covers and her on top, we finally kissed for the first time.

We held each other's faces, swore our eternal love, and kissed again. At dawn, she ran back to the main house. Our secret meetings recurred over and over during visits to Fujisawa until the end of summer when her parents understood our bond was more than a friendship.

At that point, I could feel the tension in the family and was no longer welcome.

Even so, Keiko's father told me, "When you go back to America early next year, see how you feel. If you still are in love with my daughter, then you may come back for her and I will give you permission to marry."

I believed him but I also sensed that he thought I'd never come all the way back to Japan. Regardless, Keiko and I continued to see each other in parks and cafés of Tokyo through the fall and winter. We could not hold hands nor kiss, so we wrote and recited poetry.

In February of '55, my Japan assignment in the U.S. Army ended. I saw Keiko once more before my ship sailed from Yokohama; she took off one of her earrings, saying, "You keep this one earring and I'll keep mine. When you come back, you can return it to me. I know there will be thousands of faces watching your ship sail, but look carefully and I will be there." I looked and looked but never saw her face.

On the 14-day trip back to San Francisco, I thought of Keiko endlessly. I'd read her poems over and again, looking at the earring she gave me. Meanwhile, since I had been a corporal for several months already, I was able to avoid all unpleasant duties and work instead on the mimeograph machine for the ship's newspaper.

Approaching California, my thoughts were focused on how I could raise money to go to New York to pitch my ideas to Black Star. I wondered if Kurt Kornfeld would like my two essays.

Thinking of southern California, I knew I had no one to go back to. For me, working again for Joe Pazen was not an option, and from my sister, I discovered my friend Claude had returned to France, homesick.

In the last week of February, we sailed into San Francisco. At Fort Ord, on March 1, 1955, I received a National Defense medal, Good Conduct medal, Honorable Discharge, and $300 in "mustering-out pay." Unlike the French Army, the U.S. Army let me keep my boots, clothing, and all my uniforms.

CIVILIAN

VACUUM CLEANER SALESMAN, GAS STATION ATTENDANT

SAN FERNANDO VALLEY, CA 1955

During two years of active duty, I managed to buy a used Rolleiflex camera and new Leica, I had seen a new country, and had fallen in love. In a way, things were looking up. Yet it felt like time was running out: I was 26 and had no paying job in sight. I thought I'd better manage my anxiety quickly and get into action.

With another ex-soldier heading south, I walked out of Fort Ord. At a used car lot, my friend helped me find a car. We checked several vehicles by putting our fingers in the transmission to detect sawdust in the gears, as some dealers softened the noise of a bad transmission by filling it with sawdust. We also gunned accelerator pedals to the floor for several seconds to see if engines knocked and smoked.

For $50, I settled on a gray four-door 1940 Dodge, once probably white, and my friend shared the cost of gas to Santa Barbara. After dropping him off, I headed straight for the San Fernando Valley and drove to a cheap motel. Remembering the cherry pies I loved, I found a restaurant and had two helpings to cheer myself up. I was a civilian again. Accustomed to the Army's free room and board, it took a while to adjust to my new freedom.

Looking for a job, I visited Major Douglas Parker at the 146th Fighter Group Air National Guard in Van Nuys. Always a generous man, he said, "Though your photo job was taken while you were away, there's an opening in base operations." I took the job immediately and started working from 5:00 P.M. to midnight as a flight planner, helping pilots with all weather, takeoff, and landing information needed for flights.

To earn enough for a trip to the east coast and the $400 boat fare to Japan, I needed more than one job. After looking around, I was hired as a Texaco gas station attendant and worked from six in the morning till noon. Then I noticed a want-ad for a door-to-door vacuum cleaner salesman; I applied and began working from noon till 4:30 in the afternoon.

Selling vacuum cleaners door-to-door was the hardest job I ever had, as it meant selling people machines they did not necessarily need. Though I hated to recite the virtues of my vacuum cleaners, I sold four machines in my first week. My manager was so impressed, he asked me to give a speech to his regular salesmen. He told me to "explain your methods to them," but I had no methods. Perhaps I sold more because customers sensed I was not a salesman, and they felt sorry for me.

An executive from a major Hollywood studio bought two vacuum cleaners, one for his home and one for his summer house. He and his wife thought I was a student, but when I told them I was a photographer, he offered me a job as set photographer. I thanked him but explained my calling was strictly photojournalism.

Not all attempts at sales went so well. Our vacuums had a device to shampoo carpet, which often helped close a sale. On one occasion, as I demonstrated this feature, shampooing a stain on a worn-out Persian carpet, the polisher slowly dug a hole in the carpet before I could stop it. My potential customers looked at me in horror.

Holding three jobs meant I didn't sleep much. I led a frugal life, saving as much as possible for New York and Japan.

Around that time, I came upon a Department of Defense ruling that allowed a reservist to transfer to another branch of service if an individual's service was requested, so I asked Major Parker if he could help me transfer from the U.S. Army Reserve to the Air Force Reserve. I always loved being around planes, and since I had a five-year obligation to the Army Reserve, I thought if recalled, I'd rather be in the Air Force Reserve.

Major Parker made the request and I was transferred. To my surprise, I discovered my new status offered an unusual opportunity to reach New York in the copilot's seat of F-80s flying on training missions.

All dispatchers, aware I wanted to go to New York, would inform me as soon as they knew of a two-seater fighter plane with a single pilot who could fly me to the east coast. I wrote Kurt Kornfeld at Black Star about my plans to show him, Ernest Mayer, and Howard Chapnick my two essays on Japan, and Kurt let me know they looked forward to seeing me again after nearly five years.

While waiting to hear of an available flight, I wrote to Keiko on weekends and would rest at every opportunity. With three jobs on weekdays, I slept an average of four hours a night.

With no family in California, I was in a sense adopted by a first lieutenant in the California Air National Guard, Robert P. Boal, along with his wife Catherine, and children, Mike, Jim, Stephanie, Patty, and Joanne. Bob Boal was a technical writer at Lockheed who lived with his family, in a ranch house with many bedrooms and a large kitchen-dining room, where an extra plate was set for me on Saturdays, even when I failed to show up. When I could, I'd bring a bottle of French wine though nothing was ever expected, except perhaps stories about France and the U.S. Army.

From March to August 1955, most of my stories involved adventures of a vacuum cleaner salesman. Demonstrating a cleaner at their home, photographing the event from the viewpoint of a salesman, using all the kids looking on as I vacuumed the floors, I wrote a text on the sad life of a vacuum cleaner salesman. Though hardly on a par with Arthur Miller's *Death of a Salesman*, the pictures and text sold to a Sunday supplement.

On weekends, late into the night, Bob and I would discuss philosophy, politics, and America's greatness as well as its weakness, which in Bob's opinion began with Franklin Roosevelt's "New Deal" and "the bleeding-heart liberals and Commies." That disturbed me because Roosevelt was my father's hero as well as mine—Roosevelt and Eisenhower, followed by Winston Churchill, were "architects of my freedom."

For me, it was inconceivable my friend could criticize Roosevelt yet praise Eisenhower, both great men, but Bob remained a dedicated Republican and erudite man who could quote Aristotle and carefully explain checks and balances of the Constitution and Bill of Rights.

He'd blame liberals for America's problems yet recommend *Harper's* magazine where I found America's best writers. In 1955, as a new American, I had yet to shape my American political convictions and had yet to vote in an election.

In France, my political views as a boy and teenager were simple: they were my father's views. "The politicians and establishment in France sold out to the Germans, to the Nazis," father told me. "The French bankers and industrialists voluntarily propositioned Hitler to include them in the New Order of Europe. The ruling class wanted order and thought they must crush the social progress that the proletariat had established in 1930s France."

My father's beliefs were reaffirmed by Vichy France. Pétain and his Vichy government created a law-and-order state inspired by the Nazis; imitating Hitler and his Hitler Youth organization, he created the Pétain Youth, compelling children in French schools to sing, "Maréchal, nous voilàs." ("Marshall, here we are.")

I wrote to Keiko that I was working to return to Japan. Finally, in late April 1955, dispatchers told me a T-33 "T-Bird" jet trainer was scheduled to fly to New Jersey and asked if I wanted a round trip ride. I responded, "Absolutely!"

Major Parker agreed to let me go during the week if I made up lost workdays on weekends, so I called Kurt Kornfeld in New York and asked him to book me a room at the YMCA, saying I'd see him next week. He replied, "Wonderful."

A few days later, changing from Air Force uniform into a flight suit, a jet pilot and I took off and headed eastward toward Oklahoma City. I had flown in a T-33 before and welcomed the chance to do so again: there was something exhilarating about being in the copilot's seat, armed for possible ejection, adjusting my oxygen mask, watching the dials, lifting off with 95 percent power on a single engine.

With a good tailwind, we wouldn't have to refuel after Oklahoma City and could land in the evening at McGuire Air Force Base in New Jersey, some 30 miles south of Manhattan. It was a perfect flight: the pilot even let me fly the T-Bird over the Midwest, which looked like patchwork divided into even square miles. After nearly 3,000 miles, the pilot made a flawless landing, touching down main landing gears and easing the nose gear down gently. I thanked the pilot, agreed on a takeoff time for three days later, and took a bus to the YMCA.

The next day, I walked again to Black Star by way of Central Park, all green. I talked to the trees, to the squirrels, and sat by a pond. I told the trees I was a new American and confessed I was still nowhere in my career.

As a boy in the forest of Marly, I had always found solace in my hole, talking to the trees; to cope with my anxiety now, I sought out the trees in Central Park. Sitting under their green canopy, I rehearsed my presentation to Black Star.

On that spring day in 1955, I walked into Black Star's office to begin—I hoped—my destiny. Kurt Kornfeld greeted me warmly with an embrace and introduced me to Ernest Mayer, president of Black Star, whom I had briefly met five years earlier. I also met Howard Chapnick who later became one of my dedicated mentors.

Sitting close to Mayer's desk, I pulled out my essays on Japan. Although Black Star had sold minor picture stories of mine, it was the first time I had shown my work in person. First, I displayed my Kyoto-Tokyo Express photographs. It was a tense moment as I watched all three faces passing my photos to one another. All three seemed to like them without giving me a rave review. I would learn over the years that photographic agents were stingy with their praise: great work would seldom get more than "Good work."

Then I presented my "Shadows of Kyoto." The photographs were subtle, open to the imagination, portraying shadows that were playful, flirtatious, amusing, and mysterious. The executives wanted to know about the Gion district of Kyoto, and I explained how the geishas were sophisticated entertainers for men, teasers yes but prostitutes no. An enthusiastic Kurt Kornfeld said, "This has to be a 'Speaking of Pictures' for *Life*," and all agreed. Kurt added, "It's wonderful. *Life* will love it." Kurt spoke with a heavy German accent, and though I hated the German language during the war years, his accent was New York German and not threatening.

Ernest Mayer then expressed his reservations. He thought going back to Japan was a mistake and I should instead finish my college education using the GI Bill. I said, "In a few months, I'll be 27. I can earn a degree in about two years but then I'll be nearly 29. What will a degree do for me as a photojournalist?" I went on to describe how foreign policy had changed since the Korean War, and that it was obvious that America would speed up the recovery of Japan as an industrial power instead of the agricultural nation the victors intended in 1945. Japan would rebuild rapidly just as Germany was rebuilding with America's blessing, and as it did, Japan would provide plenty of material for stories. Interest in Japan's exotic culture and recovery would inevitably grow.

I mentioned my talk with John Taji of Pan Asia in Tokyo. "For 50 percent of my income after Black Star," I said, "he's willing to let me have an office and use their photographic lab."

It was a passionate and logical presentation. Black Star didn't have a correspondent in Japan, so I asked, "Why not me?" After a long silence, Mayer said, "Let us think about it."

That afternoon, Howard Chapnick took me to lunch and said he and Kurt liked the idea. "Be patient. Kurt and I will work on Mayer. Your logic about America's Japan policy got to him. In the meantime, have a good flight back."

I walked again through Central Park and sat by a pond, feeling rather happy but keeping optimism in check.

Next morning at the McGuire Air Force base in Jersey, we were cleared for takeoff, and the pilot requested an overflight of Manhattan as a favor to me. From several thousands of feet above, I looked at the soaring optimism of Manhattan in a hazy spring light.

After landing at March Air Force base in Riverside, California, I thanked the pilot, found my old Dodge, and drove back to Van Nuys. There I found a disturbing letter from Keiko, telling me my last four or five letters were confiscated by her mother. Keiko asked me to write instead to the address of her "best friend."

The next morning, it was back to pumping gasoline from six till noon, selling vacuum cleaners door-to-door from 12:30 to 4:30, then flight planning from five till midnight.

Every night after work, I'd drive to a small café close to the end of the runway to order a cherry pie and vanilla milk shake. That was dinner for months. After four hours of sleep, it was shower, shave, coffee, toast, ham, cheese, and back to the Texaco station.

Following what seemed an eternity, I received a letter from Kurt informing me that *Life* had held my "Shadows of Kyoto" for a long time, but the editors decided it was too subtle for their readers. The good news was that "Shadows of Kyoto" had been sold to a "men's magazine" for $600.

Kurt said, "Mayer, Chapnick, and I want you to return to Manhattan to discuss your becoming Black Star's Japan correspondent." He cautioned that I was unknown in photojournalism, but my two essays held promise.

That morning, full of joy, I applied for my first American passport. When it was delivered by the State Department on May 23, 1955, I noted it was not valid for travel to Albania, Bulgaria, China, Czechoslovakia, Hungary, Poland, Romania, and the Soviet Union unless specifically approved. Though we were in the years of the Cold War, I hated any restrictions on my freedom.

Again I got a copilot seat on a T-33 to New Jersey and made my way to Black Star. Greeted warmly by Kurt Kornfeld, I was led to Mayer's office. He was happy to inform me that "Shadows of Kyoto" sold for $600, so I'd be credited with $300. Extremely pleased, I thanked him.

Then I asked to see the "men's magazine" in question. It was immediately obvious the geishas in my photos were being presented as whores in captions riddled with innuendos. Furious, I insisted the sale be called off. Seeing his commission evaporate, the salesman argued that I was being puritanical. "I may be a puritan to you," I said, "but I don't want one of my first essays in photojournalism to be published in a pseudo-porno magazine."

To my surprise, Ernest Mayer told the salesman to retrieve the essay immediately. The salesman returned with the dozen 11x14 photos I had so lovingly printed and handed them to me with great contempt. As he glared at me, I tore up the prints and threw them all on the floor of Mayer's office. Mayer, Kornfeld, and Chapnick were stunned.

We had yet to discuss Japan, and I was in a storm of my own creation. Then Kornfeld eased the tension by siding with me, saying, "It's a beautiful essay. *Life* should have published it. Since they didn't, I will start a new magazine myself for your lovely photographs."

We all laughed. Then Ernest Mayer led the business discussion. "As you know Johnny, our photographers work with us on a retainer or weekly guarantee based on potential production of each photographer. The guarantee gives you some security, and of course, we get it back from your assignments and sales. We expect our photographers to send us ideas for picture stories. We try to sell the ideas to editors, but this only works with name photographers. Since you are unknown, you'll have to shoot your projects on spec, after you submit your ideas. If we approve, we'll share your expenses 50-50. If you go to Japan, all travel and settling expenses will be yours—we can't help you on that score. Is that clear?"

"Yes," I said. He continued, "Now, for your guarantee, we don't think you can cover more than $20 a week. Of course, if your work goes well, we'll raise it to your potential."

I was in shock. Their offer was less than I made as an Army corporal in Japan, and the Army paid for my food and lodging. Even then, I barely made it in Japan on my military pay of about $150 a month. I protested that if Black Star received 50-percent commission on a $100 sale, and Pan Asia took 50 percent of my commission, $50 would go to Black Star, $25 to Pan Asia, I would be left with only $25 to cover my guarantee.

Trying to inject a humorous spin, I said, "The Japanese are poor, so I can't panhandle on the Ginza, which is what I'd have to do on $20 a week." But nobody laughed. I wasn't sure if my three interlocutors knew much about Tokyo's Ginza in 1955.

Eventually, the guarantee was raised to $25 a week, then $30, and finally Kornfeld raised it to $35. As I was an unknown, I took the offer but it was sheer folly. I had no idea how I'd survive on so little. Even our Japanese caretaker who made our bunks in the Army made twice as much.

A renewable contract was drawn that afternoon. I kept the right to distribute my work directly to our European agencies, but at that point in my career it was meaningless.

Dictating a letter of accreditation addressed to the Japanese consulate in Los Angeles, I requested a correspondent's visa. Mayer signed it and embossed it with Black Star's corporate seal. Kornfeld wanted to know when I'd return to Japan. "During the next three months," I said, "I'll prepare for the assignment. Hopefully, I'll sell enough vacuum cleaners to buy a ticket on a cheap freighter in Los Angeles or San Francisco."

Then Ernest Mayer and I signed my first Black Star contract, and we all shook hands. All said, "Good luck." Howard Chapnick took me to a nearby bar, bought me a drink, gave me a pep talk, and said, "A couple of our biggest names make as much as $10,000 a year." At that point, he might as well have said a million.

After thanking Howard and saying goodbye, I checked if there were any flights from McGuire. There were none, but a dispatcher told me there was a World War II B-17 at Andrew's Air Force base near Washington, D.C. scheduled to fly to Edward's Air Force base the next day. Andrew's base operations confirmed the flight but informed me the B-17 was stripped bare. I'd have to sit on the bare deck. "That's okay," I said and took a night Greyhound bus to Washington, arriving in time for takeoff.

After meeting the pilot, copilot, and flight engineer, I was told it was the B-17's final flight to a graveyard in California. Except for basic flying instruments, the old plane had been gutted: the bomb bay was empty and machine guns had all been removed. It was no longer a war machine. Delayed for clearance, we idled near the end of the runway. The heat inside the B-17's aluminum body rose to 107 degrees Fahrenheit as I sat up front behind the pilots, sweating. Finally we took off. As we gained altitude, the heat turned cold, and the crew and I put on higher altitude suits to keep warm. As we climbed to cruising altitude, we put on oxygen masks.

Heading west in the old, scarred B-17, I remembered how as a kid during the war, I had seen thousands of bombers filling the skies on their way to destroy Germany. I thought of the imprint of the young American airman in the soft grass of Marly and tried to imagine what his fears might have been flying into a storm of flak explosions, but I could not. I had been shown how to use my parachute and again tried to imagine what it was like for him to bail out of a ripped and torn flying machine falling to the earth, but I could not.

Instead, my thoughts wandered to the childhood I never had in France, to the four years of German soldiers in my life, to France's betrayal of her people, to postwar denial of Vichy France, a myth orchestrated by General de Gaulle. In my experience, France had never been democratic. After great republican ideals of the French Revolution were established in 1789, it took almost a century before a permanent republic was founded in 1875.

By 1955, I was an idealistic American from France. I had read Alexis de Tocqueville's *Democracy in America* in English and found enough in his writings to affirm my beliefs and convictions. I related to the passage: "Nothing is quite so wretchedly corrupt as an aristocracy which has lost its power but kept its wealth and which still has endless leisure to devote to nothing but banal enjoyments." Though written in the early nineteenth century, it was still true in 1940 France.

As we cruised at about 175 knots, the flight back to California seemed endless. I thought about the fate of the old B-17, doomed to be broken into scrap in some desert graveyard. It had been hit often but survived many bombing runs from England to Germany. It had been flown by many young American crews and most had survived—after all, the old bomber was still around—but some of its airmen surely had died or been wounded in its gut. In old age, even the glamorous painting of a Hollywood pinup on its fuselage was erased.

I worried about my own future, starting with my assignment in Japan. I wasn't sure how I'd survive on a $35 weekly guarantee. Because my contract was renewable after a year, I'd have very little time to break through, show more than promise, and have my contract renewed.

Upon returning to my very small studio in Van Nuys, I found another disturbing letter from Keiko. Apparently her "best friend" had betrayed her trust by giving my letters to Keiko's parents, and then had lectured Keiko about her filial duties. "How could she do that in the name of filial duty?" Keiko asked me.

I was not able to phone, write, or cable Keiko, not even to tell her I had a contract from Black Star to be the agency's correspondent in Japan.

In the meantime, it was back to my three jobs. Evening work at base operations was sometimes hectic when aircraft traffic was heavy, but generally I had time to think, read, and at best erase the memory of selling vacuum cleaners earlier in the day.

Ringing doorbell after doorbell, making a sales pitch for a good product that was often unnecessary made me ashamed at times. Sometimes I'd drive around the same block, not ringing a single doorbell, but then the cost of financing my trip to Japan would enter my mind, and I'd stop the car, start ringing bells, and make the sales.

Each time I drove back to the Van Nuys air base, my dignity would begin to return. I loved planes but mostly in my camera's viewfinder: there was something beautiful about a plane lifting off, taking flight.

There, at base operations, I planned my trip to Japan, and Major Parker let me keep my job until my departure. Like First Lieutenant Robert Boal, Major Parker belonged to that "greatest generation" that had endured the Depression, a time when people took care of each other and moved on to fight in World War II.

Both men in different ways shaped my early American years, enlightening me about American democracy in the early 1950s. Parker, the Democrat, and Boal, the Republican, were both very generous men.

Finally, in June 1955, I secured a three-year "correspondent visa" for Japan. I then received a letter from Keiko saying her family never left her alone: she could write but had no way to mail her letters. I imagined how her mother objected to my spending those idyllic days in their summer home and would not let her daughter out of her sight.

Trying to contact Keiko, I began writing her through Pan Asia where my letters would be stamped "Tokyo" without a return address and forwarded with Keiko's address written in Japanese. I limited my letters to one page so they wouldn't appear bulky and would hopefully not be opened by her mother.

The cheapest way to cross the Pacific was on freighters that had accommodations for up to 12 passengers. In late July, for $350, I booked passage on a Greek freighter due to leave San Francisco in August. The date would be fixed after the freighter was fully loaded.

I had few belongings, so all my luggage fit in a $10 travel trunk from Good Will Industries. The old trunk, once luxurious, was covered with faded labels from the Cunard and Transatlantique Lines, and I speculated about its wealthy owners of past times. On one side of the trunk, I could hang several suits, while the other side had drawers for clothes and shoes. I used half the drawers for strobes, processing equipment, and rolls of black-and-white, 35-mm film worth $200. I put everything I owned in that trunk, and it was still half empty.

With my sailing day less than two weeks away, I received a small packet from Keiko. It contained an earring matching the one she had given me months before— the earring she promised to "treasure until both can be matched when you return."

Her letter, very short, was essentially a poem that spoke of "a leaf in the wind, a spring breeze, a summer storm, a winter wind," followed by, "I will always love you." She signed it "Keiko, your beloved."

In my head I understood it to be a Japanese farewell, but in my heart I refused to believe it. Many questions remained: Did her father change his mind about his promise of an eventual marriage if I returned to Japan? Did she get my letters forwarded from Tokyo? A leaf in a summer storm and a winter wind sounded ominous.

THE NOODLE YEARS

BLACK STAR CORRESPONDENT

TOKYO 1955

When it was time for goodbye, Major Parker, Lieutenant Boal, his family, and several friends wished me luck.

On August 12, I drove north to San Francisco and sold my old 1940 Dodge for $10. August 14, I boarded a rusty Greek freighter bound for Japan, and for the third time in my life, I sailed under the Golden Gate Bridge.

The ship's 12 passengers were assigned to the freighter's six cabins with portholes. I was paired with an elderly Japanese-American lady named Fumiko, who had saved her pennies for years to visit relatives she had not seen since 1940.

When she discovered I had been in Japan recently, she asked me about the city of Kobe where her relatives lived. I covered Kobe for the U.S. Army, so her questions were endless.

Feeling awkward at bedtime, we devised a ritual for going to sleep. I'd step out while she undressed, and when she was under the covers, she'd knock on the door; next, I'd enter the cabin and undress while she looked away—afterward we'd both laugh. The ritual would then be repeated in the morning.

Other than Fumiko, all passengers were male students or crewmen from other ships. We shared meals with the captain and first officer who spoke Greek and halting English. The dining space was a multipurpose area with a game room and what the captain called "a library," consisting of two shelves of pulp fiction novels. The hull of the ship was rusty but the dining room was made of fine, highly polished wood. It was warm and pleasant to sit there looking at the ocean through large rectangular windows.

From the first day, I volunteered to produce the freighter's mimeo newspaper. Each day in the radio room, listening to BBC news reports, I wrote a couple pages for everyone to read at dinnertime.

For our last dinner, I published an apocalyptic issue. Nearly every news report announced a catastrophe. "A heat wave in New York reaching 147 degrees Fahrenheit paralyzed the city just as a breakdown of negotiations in Geneva brought Soviets and Americans to the brink of nuclear war."

As we all gathered for cocktails, the passengers read the latest world news in my mimeo papers. There was silence, then exclamations of great fear and excited conversations. All heads turned to me as I said, "Why don't you read the last line?" I had written in French, "All you have just read is pure fiction and designed to animate our last conversations on board." No one understood French, so I translated it into English. Relieved to know the world was not plunging into disaster, they all ribbed me as we laughed and toasted each other.

Fumiko and I became good friends. She and her husband were landscape gardeners in America. Her relatives in Japan survived the war, but her family in America had been afraid, often pretending to be Chinese to escape anti-Japanese sentiments in Los Angeles, as many of their friends had been interned. When I asked her to explain, she uttered something about racial prejudice and abruptly changed the subject.

Only years later did I learn that the U.S. government removed 120,000 Japanese Americans from the West Coast and subjected them to years of confinement in internment camps despite every sign of their allegiance to the United States: that shameful action remained in deep national denial until 1987. Then the U.S. House of Representatives, acknowledging "a grave injustice, caused by racial prejudice and war hysteria," apologized and authorized $1.2 billion in reparations. Over the years, my idealistic idea of America suffered many blows.

I showed Fumiko pictures of Keiko, hoping she could interpret the hidden meaning in Keiko's last letter. She acknowledged the return of the earring was symbolic but said, "All will change when she sees you again." Fumiko, I suspected, had become more American than Japanese.

After 14 days on the Pacific, we docked the early afternoon of August 28, 1955, at the port of Yokohama. Greeted by John Taji, Director of Pan Asia, I was told his office found me "a four-and-a-half tatami," a familiar straw-mat room, in an elderly widow's house for 8,000 yen or, at the time, $22 a month. John suggested, "You'd better have a dictionary, because the landlady doesn't speak a word of English."

I thanked him for finding a room with such low rent though I knew it would not be much larger than a prison cell. John warned, "You know, sleeping on the floor in a four-and-a-half tatami room will be spartan, more austere than you can imagine." I said, "I'll be all right." I was more interested in knowing whether I had received any letters from Keiko. He told me, "You have mail from Black Star but nothing from Japan."

John escorted me to my flat at Mrs. Watanabe's house in Nakano-ku, a poor district in western Tokyo where houses were small and Westerners did not live. He introduced me to my landlady, a short, old woman whose spine was curved at the shoulders. She looked like women I had photographed whose backs were bent from years of planting rice.

After bowing, I said, "Konnichiwa" ("good afternoon"). Mrs. Watanabe began speaking quickly in Japanese until John explained that I only a spoke a few words. I was shown my room and was shocked by its size. Covering assignments in Japan for the U.S. Army, I had lived in spacious Western style—we even had a boy making our beds. Now I was moving into a space no larger than the walk-in closets in California.

In the tiny kitchen, I found a cold-water sink and two gas burners. The toilet was the squatting kind with a bucket of water for flushing. Opening my trunk meant there was just enough room for my bed.

After my brief inspection, we all sat on the floor around a *kotatsu*, a small square table covering a square hole in the floor where one would put one's legs—in the hole was a small charcoal burner covered by a wooden grill for your feet. In winter, we could sit around the table and keep our feet and calves warm while our backs froze.

Before I made the mistake of offering rent money in cash, breaking a Japanese rule of etiquette, John produced an envelope specially designed to hand over money politely. I left the envelope of cash on the corner of the table.

As Mrs. Watanabe served us tea, she saw the envelope, bowed to me, and said, "Arigato, gozaimasu sumimasen," or "Thank you, I'm sorry." She then told John I should call her *Oba-san,* meaning "honorable aunt" or "dear lady."

Leaving bilingual instructions on how to get to the office, John said, "Since you don't have a phone, we'll telegraph you if something urgent comes up. It'll take you over an hour to reach Pan Asia. Expect the trains to be packed." That was an understatement.

Tokyo in August could be unbearably hot and humid, so when John left, I sat facing Oba-san's tiny garden, reluctant to move for fear of adding one more drop of sweat to my body. In that summer of 1955, two hours away from Keiko, I felt a deep longing for her yet was intrigued to be living so close to the grassroots of Japan.

During Army assignments in Japan, I saw places reflecting a profound sense of aesthetics, carefully tended gardens where wind blowing on shimmering, colored-glass tubes created illusions of a cool breeze. All of that became just a memory on that hot August day—the day I knew I'd have a chance to feel and comprehend a Japan I had never known before.

My education began when the absence of a bathroom in the house meant that I'd have to go around the corner to a public bath, which Oba-san said would "cost almost nothing." In the evening, I bought a pair of wooden clogs and went to the steamy public bath. I didn't know what to expect: I heard about "mixed bathing" in Japan but would learn that was more likely to occur in small rural communities or certain resorts than in cities.

Although there was a common entrance at the public bath, I noted males and females went into separate changing rooms. They'd bathe separately in what amounted to hot tubs as big as swimming pools.

As custom required, and imitating other new arrivals on the male side, I sat on a tiny stool and washed and rinsed myself with several buckets of water. When I stepped into the communal bath wearing a handkerchief-sized towel, other bathers giggled in amusement as I screamed in reaction to the scalding water.

A couple of men came over, and I understood they were telling everyone that a *gaijin*, "a foreigner," could not take the heat of the water so quickly. They helped ease my feet, legs, and then my whole body into the water: everybody was curious to watch the foreigner descend into the hot bath.

I stayed until my body turned lobster red. Stepping out, I waved to the crowd and said, "Oyasuminasai" ("good night"), and they all said, "Oyasuminasai" in return. That night, I became the *gaijin* of their communal bath, and after that, they took me in as much as the Japanese can embrace a foreigner in their midst. Whenever I went back, I felt welcome. As I became accepted, I thought the public baths in Japan created a sense of community where social ranks disappeared for a while in the nakedness of bathing.

When I returned to my flat, Oba-san was pleased to see that I was red as a lobster and immediately made some boiling tea, trying to explain that drinking hot tea was good for you when you were hot. Through gestures and my dictionary, she said she'd warm my water for shaving the next morning.

That evening, with heat and humidity still oppressive, I went to look for a restaurant. I couldn't read a menu but many restaurant windows displayed artistically crafted dishes made of plastic that looked more appetizing than the actual dishes.

I decided to splurge by ordering sukiyaki—thinly sliced beef cooked in an iron pot with green onions, noodles, tofu, and shiitake mushrooms served over a beaten raw egg. After studying prices in windows, I understood that would be my last sukiyaki for a long time.

On $35 a week, I'd set aside $20 for work, transportation, and expenses on all speculative stories. Fortunately, Oba-san did my laundry, which was included in the rent. After calculating restaurant prices, I realized all I could afford were noodle dishes, though once a week I'd have yakitori—barbecued chicken on a skewer with a bowl of rice—and maybe a beer. Eventually, I'd buy a can of corned beef from Argentina and mix it with soba noodles.

Those were lean times—it would have been comforting to know that I would in time become one of the highest earning photojournalists in the world.

The next day, I took a train to Tokyo's Central station. As a U.S. Army photographer on assignment, I had been spoiled with cars and drivers at my disposal and priority on military flights.

Suddenly I was one of millions swelling in Tokyo's population in the morning rush hour. As numbers in the crowds grew at each station, "pushers" with white gloves and uniforms squeezed passengers into hot and unbearable trains. How they could push so many people into overpacked cars was beyond my imagination.

There was something suffocating about the body heat of hundreds of passengers in the sweltering Tokyo summer. Fortunately, at five foot eleven, my head was above the crowd, so I could see, and my nose wasn't pressed in anyone else's face.

After that first inhumane commute, I got off at a station near the headquarters of the Asahi-Shimbun newspaper where the Pan Asia offices were located. There, John Taji introduced me to all his staff, who, thankfully, were bilingual.

I had thought Black Star's offices were crowded, but when I saw my desk at Pan Asia, there was barely room to reach my seat. It was difficult to imagine writing in such a claustrophobic space, but eventually I learned.

To the staff, I explained that in addition to English editions of the *Asahi-Shimbun*, *Yomiuri*, and *Mainichi* newspapers, I needed to see their translations of human-interest events that might appeal to American or European readers.

Gloria-san, a good-looking woman who served as Pan Asia's executive secretary, had been forwarding my letters to Keiko and perhaps guessed at my dilemma. As I waited, she placed a call to Keiko's summerhouse in Fujisawa.

Because Japan's telephone system was primitive in 1955, we waited a long time for a connection. In my best Japanese I asked for Keiko, and the housekeeper asked me to wait. She came back a few seconds later and said, "Keiko's not here. I'm sorry." Later Gloria-san called for me, but Keiko was still not permitted to answer.

Unable to reach Keiko, I spent a few days trying to find work, calling on all American, French, and British offices with correspondents in Tokyo: Time-Life correspondent James Greenfield explained his bureau had an assigned set of photographers; Jun Miki was *Life*'s first choice for black-and-white photos and Horace Bristol for color; the *New York Times, Newsweek, Paris Match,* and other bureaus had their own lists of photographers. I saw little hope of getting on anybody's list.

After a week of phone calls, it became obvious I'd have to create my own projects and ship them to Black Star in Manhattan and to Paris where Rapho Presse agreed to represent me in France.

Thinking of stories, I became fascinated with "soba men," the noodle men of Tokyo. Each of them wove through traffic on bicycles carrying a huge tray of 60 or 70 bowls of hot noodles to offices in central Tokyo.

Eating noodles myself twice a day, I began to admire the balancing act of the daring bikers. How they moved with such speed and grace in all the traffic seemed amazing. I decided it was a story for a Sunday supplement and Black Star agreed. But first I had to reach Keiko.

I called several times but was told Keiko was not in. I knew it wasn't true, so on a mid-September weekend, I went to Fujisawa even though I was sure her family would be there. It was hot and humid, and typhoon season had arrived.

At Pan Asia, Gloria-san gave me bilingual instructions to get to Fujisawa, some 25 miles south of Tokyo on the Pacific. Saturday morning, after two hard-boiled eggs, a bowl of miso soup, and cup of green tea, I caught a train to Fujisawa.

During the two-hour ride, I found solace in recalling Fumiko's words spoken during our voyage on the rusty old Greek freighter, "All will change when she sees you again," but as I approached Fujisawa, I was troubled by foreboding thoughts. What if Keiko's parents asked me, "Can you afford a wife? Where will you live?" How would I explain my tiny room in a poor district in western Tokyo? How would I explain my $15 weekly budget for living expenses to a wealthy family spending hot months in their summerhouse near the ocean?

As the train rolled on, I decided to say nothing about my financial straits. Instead, I'd say I expected to be ready for Keiko in two years. At least, I wanted to believe that—it was wishful thinking, but I knew I'd fight to make it by 1957.

From the train station, delaying my walk to her house, I headed for the Pacific. Ignoring the crowded beach, I found a quiet place on a rock looking east to California. A few months earlier, I had looked west to Japan from a cliff in California.

Then I walked to Keiko's home. The garden door was open—I remembered how enchanting the garden had been the year before. Through the trees and manicured paths, I could see the house with its paper screen doors open to the garden. "Anyone home?" I called out. Still using my French first name in 1955, I continued, "Keiko, Keiko. It's me, Jean. I've come back."

I felt ill at ease and embarrassed, and my English was stilted. There was a long silence. To avoid removing my shoes, I sat on a tatami mat with my feet in the garden. I was ready to wait for the rest of the day.

Then I heard shuffling of feet and saw Keiko followed by her mother. They knelt at the edge of straw mats overlooking the garden and said nothing. I remembered from previous walks in Kyoto how Keiko told me never to display emotions, but I couldn't contain myself. I burst out, "Keiko, I promised to return. Look at me, at least!" And as she did, I saw unbearable sadness and resignation in her eyes. She had lost a great deal of weight, and as she adjusted her yukata under her knees, her hands were trembling. Her mother kneeling next to her never looked at me; her eyes were downcast and remained there.

Outraged, not comprehending a thing, I cried out, "Keiko, speak to me! Speak, speak!" Then her older brother entered the room; he shook my hand, put on sandals, and took me to a secluded part of the garden.

I took my anger out on him and said, "Your father promised me if I came back, and after a reasonable courtship, I could marry Keiko. I am back." I was hurt that no one had said a word to me, not even hello. I exclaimed, "Keiko looks ill. Your mother doesn't even look at me. Your father is a liar! He has broken his word, a gentleman's word as he called it."

"Jean," Keiko's brother said, "I am very, very sorry." "Yes," I answered, "the Japanese are always sorry, that's what I hear all the time!" He waited for me to calm down and went on, "In our culture, the children owe absolute obedience to their parents. It is our filial duty." I pressed on, "Keiko isn't disobeying anyone. Your father gave her permission if I returned."

"Yes," he said, "that's true, but she'd be disobeying our mother who thinks her daughter marrying a foreigner would bring unforgivable shame to our family. Father discussed it endlessly with her, so did Keiko, but in the end, mother's will ruled, because she swore if Keiko insisted on her courtship with a foreigner, she'd commit suicide. And all of us knew she would have taken her life rather than dishonor our family name. In our culture, our mother's response is classical. Keiko had to sacrifice her love for her mother's sake. Again, I am very sorry."

Stunned, I ran back to the house just in time to see Keiko disappear behind a shoji screen. Not a single word had been spoken: it was the last time I saw her. Sending the second earring to me had indeed been a Japanese farewell.

I left the garden. The brother led me to the gate, shook my hand, and again said, "I am sorry." I could not articulate a single word.

I walked back to the Pacific Ocean, sat on my rock looking east to California and wondered, "What the hell am I doing in Japan?" The geopolitical arguments I had made in New York about Japan to owners of Black Star a few months earlier seemed abstract on that day as I wondered what kind of hell Keiko had gone through during the last five months.

Taking a pre-World War II train back to Tokyo Central, I felt the steel wheels beating against each section of the track, steel to steel, each pounding beat driving pain and anger in my heart. I hadn't expected an ancient culture in a stubborn old mother's head to alter my destiny. When I got off the train, I wasn't sure I wanted to be in Japan at all.

How could a mother give her daughter so little choice? My own mother had insulted my intelligence during my childhood, but she never threatened me with her own life. Had she, I would have also obeyed.

The idea of going back to my room in Nakano-ku with no refrigerator, no cold beer, radio, or music depressed me, so that evening I went to the Asahi-Shimbun building's Associated Press floor. There I listened to telex machines spewing out news of the world. There was something soothing in the flow of news, in the click-clack of words, signing off of dispatches far away, and the world going on with its business, and at last I calmed down.

Walking out of the building, I bumped into Sid White, correspondent for the International News Service. Sid said, "You look very pale," and invited me to the Foreign Correspondents' Club of Japan. I summoned the courage to tell him I could not afford the membership fee, so Sid invited me as his guest.

Over drinks, I told him, "off the record," of my idealistic romantic love story that had just ended. Nursing me with drinks, Sid spent the whole evening sympathizing, cheering me up, and speaking of "a clash of cultures," and though Sid often wrote features, he kept my story confidential despite its obvious appeal to his readers.

Again waiting up for me, Oba-san said when I arrived that I looked sorrowful, and I nodded my head as she made me green tea. She had already unrolled my futon and centered my pillow, and I bid her goodnight. Still high on Sid White's drinks and generosity, I fell asleep.

The next morning I woke with a hangover, so Oba-san made me green tea. The reality of yesterday began to set in, flooding my thoughts. Such a tragic denouement had never entered my mind in my last weeks in California.

I had worried about parental pressure but thought it could be eased by Keiko's independent personality and faith in my ability to convince her parents of my sincerity. I hadn't imagined her mother threatening suicide if Keiko didn't sacrifice her love.

My thoughts drifted to her girlfriend's betrayal in turning over my letters to Keiko's parents, the silence that followed, and the return of the second earring. Since Keiko's mother didn't speak English, it must have been the father or brother who read my letters announcing my return. I suspected the whole family turned on Keiko. The father's promise to me was made on the assumption that once in America, I'd never return. After news of my return, Keiko must have been unable to travel or be alone—she must have suffered deeply. On that Sunday morning, I joined her in her suffering.

After tea, I closed my shoji screen but my room became unbearably hot. To keep from idling and reminiscing, I went out to explore Nakano-ku and told myself that from tomorrow on, I'd start shooting my stories.

For the next few days I photographed soba men on bicycles, focusing on their skill in avoiding collisions in chaotic traffic. In 1955, driving in Japan's traffic was like playing a "chicken game" where whoever cut you off first would win. The nation's famous rules of courtesy and politeness collapsed: no one bowed to anyone.

On commuter trains, it was the same: everyone shoved, pushed, and squeezed through the doors, and women and children had to avoid rush hours or they'd be crushed like all the others. Japanese railroad authorities later set up special cars for women with special attention to mothers.

It was fascinating to see a highly disciplined society lose all its sense of order in traffic and public transportation, but my "noodle men," as I fondly called the

soba bikers, defied chaos, leaned right and left, straightened their loads, and made deliveries. Often they'd fall or come close and then recover in a deft balancing act: it was like a free circus performance in central Tokyo.

After their deliveries, I ate with my noodle men. I enjoyed our quick lunches as they taught me to noisily slurp my noodles in a sign of appreciation, a custom I avoided in Western circles.

My noodle men were amused and perplexed by my joining them for lunches. Like many Japanese in 1955, they thought all Americans were wealthy: I never told them that in the evening I'd be eating noodles again. In time, as I prospered, I'd always think of 1955 and '56 as my "noodle years."

After a week shooting, I made 10 11x14-inch prints of my best shots and wrote a 500-word text, which began, "Rain or shine, the soba men of Japan deliver daily hundreds of bowls of hot noodles to office workers of central Tokyo." I sent my first story as a civilian to Black Star by airmail.

My photos took a week to reach New York and another week for Ernest Mayer to respond. "Dear Johnny, Thanks for your story on Tokyo's noodle men. Next time you shoot such a mediocre story, please do not use airmail. Instead send it by sea mail. That's all your first project is worth, if that."

He went on for three pages critiquing every weakness in my work and what was lacking in my reportage. He wrote, "In your text you say 'rain or shine,' but where are the photographs of your soba men in the rain? You mention that near falls and collisions often happen: if they do, you must stay with your noodle men until an accident occurs."

The list went on and on, and I felt devastated. I was ashamed to show John Taji Mayer's letter, but this letter was in fact a hard but basic lesson in photojournalism. After the initial shock, I went out again with my noodle men. I stayed with them through rain and wind. Eventually, working in a typhoon, I witnessed a soba man falling from his bicycle and splashing his noodles all over a small Tokyo alley. I saw him laughing, but in Japan, people often smiled or laughed when they wished to cry. Despite feeling uneasy, I took my pictures.

Again I shipped my work by airmail, and this time it was sold to a Sunday supplement and distributed in Europe. After Black Star's 50 percent and Pan Asia's 50 percent of my share, my first civilian project in Japan barely covered my first month's guarantee.

Nonetheless, I celebrated by buying a radio. At last, I could listen to news and music on American Forces Radio as well as broadcasts by Japanese stations.

Oba-san, who loved songs like "Fly Me to the Moon," often listened to the radio with me. I put markers on its horizontal band so she could dial her favorite stations despite her failing eyesight.

This old lady, who had bent her back during years of planting, who lived close to poverty despite my meager monthly rental contribution, treated me with a gentle kindness and understanding rarely shown by my own mother. She pampered me and every day shared her miso soup with me.

Oba-san waited up when I was late coming home, even when I had Pan Asia send a message saying she should not wait up; in a way, she became the grandmother I never had. She never really knew about Keiko because I couldn't explain it in Japanese, yet she managed without words to ease my pain.

I tried to find out about her life. I understood she was widowed but wasn't sure if she had any children. When I asked, she didn't answer. In the winter of 1955, when we sat with legs under the *kotatsu* as charcoal warmed our feet and our backs shivered, I told her, "Thank you" in Japanese, and she said she understood. Our feelings transcended our languages.

For a number of weeks I submitted story ideas directly to *Life* magazine but soon realized editors in New York would not give me assignments. For routine coverage of events in Japan, they had a pool of competent Japanese photographers whose daily fee was half my American rate.

Those were profoundly discouraging times. My first journalistic contacts, years ago in Paris, had been with Time Inc. publications. *Time* and *Life* were the most important magazines in the world; their weekly readers numbered in the tens of millions; yet I stood on the outside, barely able to glance within.

Strangely enough, my big chance came because of Time Inc.'s cofounder and editor-in-chief, Henry Luce, and his strong antipathy to "Red China." His magazines railed against communist leaders who, in 1949, had taken power in the land of his birth. The son of a missionary, Luce was the most influential supporter of former Chinese leader Chiang Kai-shek and his ambition, from his new headquarters on Taiwan, to overthrow the communist mainland government.

Consequently, in October 1955, *Life* was barred from covering a trade fair in Tokyo staged by the Chinese to sell their goods to the outside world; therefore, the magazine turned to me, a virtually unknown freelancer, to infiltrate the fair, so to speak.

My one-day assignment was to focus on the Chinese "Chi Pao" dresses that revealed the upper thighs of women. Such dresses were banned in China and condemned as "decadent" by the Chinese Communist Party, yet they were being modeled at the trade fair to sell Chinese silk.

In puritanical China, acceptable clothes for women as well as men were the plain, unrevealing "liberation uniforms." Time Inc.'s Tokyo bureau chief, James Greenfield, told me *Life* wanted photos contrasting Chinese women at the fair wearing "liberation uniforms" with Chinese models in the sexier dresses.

I wanted the assignment but was nervous about the ruse that I was not shooting for *Life*. I told Greenfield I would do the job "but only if I can use an alias for myself without the name of Black Star and only if Black Star approves." Greenfield agreed.

So, as "Jean Renoir, independent correspondent from Paris," I introduced myself to the public relations officer at the Chinese trade fair and offered my phony business card printed in French and Japanese. Surprised to find an official who spoke French, I said my work would be submitted to communist publications in France, so he gave me a pass to cover the fair.

To give myself credibility, I spent a little time photographing other exhibits before getting to my assignment. Though it seemed hostesses in "liberation uniforms" were briefed to stay away from models wearing Chi Pao dresses, the uniforms and dresses finally crossed paths.

My best picture was published in a half page with text in the November 14, 1955, issue of *Life*. The editors respected my wishes for an alias, so after years dreaming of seeing my work in the great picture magazine, my first *Life* photograph was not credited to me but to a fictional "Jean Renoir."

Still, things were looking up. In that same month I received a five-day assignment from Time Inc.'s *Sports Illustrated* magazine to photograph the New York Yankees on their first visit to play exhibition games in Japan.

For a moment I panicked: I knew nothing about baseball and had never been to a game. At most, I had seen kids playing with gloves and bats, catching and hitting a ball, so I was very relieved to discover my assignment would focus not on baseball itself but on Tokyo receptions and parties for the Yankees.

In convertibles and open jeeps provided by the U.S. Air Force, the Yankees made their way to central Tokyo where Japanese crowds massed along the roads shouting, "Yogi Berra-san, Mickey Mantle-san, Cassey Stangel-san," as they welcomed the American sports heroes.

The Yankees were honored in a ticker-tape parade. I was amazed thousands of Japanese lining the streets seemed to know each player's face and name, while I barely knew who was who, but I quickly got to know the players and their wives at official dinners in classical Japanese restaurants. As playful geishas strummed three-stringed samisens, the greats of baseball, no doubt graceful on playing fields, clumsily tried to cope with chopsticks. Their efforts produced hilarious photographs of delicate geishas coaching huge Americans on the skill of feeding themselves Japanese style.

Before the first game, a Japanese writer at Pan Asia explained to me the finer points of baseball, such as a home run. One of my photos captured Yogi Berra running from first base and sliding home in the fifth inning. In the end, however, it was my coverage of the Yankees amused by geishas and cheered by enormous crowds that got more space in *Sports Illustrated* than the sport itself.

The only other assignment I received in 1955 was from French *Vogue* to cover a traditional Japanese wedding. Suddenly, it was Christmas Eve in the streets around the Ginza and near the office, and revelers and drinkers filled the many tiny bars. Japan had begun to commercialize Christmas as a time for men and only men to have fun and ease the stress of long working days.

It was a time to get drunk, flirt, and be entertained, caressed, served, and pampered by submissive, sexy "club hostesses" paid by the hour. None of this had anything to do with Christmas—it was carnival time.

At a little shop, I bought a bottle of *umeshu*, plum liquor, gift-wrapped for Oba-san. I thought of going to midnight mass but knew it wouldn't finish in time to catch the last train to Nakano-ku. Upon my return, Oba-san unwrapped my present as her eyes asked me, "Why?"

I explained that December 25 was a big American holiday.

I had bought myself a small bottle of gut-wrenching Japanese whiskey and encouraged Oba-san to join me in a toast. I thought mournfully of Keiko in Fujisawa and my uncertain future on that Christmas Eve, yet I still could say, "Merry Christmas to the world."

Oba-san spent the last days of 1955 cleaning every nook and cranny of the house—she even had the paper on my shoji screen replaced—and by New Year's Eve, the place was immaculate. She was honoring an ancient Japanese tradition of finishing the year in pure cleanliness, without debts.

As for me on December 31, I was in debt to Black Star for $404.34 despite having my every story published or sold. Given I was also in debt to Pan Asia, my situation seemed unmanageable.

During the long Japanese New Year holidays, Pan Asia's office was quiet and almost empty, but I knew they would be heated, so instead of freezing at Oba-san's house, I decided to spend a number of days at the office creating half a dozen story suggestions for Black Star.

There my thoughts turned to my family, whom I hadn't seen for five years. In a long letter, I wished them Happy New Year, told them to look for my Japanese classical wedding story in *Vogue*, and hinted they might see me soon.

Five years earlier, all my friends and family except for father predicted I'd soon be back in France, but they were wrong. Not long after my departure, I learned from my sister that my father, deprived of my paycheck, had to work seven days a week except for Sunday afternoon. My family was living at the edge of poverty and so was I. When Rapho Presse, my agency in Paris, told me currency regulations made it difficult to send my *Vogue* earnings to Japan, I said they should be sent instead to my parents.

Through the winter and spring of 1956, I shot a few stories Black Star approved. For *Life*, I photographed Secretary of State John Foster Dulles inspecting Korea's demilitarized zone, followed by two other assignments. For *Sports Illustrated*, I did a story on the martial art of Kendo.

In June, the U.S. Army invited me to join a group of American correspondents to witness a simulated "atomic-supported attack" on Iwo Jima, an island 700 miles southeast of Tokyo. On Iwo Jima in 1945, one of the fiercest and costliest battles in American history was fought. After a month of combat, 22,000 Japanese were killed or captured while Marines and other American fighting men suffered 21,000 casualties, including 4,500 "killed in action."

Eleven years later, U.S. forces would perform a simulated attack on the island but with atomic weapons, followed by amphibious landings. I photographed two low-flying A-26 bombers dropping two mock-atomic bombs that instantly mushroomed above the black volcanic sands of the island's western shore.

The mushroom clouds were so realistic that late into evening, many of us discussed dangers of the Cold War and the frightening new era of atomic land warfare that our forces were training for.

Later, I climbed 546 feet up Mount Suribachi to see where AP's Joe Rosenthal photographed the Marines raising the U.S. flag of victory in 1945. Reprinted on stamps, paintings, and recreated in statues, his celebrated image became part of American history.

On Iwo Jima, I befriended McGraw Hill's correspondent in Japan, Dan Kurzman, who became my first "real American friend" in Japan, a witty character with an unforgettable laugh coming from deep within. We laughed all the way back to Tokyo. From him, I later received many assignments from *Business Week* and other McGraw Hill magazines.

I also met a bright young Army captain and public relations officer who would make minor purchases for me at the PX. Japanese duties on all American products were extremely prohibitive in those years, and Japan's protective trade barriers were immovable, so American film stock sold at exorbitant prices. The young captain informed me that as an Air Force reservist, I could avoid Japanese tariffs if Black Star shipped film stock to an Army Postal Service "APO."

Coffee was prohibitively expensive in Japan, so from the PX, I immediately ordered instant coffee. It was my first coffee in 10 months. With coffee instead of green tea, mornings were less gloomy and more cheerful. I made coffee for Oba-san but she thought it was terrible.

In August, my next assignment took me to the Bay of Miyazu, one hundred miles northwest of Kyoto, where there was a mythical, beautiful sandbar called *Ama no Hashidate*, or the "Bridge of Heaven."

Frank Iwama, *Time*'s permanent correspondent in Japan, said it was one of the three most beautiful places in Japan, seen by thousands of Japanese each year. "But to appreciate its heavenly beauty," he said, "it has to be viewed upside down. The connoisseurs of the art of viewing scenery have to bend over and look at the two-mile-long sandbar through their legs."

I laughed as I imagined all those heads looking through their legs, their butts facing heavenly beauty. With *Life*'s approval, Frank and I set off for the Bridge of Heaven by boat. We immediately spread our legs, bent over, looked at the sky and beautiful sandbar through our legs, upside down.

We waited but failed to see the bridge spanning the heavens. When we admitted our failure to a Japanese viewing aesthete, he said, "You must first understand Zen Buddhism. Think of the sea as the sky, then think of the sky as the sea. Concentrate deeply and the sandbar bridge will span the heavens." I discovered that if one stayed in an upside-down position with blood rushing to the head long enough, dizziness would set in, and the bridge would indeed appear to be floating.

For a few days I photographed men, women, children, pilgrims, Buddhist priests, and wealthy men with geishas. The geishas dared lift their kimonos high enough to see the Bridge of Heaven between their legs; shyer women in kimonos tried to look under their large sleeves, while amateur photographers took pictures between their legs, cameras upside down, hoping for a miracle.

I photographed a young bride on her honeymoon trip shading her husband with a parasol while he looked between his legs for what seemed an eternity. When he finally stood up, his face was tomato red. Frank Iwama asked if he had seen the bridge spanning the heavens. "Yes, yes," he insisted, though he looked faint. The Japanese people never ceased to amaze me.

It was a fun assignment with lots of laughs, and the story was published in a "Speaking of Pictures" feature in the October 26, 1956, issue of *Life*.

Another typhoon season began at the end of August. In the first week of September, Japanese press reported that "Emma," said to be the worst typhoon to blow out of the Pacific, had devastated Japan's island of Okinawa.

EYE OF THE STORM

INSIDE TYPHOON EMMA

TOKYO 1956

Looking at newspaper coverage of Emma, I noticed that all pictures were of the aftermath but not the murderous typhoon itself. With hundreds of cumulonimbus clouds full of violent rain spiraling in the "eye" of the typhoon's vortex, Emma was a great killer in action. She was moving northwest about 10 to 15 miles an hour in a huge mass, possibly larger than New England, unleashing 125-mile-an-hour winds.

I called the 56th Weather Reconnaissance Squadron of the U.S. Air Force in Yokota, west of Tokyo, and requested permission to fly on one of their daily missions tracking and measuring typhoons.

The Public Relations officer gave me a position report and said, "Permission should be forthcoming, especially since you are a USAF reservist." I contacted Time-Life bureau chief Curtis W. Prendergast: "*Life* can get all the pictures of victims and destruction on Okinawa, but I want to photograph the 'killer in action.' I've been assured the Air Force flight crew can take me to maximum height, so I'll have a good chance to photograph the 'eye of the storm.'"

Curt answered, "John, it's a good idea but it sounds dangerous." He hesitated a long time. Impatiently I insisted, "These B-50 bombers converted to weather planes are powerful four-engine airplanes, and it'll take more than a typhoon to destroy one." Though apprehensive, Curt was convinced and telexed *Life* in New York. Answering quickly, *Life* offered me a $200 guarantee.

On September 9, I set out for Yokota Air Force Base for an early briefing while informing Curt I expected to take off at dawn on September 10. But at the briefing, a weatherman studying the latest reports told me, "You should take the night flight tonight because tomorrow, by the time the morning flight reaches Emma, she might be downgraded to less than a tropical storm."

Taking the night flight seemed illogical because to photograph the typhoon, I needed morning light. Then Captain William Martin, commander of the evening flight said, "Come with us. We have clearance for several extra hours of flight, so tomorrow at dawn we'll climb high enough in the eye so you can get your pictures." Convinced, I switched flights but was unable to reach Prendergast to inform him of the schedule change.

After reviewing flight-radio procedures and checking lifesaving equipment, dinghies, parachutes, and "Mae West" life jackets, affectionately named after the bosomy movie star, we buckled in and taxied for takeoff.

At 19:14, we lifted into the night while Tokyo below, garish with neon lights, fell away. We flew in a calm, blue night with a crescent moon shining, intoxicated by the kind of beauty that inspired Antoine de Saint-Exupéry's *Night Flight*.

It was enchanting and exhilarating even as we realized that 400 miles ahead, "the Pacific's worst typhoon in memory" was raging over Japan's southern island of Kyushu and the small island of Tsushima.

When our aircraft leveled at 10,000 feet, we unstrapped our parachutes as an airman served tea. I lit a cigarette and relaxed, but not for long: suddenly the plane jerked, vibrated, and buffeted as we hit "Emma's northern wall" of wind and water, aptly called a wall because penetrating it felt like hitting concrete.

As if we were skimming the Sea of Japan, waves of rain washed over the cockpit, wings, and fuselage. The converted bomber was tossed about like a toy, while the pilots, after switching off autopilot, struggled with controls.

I quickly buckled my shoulder and belt harnesses as Airman Keeler, the flight mechanic, plugged in a high-powered spotlight and aimed it through the porthole at leading edges of the wings. I asked, "What are you looking at?" He said, "To see if rivets have popped out in any large sections."

For two hours, the plane shook in extreme turbulence. Needing to do something, I photographed the pilots while the radar man clutched my legs. Then the temperature rose 29 degrees Fahrenheit and buffeting eased: we had entered the calm breeze of "Emma's eye."

A perfect eye was about 15 miles in diameter. In its calm, we had coffee. Suspended by parachutes, "drop-sounds" were released as they had been in the storm; the little radio boxes relayed data to the plane till they disappeared in the sea.

We'd been flying for 10 hours and 16 minutes and reached Emma's opposite wall at 5:30 A.M. The crew measured the 125-mile-per-hour winds for "a final fix" of the mission.

Captain William Martin called for clearance and permission to climb to 19,000 feet. Permission granted, the copilot, Captain Olbinski, turned to me and said, "Now you have a 10-hour lead on the morning flight. The mission is all yours. By the way, we get hazardous pay for dangerous flying. What do you get?" I answered, "I hope to get a double page in *Life*."

Flying upward out of the calm of Emma's eye into the violent spiraling wall, I kept looking at the altimeter. "Soon we should be in the clear," Captain Martin said as our altitude reached 19,000 feet.

As we circled into the wall, the plane took a tremendous beating for another 90 minutes while I figured we'd soon reach the western edge of the eye where I could photograph the typhoon using eastern backlight for contrast.

Then the number two engine coughed and quit. The engineer immediately feathered the propeller blades so the engine would not tear off the wing.

Engine number one began splashing oil on the dome I was photographing through; then engine number four started sputtering. Captain Martin turned to me and said, "Sorry *Life*, that's the end of your mission."

Entering a state of full emergency, I crawled through the tunnel to the back of the plane as Airman First Class Charles Keeler adjusted my parachute straps and gave me a thorough briefing on bailing out.

Tightening my harness, I kept one Leica sticking out of my flight suit in case I had to photograph the old bomber falling to sea. I did not know what the 11 crewmembers knew: a parachute falling into a typhoon would be instantly shredded to pieces.

The captain just said, "I don't like them silk elevators." More encouragingly, he said, "At 19,000 feet, we'll have a longer glide angle than our normal 10,000 foot missions. We're losing altitude fast, but I think we can make it to Atami near Osaka on a single pass. The 6,000 foot runway is too short for a B-50, but it'll have to do."

Descending towards Atami, we were given top-priority landing clearance. As we broke through the typhoon's wall, the plane lurched and almost shook out of control. Approaching with only one engine running at full power, Captain Martin maximized the length of the runway, hitting it within the first few feet, and at risk of blowing up engines one and four, quickly reversed the pitch of the engines in a rough and violent landing, stopping a few yards short of the rice paddies.

We cheered the pilots as we opened the exit doors and were greeted by crews of four fire trucks and ambulance paramedics. Bussed to the barracks, I booked a call to Curt Prendergast in Tokyo. In 1956, long-distance calls had to be booked in advance.

It was 7:50 A.M. when I fell asleep on my bunk. My call came through in the early afternoon: Prendergast, in disbelief and relief said, "John, thank God you're alive, alive, alive!"

I answered, "Curt, we lost one engine and power in two more. It was a close call, but I'm calling you from Atami, not heaven." It was a bad phone connection but Curt continued insisting, "But your plane was reported lost over the Sea of Japan shortly after takeoff."

Then I realized Curt was referring to the morning flight—I told him I had switched planes. All Curt could say was, "God, Jesus." I then informed the night crew about the morning flight vanishing over the Sea of Japan and felt their sorrow. Both crews knew each other and shared a bond in danger.

I thanked my crew and hugged them goodbye. The next day our story and the fate of the lost plane were reported on widely by the Associated Press. I later reflected that our climbing to 19,000 feet just for my photographs, giving us a longer glide angle, may have saved our lives.

When I saw Curt, he was full of joy but said he had felt guilty and terribly concerned. It was the start of a wonderful friendship. Curt immediately telexed George Caturani, the foreign desk editor at *Life*: "Launois was not on typhoon-chasing airplane that vanished. Launois willing to forgo $200 guarantee if *Life* gives him guarantee to do full and proper coverage of typhoon chasing out of Guam. My feelings are regardless what we do about future, we ought to reward him for his close call now."

Accidentally I saw Caturani's response in a confidential telex: "Launois was foolhardy but *Life* will pay the $200 guarantee." Outraged and insulted, I told Curt, "Tell *Life* to go to hell. Tell them I refuse their money. Since I'm an unknown, *Life* calls me foolhardy, but would *Life* have said that to Robert Capa or Gene Smith when they covered wars in Europe and the Pacific?" I instructed Black Star to refuse payment.

Curt's secretary, Harriette Watts, always gave me cookies and tea because she thought I looked "starved and too skinny." To cheer me up, she showed me a confidential telex from Prendergast to Caturani, which said in effect: "I think you made a careless mistake. I predict in near future, John Launois will become a great photojournalist surpassing all your Tokyo photographers." It did cheer me up, but *Life* never gave me another typhoon assignment.

FIRST CLASS

A LEAD STORY FOR *LIFE*

MANILA 1957

In autumn of 1956, Howard Chapnick gave me an assignment to do a story on U.S. Army Captain Edward "Ted" Bamonte for the United States Information Agency. Bamonte was a doctor who set up a 24-hour emergency station for sick and poor Koreans in villages near the DMZ (demilitarized zone), separating North and South Korea.

I was reluctant to work, even temporarily for the USIA, an agency created to convey a positive image of the U.S. abroad, as this would not be an asset to my résumé as a photojournalist. But Bamonte's work appealed to my idealistic view of American forces. At his dispensary, Korean villagers, old men, women, and many children waited on a long line each day to see the doctor. Some came for ear, throat infections, respiratory problems, tuberculosis, or intestinal diseases like parasitosis.

The majority, often arriving from remote villages, had never seen a doctor before. An old man told me he traveled "one hour of a horse's gallop" to see Doctor Bamonte. Because he had come from so far but was in excellent health, he was given some placebos.

News of the dispensary spread far and wide. Because gaining admission to Korean hospitals was extremely difficult, Bamonte's one-man operation with his one interpreter was soon overwhelmed.

More than three years after the 1953 Armistice, Korean village life was harsh. The earthen floors of simple homes, though often washed, were breeding bacteria. Villagers walked miles in the middle of the night to bring news of an emergency. At all hours, Ted Bamonte with his ambulance guided by a villager would drive to patients in distress.

Late at night, Bamonte seldom had an interpreter but did not need one once he reached a suffering person. When he made urgent minor surgical operations during my time with him, I became his nurse, resuming photography afterwards.

All too often, returning to the dispensary, he'd find another villager waiting with news of another emergency, so Doctor Bamonte got little sleep. The job seemed to be too much for one man, yet shortly before my departure, Bamonte was optimistic. "These people need help," he said. "Besides, a doctor sees diseases here that are never seen in the U.S., and I believe the Army will continue to support this dispensary even after I'm shipped home."

He shifted his attention to my physical state. "You need help with your diet yourself—you don't eat salad, you barely touch fruit, you don't eat enough altogether. Where in the world did you pick up such lousy eating habits?" I answered, "In France and Tokyo."

He prescribed daily multiple vitamins and lectured me on minimum calorie requirements. After bidding him goodbye, I flew back to Tokyo and later received praise from USIA for my story on that most remarkable man.

On November 6, 1956, President Eisenhower was reelected in a landslide. Curt Prendergast was dejected—he thought Eisenhower was in such poor health that the nation might end up with Vice President Richard Nixon, a politician he deplored.

Curt and his wife Libby had planned a victory party for Eisenhower's democratic opponent Adlai Stevenson, but they had to settle for a "wake party" or "mourning party" for Stevenson instead. At about the same time, Black Star raised my weekly guarantee from $35 to $55 and reduced its percentage from 50 to 35 percent.

While Stevenson lost the presidential election, I won a vote of confidence from Black Star and went to Prendergast's "mourning party" in an elated mood: it was my first social invitation in Tokyo.

The couple lived in the biggest Western-style house I had seen in Tokyo. An enormous black wreath was hung on their door, so despite my own good news, I thought I should try to look solemn and not offend the mourners inside.

But the party was full of laughter, and guests were keeping barmen and waiters busy. Curt introduced me to his beautiful wife, Libby, who, in turn, introduced me to their friends as John, "who has just survived a harrowing flight into typhoon Emma."

I explained to Libby that my typhoon adventure was nearly two months old, but she took me by the arm and said, "That's just like yesterday." In her slightly southern and most delightful accent, she introduced me to diplomats, Japanese politicians, and correspondents for leading publications in America and Europe. I wondered how she could remember all their names.

American, French, and Japanese hors d'oeuvres and dishes were passed while waiters always on hand served trays with glasses of champagne. Busy bartenders served me Scotch and water, which I sipped all evening.

In 1956, I was still terribly ignorant of American politics and not even registered to vote, so at the party I listened in on conversations and heard that Adlai Stevenson was a humanist, brilliant writer, and orator, perhaps "too articulate to reach the grassroots of America." Eisenhower was tolerated, Nixon despised.

It was a long way from my world in Nakano-ku with Oba-san. I mingled with American correspondents who seemed to have unlimited expense accounts. They were Democrats who worked for Republican-owned newspapers and magazines that had endorsed or favored Eisenhower. I noted that they were inclined to view photographers as an illiterate bunch, as if we were only useful to illustrate their brilliant texts: it was a perception I wanted to change.

Curt, Libby, and I ended the evening talking about France during the occupation. Discovering I had missed my last train to Nakano-ku, they looked at a Tokyo map, found Nakano-ku, which they had never heard of, and drove me home.

I told them my street was too small for an American car and had them drop me off at a nearby train station: I didn't want them to see the tiny house I lived in. Shaking hands, I thanked them for their kindness, and Libby kissed my cheek. Oba-san was incorrigible—it was three in the morning, and she had waited up for me again.

On Christmas, I repeated last year's ritual: she had her plum liquor, I had my Japanese gut-wrenching whiskey, and the two of us again toasted the "American holiday."

In the new year of 1957, I received through Black Star my first assignment for *Look* magazine, *Life*'s chief rival, to photograph in color U.S. Marines exercising at the base of Mount Fuji. With a $1,200 guarantee plus expenses, it was the highest paid assignment I had ever received. *Look* published my pictures, and I learned the editors were very happy with the results.

Through Pan Asia, Curt Prendergast left a message to drop by his office. Imai-san, Time Inc.'s office manager in Tokyo, whispered, "Curt is angry about your expense report for your Kure shipyard assignment."

The bureau chief handed me my expense report and said, "I can't approve such expenses." Embarrassed, I said, "Hey, Curt, I kept my expenses to a minimum as I usually do." "That's just it, John!" he said, "I see here that most of your meals are noodles. What are you trying to do, shame Time Inc.?"

He smiled and explained, "When you're on assignment for *Life*, I expect you to travel first class, stay at first-class hotels, eat first class—first-class everything! I don't want you eating noodles, I want you eating Kobe beef." That beef was the most expensive in the world because before slaughter, Kobe cattle were massaged for tenderness and fed beer for two months. On my next assignment, I found it easy to protect Time Inc.'s image and prestige. It looked like my noodle days were finally behind me.

On March 17, 1957, the aircraft carrying Ramon Magsaysay, president of the Philippines, crashed on the island of Cebu, 350 miles south of Manila.

I knew the death of Magsaysay would be a lead story for *Life*. A staunch anti-communist, Magsaysay was a charismatic figure who calmed peasant rebellions in the Philippines through his humanism and opened doors of the presidential palace to all the people.

On March 18, *Life*'s foreign desk editor cabled Time Inc.'s Tokyo bureau, saying in essence: "John Dominis cannot be reached in Indonesia. Please have Launois proceed immediately to Manila to cover mourning and funeral of President Magsaysay."

The bureau booked me on the next available flight to Manila, departing from Tokyo the following day. I reasoned that a professional like Dominis, traveling with *Life* Asia editor Scot Leavitt, would somehow hear about Magsaysay's death and reach Manila before my departure.

Life would then cancel my assignment, so I asked Imai-san to book me that night on Pan Am's 23:59 flight to Hong Kong, arguing that from Hong Kong, I'd easily catch a flight to Manila in the morning. If I was already in Hong Kong, I told myself, *Life* would probably ask me to join Dominis in Manila.

I quickly secured a visa for Hong Kong and another for the Philippines, and at midnight, took off on a Pan Am Clipper, flying first class. In a spacious cabin, a stewardess tucked me into my comfortable bunk bed for the eight-hour flight.

In the morning, there was a Tokyo telex in *Life*'s Hong Kong office telling me that the magazine had cancelled my Manila assignment, but "Since Launois is already in Hong Kong, have him proceed to Manila and work with Dominis." My gamble paid off, and I'd have the chance to work with John Dominis, one of *Life*'s top photographers.

Dominis immediately struck me as a generous man, secure in his own talent and more than willing to answer a newcomer's questions. Scot Leavitt explained that we had a time problem because the president's coffin wouldn't return to the capital until March 20, and our story had to be on newsstands by March 25. Meeting *Life*'s deadline would be a remarkable feat.

Moving photos to publication was slow in early 1957: rolls of exposed film for big publications in New York had to be flown across oceans and continents for processing and editing. It was just before the age of jet airliners and long before today's instant transmissions of global images via satellite and the Internet.

To give us maximum shooting time, Leavitt hired the Kodak factory in Manila to process final prints and directly ship them to the Donnelley printing plant in Chicago. There, editors flown in from New York would prepare layouts using rough radio transmission copies of selected photographs.

The cost of hiring the Kodak plant exclusively for several days was astronomical, but that was the *Life* style: be first, best, and damn the cost. Dominis and I worked without stopping for several days: we photographed the hearse carrying Magsaysay in a flag-draped coffin as it inched its way from Manila's airport through immense solemn crowds to the presidential palace and then to Luneta Park overlooking the Pacific.

Thousands upon thousands wept openly—it seemed the whole nation was in tears. I had never witnessed such national sorrow. We delivered the lead story for the next issue of *Life*, dated April 1, in which John had two pages, I had five, and the lead photograph was mine: a woman collapsing in grief, being helped to her feet.

Dominis congratulated me by saying, "Good for you"—in his own generous way, he meant it. My performance in Manila radically changed my status with *Life*. Suddenly, my assignments were no longer confined to Japan and Korea but spread to stories all over Asia to the Philippines, Laos, Cambodia, Thailand, Burma, Malaya, Indonesia, India, Goa, Guam, and Vietnam. I was on my way.

L'ÂME ENCHANTÉE

A STEWARDESS NAMED YUKIKO

TOKYO 1957

On April 26, 1957, another assignment in Manila changed my life once again, personally and profoundly. In a fateful romantic encounter, I took off for a return flight to Tokyo on Air France's Lockheed Constellation.

All I heard at first was her voice welcoming passengers on her flight. Then I looked up to discover inquisitive expressions radiating from her lovely, almond-shaped eyes.

With only a few passengers in the first-class cabin, I introduced myself to the lovely stewardess. I told her I recognized in her the eyes of a fawn I had seen at twilight while driving through a forest road near Nara, an ancient capital of Japan. Her name was Yukiko.

While much of the world was enamored with Marilyn Monroe in the 1950s, it was Audrey Hepburn who embodied the beauty I sought, and there, cruising with me at 16,000 feet, was a young Japanese woman more beautiful than the slim and graceful Hepburn herself.

I was fascinated by Yukiko's grace and her charming voice fluent in French. Enchanted, I could feel myself falling in love and that familiar emotional pain beginning to ease. Between serving drinks to other passengers, she sat next to me and spoke in French. For nearly seven years, I avoided speaking French in an attempt to leave France behind, but with Yukiko, I once again spoke in the language of my birth.

I discovered that Yukiko had graduated from Osaka University with a degree in French literature, and she spoke of her love for great novels like Romain Rolland's *L'Âme Enchantée* (*The Enchanted Soul*), Stendhal's *La Chartreuse de Parme* (*The Charterhouse of Parma*), and Jacques Chardonne's *L'Amour, C'est Beaucoup Plus Que*

L'Amour (Love, It's Much More Than Love), from which she quoted, "Once you have loved, your life is not in vain." She was idealistic and to me, as pure as falling snow.

Impressed with her exceptional education, I asked why she did not teach French literature. "In Japan," she said, "a woman is not expected to have a career. Even with a degree, at best, what a woman can get is an office job serving tea all day. But as a stewardess, I can travel and perhaps one day live in Paris."

We talked for nearly the entire flight, and landing in Tokyo, I escorted her to her cheerful rented room and made a date for the next day. I didn't know it then but Yukiko's dream was to marry a French romantic like the hero in Romain Rolland's *Jean Christophe*—and she had just met in the sky a man named Jean from Marly, France. That night, she wrote her mother in Sakuragaoka near Osaka and told of her encounter with her destiny.

In following days, we discussed humanistic values. She spoke of the dangers of materialism and how greed could destroy purity of spirit, while I told her about my last 19 months with Oba-san in Nakano-ku. In my stories of hardship in France, rebellion against injustice, early tales of pain, struggle, outrage, and my voluntary exile from France, she saw heroism, but those experiences only reminded me of lonely decisions.

After two days, she returned to the skies and flew to Saigon, while I began another assignment.

In spring, while photographing Manila from a Filipino Army helicopter and keeping track of Yukiko's flying schedule, I saw her Air France Constellation touch down at the airport. I told my pilot to land next to her plane and climbed out of the chopper in my flight suit, while Yukiko saw me and waved. As she stepped onto the tarmac, we shook hands and I told her, "I've come to buy you a milkshake."

Air France's crew was surprised at my landing, but they loved the romanticism of it, and I invited my pilot to join us. "Thanks," he said, "but you two should be alone." After finishing milkshakes, we again shook hands: honoring Japanese customs, we did not kiss in public. Yukiko escorted me to my chopper, and we waved goodbye as whirling blades lifted me away.

Between meetings, we exchanged telexes, some in poetry, coded with messages of love. Keiko's sacrifice 19 months before had left me vulnerable, and I knew love was fragile, but the pain receded each time I saw Yukiko.

But I felt insecure: I had to anchor our love and protect it from that ancient culture with its sacrificial rituals. On June 5, 1957, just six weeks after our first meeting, I gave Yukiko an engagement ring.

I didn't learn the extent of her feelings until 40 years later. Yukiko at the time wrote in her journal, "Jean Launois loves me! This reality frightens me. It came much too soon. A little while longer, please let me dream. Why did my happiness come so soon? It won't be easy to live together and love one another all our lives, but it's so fortunate we can start our life together when we're still young and unfinished. A whole life lies before us unexplored. I am grateful to the fate that tied us together, two souls united on my finger shimmer with secret passion, a marriage of the souls."

I believed I had met the missing part of my soul in Yukiko. Engaged, we lived in an elevated idealistic realm, a state of purity. We had only kissed, and in the streets of Tokyo, we just held hands.

Seeing the two of us together, Japanese men insulted her for being with a foreigner. They called her "Butterfield 8," referring to the call girl in the movie starring Elizabeth Taylor. Yukiko restrained me from fighting, saying, "They're just primitive, lost in racial prejudices." From then on, we walked together in Tokyo but no longer held hands.

Difficult as she found it to be insulted in the streets, she was upset more by my pain than her own. As a result, our love grew more spiritual, and our souls fused though our physical selves had not.

In summer, I managed to see Yukiko several times in Manila while on assignments covering Filipino politicians campaigning across the Philippines.

At political conventions, I photographed Filipino delegates removing handguns from their holsters. They checked their weapons the way people in other countries checked their coats.

As food was passed around, I noticed delegates removing peso bills that had been carefully placed inside their sandwiches—only then would they bite into their ham and cheese. None of the delegates objected as I photographed mass bribery.

By August, after so many takeoffs and landings on grassy airstrips wedged between coconut trees, I grew accustomed to seeing the graceful stewardess on the domestic airliner that took me from island to island. She'd ask me for my weapon as she collected handguns in a woven basket before takeoff, but I never carried weapons, only cameras.

After my engagement to Yukiko, I gradually learned she had grown up in a very privileged, highly cultured family. Before World War II, her grandmother often invited international orchestras from Europe to play in Japan, and her father, very pro-British, loved traveling through England.

Though Yukiko confided in her mother, she kept our engagement secret from her father. We wanted to get married in October, so I moved into a modern Japanese apartment and had to say goodbye to Oba-san, who slowly realized I would always be far away.

In the months before I moved out, Oba-san stopped waiting up for me and no longer made me tea. She didn't understand why I seldom came home any more. On maps, I showed her where I had traveled but it meant nothing to her, for she had never ventured outside of Nakano-ku.

It was difficult to say goodbye because she had been so kind to me. I bowed to her, much lower than a foreigner should, and she tried to bow lower, as was the custom, but she was too old. Had she been American or French, I'd have given her a hug or kiss on the cheeks, but instead, I held her hand and said, "Arigato. Gomennasai," for "Thank you. I am sorry."

After our engagement, I met Yukiko's father, Ei-ichi Iwao, an executive of the Osaka Power Company. He adored his only daughter, but in the cultural mores of Japan, he never hugged her, touched her hand, or kissed her cheek. His love was unspoken and powerful.

Father and daughter had seen the recent movie version of *War and Peace* starring Audrey Hepburn, and he told Yukiko she could have been Natasha. I agreed with him on that, but otherwise he struck me as stern and authoritarian.

My status in the world had changed since I courted Keiko. Now a full member of the Foreign Correspondents' Club of Japan, I was on financially sound ground. I had a small French Renault assembled in Japan, thousands of dollars of credit at Black Star, and major photographic assignments lined up.

Mr. Iwao and I greeted each other formally. We sat around a tea table, but I never had a chance to explain my credentials. Though fluent in English, he spoke in formal Japanese in the tone of a samurai warlord speaking to one of his lowly warriors.

In French, Yukiko translated. In essence he said, "You never answered my letter in which I explained why such important matters cannot be rushed." Away on assignment, I missed his letter and had not responded, which he thought was rude and offensive. "You have known each other for less than four months, and since both of you have been traveling to different countries so often, you don't even know each other. Yukiko has filial duties to respect her father, and you have to respect our cultural differences."

His tone was harsh and haughty, his voice that of a man accustomed to giving commands. As she translated, Yukiko seemed to soften the content of what he said.

"In Japan," I responded, "most marriages are arranged. Most newlyweds in your country, sir, have only crossed paths two or three times in a garden. After a few looks at each other, they're married by their families regardless of personal feelings. They don't even know if they have any ideas in common. Yukiko and I share many values, Western values, love of great English, American, French, and Russian literature. It was you who approved of her studies in a university."

For a moment he thought to himself and then in English said, "That was probably my biggest mistake. But children have a duty to their parents, and they must obey." In English I replied, "Sir! Look into my eyes and swear to me you've never disobeyed your parents." Choosing not to answer my question, he said, "I will never approve this marriage."

In her journal, Yukiko wrote, "Father is so stubborn and will not give in. I feel tears swell in my eyes. Joining me for a cup of cold tea before bed, mother held me tightly in her arms and whispered, 'You have nothing to worry about.' Still holding me as I cried, she said, 'Everything will work out.'"

As Yukiko and I bid each other goodbye, we exchanged imaginary kisses and an embrace. Greatly worried, I flew back to Tokyo, remembering what had happened nearly two years ago when an old lady had forced her daughter to sacrifice love for duty. Suddenly a modern-day samurai lord stood against my love for Yukiko, saying he would never approve our marriage.

How far would he carry his threat? I knew he loved his daughter, and I reasoned he would not break her heart. Knowing my future father-in-law was pro-British, I asked my friend Alex Campbell, Time Inc.'s recently appointed Tokyo bureau chief, to write a character reference letter to Mr. Iwao on my behalf.

Alex was delighted at the news of my engagement to Yukiko. On Time-Life stationery, Alex wrote an eloquent letter describing me as a man of extraordinary character and talent. Though Alex was Scottish, his letter was understated and very English—it worked.

Less than two weeks later, Mr. Iwao answered Alex's letter. In essence it said, "I will never approve this marriage between my daughter and Mr. Launois, but I will be present at the wedding ceremony and reception at the Foreign Correspondents' Club. Do not misunderstand, my presence will not mean approval."

On October 10, 1957, in Tokyo's Saint Ignatius Church, Yukiko's father in a morning coat walked her to the altar, but he and I barely acknowledged each other. Many members of the foreign press corps who hadn't been in a church for years were there for our wedding.

Photo by Masamichi Kanda

Yukiko's father stood like a statue of a proud man, listening to the rites of the Catholic Church as his daughter said "I do" to the American priest who married us. In church, we kissed but our lips barely touched.

At the reception, Yukiko introduced Alex Campbell to her father, and they spoke of England, which her father knew well and loved. Much later, Yukiko's father visited our house in Tokyo. Seeing his daughter happy, he spoke to me in a civil tone for the first time.

Though Yukiko and her father continued to express themselves with a love unspoken, he never gave her a wedding present, because that would have meant approval. It was left to me to pay for all wedding expenses.

But we received countless gifts from our American, European, and Asian friends. In a Time-Life Ford with "Just Married" painted in huge white letters, we drove off in the din of tin cans tied to the bumper.

As a gift for our honeymoon, Adrian Zecha, later the publisher of *Asia Magazine*, lent us his romantic cottage by a private beach in Enoshima, facing the Pacific south of Tokyo. We settled into our enchanting retreat by the ocean, delighting in the knowledge that there was not a single person on earth who could see us kissing. At last we were alone.

Unfortunately, puritanism of the 1950s, our limited experience, and denial of affectionate expressions in Japanese culture left us ill-prepared for intimacy, and our physical union was awkward. We were anxious and unable to consummate our marriage until days after our honeymoon. Instead, we took flight into the church-approved marriage of our souls and just spent a few idyllic days dreaming and planning for the future.

Despite the beauty of the place, I grew restless. I felt guilt in leisure and had never learned the art of idleness. After our honeymoon, I received an assignment to shoot some color brochures and posters for Northwest Airlines. The contract paid $1,200 plus expenses, including a first-class seat for Yukiko, my new assistant, who wrote captions for me in French, which I translated into English. On an extended honeymoon, we stayed at the best hotels and had the best meals, though sometimes I missed my noodles.

One time in Japan, Yukiko accompanied me as my interpreter on a *Business Week* assignment. As I was photographing the chairman of the board of a major Japanese trading company, he asked her, "Are you Yukiko Iwao?" "Yes," she answered. "How did you know?" He said, "I know your father." Later Yukiko learned from her mother that her father had tried to arrange a marriage between Yukiko and the son of this chairman of the board.

Yukiko was happy accompanying me on trips, but some assignments were too dangerous. In September 1958, *Time* magazine asked me to cover the conflict in Quemoy, later known as Chinmen Tao, a small island southwest of Taipei, Taiwan, close to "Red China." Taiwanese soldiers there lived underground, since Quemoy was regularly bombarded with shells from China's long-range artillery guns in a test of wills between Mainland China's Mao Zedong and Taiwan's Chiang Kai-shek.

I promised Yukiko to be careful. On September 11, 1958, I borrowed one of Time-Life's airport-issued armbands so that she could accompany me through customs, immigration, all the way to the side of the aircraft. As I took my first boarding steps on the mobile staircase, I impulsively turned and said, "Embrasse moi, chérie!" ("Kiss me darling!") Yukiko hesitated, then stepped up to embrace me, and for the first time in public, we kissed.

In her diary, Yukiko wrote, "John is going to war. I may never see him again, so I had to kiss him. What if it was our last kiss?" Her daring surprised me. After ground personnel around the plane reported our "indiscretion," she and my perennial assistant, Kanda-san, were ordered to report to customs and immigration authorities.

Immigration officials subjected Yukiko to endless insults because she had "committed fraud" by using a journalist's armband. Worse than that, she insulted Japan and the many watching the flight's departure who had seen us kiss.

She had broken an old taboo in Japan: kissing in public, particularly a foreigner. Loyal Kanda-san bowed constantly, saying over and over, "Sumimasen!" (I'm sorry!), while Yukiko endured hours of grilling and finally signed a formal letter of apology, knowing it was the only way to be released.

Once again, Alex Campbell wrote a letter on my behalf offering apologies. Our armbands were confiscated and airport privileges were suspended for several months, but Alex was delighted by the whole incident and made it a favorite story to tell visitors from America and Europe.

On Quemoy, I boarded an old C-46 cargo plane, a gift from the U.S. to Taiwan, to join a group of journalists for a flight to a landing strip under fire by cannons of "Red China." I soon realized how untrained I was in the skills of war coverage.

ARTILLERY FIRE

AN ISLAND UNDER SIEGE

QUEMOY 1958

To evade mainland China's radars, we flew so low that waves from the South China Sea sprayed against our portholes. With a good idea of where China's guns were pointing, the pilot touched down and immediately reversed pitch on both engines, braking to the maximum just one hundred yards ahead of the blasts of 155-millimeter shells, and we quickly taxied between high rows of protective sand bags.

After a briefing from the military the next morning, I managed to get a ride to a beach where green little flags marked the mine-free zones. As supply ships approached, I took cover by a building for protection from incoming shells. Associated Press's Woody Edwards, crouching deep in a shell-blown hole, saw me and screamed, "Run to my hole you stupid fool! That's the radio station. They'll blow it up any second now!"

I ran to him. Just as I jumped into Woody's hole, the radio station was hit with a full salvo, and the walls of the building collapsed. Woody, a veteran who covered many battles, had saved my life, and he briefed me that day on how to survive on an island saturated with artillery fire.

Woody and I became good friends. The following day, we saw Taiwanese supply ships destroyed by artillery fire, and we later learned that 30 journalists from all over Asia were on one of the ships. Taiwanese press reported, "All are believed dead."

That afternoon, *Life*'s John Dominis and I witnessed something unbelievable. A Japanese ex-Olympic swimmer swam through a sea of exploding shells with cameras around his neck, reached the shore, walked through minefields, and approached our bunker. With his clothes soaking wet, he identified himself in halting English as a newsman from Japan. Giving us his business card, he bowed, collapsed, and was rushed to a military hospital. Because his business card was in Japanese, we never learned who he was, but we heard news that he survived.

I had trouble photographing shells falling on the bunkered island, so my coverage for *Time* was not published. Only Dominis had the brilliance to shoot time-exposure photographs capturing the terror of tracing shells in the night from the bow of a supply ship.

With no planes available to ship his film from Taipei to Tokyo, he telexed *Life* saying he'd have to charter a DC-6 to Tokyo for $7,000. *Life* cabled back, "Charter plane if you think coverage is worth it."

John's experiments with time exposures were bold, but he couldn't be sure the technique had worked. However, after thinking about it, he said, "I risked my life all night. Hell, yes, a $7,000 charter is worth it!" His coverage made the following week's lead story.

The day we were due to leave the island, I watched our small group of journalists board a C-46 plane and reach for their "Mae West" life jackets, but I was puzzled at why they threw the life jackets back on the pile instead of putting them on. I understood when I saw about 30 wounded Taiwanese soldiers lying on the bare-aluminum floor of the cargo plane: many were teenagers without legs or arms, moaning in blood-soaked bandages.

As soon as I saw the fear in the eyes of the young men peering through their bandaged faces, I threw my life jacket back on the pile. If our plane ditched in the ocean while flying dangerously low over the South China Sea, none of those injured men would survive. No one wanted to seed the "fear of ditching at sea" in the minds of those soldiers, so we went without life jackets.

We made it to Taipei, and I celebrated by attending a reception for American newsmen at the U.S. Embassy. On Quemoy, I had been eating mostly bananas and canned lichee fruits, and now, feeling sick at the party, I couldn't eat a thing. Old timers told me it was "delayed fear."

Despite my many dramatic photographs of wounded and dead Chinese Nationalist soldiers, I was not published. Unhappy, I flew back to Tokyo, where Yukiko met me at the airport, but this time did not kiss me. I was angry to hear how she had been treated just for a kiss.

We spent a few blissful days together and many wonderful evenings at the Foreign Correspondents' Club, where diplomats and businessmen were "associate members." Fresh from my noodle years, I delighted in the exclusivity of the club and the chance to listen, learn, and share experiences with seasoned journalists. Keyes Beech, who won a Pulitzer Prize for his reporting for the *Chicago Daily News*, was one of my mentors. Though I was close to 30 years old by the end of 1958, I was one of the youngest members of the organization.

THE BACK DOOR

A FUTURE EMPRESS

TOKYO 1958

As much as I enjoyed friendships forged at the Foreign Correspondents' Club, I was aware we all worked in a very competitive atmosphere, and plans for covering any story not obvious or routine had to be jealously guarded.

I was particularly wary of television reporters, because TV had become a fierce competitor in recent years. A story on television could break well before *Life*'s publication unless we had an exclusive that would last for a week.

Though Peter Kalisher and Wade Bingham of CBS News were close friends from shared drinks and heated conversation, I was extremely cautious with them and never spoke of my projects until I knew *Life* was about to hit the newsstands in America.

By October 1958, all news organizations covering Japan were waiting for an announcement in November of Prince Akihito's choice for a bride, the future empress of Japan.

As had been the tradition for 2,600 years, she would not be selected by the future emperor nor his family but by the bureaucracy of the all-powerful Imperial Household Board, an institution that ruled over the Imperial Family's every move. For state occasions, it dictated protocol rules down to the last gesture.

Rumors were rampant. It was said the choice for a future empress was between an unnamed old-line aristocrat and, more interestingly, the 24-year-old daughter of a wealthy businessman, Michiko Shoda, a "commoner" and frequent tennis partner of the prince. Michiko was said to be Prince Akihito's personal choice, but as independent as the prince might have been, he would not have much say in the choice of his princess.

The search for Prince Akihito's bride began seven years earlier and had already cost almost a million dollars. At last, a choice was to be announced.

Though it was a big story for *Life*, it looked as if we'd be limited to a predictable, formal portrait, authorized by the Imperial Household Board: whatever we photographed would be dull and shared with hundreds of photographers and television cameramen.

To compete with Japanese television and foreign media outlets in Tokyo, I had to find a way to interview the two candidates before the official announcement. I knew the candidate not selected would lose face in Japanese culture if we published her pictures alongside the chosen bride, so I reasoned I might have a chance for a private meeting with the two candidates if I gave my word of honor along with *Life*'s word not to publish the name of the loser nor show her picture.

Alex Campbell thought it was a long shot but worth a try, and drafted a confidential telex to the editors who assured us my word and theirs would be honored. From Campbell, I requested the help of a smart and savvy reporter on the permanent staff of Time-Life's Tokyo bureau, Arthur Kawabata, who had unlisted phone numbers of both families.

Both mothers were fluent in English and diplomatic language. After a long conversation by phone and what appeared to be even longer silences from the two mothers, I convinced them to grant me a private photographic session with their daughters before the official declaration of the future empress was announced.

I was certain they agreed due to my swearing that the photographs and name of the unselected candidate would not be published or used in any form. I even offered to put the agreement in writing, but for both mothers, my word of honor was enough.

Photographing the young aristocrat was difficult enough, given the need to avoid our competitors, but getting an exclusive session with "the commoner" was like slipping through an army obstacle course. Outside her residence, photographers and reporters set up what resembled a messy military bivouac—some newspapers actually provided tents for staff. Kawabata and I therefore arranged to reach the house through the gardens.

To avoid being seen carrying camera cases, we wrapped our equipment in three *furoshikis*, a one-meter-square cloth used to carry goods by knotting its four corners. Kawabata said, "This way, if neighbors or the Japanese press see us, we will look like country cousins."

After gingerly walking through the garden, we were let in by a servant and greeted by Mrs. Shoda. She introduced us to Michiko who spoke fluent English. Mrs. Shoda complained about the Japanese press: "They watch us 24 hours a day. They eat and sleep here on our front street. We can't use our front door anymore."

Discreetly looking through the front window, I estimated the number of press people at over a hundred. We decided to use a smaller room at the back of the house, so our strobe flashes wouldn't give us away.

My lighting was a little harsh, but I had no room to set up a key light. I had Michiko, dressed in a formal silk kimono, kneel on the tatami with her hands crossed over her thighs in the formal way Japanese women knelt. Mrs. Shoda implored us to finish quickly. After two and a half rolls of film were shot, we wrapped our equipment in the furoshikis and left through the garden unseen by any newsmen—surprisingly, no one was watching the back door.

My pictures of the two women were selected for printing well before the official announcement, so once word of the "Imperial" choice hit international wires, *Life* immediately printed my picture of Michiko Shoda, "The Future Empress of Japan," for the cover of *Life International*. The December 15, 1958, issue of *Life* in the U.S. ran the same photograph followed by a picture of Michiko leaving the Imperial Palace in her limousine.

As promised, *Life*'s editors shipped back all negatives, prints, and transparencies of "the loser," and I personally returned them to the mother. Despite her disappointment, she was pleased to have pictures for the family album.

When *Life International* hit Tokyo newsstands with our big cover story, Alex Campbell, normally very reserved, congratulated me: "John you have the only exclusive with the future empress of Japan. That's simply great." I had seldom seen him so elated. Neither of us anticipated the fury of the Japanese press corps aimed at me, *Life,* and the Tokyo bureau, and I had to face the outrage of Japanese colleagues. The all-powerful Press Club of Japan, where all foreigners were excluded, demanded to know how it was possible for a foreign publication to get an exclusive with the future empress before the official announcement.

Alexander Campbell seemed to thrive on the criticisms we received. In high spirits, he said, "John, once again you've created a national scandal. You got a world's first. But in Japanese culture, the nail that sticks out in a thousand nails has to be hammered down. It's a cliché, but it's true. God knows how many letters of apology I'll have to write for you and *Life* this time, to the Japanese Press Club, the Foreign Office, and the Imperial Household Board. I'm getting to be an expert at writing letters of apology on *Life*'s behalf and yours."

In my French and American cultures, it was unheard of for a journalist to apologize for an exclusive, but since it was Japan, I reluctantly went along with official apologies.

For 46,780,000 Japanese women, it was an unprecedented dramatic break with ancient tradition to choose Michiko Shoda, a "commoner," as future Empress of Japan. For many, "Michiko-san" was a welcome symbol of the beginning of women's emancipation.

Time's editors assigned me to do a color essay on "New Freedoms Amid Old Customs."

With Yukiko as interpreter, we traveled all over the main islands of Japan in pursuit of the story. Though we found a few women who entered specialized professions , sciences, literary fields, and higher education, the majority was still subservient to men.

The rural women of Japan were still working an average of 14 hours a day and had to treat their husbands as "Master" or *Dannasama*. A refrain we heard from a great number of farmers' wives was, "Up before dawn and the last one to sleep." Many admitted, "Michiko-san represents a breakthrough against ancient tradition, but her selection as future Empress will not change our lives. Besides, she'll have to be very obedient with even more duties than we have. She is a privileged commoner, and we are the genuine commoners."

Future Empress Michiko had attended Tokyo's Sacred Heart School where names of the girls enrolled read like a roll call of Japan's wealthiest families. Michiko was clearly an uncommon commoner.

The March 23, 1959, issue was my first bylined essay in *Time* and the magazine's first eight-page color spread in its history. It came out just a few weeks before Prince Akihita and Michiko were married on April 10. At the wedding, there were no family members or witnesses in the "inner sanctuary" of the moat-protected Imperial Palace where a Shinto priest waved a sacred branch above the newlyweds to purify them.

Though some women had seen Michiko as a symbol of their emancipation, others saw her new life behind the high walls of the Imperial Castle ruled by the Imperial Household Board as the end of her freedom.

To organize coverage of the couple being transported in an open, horse-drawn carriage during the procession, *Life*'s Asia editor, Scot Leavitt, and John Dominis flew in from Hong Kong to join me.

The organizers and Japanese newsmen staffed every possible vantage point along the procession route, ruling out our moving from one position to another. When we complained, the Japanese simply asked, "Why can't *Life* staff each position?"

There was no way to outdo the Japanese in their mass-saturation coverage of the procession. We decided Dominis, atop a high building, would use long-telephoto lenses to get overall coverage of the Imperial Palace and procession, while at street level, I'd position in the bleachers. It was a good place to be when a fanatic traditionalist, objecting to the wedding, broke through crowds and began hurling rocks at the passing procession.

I captured a sequence of the man throwing stones at the newlyweds before police threw him to the ground. Luckily, no one got hurt, and our coverage made the next April 20, 1959, issue of *Life*. Decades later, in the fall of 1990, Prince Akihito and Princess Michiko at last became Emperor and Empress of Japan.

The spring of 1959 ended, and by August I finished several minor assignments from Black Star. My career was underway, but my fears of not having enough work were deeply ingrained, so I continued researching and suggesting twice as many projects than I could have physically realized. Unsurprisingly, Yukiko found me "restless and unable to stand still."

THE SMALL KINGDOM

JUNGLE WARFARE

LAOS 1959

I n the heavily polluted, steamy August heat of Tokyo, it was nearly
impossible to sleep in our flimsy, Western-style house without wet
towels over my face. Because severe attacks of asthma often left me
exhausted, we shopped around for the most powerful air conditioner
in Japan.

Technicians who installed our unit claimed that it was designed to air-condition
a room twice the size. In fact, it would only cool the lower half of our room, but to
us it was pure luxury.

Lying in bed, we found the cool level met the warm level just one foot above our
heads, so when we sat on the bed, our heads and shoulders were in the steamy
half of the room. That led to playful games, sitting up laughing in the heat, then
quickly dropping to the comfortable cool level, and repeating—rising and dropping
to what we called the levels of "misery" and "pleasure." I joked that the only way to
move in our bedroom was by crawling on our knees, which I did with some hilarity,
sticking my head in and out of the hot zone. A second unit would have solved the
problem, but we were already straining the house wiring. Nonetheless, my asthma
eased in our four-foot-high world of air-conditioning, and at last I could sleep.

The next *Life* assignment took me to Laos in South East Asia where skirmishes
were erupting between the Royal Laotion Army and Pathet-Lao guerrillas led by
a prince inspired by the Communists. According to news reports, the conflict
escalated when some 2,500 well-armed North Vietnamese regular soldiers
overran half a dozen Royal Laotion Army outposts.

On August 27, 1959, I left the steamy city of Tokyo for hot jungles of the small
kingdom of Laos, and as the flight to Hong Kong leveled off, I noticed my asthma
almost disappeared. Down below, I looked at belching smoke stacks, new symbols
of Japan's dynamism. Factories around Tokyo and Yokohama spewed thousands

of tons of particle pollution over its inhabitants, and many citizens had begun wearing gauze facemasks to filter filthy air, but complaints were few, because Japan had entered its own miraculous postwar economic recovery.

The ever-increasing number of people with respiratory diseases in Tokyo necessitated the opening of several "clean-air clinics" to treat them, so going to cover war in Laos was a relief to my lungs. Despite the oppressive hot air of Laos, by the time we landed in Vientiane, capitol of Laos, I regained my full breath.

In the center of Vientiane, an ex-French colonial town on the Mekong River, I met Jim Wilde, *Time*'s correspondent for South East Asia, at the Constellation Hotel. Jim was a tall, lanky Canadian with the classic look of a foreign correspondent: strong chin, a face carved in marble, and piercing, questioning eyes. He was my idea of an individualist and a man I knew I could trust.

"Somehow we have to get northeast to Samneua," Jim explained. "That's where the action is. It's about 120 miles southwest of Hanoi where the North Vietnamese attacked several Royal Laotian outposts. Laos has no roads going northeast. About 2,300 feet above sea level, Samneua has a dirt runway that runs uphill, then down. The Americans gave the Laotians a couple of old C-47s, and we have to get on one of them. The CIA, which calls itself 'Air America' in these parts, runs C-46 flights to the Plain of Jars and a few other strips, but the CIA is not about to take *Time* and *Life* to the battle."

All we knew of the war came from briefings by government officials in Vientiane. It was obvious we and other foreign newsmen were stuck in the capital without any prospect of getting near the fighting.

Nonetheless, Jim got us on a C-47 supply flight to Samneua, saying, "The pilots will take us but won't promise a return trip because they have to fly civilian refugees out of the war zone." Our two pilots looked like teenagers, but Jim assured me they were older. As the C-47 was loaded with rice bags and ammunition, I noticed heavy oil splashes on both engines and checked the rudder and flaps manually. Hoping for the best, I climbed on board and sat on a sack of rice next to Jim.

The young pilots raced the two engines and released the brakes as we headed northeast. As we leveled at 6,000 feet, I made conversation with the pilots in the cockpit, who said they had over a thousand hours of flight time. It wasn't much experience cruising at 110 knots on a C-47, but at least they weren't novices.

I looked at the dials, particularly oil-pressure gauges: all were normal. Below was dense jungle, forbidding territory, lush, dark, and primeval without a single road or trail. After a half hour of flying, we descended through clouds and saw Samneua's dirt runway cut at the bottom of a valley surrounded by mountains in the jungle.

During final approach, an army of civilians were tamping down small rocks and dirt with their bare feet to fill huge holes in the runway. As we got closer, they scattered and resumed their work as we taxied to a stop. Thanking our pilots, we promised them, "a great dinner when we get back to Vientiane."

The jungle was infested with Pathet-Lao guerrillas, while Samneua's Royal Laotion Army headquarters consisted of about two dozen thatched-roof, elongated huts surrounded by civilian huts. People were fleeing, carrying what little they possessed. With a pole braced on shoulders, a man and his wife carried a hand-driven Singer sewing machine as well as pots, pans, and small bags of rice, while little children followed, running to keep up.

Many refugees milled about, waiting patiently at the airstrip, but with so few planes, very few would be airlifted some 80 miles south to the Plain of Jars. Most took their chances, heading south on jungle trails. The sight of those people fleeing their primitive huts and tiny plots of land, possessing almost nothing of their own but abandoning all to save their lives, was heartbreaking to witness and difficult to photograph.

A sergeant took us to headquarters where we met General Amh-ka, the commander of the whole region, who gave us a room to sleep and invited us to share his meals. After a full briefing, we received permission to go on patrol with a squad of his soldiers.

For hours, we walked on jungle trails. Visibility was poor, on the technical edge of my fastest black-and-white film—if the North Vietnamese overran the outposts we were passing, we would never see them coming. I photographed anxious and exhausted soldiers who explained they were always on alert 24 hours a day, "catnapping at best." Dusk settled, and the cacophony of millions of insects and creatures became deafening: I wondered whether the sounds of the jungle would cover the invasion of an enemy army.

Heading back to headquarters by nightfall, I told Jim, "I've got the feeling bugs are crawling all over my body." "Yes," Jim said. "They're leeches sucking our blood. By the time we get back, they'll have sucked so much blood, they'll be as big as your small fingertip. But don't try to remove them or you'll get infected. They have to be removed with a glowing cigarette."

At General Amh-ka's headquarters, Jim and I stripped, and sure enough, our bodies were covered with blood-puffed leeches. Lighting cigarette after cigarette, sucking hard to create a red-hot glow, we applied them to the leeches on each other's bodies. Reacting to heat, the heads of the leeches retracted, and the terrible worms fell to the earthen floor of the general's living quarters.

An orderly cleaned up the mess as we put on clean t-shirts and drank warm Cokes flown in on our flight with rice and ammunition. Coca-Cola had found its way to one of the most remote places of the world.

145

THE SMALL KINGDOM

In the evening, we ate rice and boiled chicken drowned in a reddish spicy sauce. General Amh-ka briefed us on the war: "To the west, the jungle is nearly impassable, so our left flank is secure. Our rear is an open field. Vietnam is to the east, so we have to permanently patrol our right flank. It's difficult to know what the North Vietnamese are up to because they observe radio silence at all times. We don't hear them, and we don't see them—when we do, it's too late. But last week, we ambushed a small group of North Vietnamese, and shots were exchanged. Most fled into the jungle, but we captured a few prisoners." At the airstrip, I photographed the prisoners splitting rocks for the runway.

I had to get out of Samneua. My coverage had become repetitive and I needed to ship my film to New York, so Jim befriended the sergeant in charge of airstrip operations who had sole authority to decide who got on the refugee flights to the Plain of Jars.

We waited at the airstrip with Stanley Karnow of *Time* and Joseph W. Alsop, a famous American columnist whose advice was purportedly heard in "presidential circles." Alsop was determined to get out that same day.

Arguing in French with the sergeant, Alsop insisted he should be first to fly back to Vientiane. When Karnow overheard them, he blew up and said, "Joe, I heard your conversation with the sergeant. If anyone gets out of Samneua today, it'll be Jim and John. They've been here for days. You'll take your turn, just as I will." Karnow's outburst in English and French left both Alsop and the sergeant speechless.

While we all waited, the sergeant packed some 40 small children onto the deck of the C-47 and had them carefully sit on the floor and tuck their knees under their chins to make more space. Along the stripped fuselage, I saw many little heads looking around with inquiring eyes, not understanding.

The sergeant tucked in one last child and motioned to all four of us to climb on board. Sitting down with the kids, we took off for the Plain of Jars where the children would be met by humanitarian groups.

The sky was filled with dark thunderclouds. Leveling off, we entered a violent storm, and were hit by bolts of lightning racing to the plane's rudder. With each flash of lightning, we saw the children's frightened eyes.

I was scared myself, so to ease my own fears, I got on my knees and began clowning around for the children. Pointing to the front of the plane and the back, I'd spread my arms and clap my hands with each thunderbolt, screaming, "Bang! Bang!" Laughing loudly, I swung my head wildly from left to right like a broken puppet. I must have looked like a rather pathetic mime performer, but suddenly the children were laughing as well, though I could never time my movements to the thunderbolts. Because I was out of sync most of the time, the children laughed even harder as they forgot their fear and I forgot mine.

The flight only lasted about 40 minutes. Disembarking at the Plain of Jars, I photographed the children who gathered around me. Their eyes begged me for more laughs, but it had been a rough flight, and my performance had tired me out, so I ruffled their heads instead. As they waved, I motioned goodbye and boarded the C-47 for the capital. My pictures of embattled Samneua got three pages in the September 14, 1959, issue of *Life*.

In Vientiane, Jim left on another assignment for *Time*, so I was on my own from there. I would miss Jim's savvy and knew my chances of getting on another C-47 to the war zone were slim.

In Samneua, I had seen a lone pilot unloading supplies and taking off in a single-engine Canadian Beaver plane, so I set out to find the pilot in Vientiane, which was more a village than a town.

The Constellation Hotel's owner pointed out the pilot's usual table in the restaurant. There I met a man in his early 50s who said his "nom de guerre" was Marold, a name he said he selected after World War II when he joined the French Foreign Legion in Marseilles.

"Though I'm Austrian born," Marold told me, "I am a French citizen because of my services in Indochina. I flew countless C-47 missions supplying the besieged Dien Bien Phu where France lost Indochina in 1954."

I asked, "Where were you born in Austria?" He said, "In the middle." "What is your real name?" I asked. He answered, "I am Marold. When trouble started in Laos, I was hired as a pilot to fly supply missions." "When was that?" I asked. He replied, "Why do you want to know?" I avoided the question and asked, "So, you are a mercenary pilot?"

Marold said, "Yes, and a well-paid one. But I'm getting too old for this kind of flying. In a year or so, I'll retire to my little place on the French Riviera. Now what did you want to see me about?"

"I noticed in Samneua you were flying alone and your copilot seat was empty, so I'd like to go with you on your missions, because I doubt the Royal Army will let journalists fly on their C-47s again."

"Fine," Marold said immediately. "It'll be nice to fly with someone who speaks French. Meet me at the airport at 6:00 A.M. tomorrow." He finished his Pastis, and I drank my Scotch. It was Scotch without ice, because ice cubes in Vientiane were prime carriers of innumerable diseases; I never drank tap water nor ate salads, and I brushed my teeth with boiled water.

For the next few days, I flew supply missions with Marold to various outposts in northeast Laos. Landing on short strips, often less than a thousand feet long, we'd watch as soldiers removed ammunition and rice bags. While I photographed their frenetic unloading,

Marold kept his engine running so we could take off immediately, as we were often fired upon by Pathet-Lao guerrillas or North Vietnamese regulars.

The roar of the engine drowned out sounds of machine gun bullets hitting the wings' fuel tanks, fuselage, and cockpit, so in flight, we felt and heard nothing. It was only when Marold pointed out fuel gauges going down that I realized we had been hit.

Each time we made it back to Vientiane with fuel tanks near empty. Surveying the damage, Marold ordered repairs, and the next morning the Beaver was ready for another mission, though mechanics never bothered with the bullet holes in the fuselage. There were two steel plates under the seats of the cockpit, so when aloft, we felt relatively safe, but I still worried about our leaking fuel tanks.

In our fastest delivery of rice bags and ammunition, Marold landed on a small mountaintop in the northeast between two rows of Royal Army soldiers aiming rifles downward toward the enemy below.

After unloading, Marold immediately took off and explained, "Only the airstrip is secured. The guerillas control all sides of the mountain." The wing tanks were hit and again we landed in Vientiane with fuel gauges near empty.

With too many holes in the plane and too many marginal photographs, I quietly decided that I had flown my last mission with Marold. Cabling *Life*, I suggested covering a stately ceremony at the Royal Palace in Luang Prabang where world opinion was sought on the question of aid to Laos.

At dinner, I told Marold I'd probably go to the royal capital the next day but didn't say I had pushed my luck too far after our last adventure on the mountaintop. During a long dinner, easy conversation, good French wine and cognac, we felt the comfortable camaraderie of men who shared the same dangers. We shook hands and said, "To next week."

During the next week, according to Laotian government sources, Marold was shot on one of his missions. Seriously wounded, he was flown in a chartered medical plane to Marseilles—not very far from Marold's "little place on the French Riviera"—where he died several days later.

Later at the Constellation Hotel in Vientiane, looking for more information about Marold, I saw his empty table and sincerely missed him. It struck me that

though we were together for a week, I knew almost nothing about him, not even his real name.

I remembered Marold laughing out loud during our last dinner when I told him about burning leeches in the general's living quarters. "What a scene!" he said bursting out in greater laughter—it was the last laugh I'd hear from him.

I sent out my film of the royal ceremonies in Luang Prabang. Two pages ran in *Life*'s September 21, 1959, issue showing Crown Prince Savang Vatthana shaded by a huge white parasol, headlined: "Stately Maneuver in Midst of Crisis." *Life* wrote: "A unique honor reserved for the head of the Laotian Kingdom preceded by ceremonial swords and flanked by spear carriers...An aide carries a flower arrangement under a conical cover as a sacred offer...to the sacred altar of Buddha."

Flying back to Tokyo, I thought of a brave mercenary pilot flying deadly missions for a little place in the sun, exhausted soldiers searching for an invisible enemy, peasants fleeing with children, and an ancient kingdom in all of its royal splendor, asking the world to help save its privileges.

TYPHOON

"HAVOC IN JAPAN"

NAGOYA 1959

On the Hong Kong-Tokyo leg of my flight, a route I had flown many times, the Pan Am crew greeted me as a regular. The stewardesses made a point of looking in *Life*'s credit box for my name and saved my coverage of the war in Laos: as I boarded, *Life*'s September 14 issue was already in my favored seat in first class.

On route to the Laos assignment, I had ignored the luxuries of first class, deep in thought, imagining scenes I had never seen while reading the few files and clippings I had gathered before departing. After two weeks in the jungles of Laos with leeches, bullet holes in our plane, marginal meals, and stifling heat, the pampering of first class felt rewarding and earned since I had been published. In my upbringing, rewards came after work and effort, never before.

In a few months, Pan American World Airways would enter the jet age, but in the meantime, its older propeller-driven classic "Clippers" lumbered across all parts of the earth. Clippers could not fly above high-weather fronts, so the turbulence on our flight suggested we were feeling the fringe winds of a typhoon.

It was September and typhoon season had begun. Since 1956, when I took that flight inside Typhoon Emma's eye, facing the typhoon season had become a kind of ritual in my life as it had with millions of Japanese and South East Asians. It was a cyclical, often deadly ritual of life, and together with earthquakes played a major part in shaping the stoicism of the Japanese people. Typhoon season had none of the enchantments of the seasons of my childhood when long days of summer meant ripe fruit to be picked and preserved for winter, and autumn meant gathering chestnuts for winter. During four long years of Nazi occupation, winter had always meant the promise of spring and freedom.

With steamy heat, dark heavy clouds, and violent winds, typhoon season in Japan held only ominous promises of destruction, and for wood and paper houses in its path, promises of death.

At Tokyo's Haneda airport, I was met by Yukiko, who had heard little news from me while I was isolated in Laos. Spending a few delightful, tender days together, I could again put ice cubes in my Scotch and sleep late in our partially air-conditioned bedroom, keeping my head in the "pleasure level."

Days of leisure, however, were brief, for on September 26, 1959, Japan suffered the worst storm disaster in its recorded history. In Nagoya, 180 miles southwest of Tokyo, the city's 1.3 million people were preparing to celebrate the 70th anniversary of their city with music, floats, flowers, and fireworks, when a typhoon from the south struck with terrifying force.

Immediately assigned by *Life*, I requested assistance of the bright and resourceful Arthur Kawabata, because we made a good team. On the outskirts of Nagoya, Arthur persuaded a fisherman to take us in his small boat to a temple on higher ground, which had been transformed into one of the numerous makeshift morgues of the devastated city. Arthur and I then made a raft with scrap lumber and guided it with bamboo poles. What we saw and photographed was beyond imagination.

Rain and winds roaring at 125 miles per hour had tossed heavy cargo ships from the harbor to the shore. The sea, rushing in through broken dikes, drowned people and livestock and wiped out entire villages, while logs from Nagoya's lumberyards crashed through flooded streets like battering rams. Some 25,000

Evacuees running toward a rescue helicopter.

people were stranded on roofs of their homes, waiting for Japanese and U.S. Army helicopters to rescue them before they were drowned by floods.

Arthur and I stopped counting dead, bloated bodies floating in the water rushing through the streets. The stench of death was suffocating, so medical rescue teams gave us surgical masks to ease our nausea.

After the typhoon passed, hunger, disease, and looters soon followed, so many victims wanted to stay on the roofs of their battered, flooded houses to protect their possessions. It was a scene of utter desolation. Early estimates claimed that there were 5,000 dead or missing, nearly 400,000 homeless, and over $750 million in property damage.

I had flown inside the violence and fury of a typhoon where our B-50 weather plane was tossed about like a toy. In an emergency landing, we had been lucky to survive, but I had no concept of the magnitude of destruction a typhoon could cause at ground level.

Driving back to Tokyo, Arthur and I were convinced I had enough pictures of devastation, grieving people, moments of profound stoicism, and poignant scenes of elderly people more frightened of rescue helicopters' whirling blades than of the rising waters. With so many images of heroic rescue, I felt sure that editors would give us at least six to eight pages in *Life*'s section, "The Week's Events."

Instead, the magazine gave the 5,000 dead of Nagoya only two pages in the October 12, 1959, issue under the title, "Typhoon's Havoc in Japan." The cover and a 10-page essay were devoted instead to doctor-patient relationships—Arthur and I were stunned.

We couldn't understand the editors' decision nor comprehend why a few months later in a December issue, the 433 victims of a dam burst in southern France got six pages of reporting and an editorial note saying, "We salute the townsfolk of devastated Fréjus in France where dam-released waters would have claimed even more lives except for their quick-thinking heroism."

After *Life* returned my Nagoya negatives, I composed a 20-page "dummy" layout for Arthur and myself. The exercise did not ease our sense of injustice, but it did give us closure to the immensity of the tragedy.

The death of so many thousands of men, women, and children took its toll on me. One of the last scenes I photographed was of a man opening coffin after coffin in a Shinto temple as he searched for his wife and three children. Eventually he found all four dead and broke down in such agony that the magnified scene through my telephoto lens brought tears to my eyes.

When the man saw me, he murmured something and regained his composure. Ceremoniously with great dignity, he joined his hands in prayer before each coffin. As I left him with his gods and sorrow, my conscience told me I had violated his grief, and I vowed to one day stop covering hard-news stories and focus on essays and documentaries instead.

The year ended with a few minor assignments. Yukiko and I spent a quiet but cheerful Christmas at home and a noisy New Year's Eve at the Foreign Correspondents' Club of Japan.

THE DEEPEST OCEAN

THE *TRIESTE'S* HISTORIC DIVE

GUAM 1960

O n January 4, 1960, I left for the island of Guam in the Pacific to cover what *Life* would call "The Ultimate Adventure on Earth." Swiss scientist Jacques Piccard and U.S. Navy Lieutenant Don Walsh would dive some seven miles down to the unexplored bottom of the world's deepest ocean in the Mariana Trench. They'd make the trip inside the *Trieste* bathyscaph, a strange underwater vessel conceived and designed by scientist Auguste Piccard and his son Jacques and purchased by the U.S. Navy in 1957 to conduct deep-underwater experiments.

The bathyscaph was a self-contained, deep-sea research vessel. Its manned observation capsule, fixed to its underside, was made of three-and-a-half-inch steel to withstand the fantastic pressure of the abyss. The craft was a small, oddly shaped submarine, something Jules Verne might have dreamt up.

It was going to be the *Trieste*'s seventieth dive, and if Walsh and Piccard succeeded in descending some 36,000 feet into the ocean depths, it'd be the deepest dive in history.

Climbing on board the bathyscaph, I was introduced to Piccard who anticipated my many questions. "For buoyancy," he explained, "the *Trieste*'s flotation tank is filled with lighter-than-water gasoline, so when we want to descend, we release the gasoline into the ocean. The flotation tank has an opening through which seawater enters to equalize water pressure inside and out. On top there's a small, battery-driven propeller engine enabling us to maneuver under sea. The *Trieste* carries eight metric tons of iron shot for ballast, so we gradually drop ballast into the ocean when we want to rise."

Through the conning tower, I climbed 18 feet down to the passenger chamber, only 6 feet, 4 inches in diameter, crammed with instruments and extremely

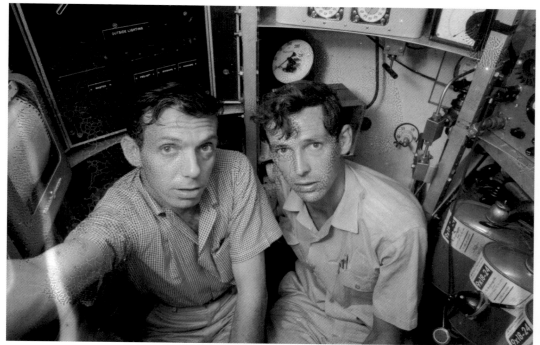
John with Jacques Piccard inside the *Trieste* after the dive.

claustrophobic. There I installed a motorized camera, so the two explorers could photograph themselves when they reached the bottom.

Because the *Trieste* was not designed to sail, it was towed by U.S. Navy tug, *Wandank,* at about two miles an hour to the world's deepest ocean, nearly 200 miles southwest of Guam Island. Piccard invited me aboard the *Wandank* for the four-day ride and introduced me to "master-mechanic" Giuseppe Buono, an Italian with a delightful Neapolitan accent whom Piccard treated like family.

Giuseppe, who supplied mechanical genius to each dive, spoke of his travels in America and how he had fallen in love with "the upper U.S." With his accent it sounded like he was saying, "I have traveled in and loved the upper your ass," so during the four-day trip, the *Wandank*'s crew repeatedly asked Giuseppe to tell us about his travels in "the upper U.S." No one explained to him why the crew laughed so hard, but he laughed with us, and his good humor put the entire crew in a good mood before the dive.

On route to the Mariana Trench, I tried to understand why two men actually wanted to descend into the pitch darkness of the planet's deepest ocean. I often dreamt of trips upward into outer space, so I understood and admired their need to explore the unknown. Walsh was a submariner, Piccard an oceanographer, and I was a photographer in love with light, not darkness. Regardless of our differences, I was seduced and swept up in the prospect of another adventure.

Days before the dive, Tom Abercrombie of *National Geographic* arrived, and we became instant friends. He had the intelligence of a very good photojournalist with wit, quick perception, and the ability to see humor in conflict. Together we pressured the Navy to supply us with a motorized rubber boat exclusively for our use.

On January 23, 1960, Lieutenant Walsh and Jacques Piccard locked themselves in their steel gondola. At 8:23 in the morning, the *Trieste* disappeared into the blackness of the sea.

For almost five hours we waited. Then at 1:06 in the afternoon, Walsh and Piccard contacted us: they had reached the bottom at 37,800 feet. If the Mariana Trench geologically remained the deepest point in the ocean, the dive of the *Trieste* would stand as the world record for manned deep-sea exploration.

At the bottom of the ocean for 20 minutes, the two explorers saw a sole or flounder about one foot long under a powerful spotlight, as well as a bright, red shrimp about one inch long. How creatures could live at such depths was beyond explanation. I expected reports of sea monsters or giant octopuses, but all they saw were one fish and one shrimp.

While we waited over three hours for the *Trieste* to complete its ascent, Abercrombie and I and an officer from the U.S.S. *Lewis* bobbed about in our rubber boat for two hours. Riding 20-foot-high waves, we were escorted by sharks some 30 feet behind our outboard motor; our only concerns were keeping our cameras dry and not falling overboard.

We were only a few waves away when at 4:25, the *Trieste* resurfaced after more than eight hours under sea. With the bathyscaph rolling on top of a huge wave, Walsh and Piccard emerged from the conning tower. Their moment of triumph made a dramatic, double-page picture in *Life*, and the story made six pages and the cover of the February 15, 1960, issue.

On the U.S.S. *Lewis*, Walsh and Piccard were given a heroes' welcome. As Lieutenant Walsh wrote for *Life*, "The feat of the *Trieste* puts the U.S. on the threshold of a new era in oceanography....if the ocean's depths are to be the potential battleground of the future."

Since no alcohol was served on the U.S.S. *Lewis*, celebrations had to wait until we reached the Officers' Club on Guam. Returning ashore, Abercrombie and I headed for the club for what we felt was a well-deserved drink.

A young lieutenant stopped me at the door. "Sir! I'm sorry," he said. "Shorts are permitted but only with Bermuda socks, which must come up just below the knee.

Your socks are down at your ankles. I cannot let you enter. It's regulations, sir!" I argued, "I'm not in the Navy. I'm from *Life* magazine." But the lieutenant insisted.

Amused and annoyed, Abercrombie told me to remove my shoes. With his Swiss knife, he cut the toes of my socks and pulled them up just below my knees. Facing the lieutenant, he said, "Lieutenant, these socks are now regulation." The lieutenant was not amused but reluctantly, he saluted and welcomed us into the club.

While celebrating the success of the dive, I took the opportunity to ask Piccard about events in France, as the Swiss kept their eyes on their neighbors. I asked, "Were the glowing reports of economic recovery in the French press typically exaggerated?" He said, "I'm not sure, because France is at war in Algeria right now, but I believe France has developed far beyond its prewar standard of living."

I had meant to ask them about encounters with sea monsters, giant octopuses, and what they would have done if the *Trieste* had been wedged between rocks at the bottom of the ocean, but in the euphoria of the moment I forgot. Years later, he told me, "The Navy, Walsh, and I did not put much credibility into sea monster stories, but we knew giant octopuses have powerful tentacles and could easily have immobilized us. But we also knew octopuses don't swim that deep, and even if one had somehow immobilized us, we believed it would have soon released us because an octopus could not possibly find the steel of our gondola to its taste." I asked, "What would have happened if the *Trieste* had been immobilized at the bottom of the ocean?" Piccard replied, "It's simple. No one could have saved us. We had only 24 hours of oxygen and a few candy bars. So we simply would have savored our chocolate bars, exhausted our oxygen to the last breath, and died. And no, we had no suicide pills."

After the assignment, I left the island of Guam in one of Pan American's new 707 jets. I decided it was time to visit France and see my family after nearly 10 years of absence. I especially wanted to introduce them to Yukiko, as they had only seen her in photographs.

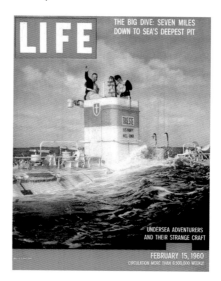

THE BIG DIVE: SEVEN MILES DOWN TO SEA'S DEEPEST PIT

UNDERSEA ADVENTURERS AND THEIR STRANGE CRAFT

FEBRUARY 15, 1960
CIRCULATION MORE THAN 6,500,000 WEEKLY

HOMECOMING

FAMILY REUNION

PARIS 1960

When I left home in November 1950, I swore to my mother I would not visit France again until my name appeared in Life magazine. By 1960, my work had been credited regularly in *Life*, *Time*, and numerous other American, French, and European publications.

For more than four years, I sent my mother magazine issues of my best work to make a point, to prove her wrong for having too often called me "worthless." It seemed I was trying to heal a deep wound, yet I never wrote her a word of reproach. Instead I addressed my mail only to her, usually with a note, "Dear Mother, I thought you might wish to see my latest story and share it with Papa and the family."

By 1960, I only sent her selected stories, believing I no longer had to prove anything to her and all the others in Marly who had wished me "good luck" but secretly hoped I would fail in my American endeavors and return to France.

Yukiko was delighted by the idea of seeing Paris for the first time. Honoring Japanese tradition, she bought hand-painted lacquered boxes and classical Japanese dolls made for display, not for play, to offer as gifts to her in-laws—the gifts required an entire extra suitcase.

My presents to mother were a copy of *Life*'s story of the *Trieste* and *Life International*'s April 4, 1960, issue with my eight-page bylined essay on the Japanese movie industry's directors, stars, and producers.

The new Boeing 707 cut travel time to half to anywhere on earth. From Japan, the shortest route to Europe would have taken us westward over Siberia, but because of the Cold War, we flew to Alaska, then Copenhagen, and on to Paris.

Some 25 hours later, we landed at Paris's Orly Airport in the late morning of April 1, 1960. Yukiko was thrilled to realize her dream of seeing Paris at last, and my younger brother Jacques, affectionately called Jacquot, was there to meet us. The

last time I had seen him, he was only 11 years old, so when I saw a soldier waving, I looked twice before realizing it was my brother in a French Army draftee uniform.

We hugged and Yukiko got two kisses on both cheeks, as in 1960 France, it was customary to receive four kisses per encounter. Over the years it was reduced to two, but not everywhere.

Surprised at the display of public affection, Yukiko was somewhat embarrassed, so I told her to expect 36 more kisses that day from her in-laws, nieces, and nephews. I informed her that the ritual would be repeated each day during our entire stay. Paris was a long way from Japan where public or private greetings were never more than several bows.

Surprised at Yukiko's fluency in French, Jacquot repeatedly exclaimed, "Incroyable!" ("Unbelievable!"). Jacquot's commanding officer granted him permission to use his Peugeot to pick up his "American brother" at the airport, so as he drove from Orly with Yukiko in the front seat, I instructed Jacquot from the back seat which streets to take. Because I had delivered packages all over the city, I was more familiar with Paris than he was.

Though cars honked impatiently, I had Jacquot cruise slowly so Yukiko could take in the Arc de Triomphe, Eiffel Tower, and the Champs Elysées along the route to our hotel. I expected to feel profound emotion seeing Paris again after a full decade, but I was indifferent. I only noticed that there were more private automobiles than in 1950, that people were better dressed, and women more elegant. Though pleased to see Yukiko so enchanted, I felt no sense of my long absence, perhaps because Paris had always inspired a feeling of permanence, an eternal physical presence. It was as though I had never left.

Life booked us a suite at the Elysée Park Hotel on the Rond Point des Champs Elysées. It was intimately small, plush, luxurious, but not ostentatious. Checking in by the hotel's small lounge, we were surprised to see a famous actor and film director reading a newspaper. Yukiko whispered, "That's Orson Welles! God, he's so huge. He's enormous." I agreed and said, "Orson Welles is larger than life."

We invited Jacquot for a drink as we were ushered into our tastefully decorated suite. All windows opened onto running balconies with views of Avenue Matignon and the Rond Point des Champs Elysées. Yukiko ran out to the balcony saying we had to see the horse chestnut trees in full bloom. It was spring in Paris, showers and sun, light and rain, Yukiko's romantic idea of the city of her dreams.

I was taken in by the quality of light as I shared the enchanted scene. I realized that in the 19 years I had spent in France, I had no idea such luxurious living existed. It was Yukiko's first stay in a Paris hotel and mine as well.

How odd, I thought. On *Life* assignments I had grown accustomed to traveling first class. In an abstract way, I took it for granted. I was expected to stay in the best hotels: Raffles in Singapore, Manila Hotel in the Philippines, Peninsula Hotel in Hong Kong, Ashoka in New Delhi. But I never knew gracious living in Paris.

Emotionally, I found it hard to take. Years of deprivation and other springtimes when life was hard rekindled painful memories that warned me against extravagance.

I cheered myself up by focusing thoughts on a satisfying statistic: at the end of 1959, I had $6,873 in credit at Black Star, equivalent to nearly $70,000 in the early twenty-first century, and I had several thousands more in billings. Black Star reduced their percentage from 50 to 15 percent on all color Time-Life assignments because in 1960, I was making more money for them at 15 percent than I was at 50 percent in the mid-1950s. So in April 1960, I was finally financially secure.

Our trip to France, Switzerland, Italy, England, and the United States was my first real vacation, and I believed my years of austerity were over. With a career underway, we could frequent the best hotels and restaurants, see the best shows, and still live within our means.

Returning to his Army base, Jacquot would join us at "home" where we were expected. With a brand new rented Renault Dauphine, Yukiko and I headed for Marly-le-Roi, less than eight miles west of Paris.

Before going "home," I gave Yukiko a tour of Marly where the population had grown from 2,800 to more than 16,000 in 20 years. Along with Le Louvre, Fountainbleau, and Versailles, one of Louis the 14th's four castles included the Château de Marly, whose stone outlines I showed to Yukiko. Built in the seventeenth century, it had cost more than Versailles. I explained to her that it had been a place of festivities, luxurious feasts, and lavish outdoor fêtes that would last for days.

The castle with its park and 12 pavilions had been a place of aristocratic elegance, ostentatious privilege, and great decadence, inspiring the wrath of the people during the 1789 French revolution.

Though Versailles represented the Sun King's notion of France's cultural grandeur and self-glorified extravagance, it survived the excesses of rebellion; instead, it was the Marly Château, a few miles north of Versailles, which became a prime target of the people's anger.

Standing on flat stones outlining the castle's foundation, I showed Yukiko the forest that helped soothe the loneliest moments of my personal rebellion. Down below was the lake's shore that cradled the body of the fallen American aviator during the war. Further below was the watering basin for the king's horses where I had tried to learn to swim, not far from the house where I spent my last days before departure to America.

To the left of the castle was the French president's luxurious hunting residence built when France finally became a republic almost a century after the 1789 uprising. I was offering Yukiko a simplified history of a privileged France that had discriminated against my working-class roots, the only France I knew.

Yukiko on the other hand, was brought up in upper-class Japan, in a country that had not known internal revolution nor had been powerfully influenced by the age of enlightenment. Japan's society was structured along lines of hereditary privilege.

In Yukiko's immediate family, there were countless professors in all disciplines. Her ancestors had come from an aristocratic society, which transformed into a feudal and then mass society where educational achievement was rewarded in a meritocracy.

Only through reading Zola, Hugo, Rousseau, and other French authors did Yukiko become familiar with class struggles in France. In the story of my own struggle, my self-imposed exile while reaching for the summit of my field, she found a lonely hero who appealed to her own sensibilities and won her romantic soul.

Saddled with the complexities and pain of my past and feeling great apprehension, I brought Yukiko to my family, people on the opposite side of wealth and privilege.

"Thirty-first" was a French working-class expression referring to workers who wore their best clothes on payday, the 31st day of the month. As we pulled into the driveway, my entire family was dressed in their "31sts" except father: he wore a sweater and his usual baggy corduroy pants with a side pocket for his ruler, similar to 10 years earlier when I had last seen him. Though my parents hadn't changed much, my brothers and sisters looked much older.

On both cheeks, Yukiko received two kisses from all my family, my old friend Claude, and his fiancée Ginette. I hugged my father and kissed my mother uneasily—I couldn't remember if I'd ever kissed my mother.

When I asked why my brother André was absent, there was a long silence and no explanation. I discovered he was not there because mother disapproved of his approaching marriage to Eliane, a cultured divorcée with whom he lived. When we visited the tiny house where André and Eliane were settled in marginal comfort, it seemed obvious Eliane had influenced my brother, encouraging him to pursue his evening studies in his ambition to become a contractor.

My sister Paulette who used to visit me in the forest, to whom I always felt emotionally close, had become distant: she was now 25, married to a mechanic named Georges, and a mother of three children.

Paulette, Georges, and their children lived in an apartment with little exposure and toilets in the courtyard. Six years earlier, they applied at town hall in Marly for "new and moderate housing" and were still waiting. "The list of low-income families living in appalling housing is long," Paulette explained, "but we've been promised a new four-bedroom apartment before the end of the year." By the end of 1960, they finally got their new home.

My second sister Odette was 23 and married to Maurice, a pleasant fellow who was an expert at pruning trees, but I was told he had a tendency to drink too much when trees no longer needed pruning. Together they lived with their beautiful four-year-old daughter Claudine in an apartment just as dilapidated as Paulette's and were on a waiting list for "new moderate housing" as well.

Jacquot was about to turn 21, and the French Army was sending him to war in Algeria, so we celebrated his birthday before his departure.

Lucette was an attractive nine-year-old child when I left: at 19, she was an attractive woman. She was engaged to Jacques, an engineer and officer in the French Army Reserve whose parents were financially at ease and able to help the young couple with their first house in a western suburb of Paris. Mother totally approved of Lucette's good fortune even though in the eyes of others, she was abandoning her working-class roots to live the life of the "bourgeoisie."

Father's dreams of a postwar recovery were cut short when his architect friend, owner of a small contracting firm before the war, died of cancer. Instead, when my brothers and sisters left home, father became a foreman earning a small salary.

At our "homecoming," Yukiko's gentleness and fluent French seduced the whole family within minutes. Sitting in the kitchen around a huge table covered with patés, hors d'oeuvres, apéretifs, wine, and champagne on ice, I remembered how the same table had united my family in hungry times. When there was not enough food, my parents fed the children first, knowing there would be little left for them.

While I looked in amazement at the luxury of mother's lavish dinner, Paulette said that despite the richly displayed table, our family had yet to join France's recovery. The economy was still burdened by colonial war in Algeria.

With my own economic woes over, I unconsciously expected my family to have moved up the economic ladder. It was true the postwar government made great reforms; anyone could further his or her education at night, but it was still a new concept to the French working class and not totally appreciated. In time, both my brothers would take advantage of it.

I suggested everyone could improve their lives through night education, but I wasn't diplomatic, and my siblings felt their brother, l'Américain, was patronizing and condescending. So in a few days, Yukiko won the hearts of my family, while I managed to inspire hostility in my three sisters, Jacquot, and his fiancée Danielle.

Paulette summed up their anger: "Hey l'Américain, where were you 10 years ago when we all worked to help the family? Sure, for the last three years you sent a monthly check. But for six years, you didn't raise a finger."

Like many Europeans in postwar years, my brothers and sisters assumed America meant wealth for everyone on arrival: I never told my family about my lean times in California or my "noodle years." To Paulette, I answered, "Some day I'll tell you about those six years."

During our stay, father and I reminisced about listening to the BBC during the war. With great enthusiasm, he explained to Yukiko how doing that was a criminal act during the years of Vichy France, as though we had been accomplices in some great patriotic conspiracy. It was only an act of civil disobedience, punishable by fines and jail but not the guillotine.

When Yukiko gave out gifts she had beautifully wrapped in Tokyo, there was genuine joy around the table—everyone knew the gifts were her idea. I simply gave mother my *Life* stories. She said, "I am very proud of you." It was the first time in my life my mother had ever said that to me.

That later led Paulette to say, "Your success is our burden. Before you were published, mother said you were worthless—now we're all worthless. Mother only speaks of you. You are the example to follow. Frankly we are tired of your success. The whole town knows about you. We don't exist anymore."

There was little I could do to ease the resentment my brothers and sisters felt. As for father, there was also a degree of distance. I wanted to tell him how proud I was that he was on the right side of history, but I didn't because even suggesting he could have been on the wrong side would have been an insult. Instead, we discussed the idea of a Europe ruled by the Nazis and shuddered at the thought.

I tried to explain my adopted country's two-party system. "Surely America has more than two opinions," he said. Father, the old proletarian Socialist, never understood the political views of his three sons though all had been deeply influenced by his humanistic principles.

His first son had become an American; his second, André, was a member of "L'Union pour la Nouvelle République," France's leading conservative party. Later known as the Gaullist party, it endorsed and elected Jacques Chirac in the presidential election of 1995.

Father's youngest son, Jacquot, was a card-carrying member of the French Communist Labor Union, C.G.T., and would later gain full membership in the French Communist Party. As a result, father at age 60 and until his death could not discuss politics with any of his three sons.

By the time we left France a week later, my family had found Yukiko "gracious, sensitive, and caring" while my sisters, Jacquot, and his fiancée found me "elitist" and incapable of comprehending their struggles.

They asked, "How could anyone traveling the world in jets and staying in luxurious hotels possibly understand us?" Jacquot and his fiancée were ideologically bound to the working class, so in their eyes, I had betrayed my origins.

In 1960, class distinctions in France were still deeply entrenched in a kind of apartheid system written not in laws but in mores of a nation. There was a segregation of classes: working class at bottom, bourgeoisie in the middle, and the highly educated elite at the top of the pyramid.

In Paris, Yukiko and I saw my old friend Jacques André, *Life*'s photolab chief. He had heard about me from the great *Life* photographer Dimitri Kessel for whom I made prints during my days in the French Army. Apparently, I had become *un grand pistolet* (a great gun). It was Jacques André who in 1950 loaned me $10 so I could raise my savings to $50 to start in America. After reuniting with hugs,

I reached for my wallet to pay back the loan with interest. Jacques adamantly refused my money and instead invited us to dinner.

In Paris, 14 days went by in a whirl of lunches, dinners, shopping for Yukiko, museums, and shows. One night I accidentally stumbled into a sleazy strip joint with Yukiko, Claude, and his fiancée Ginette. We made that mistake after a few too many toasts to our short reunion.

As Yukiko and I drove eastward to Geneva, Switzerland, I was relieved our family visit had ended—I honestly felt no regret leaving and no nostalgia for my roots. I found France strangely paradoxical: I learned that in France I had to restrain my optimism, understate my success, express a certain pessimism and fatalism, and anticipate one's inevitable downfall.

In the French psyche, I again felt the historical weight of too many cathedrals, castles, battles, monuments, the dead, and too many defeats: it was a place where optimism gave way to pessimistic wisdom. But for me that spring, I was 31, hopeful, and not ready to surrender to the French pessimism of my birth.

Dinner at at Jacques André's apartment in Paris.
From left, clockwise: daughter of Jacques and Monique, Monique André, Jacques André, Jacques Wolfs (husband of Lucette), Lucette Wolfs (John's youngest sister), and Yukiko.
(Photo taken by John.)

NATIONAL GEOGRAPHIC

A SUMPTUOUS PALAZZO, A STUDENT
MOB, AND A "BREAKTHROUGH" STORY

VENICE, TOKYO 1960

Driving out of France, I had to contend with French truckers who tried to push "bourgeois" car owners off the road, because in 1960, too few working-class truckers owned private cars. "Courtesy will come with ownership," I explained to Yukiko.

After lunch near Dijon, famous for its mustard, we arrived in Geneva and found a hotel on the western shore of a lake in Nyon. For a couple days, we took in sights like tourists, but Yukiko complained, "You'll never be a tourist. You approach everything like a photojournalist on assignment. Why can't you be a simple visitor?" It was true. I tended to treat each new sight as a possible story.

After two days in Geneva, we drove through the Swiss Alps and headed for Locarno, Lugano, and then Bergamo, Italy. The scenery was majestic with crystal-clear lakes and rivers, a world away from the brown and yellow Mekong River in Laos.

Through some mountain passes, carefully packed snow on both sides of the highway reached twice the height of our car. After steamy Southeast Asia, driving through high snow banks seemed like a luxury as we remembered our half-air-conditioned Tokyo bedroom.

In western Switzerland, we understood the menus written in French, but in Bergamo we not only spoke no Italian, we knew little about Italian food. Still, we managed to order spaghetti with *carne*—Spaghetti Bolognese. In Verona, we saw Juliet's balcony; then in Mestre, we crossed the Lagoon on a *motoscafo*, a small motorboat, taking us directly to the Royal Danieli landing in Venice.

In the hotel's reception hall with its grand staircase and majestic elegance, the staff greeted us with Venetian grace and warmth, making us feel that we had returned home to our own palazzo.

Ushered into our suite, we marveled at the palatial 24-foot ceilings, crystal chandeliers, gilded furniture, tapestry, tall Venetian windows overlooking the Grand Canal, and a bathroom as big as our living room in Tokyo.

Falling onto our huge canopy-covered bed, we laughed and laughed. Instantly we were lovers in Venice, far from Japan and all its codes of behavior, and for the first time in years, we felt free.

The next time I visited the Royal Danieli, our luxurious suite had been divided into two separate floors and into very ordinary double bedrooms, but in 1960 it was palatial. In the ebbing April light, we hired a gondolier to take us for a short ride through the canals before nightfall; he explained the history of the sights in broken English, which I translated into French for Yukiko.

With some 400 bridges in Venice, we went to the Rialto, Venice's first bridge, and then the Ponte Dei Sospiri (Bridge of Sighs), over which prisoners were said to have "passed from the Doges' Magistrate's Palace to the Prigione Nuova (New Prison), moaning and sighing after sentencing."

After breakfast on the Piazza Saint Marco, we walked around admiring the architecture. Suddenly more than a dozen young Venetian men in their twenties surrounded Yukiko, blowing kisses, gesturing, and gyrating, while shouting, "Bella Giapponesina!" ("Beautiful Japanese lady!")—we were literally mobbed.

I stepped in to break the dancing circle and pushed away a couple of amorous Venetians to no avail. Seeing a policeman a few yards away, I waved to him, but he only smiled and stayed in place.

I put my arm around Yukiko's waist, and we took refuge in Saint Mark's Cathedral. For a couple hours, we marvelled at the church's beauty, while Yukiko commented on its architecture, violent history, and how it was "burned in 976 A.D. in a popular revolt."

When we stepped out of Saint Mark's, the young men were still at the entrance, and their numbers had grown. The circus began again with clowning and blowing kisses, but now they cautiously stayed a few feet from my reach.

My patience ran out and it showed, while Yukiko, puzzled and amused for the first few minutes, was no longer smiling. So we walked back to the Danieli, pursued by the young men who finally left us by our hotel's entrance.

While Yukiko went up to our suite, I asked the hotel manager about the circus outside. "Normally," he explained, "they behave like that with single foreign women, not married couples. Operating from the Piazza Saint Marco, their favorite targets are American women because we have so many visiting in pairs, but we don't see many Japanese, especially beautiful Japanese women. I'm sure they were praising her beauty because your wife is an exotic sight, and I assure you their comments were complimentary. It's all in good fun, and I'm sorry if they ruined your day. But don't let them spoil your stay in Venice."

When we left Venice, it felt too soon. We departed with regret, as though a sumptuous feast had just been called off after an opening toast. Yukiko felt she had seen "the most beautiful city of all," an architectural triumph of artists over barbarians.

The manager, concierge, and porters bid us goodbye at Danieli's private launch and wished us a good journey with the warmth and exuberance Italians can express in complete sincerity. It struck me how opposite this Venetian hospitality was from the subtle, understated, and coded politeness of the Japanese.

After crossing the Lagoon and landing in Mestre, we headed southwest to Genoa, then to San Remo and Monte Carlo where we saw the theatrical guards at the entrance of the medieval Genoese and Renaissance Palace, a perfect backdrop for an operetta.

We drove to Antibes, Cannes, and spent a night in Nice with a beautiful view of the Mediterranean, but the French Riviera was disappointing after Venice, and in the morning, we headed north to Paris. Our vacation was over, but my career as a recognized international photojournalist was about to leap forward. *National Geographic* offered a major assignment, my first for that prestigious magazine. I was also due to meet with top editors at *Life* and had meetings scheduled in London, New York, and Washington.

In late April 1960, we flew from Paris to London where I became Yukiko's personal guide to the great capital.

In early May 1960, we landed at Idlewild International Airport, later named JFK, on Long Island, New York, where our Pan Am 707 flight was met by Kurt Kornfeld and Ernest Mayer of Black Star, both men in their early seventies.

In old European fashion, we all embraced, and Kurt presented a huge bouquet of red roses to Yukiko. It was a warm, enthusiastic welcome. Kurt was instantly seduced by Yukiko's grace and gentleness, while Yukiko found in Kurt a charming, old-world grandfather, a relationship that would last until Kurt's death at the age of 80.

The last time I saw Mayer was five years earlier in a tense meeting where I argued, with Kornfeld's help, for a raise of my weekly guarantee from $20 to $35. Though I could never call the more reserved agency chief by his first name, he seemed genuinely pleased to see us and greatly surprised me by renting a chauffeured car for our drive back to Manhattan.

Since Black Star's creation in 1936, Ernest Mayer handled the agency's finances through lean years, so he was often frugal. On the other hand, Kurt almost never discussed money. He tipped taxi drivers generously and always brought roses to the lady editors at *Life*—Time Inc. was his turf. The combination of Mayer and Kornfeld was good for the agency with one man watching the bottom line and the other fascinated by talent. Dressing off the rack in Manhattan's garment district, they were a far cry from Dolf Seedorf in London's agency.

As we drove over the Triboro Bridge, Yukiko was excited to see Manhattan for the first time. On the way to the city, Kurt informed us, "I've booked you at the Tudor City Hotel because it's only a few feet from my apartment, and I'm looking forward to spending a few evenings with you both." Kurt showed me a list of editors at *Life* I'd meet for the first time, including Managing Editor Edward K. Thompson and Director of Photography Richard Pollard. "No one knows your face at *Life*," Kurt said. "So it's important you meet all those people, so they can put a face to your work."

My early mentors at the agency were Kurt and Howard Chapnick. In my first two difficult years when I had to create my own projects, it was Kurt who took my work to the right editors at *Life*. Once *Life* had published a number of stories, they finally began giving me assignments.

Howard also made a list of editors I should meet at Argosy, Sunday supplements, and other publications. After several three-martini lunches that were then in vogue, I reduced my intake to a single drink per meeting. Meanwhile Kurt took Yukiko on tours of New York City landmarks before moving on to the serious business of shopping at Saks Fifth Avenue.

I met *Life*'s burly managing editor, Ed Thompson, early in the week before pressures of getting the magazine ready for "closing time" diverted his attention. A formidable figure at the most popular weekly publication in the world, he greeted me warmly while puffing on a huge cigar. He suggested dry martinis to start the afternoon and prepared them at his own office bar.

Praising my coverage of the *Trieste*, he said it had been "well received all around." Since it was a recent story, my timing was good, and my descriptions of riding in a tiny rubber boat followed by sharks made for good and easy conversation. Though I'd been nervous about meeting the "big boss" at *Life*, Ed Thompson quickly put me at ease.

Director of Photography Richard Pollard also greeted me warmly and seemed less authoritarian than his cables. Moving through every department at *Life*, I met each editor and the assistants, putting a face to my photographs, as Kurt had instructed.

In Hong Kong, John Dominis told me, "When you go to New York, make sure you meet the picture editor, Peggy Sargent. She's a photographer's best friend and a remarkable editor."

She was exceptional at her job, knew the best shots out of hundreds of choices, and had a knack for identifying a photographer's disposition. Demonstrating her skills on a few of my assignments "awaiting space," she spread out 20 or so prints of each subject and without hesitation pointed to my favorites. I was impressed she so keenly understood my mind and heart purely through my work, before ever having met me.

Days in Manhattan were spent in a whirl of lunches, nights at the theater, and a wonderful Italian dinner with Howard and Jeanette Chapnick at Antolotti's near the United Nations. Howard taught us more about Italian dishes than we had learned in Italy.

Spending an afternoon in Central Park, Yukiko and I sat by the pond where five years earlier I had rehearsed my presentation to Black Star. It all seemed so very long ago.

We spent our last evening in Manhattan at Kurt Kornfeld's place. Kurt knew of my love for a young woman in Japan when I pulled every string to work in that faraway country. I realized Kurt assumed that first love was Yukiko, so I discreetly told him of the sad denouement with Keiko. In his inimitable German accent, Kurt said, "My Gott, John, I had planned to speak of your love conquering the oceans."

Kurt was a kind, erudite man of great character. In a way, I adopted him as my grandfather, for I had never known my own: both my real grandfathers had died during the Spanish flu epidemic of 1918 before I was born. During five years in Asia, I received regular letters from Kurt encouraging me in hard times and praising me when I finally achieved success. By 1960, I felt very close to him.

Yukiko spent much of the evening answering Kurt's many questions about Japan and her culture. After many delightful hours dining, drinking, talking, and laughing, it was past midnight by the time we walked back to our hotel.

Next we flew to Washington to discuss my *National Geographic* assignment on Japan with Director of Photography James Godbold, Associate Editor Franc Shor, and Associate Illustrations Editor and photographer Bill Garrett. I had met Garrett in Tokyo on my return from the war in Laos and had briefed him on the chaotic situations he'd face there.

Godbold gave us a tour of *Geographic*'s editorial facilities. It struck me as a place of conservative wealth working at an unhurried pace far different from the energetic atmosphere of Time Inc.: the segregated cafeterias for staff, with women on one side and men on the other, was particularly surprising.

Lunching in one of the executive dining rooms, we discussed the magazine's editorial requirements. I understood my coverage of modern Japan would be extensive and that I'd need to overlap with writer Franc Shor. Other than that, I'd be on my own.

All my leading questions were answered positively: I could take as much time as required, expenses were unlimited, and immediately upon our return to Japan, I could hire Yukiko as my interpreter, and add an assistant when necessary. Assignments could be interrupted to fulfill obligations to *Life*, and yes, my fee would be based on the time I spent on the job—all the details would be worked out with Chapnick at Black Star.

Because I had always worked on deadlines, the luxury of taking as much time as needed on a story was extraordinary. To study how the magazine covered an entire country, I spent the rest of the day looking through a stack of *Geographics*.

In the evening, Bill Garrett invited us to his home in Vienna, Virginia, where we met his wife Lucy and their two young children. With drinks, a steak dinner, and good wine, our conversations continued late into the night: it was the beginning of a long friendship.

We flew next to California to visit my old friend Bob Boal and his wife Cathy whom I had not seen for nearly five years. Major Douglas Parker and his wife joined us in a grand reunion with the people who had all generously taken me into their families after I left my first mentor, Joe Pazen—the people I viewed as my early "Californian architects."

Bob barbecued dinner, and we all ate and drank too much except for Yukiko who never touched alcohol. The next evening, we invited the Boals and Parkers to the best Japanese restaurant I could find in Los Angeles. It was the first time I could invite my California friends to dinner.

After bidding goodbye to the Parkers, Bob and I stayed up late talking while Yukiko and Bob's family slept. Around four o'clock in the morning, Cathy sleepily begged us to go to bed just as she had years before.

The following day, we said goodbye to the Boals, promising not to wait another five years before our next visit. From LAX, we took off for Honolulu and then landed in Tokyo on May 25, 1960.

Normally after an assignment, I never knew when I'd work again. As a freelancer, I had lived in a constant state of insecurity, but in 1960, I knew *Geographic's* assignment would create several months of work, and a forthcoming visit by President Dwight Eisenhower meant a major assignment from *Life* as well. Elated, I was anxious to start.

On June 19, 1960, Eisenhower was due to arrive in Japan. It would be the president's last destination after an 18-month, 60-thousand-mile odyssey of personal diplomacy for peace, which *Life* had covered in capitals as diverse as Madrid, Rome, Tehran, Karachi, and New Delhi. The trip had been a triumph of personal diplomacy for the president, even in India where crowds overwhelmed him with cheers, and millions called him the "Prince of Peace."

But the shooting of a U.S. U-2 spy plane over the Soviet Union gave Khrushchev a powerful tool with which to humiliate Eisenhower. The president's prestige diminished at a May 17 summit conference in Paris when Khrushchev boycotted the conference despite last-ditch efforts by Macmillan and de Gaulle to save it.

Though it was believed in diplomatic circles that a spectacular welcome in Japan would restore presidential prestige, many observers failed to understand the reaction that the shooting of the U-2 spy plane created, particularly among leftist students on Japanese university campuses.

The downed U-2 had come from Peshawar, Pakistan, but many Japanese students were ready to believe it had come from Japan, where several U-2s were based, and antimilitary sentiments erupted in the universities around Tokyo.

Most students wanted to topple the government of Premier Nobosuke Kishi. Protesters said, "We have no voice in our government" and wanted to stop the U.S.-Japan security pact, which Eisenhower was to sign on arrival.

The student union, Zengakuren, claiming to be left of Mao Zedong, led thousands of students into streets of the capital, paralyzing traffic and wreaking havoc. Demonstrations turned into ugly riots as thousands chanted, "Anpo-Hantai" ("No Pact"). A 22-year-old Zengakuren leader, Nobuo Aruga, whom I photographed and befriended, said he was an avowed disciple of Lenin, yet he hated Soviet bureaucracy as well as U.S. capitalism. He wanted Japan "to turn its back on both superpowers and establish an idyllic neutral socialist state." Aruga explained, "Zengakuren will attack the premier's residence and stage a showdown with police at the airport if Eisenhower comes."

On June 11, Eisenhower's press secretary, Jim Hagerty, landed at Tokyo Airport and met Ambassador Douglas MacArthur II to arrange the president's journey. The two Americans were trapped in their car, surrounded by some 20,000 screaming students, while Japanese police were overwhelmed by a human tide of demonstrators waving red flags and antipact slogans.

To avoid being crushed, I stood near the trunk of the car, photographing enraged faces. In vain, students climbed on the roof of the car, trying to calm the raging mob, while others pushed and pulled, trying to overturn it.

After an hour, a U.S. Marine helicopter swept down over the screaming protesters, unsettling the mob long enough for police to help Hagerty and MacArthur board the chopper and lift them to safety—they were lucky to escape. My dramatic coverage of the rescue and tumultuous week ran five pages in *Life's* June 20, 1960, issue, entitled: "A Challenge to U.S. by Riotous Japanese."

Despite many wounded in their ranks, the next student strategy was to attack the Diet Parliament and occupy it. Confrontations with police became violent: Batons were swung. Rocks were hurled. A Time-Life armband let me run through police lines as I wore a light helmet with the *Life* logo to protect my head from incoming debris.

On Parliament grounds, I got caught between a massive police charge of hundreds against a larger countercharge of students. Sandwiched between two forces, I climbed a branch of a small tree and pulled myself up.

For two hours, four feet above the clashing melee, I photographed charges and counter-charges from an extraordinary vantage point. The violence unleashed was incredible: waves of rocks crashed against plastic bodyshields, while police batons swung wildly and crushed skulls. The sound of the fury was terrifying.

With each charge, my tree shook. After I exposed my last frame, I realized my cameras had given me a false sense of security: suddenly I felt vulnerable watching the violence without a camera before my eyes.

By nightfall, both sides regrouped. In the lull, I slid down my tree and headed for the office where a deep gash in my tibia was cleaned and bandaged. Back on the job, I managed to keep an uneasy peace with some student leaders, thinking I had some kind of journalistic immunity. With each passing day, violence increased as rioters attacked the Parliament and passions flared out of control.

Suddenly a mob of students, recognizing my Time-Life armband, closed in on me screaming, "We don't want your American pact!" I continued photographing until one rioter yanked my camera strap. I stumbled forward into a huge group of students screaming, "Anpo-Hantai!" ("No Pact!")

The mob moved in. Afraid they would lynch me, I looked at the rioter yanking my strap and screamed, "Bokuwa France Jin!" ("I am French!")

What happened next was like a miracle: the mob stopped screaming. The leader released my camera strap and said, "Gomennasai. Sumimasen," ("I am

sorry. Excuse me.") and bowed deeply several times; then all his followers bowed deeply saying, "Gomennasai. Gomennasai." Shaken, I said, "Arigato. Merci." I had remembered my roots just in time.

The students attacked the Parliament in following days, burning 17 out of 20 police trucks. With many wounded on both sides, ambulances rushed in and out through the night. Prime Minister Nobusuke Kishi's government and cabinet called an emergency session in which they bowed to the demands of the students, cancelling President Eisenhower's trip to Japan "for the sake of his own safety."

Humiliated, after a final trip to Formosa, the president returned to Washington on June 27, 1960. My pictures of the last impassioned days of the riots, subtitled, "Frenzied Face of the Violence Which Was to Wreck the Visit," were published in *Life*'s issue of June 27, 1960.

Day by day, the rising humidity of another Tokyo summer was sneaking in under the blazing flames of riots, illuminating the Parliament by night and blanketing the city with oppressive heat by morning. As ashes smoldered, the steamy heat of summer had replaced the fires of the spring riots.

Along with much praise from the editors at *Life*, I was given a $300 bonus. Black Star said it would not take a percentage because of the risks of the assignment. This time, no one at *Life* called me "foolhardy" for being in the "eye of the storm."

Though still recovering from the frenzied pace of the riots, I had to immediately prepare for my first assignment for National Geographic, quickly scripting coverage plans for Franc Shor.

When I met Shor at Tsukiji-en, one of the best traditional inns in Tokyo, I got the sense that the great writer was holding court. A portly figure at about 250 pounds, with red puffy cheeks, he seemed arrogant and pompous—I thought he looked imperial.

Rising from pillows stacked on a tatami floor, Shor offered his hand like a cardinal of the Roman Catholic Church. Not seeing a ring to kiss, I awkwardly reached for the palm of his hand and shook it.

"This guy thinks I'm his subject," I thought and wondered whether we'd be able to get along. It may have been my first assignment for the magazine, and Shor was a senior figure who held power over me at Geographic's Washington D.C. headquarters, but I knew I wasn't about to be bullied by anyone.

Shor reacted positively to my outline and seemed erudite and knowledgeable about Japan, so I relaxed. He said my outline was distinctly conscious of Japan's classical beauty coexisting with the "economic miracle" of modern Japan.

By 1960, centuries of Japan's classical past had survived the onslaught of postwar modernity. The country had entered a new economic phase, eventually creating the world's second most powerful economy after the United States. Correspondents often joked, "America won the war, but Japan will win the world's markets."

Shor suggested we visit the main islands, so together we traveled with interpreters to Kyushu and Hokkaido. Shor ordered a chauffeur-driven Lincoln for our journey, and as we boarded our car each morning at dawn, a white-gloved chauffeur held the door and bowed deeply.

Together we traveled to ancient capitals of Kyoto and Nara, the port city of Kobe from which 40 percent of Japan's products were shipped to world markets, and Osaka where "Good morning" in Japanese meant, "How is business?"

Each morning as we sat sleepily in our Lincoln seats, I began to notice Shor was enjoying the bowing of the driver and hotel staff as they lined up for our departures. I laughed to myself, thinking, "Franc loves it all." As we rode north to Hokkaido, I thought, "Maybe America has produced an emperor after all."

But Shor had redeeming qualities. I read some of his work and was fascinated— he was a good writer. As we traveled roads of Japan, he recounted his exploits with erudition, humor, and gusto in the oral tradition of a great storyteller.

His needs as a writer were different from mine. Though he told me I could stop the car any time for photographs, I argued I could not cover Japan properly from a moving car.

Duing our trip to the northern island of Hokkaido, I saw a fishing boat in Atsunai, poking its prow out of a barn where fishermen had stored it for the winter. The length of the boat was too long, so a side of the barn was cut to accommodate the thatch-covered bow. The image reflected the rugged winters of Hokkaido when seas were too rough for small fishing crafts and the island was under ice and snow for five months out of the year. It was a picture I had to take.

The driver stopped the car, and I went to work on a composition of girls mending crab traps with a background of snowy mountains and menacing skies. After I'd worked on my picture for half an hour, Shor approached me and said, "John, if you don't have this photograph by now, you will never have it." Angrily, I turned around and told him, "Franc, no one, I mean no one, ever tells me when I have my photograph or not." Stunned, he walked back to our heated car to sit and wait, while I deliberately took more time than needed to finish my picture.

On the road to Sapporo, not a word was exchanged. As we stood before the clerk to register at our inn, I ordered a separate dinner. I knew I may have hurt my relationship with *Geographic* by standing up to Shor but reasoned I wasn't telling him how to write, so he couldn't tell me how to photograph.

After relaxing in a traditional Japanese bath, I worked on research for Sapporo. While I scribbled notes about neon lights reflected on September snow, I heard a gentle knock on my shoji screen. Expecting dinner, I opened the door but instead saw Franc Shor. "John, I'm sorry," he said. "I will never again interfere with your work. You have my word." We had a civilized dinner together, drank too much warm sake, and made a lasting peace.

Several days later, we separated in Tokyo, but on his departure, Shor gave me two of his calling cards with written notes to the sommeliers of the George V Hotel and the Ritz in Paris, instructing each of them to serve me one of his vintage Bordeaux wines, which he kept in private cellars in both hotels. A year later, the George V sommelier informed me that Shor was a "connoisseur of fine wines" and so, with dinner, I savored an excellent Bordeaux, though to my father's dismay, I didn't know much about good wine in 1961.

When Shor and I parted ways, he left for Hiroshima while I traveled to Kyoto, the ancient capital. After several days, I found in the geisha district the images I needed. A motorcyclist and his girlfriend in Western dress and crash helmets shattered

the serenity of the Gion-Machi neighborhood, passing at full speed a strolling geisha and her two apprentices in wooden clogs, silk kimonos, chalky makeup, and lacquered black wigs. The motorcyclists and the geishas were centuries apart, creating an image of ancient and modern Japan, clashing yet coexisting.

My coverage of Japan for *Geographic* was broad enough to include booming industries, farmers, agriculture, art, religion, and classical and modern entertainment. The latter ranged from the drama, song, and dance of traditional Kabuki Theater to Tokyo's Kokusai Theater where dancing "Atomic Girls" emulated the famous Radio City Music Hall Rockettes of New York.

After shooting thousands of photographs, I shipped the last of my films to *Geographic*. Despite reassuring reports from the picture editor, I had not seen a single picture and felt a profound sense of insecurity. As I nervously waited for word on the final layout, Franc Shor was certain our combined words and pictures might run up to 32 pages.

Finally, editors sent me a cable saying our Japan coverage closed in the December 1960 issue with 46 pages including 30 pages of my photographs—it was like being told my name would be in lights and seen by millions of people. More than most magazines, *Geographic* honored photographers as well as writers with prominent bylines.

Mayer, Kornfeld, and Chapnick sent congratulatory cables, saying I was Black Star's first photographer to make it in *Geographic* on a major assignment. "It's a breakthrough," said Chapnick. My Japan coverage led to numerous *Geographic* assignments in far-reaching parts of the world over the next two decades.

When we saw the published story in late November, Yukiko and I celebrated at the Press Club. I never had so many pages of my work in one magazine. One full page depicted Yukiko feeding a fawn in Nara's National Park; it was an idealized picture of her, for she was more graceful than a fawn to me. Though she never touched alcohol, the photograph helped me persuade her to try a sip of champagne.

In the last months of 1960, I was approached by Tokyo-based film director, Steve Parker, to cover his film *My Geisha* for Paramount Studios. Starring in the movie was Yves Montand as a film director shooting a new version of Puccini's *Madame Butterfly* along with Shirley MacLaine playing Montand's wife. In the film, Shirley disguises herself as a geisha to seduce her husband and regain his fleeting love.

To play the part, Shirley had to learn the art of being a geisha at the prestigious Geisha School in the Gion district of Kyoto with choreographer Michio Ito. It was a stretch, to say the least: at five foot seven, the American movie star towered over the authentic five-foot geishas.

Shirley had to learn how to "slide into a room like a shadow, to be pigeon-toed and walk like a bird." Her instructors insisted, "You must walk from the knees down." They had her mince around the room in her 17-piece kimono, 6 ½-pound lacquered black wig, and a handkerchief between her knees.

Each day before shooting, Shirley endured long makeup sessions to paint her face chalky white and be fit with brown contact lenses to hide her blue eyes. Her training as a geisha produced hilarious photographs for the cover and a six-page essay in the February 17, 1961, issue of *Life*, and my photos of Shirley and Yves acting together were published in a French magazine.

Because only Yves and I spoke French, I became his reluctant confidant during production. He admitted he had fallen in love with Marilyn Monroe: featured as screen lovers on a *Life* cover the previous August, they were in fact actual lovers. Yet while he claimed to have great passion for Marilyn, a couple of weeks into production of *My Geisha*, Yves confessed his strong feelings for Shirley.

"She is highly intelligent. She knows how to see, how to understand things in life. She's so generous," Yves said. But Shirley wasn't that generous. At 2:00 A.M., after weeks in production, Yves knocked on our hotel room door. Yukiko heard him say, "John, may I speak to you?"

Yves Montand on location in Kyoto (taken by Yukiko).

Opening the door, I saw Yves crying softly and understood Shirley had rejected him—he was inconsolable. We walked to the hotel's empty bar and sat in silence. I didn't know what to say except, "All you can do is concentrate on your work." When he calmed down, I walked him back to his suite, and he thanked me for listening.

Yukiko asked me, "What happened?" I told her, "Yves is brokenhearted." On the set next morning, Yves was strictly professional. As he acted his role, none of his sorrow showed on his face. During the remaining weeks of production, he never mentioned his feelings again.

Before leaving for Paris, he gave me his private telephone number and address on Place Dauphine, so Yukiko and I met him again when I was covering another film in London in 1962, and Yves was performing a one-man musical act. After enjoying the show, we shared drinks at a private club with Yves and his wife and actress, Simone Signoret.

RIGHT TO KNOW

THE COURT-MARTIAL

SEOUL 1961

At the club, Yves reminisced about Japan with Yukiko while I had a heated ideological debate with Simone. She was outraged by my American idealism, saying, "How you, a Frenchman of working-class origin, could become an American is beyond me."

Like so many French intellectuals on the left in postwar France, Simone lived in materialistic splendor while linking France's working class to the Communist Workers' Union, not capitalistic America. Though Yves and I in Kyoto discussed the contradictions of his lifestyle of luxury and his proletarian ideals, he chose to bypass the subject that night and continue his conversation with Yukiko. Our discussions carried on into the late evening, when we bid them a warm goodbye. It was the last time we ever met.

In 1961, the third week of May, another coup d'état shattered the morning calm of South Korea. The streets were hardly clear of wreckage from the last revolution when students forced down the dictatorial President Syngman Rhee a year earlier, in an event I photographed. Violence again toppled the parliamentary government. But the coup, led by U.S.-trained Lieutenant General Chang Do Yung, immediately led to imposed martial law and closure of civilian airports. It was impossible to reach Seoul on commercial airlines.

With 50,000 servicemen stationed in Korea, the United States reluctantly accepted General Yung's new government. America's military commitment to South Korea suggested that the U.S. press corps in Japan had a legitimate reason to ask the Air Force for transport to Korea.

I joined a small group of American correspondents who contacted the commanding general of the U.S. Air Force in Japan, insisting it was the American people's right to know what was taking place in Korea, and was amazed by the general's acquiescence and his almost immediate agreement.

Within hours, we flew from Tachikawa to Seoul in an Air Force C-47. On the slow flight, I mused that no other press corps on earth could have persuaded a commanding general to supply a press plane for "the people's right to know" about a country where a military man had just taken over its legal government—a country where, ironically, the people never had "the right to know."

Once again, I appreciated that the American military obeyed constitutional laws and their commander in chief, the president, was an elected civilian.

When we reached Seoul, the cracks of rifles and rattle of machine guns had nearly ended; only the rumble of tanks remained. The former government of Premier John Chang had given Koreans the closest thing to a democratic state but had been removed by violence.

General Chang Do Yung's 3,600 reservist troops controlled all institutions in the capital. A curfew was declared and martial law imposed.

From Time-Life's stringer, I learned that hundreds of young people had been arrested and locked up for dancing all night and breaking curfew, and that all of them would be forced to appear before a court-martial.

The day of the court-martial, a press conference was scheduled by General Yung. Don Connery covered the conference for *Time* and *Life*. Since I already had pictures of the general and his backer, Major General Pak Chung Hi, preparing to address "the victorious troops" at Seoul's city hall, I decided to photograph the court-martial if at all possible.

Bluffing my way in by brazenly walking past armed Korean soldiers who guarded the court's entrance, I discreetly sat in the back benches and laid low, facing the judge and prosecutors, all military officers.

About 40 boys and girls, mostly students and teenagers, sat on benches facing the presiding judge in uniform, elevated on a platform, flanked by two military prosecutors.

There were no parents, no witnesses, no defense lawyers in the courtroom, only frightened kids facing military judges. With five cameras around my neck and shoulders, I was the only witness, trying to keep a low profile.

While all were accused of breaking curfew and dancing after hours, an additional charge was brought against the girls for having nail polish on their fingernails. Each youngster was summoned before the prosecutor and sentenced to several months in jail. The girls were ordered to show their fingernails for traces of nail polish: holding their red fingernails before the prosecutor, many of the girls broke down, sobbing.

All were sentenced to jail and led away, crying, by armed soldiers. One of the prosecutors kept staring at me as I laid low behind the benches. I got out with several pictures that would shock *Life*'s readers, revealing the outrageous military justice of South Korea's new government.

When I joined Connery later, he agreed when I said, "It's our duty to expose these military dictators for what they are. Can you imagine our kids getting sentenced to jail for having gone out dancing one night or for wearing red nail polish?"

Connery remained in Seoul while the Tokyo bureau manager, Imai-san, met my plane at Tokyo's International Airport to ship my film to New York. To editors of *Life*, I drafted a cable explaining, "My pictures are exclusive. No other journalist was in the courtroom. Morally, we have a duty to expose these dictators supported by American taxpayers, to expose them for the tyrants they are."

I expected at least two pages in *Life* for my coverage of General Yung's mockery of justice, so was surprised when my request was ignored. Instead, editors ran only a single page in the May 26, 1961, issue of *Life* with half the page devoted to generals of the coup d'état, a quarter page to "triumphant tankers rolling down Nam San Hill" in Seoul, and a small picture of ex-Premier Chang who tried to bring democracy to South Korea. The story did not even mention the court-martial.

Life's chief picture editor, Peggy Sargent, selected pictures of the teenagers at the trial and made several 11-by-14 prints, but in vain. Expressing personal regret, she told me, "Those were powerful photographs. I'm very sorry they didn't run."

As always, I felt the emptiness that came after a tense assignment. To fill the void of another story's conclusion, I went to the Foreign Correspondents' Club in Japan where I bumped into my old friend Rowland Gould. An Englishman, he was deputy director of the *U.S. Army Times, Navy Times*, and *Air Force Times* in Asia.

Rowland was probably the most generous man I ever met. When I was struggling in my "noodle years," he offered me office space in Tokyo in exchange for pictures I could take later, though I already had facilities at Pan Asia.

Such was his compassion and empathy for people's troubles that Rowland often took in strays, not cats or dogs but men or women who were down on their luck. They somehow found their way to Rowland's doorstep, which might explain why he was nearly always on the edge of financial ruin.

Because Rowland and I were not competitors, we shared information and often discussed riding the fabled Trans-Siberian Railway from Vladivostok to Moscow.

FORBIDDEN LAND

TRANS-SIBERIAN RAILWAY

SIBERIA 1961

F or 15 years after World War II, Siberia had been closed to almost everyone, especially Western journalists.

At the Correspondents' Club in 1961, I asked Rowland about our Trans-Siberian dream. "Is there anything I should know?" When he said, "Yes," I was skeptical but had great expectations.

"There's a Soviet cruise ship with Russian athletes docked in Yokohama," he said, "and I think perhaps we can convince them to let us return with them to Far East Russia and then ride the Trans-Siberian to Moscow. You can approach the Russians for *Life* and I for the *Daily Mail* of London and CBS News."

Reasoning the Soviets might be less hostile to an Englishman than an American, he said, "Let's work separately." It was a long shot: we knew Siberia was still a forbidden land, presumably full of dark secrets. For over a century, Siberia had been a deadly nightmare and final journey for multitudes of Russians, yet the more I thought about it, the more I wanted to make the journey.

Many associate members of the Foreign Correspondents' Club of Japan were diplomats from major countries including the Soviet Union, who cultivated relationships with journalists as we did with them.

Often I had heated discussions with a secretary of the Soviet Embassy in Tokyo. I forgot his name long ago but not our ideological debates nor his heavy drinking when it came to buying him several rounds of Scotch, his drink of choice.

Though we agreed to disagree on the best forms of government, we understood each other when sharing our thoughts of Nazi Germany's wartime invasions of France and the Soviet Union. We had suffered from a common enemy, his people much more than mine. Emotionally, history would bind us.

Often whiskey made him thoughtful and brought patriotic tears to his eyes. In those moments, we became friends, which called for additional toasts to peace. It was no accident that I called upon this secretary of the Soviet Embassy to help me.

At the embassy, I explained what I wanted. He remained solemn and silent for what seemed an eternity; finally he said, "I see you are requesting two visas." "Yes," I answered, "Don Connery will write for *Time,* and I will photograph for *Life*." He fell back into silence again.

From our press club conversations, I knew "my diplomat" feared photography more than writing, because photography was harder to deny as propaganda, so in an impassioned plea I said, "I assure you my photographic coverage will be fair to your country, to your people."

At last he smiled, looked into my eyes, and said, "John, I believe you. Vladivostok is off limits, but you and Connery can sail our ship from Yokohama to Nakhodka and then ride the Trans-Siberian to Moscow. I don't know how many stops will be permitted along the way, but keep in mind, many cities in Siberia do not have accommodations for visitors." Shaking hands, I thanked him. As I walked out of the Soviet Embassy, I was delirious.

For fear of raising *Life*'s expectations too high, I deliberately kept my pursuit of a Soviet visa a secret. When I finally told Time-Life's permanent reporter-translator

"Free-enterprise" flower vendors being lectured by a party official at a railroad station.

in the Tokyo bureau, Frank Iwama, he smiled and said, "At last I can show you this. It's a confidential cable that's been sitting in our files for a long time." In essence it said, "If the Soviets ever open Siberia from the Far East, please inform John Launois to go ahead. It's an assignment."

It was my first preapproved assignment. After informing editors of my visa, I received a color-photo assignment from *Time* magazine as well.

Don Connery was still in South Korea. Afraid my good news might fall into the wrong hands, I asked Iwama not to send an open cable to Connery in Seoul—we'd wait for his return. As far as I knew, the Russians had only approved visas for Rowland, Connery, and myself. I figured if that became known, all news organizations based in Tokyo would rush to the Soviet Embassy.

I met Connery at the Tokyo airport on his return from Korea and showed him a map of the Soviet Union in Japanese, on which I translated names of cities we'd pass through on the railroad. When I told him I secured two visas for an adventure in Siberia, he was overcome with disbelief—only once his state of shock subsided could he express his great enthusiasm.

On June 8, 1961, we sailed from Yokohama with a group of Russian athletes who had performed exhibition games in Japan. We were grateful to be in their company and on the ship that brought them, well aware that all Japanese and Western means of transportation to Far East Russia were forbidden. For our 5,800-mile, nine-day journey, I requested a number of stops but only two were permitted, one in Khabarovsk and the other in Irkutsk.

On June 9, 1961, we docked in Nakhodka, about 50 miles east of the top-secret Soviet naval base, Vladivostok. At customs and immigration, customs officers merely glanced at my equipment and personal baggage but immediately confiscated Rowland Gould's professional tape recorder provided by CBS—Rowland fought a hopeless fight to get it back. We speculated that authorities feared Rowland might record dissidents criticizing Soviet ideology. Ironically during our entire trip, we met only mild criticism of the government.

Rowland was allowed to keep his movie camera and a small personal tape recorder, which I assumed would not meet CBS's professional requirements for sound. As always, Rowland remained optimistic.

From Nakhodka, we boarded a train pulled by two American-made steam locomotives from the World War II lend-lease program. After a night and day, we arrived in Khabarovsk, a typical Soviet city with tree-lined streets and drab Stalinesque architecture of five-and six-story apartment and government buildings.

We checked into the Dalnyvostok Hotel where we were not allowed to eat in the public dining room. Instead we were led to a huge private room where a table was set for us with small British and American flags.

The three of us found the segregation unbearable, particularly since we could hear jazz music and sounds of laughter drifting in from the hotel's main dining room. We called for the manager and insisted that we eat with other hotel guests. When he refused, we refused to order. Eventually, he led us to a table by the jazz band and its short-sleeved musicians. With our national flags displayed on our table, the Stars and Stripes attracted immediate attention.

No one in Siberia had ever seen an American in person before. The young people in particular asked if we really were from the United States. They had all been told that Americans were imperialist warmongers intent on destroying the Soviet Union, but Don and I didn't match the clichés of Soviet propaganda. Soon we were exchanging toasts and dancing with girls—it was an exercise in grassroots diplomacy.

Between drinking and dancing to tunes like "Love Is a Many Splendored Thing," we tried ordering dinner from a 20-page menu with an endless array of dishes. I looked forward to Beluga caviar, since I had never tasted fresh caviar, but it wasn't priced. The catch was that only dishes listed with a price were available, so we settled for two of the five dishes priced on the menu.

John and Don Connery (second from right) at a collective farm in Khabarovsk.

To our newfound friends, we proposed countless toasts with vodka and marginal champagne from Georgia. As the dining room closed, we ended the night walking and singing with a group of students in the city's silent streets.

One day in Khabarovsk, after exploring the 6,177-acre Red River Collective Farm, we visited a family apartment in one of the city's newer housing blocks. The two parents, two children, and two grandparents occupied a space no larger than a typical American living room. Making do with a wood-burning stove and an electric hot plate, they said they were on the waiting list for a gas stove and a refrigerator. The Ukrainian-born grandfather, who managed a chicken farm, told us of the horrors of war in the Ukraine and on other fronts of the Soviet Union during World War II.

The 70-year-old veteran asked Connery, "Why do you Americans want to destroy the Soviet Union, its people, its women, and children?" As tears streamed down his cheeks, he asked again, "Why? Why its children?"

In his large right hand, the old soldier held up three little chicks from his farm as his 11-year-old granddaughter hugged his waist. With his left hand, he covered the child's eyes so she wouldn't see him cry as he said, "If you attack us, I'll fight. I will take up arms again. But, for the sake of our children, we must not make war anymore."

In that instant, with five cameras around my neck and shoulders, I was torn between journalism and the man's dignity. He seemed to believe we did not want war and appeared convinced we were not the warmongers portrayed in Soviet propaganda. I couldn't betray his trust and exploit his sorrow. Without regret, I'd later say, "It was the most powerful picture of our trip, and it was the one I never took."

After covering Khabarovsk for three days, we began our 2,000-mile trip to Irkutsk, the ancient capital of Siberia. Riding the Trans-Siberian Railway at 30 miles an hour, it took nearly three days to reach the city.

Despite Soviet claims of creating a classless society, wealthier citizens on the train traveled in "soft class," mixing men and women in compartments with two upper and lower berths with comfortable bedding, oriental rugs, and silk-shaded lamps on tables next to the windows.

In a pseudo-Victorian atmosphere, "soft-class" passengers ate meals in dining cars and were served tea and snacks at their seats by female attendants. But nearly 90 percent of passengers traveled in "hard class," provided their own bedding for wooden bunks, and bought their own food at stations along the way.

During our three-day journey to Irkutsk, all attempts to photograph "hard-class" passengers were met with suspicion and outright refusal. Communication was our main obstacle as we had no common language. I didn't expect to see anything resembling labor camps or the great Soviet military complex near the railroad—we would never have been allowed to take the trip if they were in sight. I simply hoped to take mood photographs of the Siberian landscape, south of the taiga.

I wanted pictures of birches, pine trees, black earth, and barren steppes, but photographing the landscape was strictly forbidden by the conductor. Express permission from authorities was needed to photograph any railroad stations, but I could never get permission in time.

When my frustration had reached near desperation, I began making countless trips to the bathroom where I managed to open a six-inch-wide window above frosted glass behind the toilets. From there, I photographed unpainted houses in muddy villages close to small rivers and streams where people carried buckets of water balanced on wooden bars across their shoulders.

Eventually, our female attendant became suspicious of my numerous visits to the toilet, visits that ceased once darkness fell. Fortunately, she moved very slowly as her girth barely made it through the train's corridor. Because she was about five feet tall and seemed just as wide, Connery and I called her "Mrs. Five by Five."

She had the shrewdness of a good Russian peasant: I could see in her smirk that she doubted my explanations of severe diarrhea as I rubbed my stomach. We knew Mrs. Five by Five had a pass key. In her suspicious mood, she could have forced herself past Connery, opened the bathroom door, and found me fully dressed with my camera and the Swiss Army knife I used to open the window, so I was taking a considerable risk. Western journalists had often been arrested and accused of spying on Russia while photographing ordinary buildings.

To bolster the credibility of my illness and countless trips to the toilet, I began adding evening trips to the bathroom. During the day, Connery would stand watch near the bathroom door, and as soon as he saw Mrs. Five by Five approaching, he'd start whistling a tune from *My Fair Lady*. That was my cue to lock the window in about three seconds and appear to be using the toilet. It was an unnerving exercise in undercover photography.

Reaching Irkutsk, I realized my essay would fail unless we found an official escort to travel with us to Moscow as an interpreter to deal with officials and explain our needs. Connery agreed after hearing me complain for a thousand miles.

Prospects improved in the city famous for being at the edge of the world's deepest body of fresh water, Lake Baikal.

I spent part of one day photographing teenage Siberian cowboys corralling cattle on the huge Lenin's Way Collective Farm.

On another occasion, talking to numerous Russians at a celebration of Irkutsk's three hundredth anniversary, Connery and I were struck by the mixed emotions of the young people. They complained of the drudgery and limited choices of their life, yet they exhibited great pride in the nation's rise to superpower status and in its achievements in space flight. Having absorbed much of the Kremlin's relentless propaganda about "American warmongers," they feared the United States, yet they were fascinated by what they knew of American culture and personal freedoms. They dreamed of the day when they might be allowed to travel to the West.

We were far from the Cold War, and none of us spoke of it. Nuclear weapons were being tested regularly in the vast regions of Siberia, but ordinary people were never informed about these activities, and our own information came a long time after that warm Siberian night in June of 1961.

It was the year John F. Kennedy was sworn into office, when it was possible to believe our young and charismatic president would somehow bring an end to the Cold War and transform the world.

In his inaugural address, Kennedy gave us reason to hope when he said, "Now the trumpet summons us again...against the common enemies of man...tyranny, poverty, disease and war itself." America and the Soviet Union should "begin anew the quest for peace." Though we did not think of ourselves as naive, we were as optimistic as our young Russian friends, even thinking our friendly contacts would help speed the end of the superpower confrontation.

Sadly, our optimism was misplaced. Sixteen months later, in October 1962, while I was at work on other stories and Connery was installed as Time Inc.'s new Moscow bureau chief, the Cuban Missile Crisis struck fear into every corner of the globe. The U.S. released photographs of Russian nuclear missiles assembled on Cuba, and the world was on the brink of war as our naval vessels blockaded the island. Though Kennedy persuaded Soviet Premier Nikita Khrushchev to remove the missiles, the possibility of an all-out exchange of nuclear weapons had been greater than we and our young Russian friends dared imagine.

As a new American in 1961, I was influenced by my two years in the U.S. Army and of course, by the media. I believed the Soviet threat to the noncommunist world was real, that Soviet-style tyranny, if not confronted, might well crush the world's democratic societies, but I never felt indoctrinated by the loudest voices opposing "the Red menace." I remained a free thinker, sometimes critical of America's shortcomings, and ready to hear all opinions. I knew how totalitarianism worked, but traveling across Russia, I did not expect to meet so many people, young and old, who were completely indoctrinated by the Soviet government's party line.

The Russia I saw reminded me of the occupied years of Pétainist France when Vichy's militia terrorized dissidents, and fear kept people from speaking out. I thought perhaps the people of Russia were cautious with us simply because we were Americans, their official enemy.

The most critical remarks from students were in calling Khrushchev "the God of Corn" and saying, "To hell with Stalin." These were people who had never known democracy or had been exposed to "the Enlightenment"; I wondered how they could ever develop the idea of individual liberty. Was it just through sheer brutality that the Soviet government succeeded in indoctrinating so many millions?

"My diplomat" at Tokyo's Soviet Embassy had told me, "World War II played a huge part in creating Russian solidarity. Nazi Germany's war against the Soviet Union unified Russians from the Ukraine to Vladivostok. When they attacked us, they made us great patriots."

Soviet propaganda convinced millions of Russians that the U.S. wanted war. America was the new enemy, so there had to be greater Russian patriotism and continued sacrifice. The government line was reinforced by the fact that the postwar generation of Russia lived far better lives than their parents and grandparents. Education and health care were free. Housing projects were going up throughout cities we visited, though conditions were cramped, and tenants on each floor often shared a communal kitchen and bathroom.

It reminded me of my sister Paulette in France who was waiting for low-cost housing and shared a toilet with others in the cobblestoned courtyard of her building on Rue de l'Eglise. After the war, France was again a fragile, elitist democracy, but Russia, despite its liberal thinkers of the nineteenth century, had never been democratic.

Since we were American and basically free, the political system we discovered in Russia was profoundly disturbing, yet Siberia was not what I expected. My mind was too full of images of exiles from the Tsarist days and of the totalitarian regime wrought by Lenin and Stalin, all suffering in a grim, frozen wasteland. But none of that was seen as I photographed "collective farms," industries, warm weather pleasures, and people rushing to work on tree-lined streets where girls and women wore summer dresses. Siberia in June was a long way from January's plummeting temperatures of a hundred degrees below zero or August's intense heat soaring up to 120 degrees.

From Irkutsk, Russian authorities normally would have assigned us a trained and indoctrinated interpreter from Intourist, the official travel agency. But Intourist's interpreters were thousands of miles to the west in Moscow and in other cities visited by Western visitors.

In Irkutsk, where Western journalists had not been seen for 15 years, all the authorities could find for an interpreter, to our great delight, was Galina Vadnikova, a very pretty 23-year-old Siberian schoolteacher. She had never met Americans before and had far more questions about Western Europe and America than we did about her life in the infamously fabled land, Siberia.

From the moment I saw Galina Vadnikova's beautiful face, hazel eyes, long delicate hands, and slender figure, I knew her gentle manners would help charm the suspicious "hard-class" passengers I encountered.

As the Trans-Siberian pulled out of Irkutsk, Galina and I immediately worked out a strategy to establish trust with some "hard-class" travelers. After I selected a compartment shared by a young woman and two men who were obviously all strangers, Galina managed to make an introduction. For a few days, we irregularly called on them for small talk.

One of the men was in the liquor business, always dressed in pajamas. The other in pants and a short-sleeved shirt said he was simply "a worker." They met on the train and had become drinking buddies to the dismay of the young woman who shot distrustful glances at her convivial companions.

I asked, "Is the young woman intimidated by the two drinking strangers?" Galina explained, "You've never seen them drunk. Like I do with you and your friend Connery at bedtime, she prepares her bed while the two men step outside the compartment. When she is safely under covers, she unlocks the door so the men can prepare their bedding under the compartment's night light and go to sleep, just like when I knock on the window to signal you and Connery to do the same. But it's an uncomfortable journey for her, because they drink so much."

With Galina translating, we began having easy conversations and sharing shots of four-star brandy. On Galina's advice, I let them use a camera to photograph each other. Galina took one of me with the group. The young woman was soon at ease with Galina and me but remained embarrassed by the men's perpetual drinking.

I was determined to photograph that uneasy relationship. Fortunately, after a couple days, no one paid any more attention to my cameras. On the third day, the two men were drinking when the young woman shot another distrustful look at them, and with a wide-angle lens, I captured the entire compartment, the woman's look, the man in pajamas with his drinking buddy and small window table with three bottles of liquor in the background. It was my first candid photograph of "hard-class" passengers. To capture the scene, it had taken three days, many minor conversations, and a quarter bottle of brandy with several toasts to peace, but it was Galina's tender diplomacy that established the needed trust. Later *Life* would run that hard-won picture on a two-page spread.

Galina and I spent most of the daylight together. As the train headed west, a few precious minutes of sunlight were added to each passing day. Watching the Siberian landscape passing before us, we were silent at times. As we looked at each other, I sensed Galina was falling in love, though I had spoken to her only of my work and the photographs I needed to take.

She constantly tried to assist with our assignment. At one point, she disappeared for a while and returned after convincing the conductor to allow us to open one of the exit doors while the train was still moving. Leaning out the door, I photographed the landscape, capturing a wide-angle shot of the train curving around a lake, which was featured in *Life* as well.

In conversation, Galina told me little of her life other than describing her delight in reading poetry around a red-hot stove in long Siberian winters. She explained, "The stove burns my face and the poems warm my soul." At my request, she recited a poem that sounded beautiful to the ears, but when I asked her for a translation, she only blushed and said, "It's about love." My questions about a boyfriend remained unanswered.

Galina asked, "Why did you leave France, the birthplace of the 1789 and 1848 revolutions?" I explained, "Throughout my youth, France was deeply divided by a class struggle where I found myself at the bottom." Though her Soviet education confirmed my story, she had a much more romantic idea of France than I ever had.

I continued, "In the oppressive days of 1943, my father assured me only America could save France from the Nazis and the Vichy government, so I created a mythical America, and when my stomach growled with hunger, I fed myself on American idealism." She appreciated the image but insisted, "Without our heroic Soviet soldiers, the Nazis could not have been defeated. Our people made the greatest sacrifice."

Galina also had hard questions about the "Negroes in America" and said, "America is deeply racist. The Negroes are segregated, without rights. They live like slaves." At the time, I was profoundly ignorant about racism in America: the only African Americans I met on assignment were Louis Armstrong, Nat King Cole, and a few other successful personalities I photographed for *Ebony* magazine.

I knew more about Japanese racism towards Koreans than I knew about my chosen country's shameful history. Since the Soviet education system naturally exploited America's greatest faults, Galina knew more about racial injustice in America than I did.

She went on to ask, "Is it true workers in America can't vote?" I explained, "That notion comes strictly from Soviet Communist propaganda."

My young brother Jacquot, a French Communist party member, had asked me the exact same question in 1981, illustrating the far-reaching influence of Soviet thinking. Jacquot already had serious doubts about the party, so it had been easy to add a few more, but Galina was different: she had been fed Soviet ideology all her life, and my gentle explanations of Soviet propaganda invoked pain in her eyes. She didn't like seeing me as the messenger of another truth.

During the nine days of our 5,800-mile journey, Galina occasionally entertained us with mournful Russian love songs. With just 300 miles to go, night fell, and our adventure on the Trans-Siberian would soon come to a close.

We slept uneasily as we approached Moscow. When first light dawned through curtains of our compartment, I stirred in my lower berth and saw Galina's beautiful face looking at me from the opposite berth with tears quietly running down her cheeks.

We knew a beautiful journey was ending. As I reached for her face and cradled her left cheek, our lips met in a gentle kiss, long enough for me to taste the salty sadness in her tears. It wasn't a passionate kiss, simply a first and last kiss. She was 23 and I was 30, a Romantic meeting a Romantic: I was enchanted and she had fallen in love. It was a love story innocent and doomed.

Galina escorted us to Moscow's Ukraine Hotel. Close to tears, she quickly left. Connery later wrote in *Life*, "She wept before our train reached Moscow....delivered us to our hotel and abruptly left us...Moscow seems to affect people that way."

He was right. Moscow exuded power and fear, but I never told Don why Galina left us so abruptly, even declining our invitation to the Bolshoi Theater. I didn't say anything, because I feared if Soviet authorities ever discovered our official escort had fallen in love with one of the enemy while on duty, she might have been punished or discredited for the rest of her life. It was a reflex I learned during the Nazi-totalitarian rule of my own country.

From Moscow, we sent the most important films by diplomatic channels to Frankfurt, West Germany, and headed for Paris on one of Aeroflot's huge Tupolev airplanes. When *Life*'s editors learned we had sent the films ahead, they told us not to ship them from Europe but to "hand-carry all film to New York."

When Connery volunteered to take my film to New York, I decided to visit my parents, but it was too complicated to call ahead. A telephone was extremely difficult to own in 1961 France, unless you had "friends in the right places." Knowing they had no phone, I simply rented a car and drove to Marly-le-Roi to surprise my parents and take them to dinner.

Father at age 61 had just retired. Thanks to the government's social reforms in the late forties, my parents received a modest monthly social security check and were entitled to free medical care, including prescriptions. They received another monthly check from my European copyrights, so my parents were modestly secure for the first time in their lives as they entered their retirement, or as they said in France, their "third age."

Father was interested in workers' conditions in the Soviet Union. After I described to him what I saw, he said, "I'd rather be poor and free in France than half poor and regimented in Russia." Mother complained, "How can you come from the other end of the world and only stay for dinner?" I promised to see the whole family again before returning to Japan.

I had given my mother $100 to send to my youngest brother Jacquot, fighting in France's colonial war in Algeria, but she decided to ration my gift in four payments over four months. From my experience in the French Army, I knew Jacquot was barely making enough for a decent dinner, so I wanted him to have the money all at once so he could invite all his buddies in his squad to a feast. To my mother, $100 was an outrageous sum, but I argued, "Jacquot is risking his life 24 hours a day. Send him the whole hundred!" Eventually, we compromised, agreeing to send him two payments of $50 each. Either way, I knew $100 in 1961 would cheer Jacquot up in French Algeria.

Seeing my family again left me feeling alone, for in a way, we had become strangers. Sending money to Jacquot "to have a feast" was misinterpreted as "my arrogance with money." My beloved sister Paulette who brought me food in the lonely forest of Marly was no longer the sister who cared for me. She said I lost her through my own selfishness, living in worlds separated by thousands of miles.

To escape mother's insensitivity and father's criticism, all my sisters married young, moved out, and were struggling to bring up their own children. They were tired of hearing mother constantly praise their older brother's "wonderful achievements."

No one in my family understood the "journalistic first" of the Siberia story and my excitement, nor did they seem to care—they certainly didn't care how people in Siberia survived. Only father was curious and shared some enthusiasm. I expected some praise but instead felt complete indifference from my family: their general reaction to my success was, "Who cares? So what?" The flight back to Tokyo via Anchorage, Alaska, was a long one.

The July 21, 1961, issue of *Life* with Connery's text and my black-and-white essay on Siberia closed at 16 pages with photography receiving the upper byline as was customary at *Life*. The story was billed; "Two Yanks in Siberia: Surprising Encounters with Grassroots Russians." It was thrilling to see my essay in *Life,* but what I loved most was being called a "Yank."

In the September 22, 1961, issue of *Time* magazine, editors introduced my eight-page color essay and Don's text as "The new Siberia....rarely visited, even more rarely photographed by outsiders."

Though Rowland Gould's coverage never appeared on CBS television, he published a series on Siberia in Britain's *Daily Mail*, a popular newspaper with a huge circulation. I was sorry about my friend Rowland's bad luck, yet gratified that *Life*, a weekly magazine, had not been scooped by CBS on such a major story.

After our trip, Soviets again closed Siberia to all Western journalists, so my photographic essay remained exclusive for a long time and was distributed widely throughout Europe.

Paris Match, the foremost French picture magazine, had hoped to get its own team on the Trans-Siberian and turned down its chance to publish my photos after *Life* at a customary rate, but with Siberia again closed, Black Star London eventually sold my essay to *Paris Match* "at a premium." The magazine published 10 pages in their April 21, 1962, issue, nearly a year after *Life*'s release.

Though all my photographs were stamped, "John Launois," the editors of *Paris Match* chose to begin their text, saying, "The most secret country in the world, usually closed to Westerners...opened its smallest doors to our reporters...From the Pacific to Moscow...here are the pictures of *Jean Launois*."

Not only had editors used my French first name, they called me "one of their reporters." I could only imagine the editors misled readers because at that time, *Paris Match* could not accept second place to America's *Life*, which had inspired *Match*'s creation in 1949.

Shortly after the *Life* and *Time* stories appeared, my pictures were published in West Germany. In a telephoto picture showing some 80 faces in an Irkutsk stadium, several German mothers recognized their long-lost sons and asked for help in poignant letters about their sons made prisoners on the Russian front, apparently shipped to Siberia as laborers, never to be heard from again.

There wasn't much I could do but tell them what they already knew from my captions. Our New York office forwarded their letters to the Irkutsk authorities and suggested the mothers try getting visas to Siberia. But it was an exercise in futility: anti-German feelings ran high in Russia, and Siberia was again closed to Westerners.

Our trip across Siberia opened my mind, roused my curiosity, and awakened my need for wider horizons: I wanted more first-hand knowledge of places and faces other than in Asia. Though China was still a land I longed to see, my applications for a visa were denied for four years. "Red China" was hermetically sealed since 1949, closed off to all Americans except a select few who were considered politically acceptable to Mao Tse-tung.

"If not China, then where?" I learned from Curt Prendergast, who had become Time Inc.'s bureau chief in Paris, that *Life* assigned stories on the Middle East as well as most of continental Europe from his office.

JAPAN'S HIGHEST PEAK AND
MIGHTIEST SUPERTANKERS

MT. F.UJI, NAGASAKI 1961

Returning to Japan, I spent a few happy days with Yukiko and discussed leaving Tokyo for Paris or Beirut. We had visited Lebanon briefly on one of our trips together, and on our last European trip, we felt liberated from the racial prejudice that our marriage had inspired in Japan. So the idea of moving, particularly to Paris, appealed to Yukiko.

Kurt Kornfeld approached Richard Pollard, *Life*'s director of photography, to request my change of location, but Pollard responded, "Europe and the Middle East are well covered from London or Paris, and Paris is fully staffed. *Life* gave John breaks in Asia and he performed. John is valuable to us in Asia. We need him there."

My heart sunk but I understood a freelancer on contract accepted certain limitations. I had to be where I was needed—only *Life* staffers could request a change of location.

John Dominis urged Pollard to offer me a staff position, but I wasn't sure I wanted to be a staffer despite the glamour attached to the job. I enjoyed my freedom as a freelancer and the fact that all my photographic rights belonged to me and not eternally to *Life*. My contract gave me the right to release all my work published in *Life*, as well as the right to work for *Geographic* and all publications except *Look* and *Newsweek*.

The magazine gave me my major breaks. *Life* always expected the best from its photographers in a culture that demanded discipline and excellence, and though I had disagreements, I soldiered on, forgot about a Paris or Beirut base, and was grateful to be part of the world's most important picture publication.

In early October 1961, on *Life*'s expense account, I purchased the best mountaineering gear money could buy to cover John F. Kennedy's Interior Secretary Stewart Udall as he climbed Japan's 12,397-foot Mount Fuji.

Thousands made the pilgrimage to the sacred summit of Fuji, but the mountain was closed to all pilgrims and climbers during the "dangerous season." The Japanese made exceptions for experienced climbers like the American politician, a famous outdoorsman.

Though I climbed a few mountain trails in the steamy jungles of Laos, photographing soldiers at war, I had no experience climbing ice-covered mountains, 12,000 feet up.

I loved looking at mountains from a distance or a plane, but I did not belong to that category of men like Sir Edmund Hillary who climbed Mount Everest in 1953 basically "because it was there."

At dawn, after a sleepless night on another assignment, I met Secretary Udall at base camp where he challenged me, saying, "John, the last time *Life* magazine climbed with me, the photographer, exhausted, dropped out before reaching the summit." I assured him, "Mr. Secretary, I will make it to the top."

Escorted by two American military mountain climbers carrying radio and other gear, the secretary set off at first light, followed by a horde of Japanese photographers falling into a long Indian-file line of men with cameras, notebooks, pencils, and some caged homing pigeons.

Despite great advances in communication in 1961 Japan, the messengers that carried a single piece of negative film from remote areas like Fuji were often homing pigeons. Motorcycle messengers in ever-increasing traffic jams were slower than pigeons and useless on Mount Fuji.

The climb started in a media circus, but slowly the large crowd of newsmen thinned as many dropped out in exhaustion. At 12,000 feet, most disappeared under heavy clouds blanketing the mountain below. Only a few of us were hanging on, breathing heavily, climbing a few feet at a time.

I made the mistake of carrying too much equipment but continued up the icy peak by following the footsteps of Don Connery of *Time,* whose only extra weight was his personal camera, notebook, and pencil. As the grueling climb ensued, I had to remind myself constantly of my promise to make it to the top.

In a final effort, I photographed Secretary Udall lifting his foot and crampon boot as he passed under the heavily iced *torii,* the sacred gateway to the summit of the mystical mountain.

Secretary Udall congratulated me for having "made it to the top," and my picture made a double page in *Life*'s November 17, 1961, issue entitled: "America's Udall-san to the Top of Fuji." It was the first and last mountain I ever climbed.

Soon after Fuji, *Life* editors cabled me to proceed to Saigon to meet Hong Kong-based Scot Leavitt and London-based Hank Walker, the celebrated war photographer, for what they called a "blockbuster" story.

By October 1961, Vietcong guerrilla penetration from the north had expanded into South Vietnam, while economic aid from the U.S. sharply increased, along with military commitment. Soon there'd be 24,000 American military advisers, officers, and men in Vietnam to advise and train 170,000 South Vietnamese forces. It was the largest escalation of U.S. involvement in Vietnam to date.

I'd rendezvous with Leavitt and Walker at the Caravelle Hotel in Saigon, later known as Ho Chi Minh City. From Walker, I knew I'd learn about covering war and combat. He'd been trained as a combat photographer serving in the Marines in World War II and for *Life* during the Korean War from 1950 to 1953.

His fame and reputation preceded him. His picture of John Kennedy and his brother Robert huddled together in conversation in a Los Angeles hotel room during the 1960 Democratic convention was considered "a masterpiece," while his reputation for being "clear headed and cool in combat" was reassuring to a novice in war photojournalism like myself.

A "blockbuster" meant 10 or more pages in the prestigious news lead section of *Life*. I was accredited to Washington's Department of Defense, providing access to U.S. trainers, and was mentally prepared for action. All-out war between the two halves of Vietnam looked certain: at any moment, the Communist North seemed ready to strike at the South.

In 1954, France's colonists in Vietnam were defeated by Ho Chi-Minh's forces at Dien Bien Phu in the north and retreated south of the 17th parallel. Later that year in Geneva, France and Ho Chi-Minh agreed to a de facto split of Vietnam. The Vietminh would voluntarily stay north of the 17-degree demarcation line—the 17th parallel.

In 1956, the Geneva Convention, which hoped to establish a unified Vietnam, recognized the north and south as separate countries. Following the peace treaty, the U.S. for the first time gave economic assistance to the government of South Vietnam.

In 1961, while there was still time for apéritifs, long lunches, and social evenings at French clubs in Saigon, the Vietcong were demanding protection taxes from French businesses still operating in Vietnam. Though old colonial habits of leisure still prevailed, an era was ending, but the French community in Saigon was unwilling to admit their lifestyle in South Vietnam was doomed, despite daily penetrations by Vietcong guerrillas.

Walker, Leavitt, and I expected a window of time for the start of an offensive. From local sources, we heard of Vietcong infiltrations close to Saigon, but there was nothing to see. At the Caravelle Hotel, we discussed daily briefings from U.S. advisers to the South Vietnamese forces and tried to determine the next move, but we heard absolutely nothing.

Day after day we waited, always alert for the first signs of *Life*'s "blockbuster." We were ready for action, but U.S. advisers had no information. All sources could say was that something was coming, but no one knew where or when.

Days and weeks went by, and we were still in Saigon, drinking at sidewalk cafés along the Mekong Delta, waiting for a mission that remained uncertain. Charged for action with nothing to do as days dragged on, our rational faculties wore thin. Needless to say, we sometimes drank too much.

By November 23, my 33rd birthday and our 36th day of waiting in Saigon for an indefinite assignment, Walker and I had photographed practically nothing. After wasting more than a month in Vietnam, Hank and I left for Tokyo: *Life*'s "blockbuster" was a bust. A few years later of course, all of Vietnam was consumed by warfare.

Landing in Tokyo, I invited Hank to my home where Yukiko had prepared a traditional Japanese dinner and reception for our "honored guest." Talking late into the night, he remarked that my Trans-Siberian essay was "a great first" and seemed genuinely impressed as he looked through a compilation of my photographs of Japan. Compliments from a top professional meant a lot and cheered my spirit. As we drove Hank back to his hotel, I had no idea our fateful meeting would lead to a significant change in my life in the near future.

The next assignment for *Life* took me to the western shore of India in December. In a military overthrow, the Indian Army put an end to Portugal's long colonial rule in Goa, otherwise known as "Portuguese India."

After hiring a driver in Bombay, I arrived at press headquarters for the conflict where a number of journalists and I would spend the night sleeping on cots. Though I paid my driver part of a large "danger fee" to drive me all the way to Goa's capital, he disappeared by morning after hearing sounds of artillery fire.

About 250 miles south of Bombay on the Indian side of the border, authorities made false promises to the foreign press about taking them to Goa, when actually they were preventing them from entering. "At any moment," we were told, "transportation will be arranged for all journalists." In the afternoon, I arrived early at the press briefing, held in a makeshift building resembling a barn. For an hour I waited alone, sitting behind the press officer's desk, spinning a French beret left on a desk. I couldn't help noticing that under the beret was a "Confidential" cable from New Delhi instructing the field press officer to: "Hold the foreign press in India until further instructions."

At the briefing, the press officer denied those instructions, but by my asking, he knew I had read the cable. Realizing we could be held up for days, I discreetly left the Indian base camp, got a ride in a dugout canoe, and crossed the river separating India and Goa.

Reaching the shore of Goa, I immediately fell in with a small group of Indian Army officers. Brazenly, I introduced myself. "It's wonderful to see you," I said. "I'm here for *Life* magazine from New York. Officials in New Delhi assured me you'd take me to the capital in Goa." Welcoming me, they said, "You're lucky you found us because there are many minefields between here and the capital." At the entrance of a hotel, we bid goodbye as I thanked them enthusiastically.

The fall of Goa marked the end of European colonial history in India. First I photographed the Portuguese soldiers who had become prisoners of the Indian Army. Then I met the new governor, the victorious Major General K.P. Candeth who commanded India's 17th Infantry Division, and posed him before numerous oil paintings of the Portuguese governors who had ruled the territory for the past four and a half centuries. The picture made *Life*'s January 5, 1962, "Newsfront" and a double page of "The Editor's Choice" in *Life*'s February 12, 1962, international edition.

After a few days of photography in Goa, I was attempting to obtain a military permit to secure a taxi to Bombay, when I bumped into the Indian press officer I had left behind on the Indian border. This time, he was escorting a group of correspondents into Goa. When he saw me, he shouted, "Our military police will arrest you, and we will prosecute you for illegally entering Goa in wartime and for reading a confidential cable, which was an act of spying. On both counts, you're liable to receive a heavy fine and jail time. That should cool your American arrogance."

I didn't want to end up in an Indian jail indefinitely, so when he quieted down, I answered as calmly as possible, "As you wish sir, but when the press publishes the contents of that cable instructing you to hold the world's press on the Indian border, you sir, will have shamed your government and you sir, will have to explain to your superiors in New Delhi why you left a confidential cable on your desk under your beret in an empty, unguarded briefing room at least one hour before your press conference."

Bluffing that I had taken photographs of the cable, I continued, "Let's be civilized. I promise you I will not file the contents of that confidential cable nor release photographs of it if you simply get me a military permit for my taxi driver to leave Goa." We shook hands and within an hour I was on my way to Bombay.

It was just before Christmas when I reached New Delhi to reunite with Yukiko and photograph Mark Robson's film, *Nine Hours to Rama,* based on Stanley Wolpert's novel about Mahatma Gandhi's long struggle against poverty, corruption, violence, and colonialism in India.

In New Delhi and Bombay, filming went on for weeks. Strangely enough, in order to buy liquor for daily cocktails, the director, his crew, cast, and I were forced by government regulations to sign a document for the city's authorities, certifying and swearing that we were all alcoholics. Yukiko, the only nondrinker in the group, was the exception.

By February 20, my coverage of *Nine Hours to Rama* was finished. Director of Black Star London, Dolf Seedorf, had already sold my story to the *London Sunday Times* "color section" magazine for a cover run and six pages in April.

In a Fleet Street pub, Dolf and I discussed further distribution while listening to the BBC's radio report on Lieutenant Colonel John Glenn's orbit around the earth. Sitting at the next table, a large group of British journalists raised their glasses in my direction. "To you, Yank," they toasted, "and to your John Glenn." It was the second time I was called a Yank. I felt moved, and with thanks toasted the journalists and John Glenn.

I returned to Tokyo where a nice assignment from *Life International* was waiting: The editors wanted an essay on Mitsubishi's giant Nagasaki shipyards where the world's biggest supertankers were produced.

I was glad to take the assignment, because an essay meant I'd have the poetic and artistic freedom I was never allowed while covering news.

Mitsubishi's management gave me carte blanche, and after securing access to research labs and the entire shipyard, I looked for reality and abstraction. While I photographed the launch of a 53,000-ton supertanker in Nagasaki, I was told it took 1,100 men to produce the colossal vessel. Chairman of the Board Kaneo Niwa agreed to let me photograph all 1,100 men on the bow of the tanker while I looked down from the top of a towering crane: organizing the shot took several hours.

I had no idea what it cost Mitsubishi to assemble so many workers for a single photo, but I suspected the chairman imagined a few pages in *Life International* was worth the expense. After a few weeks of shooting, my essay closed with nine pages in the May 21, 1962, issue.

When early copies of the magazine arrived in Tokyo, Time-Life's permanent correspondent, Frank Iwama, said, "John, before you look at your essay, let me read you the opening paragraph of the text. Because when you first came to this office more than six years ago, you had no track record. You looked starved and were a newcomer, totally unknown—I didn't see how you could break through. Now listen to this."

With emotion I had never seen in Frank before, he read me the editor's leading paragraph: "Beauty is whimsical, sprite, sometimes brazen and self-flaunting, sometimes so shy and elusive that it dwells unseen amid a thousand eyes. Its manifestations, to the rarely sensitive beholder, are myriad; among them is the bewitching dragonlike pattern on the preceding page, in prosaic reality a plastic scale model of a turbine blade undergoing tests and revealing in its varied colors the intensities of stress. The image, like the others on these and the following pages, was captured in a photographic tour de force by John Launois."

Like an older brother, Frank always helped me with story ideas though as a Japanese Canadian, he seldom showed his emotions. I was moved even more by his feelings than by the tribute to my work.

Frank added, "John, I have never seen editors of *Life* praising a photographer in the opening paragraph. I used to worry about you. But after following your work for the past few years, I can see you are well on your way. I'm proud of you."

For the first time in seven years, we hugged each other. Then we looked at all nine pages of the Mitsubishi story and saw how *Life International*'s art director made a truly beautiful layout. Upon seeing the issue, Mitsubishi ordered a thousand copies and Chairman of the Board Niwa invited the entire Tokyo Time-Life office to attend a lavish dinner. I sat next to him as "guest of honor" while graceful geishas catered to our every need and whim.

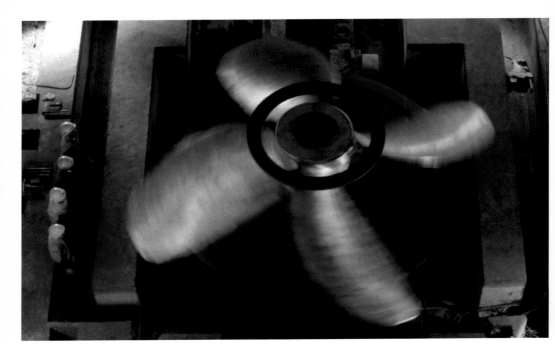

As sake and beer flowed, I asked Chairman Niwa, who seemed to be in his sixties, about his early years as an engineer at Mitsubishi Shipbuilding. He told me, "Before World War II, my very first job, sailing on British ships, was to make drawings of the English waterclosets. I was required to make precise drawings of the shape, width, interior, exterior of toilet seats and flushing systems." Laughing together, I interjected, "So you had to travel a long way before building your supertankers." "A very long way," he answered.

As the evening came to an end, we all sang the well-known "Sakura," a mournful song about the ephemeral beauty of the cherry blossom, a poetic metaphor for the brevity of life.

Sounds of the Mitsubishi party geishas playing their three-string samisens were still in my mind when I had to rush to northern Thailand to cover the arrival of 5,000 U.S. troops, tanks, planes, and helicopters dispatched to forestall a Chinese-supported onslaught by communist guerrillas from North Vietnam and Laos.

With a U.S. Marine helicopter crew, I flew to the northern tip of Thailand to photograph the Mekong River, which separated Thailand from Laos. In early May it was swollen from the first rains of the monsoon. Flying low about 250 feet under clouds, in slashing rain, the helicopter shook violently, pushed and pulled from side to side in sudden gusts of wind. Shooting with a fast shutter speed and small aperture, I captured a dramatic double page of the swollen Mekong with Thailand in the foreground and Laos in the distance under the dark and threatening clouds of the monsoon.

It was a rough ride, so when I finally said, "OK, I have my picture—let's get back to the airstrip in Udon," the pilots and crew cheered. My coverage made four pages in *Life*'s July 1, 1962, "Newsfronts," entitled, "The Mekong River: New line in the cold war vocabulary."

CITY OF SONG

THE SCHRAMMELMUSIK CHALLENGE

VIENNA 1962

O n my return to Tokyo the third week of May, I received a *National Geographic* cable inviting me to photograph the beautiful city of Vienna, Austria. Editors wrote: "The end of May and early June, a time of many festivals in Vienna, would be a good time to start if you can free yourself."

Yukiko had already read the cable and loved the idea, and I immediately accepted the assignment. Again I heard music in my head but it was the orchestral sounds of Strauss, Mozart, Haydn, and Schubert.

After checking into Vienna's Imperial Hotel, I met with Franc Shor on the terrace of the Sacher Hotel, a few steps from the State Opera. He seemed totally at ease in Vienna's glorious imperial past.

Shor greeted me like a lost old friend, and I thanked him for the excellent Château Mouton Rothschild from his private cellar at the George V Hotel. For our story, we agreed to work separately from the beginning and meet for dinner when necessary.

In Vienna, a city of such illustrious musical traditions, where in the late eighteenth century, Mozart, Beethoven, and Schubert composed many of their greatest masterpieces, it seemed natural that the first picture in Vienna would celebrate music.

Within a week, Shor introduced me to four members of the Vienna Symphony Orchestra. In a labor of love, they had brought back Schrammelmusik, once popular folk music, which Johann Strauss felt captured "the real spirit of Vienna" but had disappeared in the 1890s with the deaths of composers Josef and Johann Schrammel.

My four new friends would pick me up after concerts to take me to their favorite *Heurige* or "This year's wine." In the gardens of vineyards, the quartet played their beloved Schrammelmusik as we drank fine wine all night.

My coverage of Vienna was broad, encompassing images of the State Opera, ballet, museums, the old Danube with beautiful women of Vienna sunbathing on shore, Saint Stephan's Cathedral where I sat in a choir singing Mozart's Coronation Mass, and of course, the baroque summer residence of the Habsburg Emperor's eighteenth-century, 1,400-room Schönbrunn Palace. There, at age six, Mozart played harpsicord for Empress Maria Theresa, the mother of Marie Antoinette, who was guillotined in France in 1793.

It didn't take long to fall in love with the city, as the muddy fields of the swollen Mekong and steamy jungles of Laos swiftly receded from my mind.

Yukiko joined me from Tokyo and was soon enchanted by the charm and romance of Vienna: in our beautiful room at the Imperial, she was always delighted to find a single red rose on her breakfast tray. Following our luxurious hotel stay, we spent most of our month together at a rented apartment in the inner city.

It was amusing to see how easily Franc Shor adapted to the leisurely pace and traditional manners of Vienna. Like most Viennese men of standing, he'd kiss the hands of ladies that he encountered daily.

When he left for Washington D.C., he gave me a calling card with compliments of another vintage Bordeaux from his private cellar—this time I was actually going to miss him.

Shor was supposed to complete his text within a few months but somehow could never make it happen. His later drafts were rejected but I never knew why, so in 1962 my two and a half months of work on Vienna was shelved at *Geographic* for five years. But in 1967, Viennese-born staff writer Peter White was assigned to write the city's story again, and I returned to Vienna to complete the work.

One challenge from my first trip I finally solved. I had been stymied about how to portray the music that disappeared after the death of Josef and Johann Schrammel and was revived more than half a century later by my favorite Viennese quartet. I pondered the subject until at last I envisioned musical notes floating in the air as musicians played. To create this image I would photograph the quartet through a six-by-four-foot sheet of glass. The first few violin notes of the lost music were drawn on the glass in green colors. When the quartet saw my test picture, they exclaimed, "It's wonderful! The notes of Schrammel are floating in the air. You've photographed the spirit of Vienna." The story was finally published in the June 1968 issue with 40 pages of text and pictures entitled: "Vienna: The City of Song."

Near the end of August 1962, Yukiko and I returned to the steamy heat of Tokyo where our bedroom was still half air-conditioned. Even our glass wind chimes in the slight breeze failed to cool our minds.

I completed a few minor photographic assignments but without enthusiasm—we missed Vienna. In October, India declared a "state of emergency" when a long-simmering border dispute with China flared up in the Himalayan Mountains. *Life* immediately assigned me to cover the conflict, so I took off for New Delhi.

TIMING IS EVERYTHING

AN UNEXPECTED OFFER

TOKYO 1962

At New Delhi's International Airport, I was met by Time-Life's permanent correspondent in India, Jim Shepherd. He eased me through India's bureaucratic customs services and led me to the first-class waiting lounge to introduce me to Henry Luce, the major creator of the Time Inc. media empire and the most influential of the world's "press lords," who was waiting for a flight to Paris.

Shepherd said, "Mr. Luce, this is John Launois, here to photograph the India-China War." After we shook hands and I said, "It's a pleasure to meet you," I set about arranging my photographic gear a few feet away from Luce, while Shepherd whispered in my ear, "You better pray he catches his flight. There isn't a single hotel room available in New Delhi, so I booked you his suite at the Ashoka Hotel."

While we waited with Luce for his departure, Shepherd briefed both of us. "Primarily attacking Towang and Se Pass, the Chinese have pushed through the Himalayan Mountains. They could roll on to Indian military headquarters at Tezpur, then to the Brahma Putra Valley, Assam Plains, and even the western Indian states."

"This is very serious," Luce said. I asked Jim, "Has the bureau applied for my accreditation with the Indian military?" "Yes," Jim said, "but be prepared for heavy censorship and limited access to the front."

Unfortunately, my encounter with Henry Luce was all too brief. I wanted to tell him how his prospectus for *Life*, "To see life, to see the world, to eyewitness great events...shadows in the jungle and on the moon," inspired me to become a photojournalist at the age of 19 in France.

I wanted to tell him how I had already photographed shadows in the jungle and hoped to one day photograph shadows on the moon.

I also wanted to ask why *Life* editors shelved my pictures of the court-martial of innocent students in South Korea. But there was no time: his flight was called, we shook hands, and said goodbye.

By the first week of November, some 2,500 Indian soldiers had been killed, and the Chinese had taken approximately 2,500 square miles of Indian territory. In New Delhi, I photographed the anxious and dejected Prime Minister Jawaharal Nehru in a state of disillusionment after India's neutrality had been violated.

I photographed ill-equipped Indian soldiers still using World War I English rifles but ready for battle west of Se Pass. When an Indian press officer demanded I hand over my film so he could send it to New Delhi's censorship bureau, I quickly removed my exposed film from two cameras and switched them with unexposed rolls. Feigning anger, I pulled out the film from the unexposed cartridges and exposed them to the light before giving them to the surprised officer. He complained, "Now we'll never know what you photographed."

The India-China dispute regarding the ownership of remote mountain territories soon slowed to a halt. In normal times, the fight between the two nations with immense populations, each still struggling with widespread poverty, would have been the biggest story in the world. But events in Asia were overshadowed by October's Cuban Missile Crisis, and the horrifying possibility of thermonuclear war between the United States and the Soviet Union.

My coverage of the India-China War made 1962's November 9 and 16 issues of *Life*. The cover on November 16 was of one of the pictures that escaped the censors: a tight close-up of an Indian soldier with his rifle "ready for battle." It identified no particular battlefield and had not breached India's security. I had no way of knowing that my professional life was about to change and that picture would be my last cover for *Life*.

On November 10, back in Tokyo, I had barely unpacked and cleaned my equipment when I received a phone call from Hank Walker in London. "Grab a pen, some paper, and listen carefully," he said. "The era of Norman Rockwell covers at *The Saturday Evening Post* is ending."

Norman Rockwell was a celebrated illustrator who painted countless covers for the *Post* with scenes of an idealized America. Walker elaborated, "A new editorial team headed by Clay Blair Jr. as editor-in-chief of all Curtis Publishing Company magazines is modernizing *The Saturday Evening Post*. It's a generational change, and for the first time in its history, photojournalism will play a major part in the making of the new *Post*. I have quit *Life,* and will be assistant managing editor for photography."

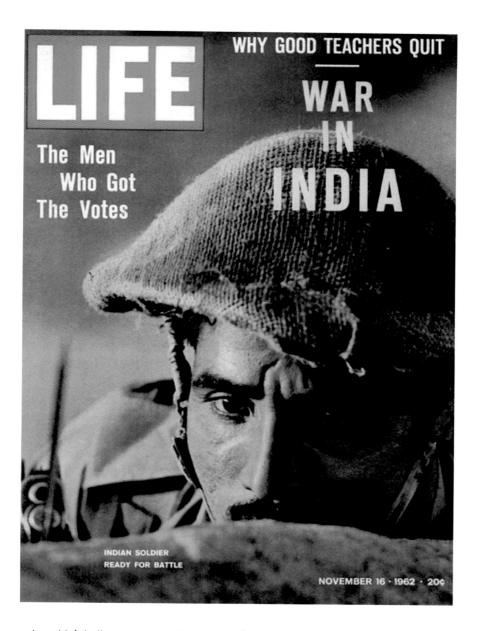

WHY GOOD TEACHERS QUIT

LIFE

WAR
IN
INDIA

The Men
Who Got
The Votes

INDIAN SOLDIER
READY FOR BATTLE

NOVEMBER 16 · 1962 · 20¢

I couldn't believe my ears. Hank Walker's prestige at *Life* after 15 years was so great, he could have demanded any base, anywhere in the world—yet he resigned. It seemed incredible.

Hank went on, "I'm proposing contracts to five American photojournalists, and you're high on the list. I can't tell you the names of the other four right now, but they are men at the top of their profession, and I know you admire them. Some you know personally."

Intrigued, I wondered who the others were when Hank said, "Here's my proposal. At the *Post*, you'll be guaranteed a yearly minimum of $20,000. And whatever your day and space rate is at *Life*, I'll double it."

It would mean my day rate would jump from $75 to $150, while my fee would increase from $350 to $700 for a color page and from $600 to $1,200 for a cover photo.

In 1962, a $20,000 yearly guarantee was equivalent to more than $200,000 a year in the early twenty-first century. Considering Black Star's president Ernest Mayer only made $10,000 a year, $20,000 was an incredible offer.

Walker elaborated, "Naturally you'll own all your copyrights for distribution in Europe and the rest of the world. You'll maintain your right to work for *Geographic*, *Newsweek*, and all publications except *Look* and Time Inc. magazines. All work will be bylined with equal points for writers and photographers. Also you won't cover hard news except for extraordinary events."

Hank assured me, "Essentially you'll be working on photographic essays, which you can script yourself. In the new *Post*, you'll belong to a new team from day one, and your voice will be heard on all assignments you take. And no projects will be shelved—damned distressing for photographers, and as you know, common at *Life*." Hank clinched the deal when he said, "Manhattan will be your base, but with your experience in Asia and elsewhere, you can expect assignments anywhere in the world."

I was stunned. I promised Hank an answer within a week. Though his generous financial offer was extraordinary for 1962 and appealing, what swayed me was the idea of being based in Manhattan, with the possibility of covering stories "anywhere in the world."

I discussed the offer with Yukiko, and although she was apprehensive about living in Manhattan, she said she'd support my decision. The idea of leaving *Life* was emotionally difficult for me as photographing for the magazine had been a dream of mine from the very beginning of my career. I had come a long way and won a measure of respect at *Life*, but truth be told, my work for the magazine was limited: Dick Pollard, the director of photography, made it clear I was "needed in Asia."

Despite Pollard's opinion, I believed my work was becoming stale in Asia, so I found myself at an impasse. To discuss the idea of leaving *Life*, I turned to my old friend Keyes Beech, the Pulitzer Prize-winning correspondent for the *Chicago Daily News* who had been in the Far East for 12 years. "I should have left Asia years ago," he said. "Now it's too late. I'll probably finish my life here."

Keyes assured me, "Your instinct is right, especially if you're afraid of your work becoming stale. Don't make my mistake—timing is everything, and the opportunity may never come again."

When I informed Black Star of my pending decision to take Walker's offer, Mayer, Kornfeld, and Chapnick all gave me their blessing, telling me, "John, this has to be the highest paying contract ever offered to a freelance photojournalist."

Black Star would continue to represent me, take care of billings and worldwide distribution, and would reduce their rate to a flat 15 percent. I called Hank in London, told him I'd like to accept his generous offer, and agreed to meet him in Manhattan in the beginning of January.

Though Keyes and Black Star gave me encouragement, no one at Time-Life's Tokyo bureau shared my enthusiasm, even my old friend Frank Iwama had reservations. I told Pollard that Hank Walker had given me the opportunity to leave Asia. Later I heard my decision had created some bitterness with *Life* editors who felt I was ungrateful, since the magazine had given me my first break. That was true, they had given me that first break, but *The Saturday Evening Post* was giving me my second: my conscience was clear.

By mid-December, Yukiko and I had sold or given away our American-made appliances and everything we didn't need. Time-Life's office manager, Imai-san, bought our "little Renault" while Yukiko and I kept our luxurious Ford V-8 until our last week in Japan—then I simply gave it to my old and often broke friend Rowland Gould for a drink and a song.

After the packers finally left, Yukiko and I moved into the Imperial Hotel and attended several farewell parties, including a lavish affair thrown by the Time-Life bureau.

MANHATTAN

TWO TUDOR PLACE

NEW YORK 1963

I t was our last Christmas and New Year's Eve in Tokyo: seven years spent in Japan and Asia were coming to a close. While Yukiko spent a few weeks with her family in Sakuragaoka near Osaka, I flew to New York to organize our new life in Manhattan.

As I rode from New York's Idlewild Airport in a limousine packed to the ceiling with 3 suitcases and 11 cases of photographic gear, I remembered the deep shame I felt arriving some 12 years earlier on the docks of southwest Manhattan as I showed the customs officer the meager possessions in my cheap cardboard suitcase. The aluminum boxes filling the limousine's passenger compartment made me think, "You are no longer a frightened poor immigrant," reassuring my insecure ego.

I remembered November 1950, my first night in America at the YMCA, the acute pain in my stomach, the anxiety, and fear of beginning with nothing on a new continent, without even my own camera to prove I was a photographer. I had no idea then how I'd begin to climb the ladder of photojournalism—to grasp the history of my adopted country, understand how it functioned, and ultimately learn how to become an American. Though I eventually took junior college night courses in literature, I wondered how I'd master a new language. Much of my limited English was the product of listening to English song lyrics.

During my early days in California, I carefully prepared my mind for a difficult journey that I'd take one step at a time. I had traveled a long way to become an American photojournalist: two years in the U.S. Army had accelerated my integration, but the road to a successful career had been rough. Seven years in the Far East introduced me to top-flight American correspondents and Pulitzer Prize winners, many of whom had been kind, generous, and helpful to the young newcomer I had been. Most were well-educated, articulate university graduates who spoke a refined American language: I learned from them, absorbed hard lessons in American journalism, and eventually could beat the best of them—at least sometimes.

Riding in my limousine, I recalled days of hardship in Japan and the noodles that had been a key to my survival. When my driver asked, "Where to, sir?" it occurred to me I could tell him, "Take me to The Plaza or The Pierre or the Waldorf Astoria." The thought warmed my heart, but instead, I instructed the driver to take me to the more modest Tudor City Hotel on 42nd Street close to where Black Star's Kurt Kornfeld lived—for Kurt had already placed a deposit for us on a spacious three-and-a-half-room apartment in his doorman building at Two Tudor Place.

A Manhattan base was the ultimate goal in my career, the place to win, the place to breathe the rarefied air of success. It had taken seven years to get invited through the front door of the city, and now I felt sure Manhattan would give me a chance to rise higher in my career.

At Tudor City, Kurt Kornfeld in his German accent said, "Welcome to New York, my very dear young friend." Seeing Kurt brought back good memories from 1960 when Yukiko and I spent time with him at his apartment and were impressed by its location adjacent to the United Nations headquarters.

Kurt had found us an apartment with southern exposure. Lucky for us, an heir to the Stevens Textiles Company was moving out of apartment 8-K. Kurt introduced me to the Stevenses, a charming young couple who invited us into our future apartment.

"God, it's huge," I thought. The bedroom looked bigger than our Tokyo living room and garden combined. The kitchen was spacious and fully equipped, just right for Yukiko: I couldn't even fry an egg, but Yukiko had elevated cooking to an art form. Remembering our Japanese apartment, I asked the Stevenses, "Do the air conditioners cool the apartment from floor to ceiling?" They answered, "Yes, of course—what a strange question." They thought my explanation of the "misery and pleasure zones" was hilarious.

The Stevenses offered us cocktails, and sipping my drink, I walked to the southern windows of our first apartment in Manhattan. From our eighth-floor view, I could see the Empire State Building illuminated just a few blocks away. "So long Tokyo," I said to myself. "Hello New York."

The next morning I met with Kornfeld, Mayer, Chapnick, and Howard's cousin, Ben Chapnick, the future chief of Black Star, who congratulated me on my contract with *The Saturday Evening Post*. The rest of the day I spent with Hank Walker, in charge of photography, and the *Post*'s new editor, Clay Blair.

"*The Saturday Evening Post* was traditionally a writer's magazine," Hank said as he poured us Scotch. "For over two centuries, the magazine published just about every famous American writer, from Edgar Allan Poe, Fenimore Cooper, and Harriet Beecher Stowe to Steinbeck and Hemingway. Artwork and photos functioned only to illustrate the writer's work. Under Clay Blair's editorial leadership, the *Post* will change radically by publishing not only America's best writers but America's best photojournalists as well. That's why you're here."

I was flattered but didn't really know if I belonged in the ranks of "America's best." How could a creative person searching for higher fulfillment ever know if he was one of the best? I knew I had reached the level of numerous photographers I had admired at the start of my career in 1955, but in 1963, the list of photographers I hoped to learn from was reduced to Eugene Smith, David Douglas Duncan, Gordon Parks, and a few others.

"All assignments approved in advance by the editor will be published," Hank promised. Many photojournalists believed a story could be entirely told through pictures with short texts and captions: that had been *Life*'s winning formula. The *Post* was going for a different approach.

I endorsed the idea. "Words and images should complement each other like a movie," I said. "Like a film director, a good photojournalist should distill thousands of words on any subject, produce the visual essence of a writer's work, and add to a shooting script the elements that words can't describe."

I was on my third Scotch. That was my limit but for Hank, built like a front lineman of a football team, he might as well have been drinking milk. Whiskey did absolutely nothing to him, while a single sip of my third left me wobbly. Hank noticed and took my drink away. Ordering coffee from room service, he said, "Hang in there John, I have to explain a few things."

After two cups of coffee, I felt better. Hank continued, "As you know, I've recruited five of the best photojournalists for the new *Post*. We have John Zimmerman, Burt Glinn from Magnum in New York, and John Bryson from the West Coast. My old friend John Dominis won't be joining us—he feels *Life* magazine is his life, so instead I'm recruiting Larry Schiller from the West Coast. For you and Zimmerman, I've decided to raise your minimum guarantee from $20,000 to $25,000."

I couldn't be sure why our guarantees were raised, other than the fact that Zimmerman and I had contracts with Time Inc. when Hank was persuading us to join. "Since the *Post* will be paying you double-space rate and double-day rate," Hank explained, "in one year from the *Post* alone, not including foreign rights, you'll probably clear $50,000."

I was stunned. A good yearly income for a family of four in 1963 was $7,000, and only 40 percent of American families had reached that level.

Hank asked, "Do you have a financial adviser?" I laughed and said, "Are you kidding? After expenses of moving here and investing in my equipment, what I'll have left is hardly what a financial adviser would be interested in."

Impatiently he said, "John, I'm telling you, this year you'll need one. Try calling Ned Beinstock. He's a financial wizard who helped make some of us rich while we were covering the world." Being rich had never been a driving force in my life, but the idea of $50,000 in 1963 prompted me to call the wizard.

Unfortunately, Beinstock had retired. After I related my conversation with Hank to Black Star's Ernest Mayer, whose salary was only $10,000 a year, he said, "John, Mr. Walker is right. You'll need a financial adviser. Get one. In the meantime, we'll deposit your credit in your savings account." Foolishly, I waited years before I found an adviser, but by then it was a little too late, an oversight I'd later regret.

I appreciated Hank trying to look out for me. Born in Canada in 1921, he was only seven years my senior, but on that first day at the Warwick Hotel, he assumed a fatherly attitude with a kind of protective demeanor he undoubtedly shared with younger members of his Marine squad in World War II combat.

On January 12, Yukiko was due at Idlewild. Though I was certain she'd love our new apartment, I worried about how she'd adapt to New York without friends, as I knew of the loneliness she experienced when I couldn't take her on assignments. In our first few years of marriage, she joined me on several assignments in Asia and was happy to share the journey of my professional and personal rise from what she called my "tragic past." I never saw it as tragic, just tough.

In the fall of 1961, after my trip across Siberia was published and read in most of the free world, Yukiko felt isolated and left out of the congratulatory receptions I received at the Press Club in Tokyo. In her diaries, she felt her life "useless" and that she could "only live in John's shadow." She wrote, "I don't have the courage to live this life. If I could be born again, I would be somebody, not a nobody, never. I used to be important in Japanese circles, but now I am absolutely nobody in John's circle of friends."

While my profession became more demanding, my career gained momentum and could not change course—nor did I wish it to—but during my rise, Yukiko's existence was careening down an emotional roller coaster.

Yukiko in 1955 was a rare woman: she graduated from the University of Osaka with a degree in French literature and dreamed of being a playwright, a theater director, or even an actress, but because of the changes created by our marriage, she never pursued those dreams. After taking her citizenship test, she was sworn in as an American on May 7, 1962, at the Southern District Court of New York. On that day, she renounced her Japanese citizenship at the Japanese Consulate in New York, and though viewed by the Consulate as a "traitor," she was issued a resident's visa so she could return to Japan.

In the first days of 1963, Yukiko moved to New York as a resident and American citizen. During lengthy discussions at social events, she'd often retreat into silent isolation: her fluent French had helped her at cocktail parties at the United Nations but in few other places, so I worried about her arrival.

After an 18-hour flight, Yukiko's plane landed at Idlewild where we kissed shyly. Insisting she wasn't tired, she wanted to see the apartment immediately. Opening the door to our new home, Yukiko exclaimed, "So much space! How are we going to furnish it?" As we made drawings of how we'd furnish the rooms, the doorbell rang. It was Kurt Kornfeld. He greeted Yukiko like a long lost daughter, and her obvious happiness to see him again was reassuring: at least she would have one good friend in New York.

Our newly furnished Tudor City apartment.

THE SATUR-DAY EVENING POST

ABOARD DE GAULLE'S PRESIDENTIAL TRAIN AND NAVY SUPERCARRIER U.S.S. FORRESTAL

FRANCE, THE ATLANTIC OCEAN 1963

Without wasting any time, Hank Walker set up a meeting with Clay Blair, the Post's editor and Curtis Publications' editor-in-chief. Before our introduction, Hank showed me some biographical blurbs on Blair: "the first reporter to ride the atomic submarine Nautilus, first to fly in a B-52, and first to break through the sound barrier in a plane."

In one blurb, Blair was quoted: "The real measure of a man is not how he performs in times of peace and prosperity but in times of adversity....I admire men who work and fight to the end under fire....I am not afraid of anything, and I feel fear is an indefensible emotion. Fear is something that a man feels when faced with the unknown, but he should probe the cause of his fear and learn what to do about it."

Reading those heroic, reckless words, I wondered how a man could feel "fear is an indefensible emotion." Years later, I learned Blair denied ever having written those two sentences: instead, they were the creation of a zealous editor at the *Post* embellishing promotional text in times of crisis.

While reading information on Blair, I glanced up at Hank. In his face I could see he deeply admired the editor. The two men had been close friends since their days in Time Inc.'s Washington bureau when Blair was a Pentagon correspondent and Walker a *Life*-staff photographer.

Walker, the ex-Marine, and Blair, a former submariner, were a formidable pair—both in good shape and standing over six feet tall—and they shared many of the same values. At our meeting, Blair exclaimed, "Welcome on board!" He said, "You'll find Hank to be a good leader and a fair one. And he's a damn good photographer, a great instinctive journalist, cool under fire. He'll be an excellent director of photography, and you'll enjoy working with him. If you have any personal problems or trouble in the field, Hank will always be there. He won't let you down."

Blair explained, "You can expect crusading journalism from the new *Post*. We'll cover stories that other publications are afraid to touch. You'll find the *Post* an exciting place to be at the beginning of a new era."

Walker acknowledged that the Curtis Publishing Company lost four million dollars in 1961 and nineteen million in 1962 but said losses were not due to the *Post* but to the archaic bureaucracy of Curtis Publishing. Walker assured me, "The *Post* under Clay Blair's direction will turn things around."

With Blair and Walker, I was part of an extraordinary team. When Hank proposed my first few assignments, it seemed as if I were on a mission. And I was not the only one elated: I felt the same enthusiasm in Managing Editor Don Schanche and Executive Editor William Emerson Jr., a gregarious Southerner who left a senior editor position at *Newsweek* to join the *Post*. Emerson had enough enthusiasm to inspire everyone, including the cleaning ladies. Otto Friedrich, assistant managing editor for text, was a brilliant writer and editor who also believed in great possibilities for the modernized *Post*. Still, he clashed with Hank since Otto believed any space for photographs or paintings would steal space from writers. Consequently Otto suffered silently when Walker was given over 10 pages per photographic essay from Clay Blair, the man who made the final decisions.

Otto also had an uneasy relationship with Art Director Asger Jerrild who designed layouts for the *Post*, as Otto would have been happy to use a single, postage stamp-sized photograph for a story. Despite conflicts, Otto commissioned the best writers and was often leaving the office with stacks of manuscripts. At home, he'd work long hours.

In the first few months of 1963, I met most of the *Post*'s 60 or so members in the editorial staff. We all felt the fever for a new era at the *Post*, inspiring our search for excellence in photojournalism, to succeed where others had failed. We believed in the magazine, and confidence among staff was contagious.

Though my first few assignments were not in a crusading mode, there were projects I loved photographing. "The Echo of Western Hoofbeats" covered thoroughbred breeding in California, south of San Francisco. I captured images of horses galloping on Half Moon Bay and photographed the Santa Ana racetrack by mounting a motorized camera low on the rail in the inner circle of the track, freezing the motion of an actual race. Lying flat, activating my camera as horses raced to the finish line, my wide-angle lens inches away from pounding hoofs made permanent the flying dirt, legs, torsos, and distorted heads of horses with trembling figures of jockeys on their backs, frozen in time.

One picture captured a million-dollar stud running at dusk on the crest of a hill in the Sierra de Salinas, lifting all its legs in the air. The great stallion silhouetted against a dusky blue sky seemed symbolic of nature unbridled. The image spoke of open space and infinite freedom. "Western Hoofbeats" closed with nine pages in the May 4, 1963, issue of the *Post*.

The Sierra Salinas were just a few miles from Fort Ord where I had prepared for the Korean War in four grueling months of basic training. Driving south, I called on my old friends, the Parker and Boal families, who wanted a full briefing on my new life. In the San Fernando Valley, we celebrated my return to America.

During my absence, I called Yukiko almost daily. Kurt Kornfeld visited her often, so she was in pretty good spirits when I returned. After a couple days together, I left for my next assignment to photograph open-heart surgery at Pennsylvania's University Hospital. In 1963, open-heart surgery was still extraordinary. While scrubbing down, the lead surgeon said, "This will be pretty graphic. Are you sure you won't flinch?" I assured him, "I'll be fine," but when I saw the patient's chest wedged open by two giant clamps and a heart beating within, I felt uneasy.

I had come across dramatic scenes in Asia, but nothing prepared me for the awesome spectacle of a human heart beating in an open chest: I had never seen a heart at work from within. When the heart stopped beating, a machine pumped the patient's vital organ for about five hours, while surgeons cut and stitched a bypass. Jolted by electric shock, the heart beat again as I photographed the organ pumping in the opened chest. Viewed through a camera lens, the scene had a surreal quality.

The picture made the cover of the *Post*'s June 15, 1963, issue with the billing: "The American Doctor Troubled by His Wealth and His Changing Image." It was my first *Post* cover.

I missed the immediacy of *Life*'s frenetic pace where my work would be published within a week or two after submitting photos, while the *Post* could take months before seeing them in print. But I appreciated the luxury of extra time that Walker and Senior Editor Marshall Lumsden would always allow. My right to edit my own pictures, to decide the sequence of photos to be shown to editors and the art director, was a welcome privilege I had never enjoyed during my seven years at *Life*.

In March of '63, Yukiko and I threw a housewarming party, inviting editors, writers, photographers, new acquaintances at the *Post*, the Mayers, Chapnicks, and Kurt Kornfeld. Our apartment in Manhattan had acquired personality, and at last we could welcome friends and say, "This is our home." In Japan, I always felt like a *gaijin*—a foreigner. America was the only place on earth where I truly felt at home.

Though some veterans from World War II still harbored anti-Japanese feelings, Yukiko never encountered such sentiments in New York. She adjusted faster than I could have imagined and escaped the severe loneliness she knew in Tokyo, largely because Kurt Kornfeld visited often and took her out to dinner, the theater, and movies. In return, she'd cook French gourmet dinners for him.

Still Yukiko was alone most of the time and felt her husband was "married to the *Post*." In a way, it was true. At the magazine, I had creative freedom and was on a natural high most of the time. During years in the Far East, I worked from cables assigned by faraway, faceless magazine editors, but at the *Post* I had immediate access to all editors in all departments—it was exhilarating.

Because of my total involvement with *Post* assignments, including editing and slide projections, Yukiko would complain, "At least in Tokyo, I had you for myself, but now when you return home, you just drop your bags and disappear for days to edit your work." Our lack of time for each other led me to discuss the possibility of having children, as I had the idea it would bring us closer together.

By April, Dr. William Sweeney III confirmed Yukiko was pregnant. It seemed so simple and yet almost frightening. I expressed great joy to Yukiko about our coming child, hiding my anxieties shaped by memories of the absence of joy in my own childhood: all I could remember of my youth were years of poverty, rebellion, and hard work at an early age. But I knew our children would not be born out of a need to support us or to work for the family's survival: they'd be born strictly out of love.

In May, Hank Walker asked me to read Don Cook's article from the Paris edition of the *New York Herald Tribune* about "The Renewal of France" under President Charles de Gaulle. The president had changed the constitution of the Fourth Republic, giving himself full power for his Fifth Republic and making France the world's fourth nuclear power. Handing me the article, Walker said, "You're my first choice for this assignment. Give me an answer tomorrow."

I had never covered my country of birth as a photojournalist and knew little of "the renewed" France except for what I read in newspapers and impressions from recent brief visits. If there was a renewal underway, I wanted to know what "the grandeur of France" meant in social terms. If de Gaulle actually helped create the beginning of a middle class, I wanted to see it for myself: I certainly knew nothing like it in childhood.

Challenged by Hank's offer, I was happy to take it on. I told him that Yukiko, who was entering her second month of pregnancy, would come to France with me. Hank agreed and congratulated me on our forthcoming child.

Within a few days, we arrived in Paris at the same Elysée Park Hotel suite that enchanted Yukiko three years earlier. Affected by morning sickness, she rested in our suite while I called on Don Cook at the Paris *Herald Tribune*'s office at 21, Rue de Berri, off the Champs Elysées. Introduced to Paris by James Gordon Bennett Junior in 1887, the *"Trib"* was the first American newspaper I had known. At 19, aspiring to become an American, I had read it with a dictionary.

Walking through halls of the *Herald Tribune* was a thrill. Don Cook, a seasoned, affable journalist and writer knew his way around Europe and particularly France. He immediately welcomed me, saying, "John, my office is yours. You'll need help with the bureaucracy, so just ask and I'll do all I can."

I informed Don, "I've drafted a rough script of my pictorial needs, and I'll need help getting access to France's plutonium reactor. Also, if I accompany de Gaulle on a presidential trip, how close can I get to him, and how long will accreditation take?"

Cutting me off, Don asked, "When did you last cover France?" "Never," I answered. "I left France in 1950 and since then have only visited the country a couple times." Don pointed out, "Well, you should know de Gaulle has been bitter with America for over 20 years. He snubbed America and Britain by producing atomic weapons without technical help from them. France's Mirage IV jets with nuclear bombs are symbolic of the country's power and independence, so you can appreciate that France's top-secret nuclear program is off limits. At this point, I can't see why de Gaulle's Ministry of Defense would cooperate with an American publication."

"French pride might get us cooperation," I suggested. "De Gaulle and his Gaullists are constantly boasting about France's nuclear *'Force de Frappe'* strike force, so why not argue that this is another historic time for relations between France and America? The first of course was French participation in America's war for independence, which by the way, was reported by *The Saturday Evening Post*—remember, the magazine is 236 years old. Why not let the same publication photograph the atomic weapons reactor, which stands as a symbol of the French nation's independence and power?"

Thoughtful for a while, Don Cook asked, "Are you sure the *Post* covered France's participation in the American Revolution?" "No," I answered, "but we can safely assume it did. I'm willing to argue the logic of that with the French Ministry of Defense."

Don was skeptical but didn't want to dampen my enthusiasm. Calling a high official at the Ministry of Defense, he scheduled an appointment with a high-ranking assistant to the minister with whom I'd make the same argument but with more subtlety.

At the ministry, I argued, "America still has an image of Frenchmen wearing berets and carrying baguettes under their arms. The *Post*'s 30 million readers are typical. They still see France as a country that produces cheese, wine, high fashion, and glorified museums. Now that France is a nuclear power, why not show it to the readers of the *Post*?"

I could tell my arguments appealed to the official's patriotic Gaullist vision of his country. Opening the *Post*'s contents page and pointing to the text claiming its 236th year, I said, "The *Post* undoubtedly reported on France's glorious participation in the American Revolution."

I knew I had touched his French pride when he answered, "It might be possible, but it will take months to conduct a security check on you." "Can't you speed it up?" I urged, "My life is an open book." Presenting my DOD accreditation card, I explained, "This is my American Defense Department accreditation. You can be sure it was issued to me only after a thorough investigation to make sure I am not a Communist or a subversive." After studying the card, he asked me to fill out several security clearance forms.

A few days later, the French Ministry of Defense granted me permission to photograph the G-2 reactor at Marcoule, north of Avignon. Under de Gaulle's administration, it had produced France's first arsenal of nuclear weapons.

I presented the documents to a surprised Don Cook, who exclaimed, "That's a first! I've never heard of an American journalist receiving French security clearance with an American DOD card, but I'll remember that one." Things were falling into place. Cook managed to get me a seat on the presidential train for a journey to the southwest provinces of France.

In preparation for the presidential trip, I read three volumes of General de Gaulle's war memoirs, *Mémoires de Guerre*, chronicling his life from 1940 to 1946 in some 2,000 pages published in the 1950s. The memoirs highlighted de Gaulle's historic call from London's BBC urging all Frenchmen to join him in England and build in exile the forces of "Free France."

In his 1940–1942 volume *L'Appel* (The Call to Duty), a line on the first page summed up the essence of what I'd hear on our four-day presidential trip: "In my understanding, France cannot be France without grandeur."

To understand the man, I read de Gaulle's words at night while Yukiko slept. I wanted to be ready for an intelligent conversation should the president make a courtesy call to the press car. No one told me de Gaulle never had casual conversations with reporters; in fact he never spoke to them at all. All questions had to be submitted to his staff before his return to the presidential palace, l'Elysée, where he'd hold a press conference.

The reporters on the journey were all regulars, habitués, and at the press conference, they dutifully asked the same questions they had submitted. Though reporters disliked being so controlled by de Gaulle's staff, they played by the rules for the sake of access.

At the start, I remarked to fellow journalists that France's freedom of the press was limited, but their reaction was hostile, so I immediately dropped the subject. For an American to suggest the French press was not entirely free was an affront, but it was obvious their freedom was compromised by censorship.

Government censors controlled the national news agency, Agence France-Presse. Though the French press was free to print some of the cruelest political satire I had ever seen, politically unfavorable television reports on de Gaulle were simply not shown on government networks.

The year before, in 1962, de Gaulle asked people of France to vote in a referendum for a constitutional amendment to eliminate the National Assembly's Electoral college and provide for direct elections of the president. The amendment won by a narrow majority, and for the first time in the history of French republics, a single party made up of the Gaullists and their supporters wielded control of the National Assembly. "De Gaulle's power is complete," Don Cook said. "No constitutional checks and balances impede him."

On the presidential train, we were scheduled to stop in several cities and end up in the Bay of Biscay's port city, La Rochelle. Traveling with the president had its perks: gourmet lunches were served in the press car, and a few miles before each stop, while we ate, drank white and then red vintage wines, the presidential train rolled back and forth along the tracks, allowing us nearly three hours to dine.

While we indulged ourselves in a long sumptuous meal as the train moved forwards and backwards, we could see armed gendarmes hiding alongside tracks to fortify de Gaulle's security. Conversations during our extravagant lunches were never about the president's politics but about the quality of food served, wines tasted, and liquors sipped. Just minutes after waiters removed our coffee cups and liquor glasses, the train would pull into the station precisely on time.

At each stop and in the plaza where *"Le Général"* spoke, thousands lined the streets: de Gaulle was received in each city as a mythical hero. I photographed the multitude of misty eyes listening to de Gaulle speak of the grandeur and independence of France. "Nobody else can become the master of our destiny," he proclaimed.

Referring to the Soviet Union and America, he said, "France does not accept that two privileged states should alone possess power and domination once and for all and forever. France will continue atomic testing for her security." In that speech de Gaulle established foreign policy for decades; he managed to persuade most French citizens to bury shameful years of the Vichy government's collaboration with the Nazis and to believe again in the glory of France.

In La Rochelle, I photographed de Gaulle extending his arms like a prophet, surrounded by tricolor flags, standing before a huge cross of Lorraine, his symbol of the "Free French," as he led thousands into singing the national anthem, "La Marseillaise." As if entreating his children or subjects, he led the adoring multitude into tears of patriotism, inspiring a spirit of nationalism.

I could understand why the Gaullist era was often compared to Louis Bonaparte's Second Empire in the previous century, for during our four-day journey, de Gaulle's behavior had an imperial style. As an American, I now felt an

WHY DE GAULLE DEFIES U
France: a new atomic pow

PROFITS FROM GRIE
You can't afford to d

POST

THE SATURDAY EVENING POST NOVEMBER 23 - 1963 20c

Why Valachi talked / Smoldering Romy Schneider / First-aid psychia

even greater appreciation for the checks and balances guaranteed by laws of my adopted country.

What fascinated me was the adulation and support de Gaulle received from the French who traditionally had never been an easy people to govern, but there was no denying he was creating a proud and confident France I had never known in my childhood.

France was seeing the creation of a large middle class, which had never existed before. There was a refrigerator in every fourth home, a washing machine in every sixth home, and a car for every seven people. Even Paulette, the least privileged of my three sisters, and her husband had acquired a used Citroën.

When de Gaulle announced his plan to give Algeria independence in 1962 after 132 years of French colonial rule, even his bitterest enemies admitted that he had stabilized France when he crushed a revolt led by three of his generals who were against Algerian independence. The country had almost plunged into civil war, so by calling on French soldiers to shoot any officers in revolt against the state, he saved France in one of its darkest hours since the years of Nazi domination.

What surprised me during four days traveling with de Gaulle was that none of the president's glorious, patriotic speeches reached or moved me despite my roots in the nation. I was a foreign observer, no longer emotionally French. The only thing I still appreciated about my French heritage was a familiarity with works by La Fontaine, Molière, Racine, Voltaire, Rousseau, Hugo, Baudelaire, Zola, and other great thinkers.

In short, my divorce from France was complete. In my mind, the poor of Europe left nearly nothing behind when they crossed the Atlantic: I left behind a family but little else. There were no cherished traditions, no patriotic memories, and certainly no monuments to my poverty.

Meanwhile, Yukiko suffered from morning sickness, often confined to her bed during our six weeks in France. Even so, she enjoyed her conversations with Pierre Cardin's beautiful Japanese model, Hiroko Matsumoto.

Fortunately, her health returned by the time my assignment brought us to Marseilles, St. Tropez, and the French Riviera, and she became cheerful again as I interviewed people between photographic takes. By the end of our trip, I remarked to Yukiko, "I learned more about France in this single trip than in my first 18 years growing up in Marly."

At the end of June, we flew back to New York. After editing thousands of color photos, I showed Marshal Lumsden and Hank Walker my selections and was gratified by their reactions. Hank invited me to the famous and costly "21," one of his favorite Manhattan restaurants. He was amused by my story of using a DOD card to obtain French security clearance, thinking it "clever if not cunning." I protested, "Hank, that wasn't cunning. I was completely sincere in my approach. That's why it worked."

Because my coverage was often physically very close to de Gaulle, Hank asked whether he ever spoke to me. "Not a word," I answered. "For the whole trip, he was completely aloof. I never saw him talk to the press. De Gaulle was emperor, and we were part of his retinue. Whenever working at close range, I always said, 'Merci mon Général,' but he never acknowledged my presence."

Aware that Hank had covered John F. Kennedy for *Life*, I asked, "What is it like traveling with President Kennedy?" He answered, "JFK could never behave like an emperor. No American politician can. Kennedy is rather graceful with the press. There are rules of course, but he always makes himself accessible."

Immediately, I said, "Please, Hank, let me cover the president's reelection campaign." I expected him to assign a more politically seasoned photographer so was ecstatic when he answered, "Good idea, I think you'd learn a lot from an American presidential campaign. It'll be exhausting but exhilarating. As soon as it's in full swing, you can do an essay on the campaign. You won't have to wait for text. Actually, during their last trip to France, Jackie was even more popular than the president, so your French background might help get you closer to the Kennedys. I know you've got a hectic schedule, but I'll assign you to the campaign at the first opportunity."

In September, after receiving clearance from the Secretary of the Navy, I began an assignment to cover fighter-bomber flights from the deck of the supercarrier U.S.S. *Forrestal* in the middle of the Atlantic.

For 11 days, with a weekend sandwiched in at the Officers' Club in Norfolk, Virginia, I flew multiple daily missions strapped in the copilot seat of an A3B Sky warrior jet piloted by Lt. Commander W.E. Bassett and at times by Commander Fred Carment.

After being catapulted from the supercarrier's deck, I photographed Phantom II fighter-bombers capable of flying up to 1,650 miles per hour. From 40,000 feet, I simultaneously directed as many as six jets in various compositions in the sky. In flight, I captured "on-deck refueling" of jets a hundred feet above a 50-mile sandbar in the Atlantic. I photographed air-to-air missile firings in flight and caught the magic of fighters taking off at dusk, as brilliant glows of afterburners illuminated the night's blue light.

Admiring the perfected skills of carrier pilots, I eventually learned to relax as our catapulted A3B, with engines at full blast, accelerated from zero to 145 knots. As afterburners kicked in, we seemed to drop dramatically, propelled from the edge of the carrier's short deck.

It was an immense thrill to land on the carrier deck's landing strip, which moved up and down several degrees as our aircraft's hook caught the middle cable in a jolt that brought our landing speed down from 145 knots to zero in three and a half seconds. I came to appreciate why a touchdown on an aircraft carrier was not called a landing but a "recovery."

From a chopper, I photographed the 5,000 men operating the *Forrestal*. I was touched and proud when officers of the Hatron Eleven Squadron presented me with a certificate reading: "Let it be known that John Launois did recover aboard U.S.S. *Forrestal* in a Douglas A3B Sky warrior piloted by Lt. Commander W.E. Bassett. For his intrepidity and complete disregard for his personal safety, he is made an honorary member of this unit and a Tail-Hooker....this seventeenth day of September in the year of our Lord, nineteen hundred and sixty three."

The Navy was extraordinarily cooperative, partly due to the political significance of the story entitled: "Fight for Survival of the Super Carrier." The *Post* wrote that the mammoth vessels were: "huge, fast, and nuclear-armed" as they displayed American power all over the world. "But their enormous cost has touched off a critical battle between fleet admirals and Secretary McNamara." The piece ran nine pages in the November 2, 1963, issue of the *Post*.

THE NEW FRONTIER

"AMERICA'S SENSELESS TRAGEDY"

WASHINGTON D.C. 1963

Even with countless projects pending, I looked forward to covering President Kennedy's reelection campaign. On November 22, 1963, assistant editor Judy Gurovitz and I had just ordered lunch at a small French restaurant near our New York office when the chef, looking dazed, solemnly said to his customers, "Three shots have been fired at the presidential motorcade in Dallas," quoting United Press International's first flash report of the attempt on Kennedy's life.

All tables fell silent as the chef raised the volume of his kitchen radio for all to hear. Five minutes later, a second report announced, "Kennedy has been wounded, perhaps fatally."

Shaken in disbelief, we canceled our orders, paid for our drinks, and rushed back to the office, repeating to ourselves, "Oh, my God. Oh, my God." Less than an hour later, a UPI news flash announced, "President Kennedy is dead."

All *Post* editors in the building gathered in Clay Blair's office. Secretaries and other personnel were shedding silent tears or weeping openly. Visibly shaken and somber, Hank Walker took me aside and said, "John, it's over in Dallas. The story is moving to Washington, and that's where I need you." Judy Gurovitz would work with me and assist our other photographers.

In Dallas, the apparent assassin, Lee Harvey Oswald, was captured by the Dallas Police.

At 3:38 P.M. , Eastern Standard Time, Vice President Lyndon B. Johnson, flanked by the widowed first lady and Mrs. Johnson, was sworn in as our 36th president aboard Air Force One at Dallas's Love Field. Minutes later the plane headed back to Washington with the coffin of our dead president.

As a relatively new American, I had an idealized vision of what an American leader should be, and John F. Kennedy fit that vision. Through those unspeakable hours of November 22, it seemed that what was best about America had been silenced. A president who sought to uplift us with hope for a just and peaceful world, drawing on the nation's highest ideals, had been apparently murdered by a nobody, a high-school dropout trained as a rifleman by the Marine Corps. Overwhelmed by grief, outrage, and sorrow, I would not fully understand for several years the extent of what John F. Kennedy's assassination meant to America and the world.

In the evening, Judy and I flew to Washington. At the Jefferson Hotel, we arranged for one of our two bedrooms to double as an office. The next day, we attended Pierre Salinger's first press briefing to the American and foreign press at the White House where JFK's coffin rested on a catafalque in the East Room. All of us were grieving as if suffering a personal tragedy: the senselessness of his murder had left even his harshest critics speechless.

In *The Saturday Evening Post*'s November 23, 1963, issue, my de Gaulle coverage was published with a cover and seven pages, but at that moment it meant nothing. November 23 was also my 35th birthday, but I was in no mood to celebrate.

The next day, as we focused on Washington events, Dallas again made the headlines: Jack Ruby, an owner of local strip joints, had freely entered police headquarters and shot Oswald, televised live on NBC.

After repeatedly watching the replay of the shooting, Judy and I were convinced that Ruby's easy access to the policemen escorting Oswald to another location was part of a larger conspiracy: the conspirators, we reasoned, wanted Oswald eliminated. He died at Parkland, the same Dallas hospital where the president had expired two days earlier.

On the same Sunday, I photographed a multitude of mourners lining the Capitol to pay their last respects to the president lying in state in the rotunda. In their faces, I saw the grief of a nation.

Toward evening, I climbed to the highest level of the Capitol just under the dome. People filing in two lines on each side of the coffin looked like tiny black points filling the frame. Though the majority of mourners were white, many were black Americans, but from where I was perched, all colors disappeared: only a mass of grieving people remained.

At about 2:00 A.M. on Monday the 25th, Hank Walker phoned and said, "As you may already know, in about nine hours the marching procession to St. Matthew's Cathedral will begin, led by six horses pulling the caisson. It'll be followed by

Jackie, Bobby, Teddy, dozens of world leaders, and Washington's political and military establishment. It's a once in a lifetime shot. If you can show all those elements in a single photograph, I promise you a full-bleed double page."

To capture that entire scene, I'd have to shoot from above. I turned to Judy and said, "I need you to find me a 20-foot sliding ladder within the hour." Anyone but Judy would have replied, "Are you crazy? It's the middle of the night!" Instead Judy rushed off saying, "I'll wake the hotel maintenance people and see if they can lend us one."

In less than an hour, Judy had our ladder, and my assistant found us a station wagon to transport it. With our ladder leaning against a streetlight at the junction of Connecticut and Pennsylvania Avenues, I tried to compose a picture in the dark and deserted landscape of the city at night.

To frame the shot, I had my assistant run up and down, left and right, to draw an imaginary rectangle frame, which theoretically would capture the procession in a single photo. It was dawn by the time I felt we had found our angle. Tying the ladder to the streetlight, I left my assistant to guard our position.

By Monday morning, a quarter of a million people had filed by John F. Kennedy's catafalque. Just before noon, I positioned myself 20 feet up on the ladder. Within minutes, I saw uniformed riders and six horses pulling the caisson bearing JFK's coffin, followed by a seaman with the presidential flag and Black Jack, the horse without a rider, carrying a reversed boot on the saddle, symbolizing the departed rider.

"The departed rider" was followed by Jacqueline Bouvier Kennedy, flanked by Robert and Edward Kennedy, accompanied by leaders of the world and hundreds of men and women of Washington's elite. They all filled the empty frame I had imagined in the middle of the night and came into focus for a fleeting instant.

"If you succeed," Hank Walker had said, "you will have shown our departed president, his family's sorrow, a nation's sorrow, and the world's sorrow in a single photograph."

In the December 14, 1963, issue of the *Post*, the picture of the procession was the only double page featured in its 25-page coverage of "America's Senseless Tragedy." The caption read: "Historic assemblage marched behind caisson to funeral march in Washington."

As I left the cortege at St. Matthew's Cathedral, thousands of weeping mourners gathered along Pennsylvania and Connecticut Avenues. When we passed the Lincoln Memorial and Memorial Bridge, heading for Arlington National Cemetery, I asked my assistant to slow down so we could see the estimated one million

people lining the route to Arlington. Through my telephoto lens, I saw people of all ages and was amazed at the sheer number of grieving young men and women paying their final respects to their lost young president. Their somber faces were illuminated by crisp, sunny afternoon light.

As always during tragic events, my cameras provided an emotional shield, allowing me to keep my own grief in check, but the finality of the burial at Arlington made it hard to maintain my composure.

With the president's casket perched on a stand, mourners assembled around the grave. Behind the Kennedy family, I saw Lyndon B. Johnson, our new president, but emotionally, I felt John F. Kennedy was still my president. Closer to the grave were former Presidents Truman and Eisenhower, but I took particular note of Charles de Gaulle at the foot of the grave. Born on November 22, 1890, his 73rd birthday coincided with Kennedy's slaying. Focusing my 300-mm telephoto lens on his face, I wondered if he reflected at all on how lucky he had been to survive four assassination attempts. On November 9, 1970, de Gaulle's life would end at the age of 80—by that date, Kennedy would have been 53.

At the president's burial, I was overwhelmed by the ceremonial mystique of the military funeral. Representatives from all branches of the armed forces were there to bid farewell to their commander in chief among the lachrymose sounds of the fifes, drummers, bugler, and Air Force bagpipers. The Marine band played the national anthem, and the Navy played the national hymn. While thousands lamented our loss on hillsides surrounding the young president's grave, Army soldiers shot three volleys of rifle fire into the air.

Fifty F-105 fighter jets representing each state in the Union soared in the air and flew low over Arlington in a V-shaped formation, leaving an empty space at the head for their fallen leader.

Colonel James B. Swindal, who piloted Air Force One for JFK, flew the Presidential Boeing 707 some 500 feet above the grave and tipped the jet's long wings from one side to the other in a final salute.

I felt my stoicism falter as I watched through my long lens the eight Army men in white gloves lift up the American flag that had covered Kennedy's coffin. They folded the Star Spangled Banner and handed it to Arlington's Superintendent Jack Metzler, who presented it to Jacqueline Kennedy, saying, "Mrs. Kennedy, this flag is presented to you in the name of a most mournful nation."

As she held the red, white, and blue triangle against her dark dress, I could see her face behind a transparent black veil: her puffy eyes swelled and blurred in my lens as my own eyes filled with tears. In a blur, I watched as she lit her husband's eternal flame.

After finding Judy Gurovitz at the bottom of the hill, the two of us rushed to Washington's National Airport. Physically and emotionally exhausted, we remained silent on our flight back to La Guardia Airport. All I could think of was how John Kennedy had inspired in me and so many Americans a noble vision of patriotism.

JFK had surrounded himself with brilliant and cultured people trained to find solutions for the great dilemmas of the world. An extraordinary number of his ambassadors were fluent in the foreign languages of countries to which they were assigned, most notably Ambassador to Japan and Harvard Professor Edwin O. Reischauer, who won praise from the Japanese press when he addressed them in flawless Japanese on his 1961 arrival at Tokyo's International Airport.

Kennedy inspired what was best in America just as he moved men and women of all ages to readily volunteer for his Peace Corps: I wondered if those noble feelings and aspirations would disappear with his death. Would borders of the "New Frontier" close and high ideals it inspired be forgotten? What else died in America on November 22, 1963? In the last hours of our farewell to John Kennedy, I had no answer.

AMERICAN SON

CHRISTOPHER MARK LAUNOIS

NEW YORK 1964

I n the first week of December, I accepted a *Ladies' Home Journal* assignment on "Women Diplomats of the United Nations." This was welcome because it would keep me close to Yukiko as she entered her ninth month of pregnancy—I could walk to work with the U.N. a mere 500 yards from our apartment. For the first time in my career I had a project at my doorstep.

When Dr. Sweeney told us the baby might arrive before the end of the year, I said, "That's fine since I'm working close to home." But on December 15, Hank Walker asked me to shoot a Christmas story on the Caribbean islands, assuring me I could fly back any time to be with Yukiko.

So for Christmas in St. Thomas, I photographed the island's advertised "beautiful beaches in paradise" and gaudy tourists on cruise ships, while Yukiko spent the holiday with some of our friends. On Christmas night, I tried to call and counted 93 rings before the international telephone operator on St. Thomas answered the phone. I exclaimed, "Do you realize, Miss, it took 93 rings before you answered?" She said, "Too bad," and hung up. It took another 90 rings to reach another operator: this time I politely and sweetly gave Yukiko's Manhattan number.

It was two o'clock in the morning by the time I reached Yukiko to wish her "Merry Christmas!" She sounded anxious, fearing I'd miss our baby's birth, so to be sure I was home in time, I flew back to New York on December 27.

We spent a quiet New Year's Eve with Time-Life friends from our days in Tokyo, Fernando and Anne Marie Casablancas. Soon after, at 4:00 A.M. on January 7, 1964, we checked into New York Hospital on East 68th Street. Doctor Sweeney thought I should witness our child's birth and had me gowned, gloved, capped, and masked. Meanwhile, Yukiko went into agonizing labor pains for several hours.

At 7:00 A.M., Dr. Sweeney said, "I'm sorry, but you can't stay. Yukiko is small. I don't think she'll need a cesarean, but an incision will be necessary. I don't expect your child to be delivered till noon, so try to relax. Both mother and child are safe." I could see the stoicism of Yukiko's culture as she suppressed the pain while nurses told her to "push, push." I said to her, "They told me I have to leave, but Dr. Sweeney assures us that you and our baby will be fine."

It was close to dawn when I left the hospital and walked northward to a small park overlooking the East River. I wondered why giving birth was so painful. I questioned whether I was ready for fatherhood and how a child would change our lives. I asked myself, "How can a man who constantly travels from home be a good father?"

If we had a girl, we'd call her Maya; if a boy, he'd be named Christopher. Yukiko and I didn't like the American habit of shortening first names but thought Chris sounded fine.

Around 10:00 A.M., I returned to the hospital, but our child was not yet born. Dr. Sweeney and his team had been up all night; from behind the curtained operating room, he came out and said, "John, it won't be long now."

Finally at 12:32 P.M. on January 7, 1964, Christopher Mark Launois, weighing seven pounds, ten ounces, was born. Yukiko was wheeled to a private room. As I held her hand and kissed her forehead, she appeared completely exhausted. She fell asleep as I told her, "I want to see our son."

When a nurse brought me to Christopher, all I could think was that he looked as bald as Eisenhower. As his tiny fingers held my pinkie, I suddenly remembered the birth of my two brothers and three sisters who had been delivered at home in France by a midwife. At the time I was unable to relate to them, suspended in an emotional vacuum: disturbingly, I now felt the same with my own son.

I expected to experience a deep emotion and immediate bonding, but I felt empty. During the reverie of a long night, as I reflected by the fast-flowing waters of the East River, I imagined having a conversation with our newborn child in which I'd say, "Welcome to the world. I'll often be away, but I'll show you the world." Of course, I didn't expect a newborn to say, "Hi, Dad, how was your trip?" but I almost did. Of course, Christopher soon acquired a personality of his own, and my early indifference to him disappeared—in little time at all, I fell in love with my son, my only child.

Over the next three days, I visited Yukiko and Chris twice a day and took them home on January 11. After hiring a nurse to look after them, I returned to the Caribbean islands to complete my essay by February, and the story made the cover of the March 14 issue of the *Post*.

Chris was over a month old by the time I returned home, but I had only seen him for five days. The sad truth was I would not see much of him in his early years. He'd crawl, talk, and walk without me, as I missed most of his infancy and early childhood.

Though the *Post*'s financial health was in question in January 1964, projects were quickly accumulating. While I could choose assignments, many were suggested by Hank Walker when he felt a story was "tailor-made" for me. Hank often selected assignments he instinctively knew I'd love. When he showed me an article written for the *Post* by former President Harry S. Truman, entitled: "My First Eighty Years," Hank said, "We'll need a cover on old Harry." I had photographed Truman at Kennedy's funeral but never met him, in fact, I had never met a president of the United States. I immediately accepted Hank's offer.

GIANTS

HARRY TRUMAN AND AMERICA'S STEEL INDUSTRY

MISSOURI, KENTUCKY 1964

When I met Harry Truman at his Presidential Library in Independence, Missouri, I found the former president affable, open, unpretentious, and obviously a man of the people: he won me over immediately. It occurred to me a man of such humble roots could never have been elected president in the elitist government of France.

Since the background of the library was too formal, I suggested photographing the former president in front of his modest home, the kind of house seen in works of American prairie painter, Grant Wood. President Truman immediately agreed.

After the shoot, he invited researcher Andrée Abecassis and me to have cookies and coffee. He introduced me to his wife "Bessie." She insisted, "Young man, I recognize you from our days in the White House." I responded, "Please forgive me, Mrs. Truman, but you must be mistaken. When Mr. Truman was elected President in 1948, I was only 20 years old and living in London. Four years later, I was in California about to be drafted into the U.S. Army."

Mrs. Truman simply said, "Young man, you can't fool me. I never forget a face." I smiled and wondered who looked like me in the White House Press Corps during the Truman years.

In relaxed conversation with the former president, I related how my father and I in France had been saddened by the death of President Roosevelt on the eve of the Allied victory, and how my father had wondered, "How can Vice President Truman possibly succeed the great man?" But I assured Mr. Truman, "After we learned more about you, we came to admire you as well"—the former president just chuckled. He afforded us nearly half the day, and in the end gracefully signed the two volumes of his memoirs I had brought with me. My photo of Mr. Truman made the cover on the June 13, 1964, issue of the *Post.*

For the *Post*'s series on "America's Great Industries," I spent six weeks photographing changes in the American steel industry based on David R. Jones's critical analysis of the American economy's "humbled giants." Two years earlier, President Kennedy had challenged the steel industry after they had betrayed their promise of a modest wage increase that the administration had negotiated with the unions. After the industry unreasonably and excessively raised steel prices to compensate for rises in labor costs, an angry Kennedy had appeared on national television and excoriated the "tiny handful of steel executives and their pursuit of private power and profit."

Because the American people widely supported JFK, the "majors" backed down. Foreign competition in 1964 further humbled steel makers by forcing executives to modernize their industry to keep prices competitive.

For 40 days and nights, I shot in the midst of U.S. Steel, Jones & Laughlin, Bethlehem Steel, and other major firms. To focus on the industry's recent innovations, I captured on film what was then the world's largest blast furnace: at 234 feet high, "Amanda" produced 3,340 tons of iron a day, roaring through the night on Armco's Ashland, Kentucky works by the Ohio River.

The nine-page story was released in the *Post*'s June 27–July 4, 1964, issue as: "Steel the Giant Under Fire," with the subtitle; "The customers no longer wait in line and the Lords of Steel are learning how to scramble for business." The cover featured my photo of a rugged, dirty, young steelworker whose face was prematurely wrinkled and baked by the intense heat of blast furnaces, as he shouted orders to a crane operator, while cascades of molten iron seethed in the background.

After the story was released, the steelworker on the cover filed a lawsuit against the *Post*, claiming I had photographed him without his knowledge. However, when our lawyers proved in court that I had taken more than 72 photos of the same worker in various poses, it was obvious he knew he was the subject, and the lawsuit was dismissed.

During the "Steel Giants" assignment, I visited Yukiko and my son on only two weekends. By then, Christopher was already four months old, and I had seen him for less than two weeks. Yukiko was deeply unhappy and our marriage was in trouble, yet I was blind to the enormity of Yukiko's distress. She would later reflect:

"Our marriage was in trouble long before Chris was born. During my eighth and ninth month, the rift between us was already deep. Professionally, John was at the top of the world—the possibilities for his future seemed without limit. Meanwhile, I was moody and often depressed.

He did not enjoy coming home to a nagging, pregnant wife and often didn't show up until dawn, after drinking all night with colleagues. On the rare occasions when he was home at night, we had very painful conversations, and he expressed a desire to be free. Accustomed to Asian women, he found American women's chiseled faces so beautiful, so alluring. At work, he was surrounded by these attractive but also intelligent young women with the highest education who adored him.

He didn't mean to hurt me by admitting this: he was just being honest. But he had no idea how much it hurt me. I was in despair and so lonely.

One night, I could no longer bear to be alone in the apartment and slipped away at about 2:00 A.M. I thought of death, but it was wintertime and the idea of throwing myself into the East River did not appeal to me, so I just walked around 42nd Street hoping someone would attack and kill me. I encountered a couple of homeless men at Grand Central Station, but nobody attacked me.

It was freezing, and I had no place to go, so I came back to the apartment at around 3:00 A.M. John wasn't home yet. All I wanted was for John to come home, to worry about me, or to come looking for me—but that didn't happen.

The situation did not improve even after the birth of the baby, and Kurt Kornfeld advised us to separate since we were so unhappy. When I lived alone with Chris, Kurt came to dinner at least once a week and called me on the phone every single day.

John wanted to have his own apartment to be free. He told me he had confided in Hank Walker, and Hank had said to him, 'You took Yukiko out of her culture and transplanted her in a strange culture. Whatever you do, I want you to do the honorable thing.'"

Caught up in my own creative ambition, I couldn't see the terrible depth of her unhappiness. Yukiko and I discussed our marital problems but found no solutions. To ease the tension, I promised we'd take a vacation and learn to ski in the French Alps: we were drifting apart, yet all I could offer was a skiing holiday eight months away.

By mid-May, the weather was beautiful in New York. I hoped to spend a full week with my new family as soon as my pictures were edited, but that promise was postponed because of an assignment to cover the Beatles. The group was to tour New Zealand and Australia in June, followed by their second U.S. tour, performing in 25 cities over five weeks, beginning on August 19, 1964.

HARD DAY'S NIGHT

THE BEATLES

LONDON 1964

Because the *Post's* editors wanted a Beatles cover on the newsstand at least two weeks before August 19, the band had to be photographed in late May. Bored of pictures of the Beatles performing among throngs of teenage girls, Hank Walker wanted "something different."

Instead of concentrating on "Beatlemania," I focused my attention on what appeared to be the Beatles's humorous contempt for the British establishment, particularly the English aristocracy. I remembered an anecdote that during a royal performance, instead of singing, "God Save the Queen," John Lennon mischievously sang, "God S-A-A-A-VE the CREAM." To the audience, he sarcastically said, "For our last number, I'd like to ask your help. Will the people in the cheaper seats clap your hands? The rest of you, just rattle your jewelry."

Discussing ideas with Hank, I said, "If I can show their irreverence and disdain for the British upper class in a single picture, we'd be on to something. What we need is a situation in which the Beatles can visually spoof and satirize the establishment." I thought about how John Lennon had recently bought a racehorse for his father's 62nd birthday and how all four of the boys were riding around in chauffeur-driven Rolls-Royces with tinted windows—it seemed the Beatles had become millionaires overnight.

An idea dawned on me. I said to Hank, "Why not ask the long-haired Beatles to dress like the financiers in London's financial district? Dressed in classic black suits, bowler hats, gray gloves, and ties, with black umbrellas and the *Financial Times* under their arms, the Beatles would be mocking the establishment while becoming part of it."

Hank had lived in London and often saw the dressy financiers. "That's a great idea," he said, "I'm sure the Beatles would love to make fun of them."

On May 22, 1964, Judy Gurovitz and I took off for London. In the office of Beatles manager Brian Epstein, we met "the four lads from Liverpool." Epstein was unenthusiastic, but the Beatles, having come from a poor Liverpool background, instantly loved my idea. They humored their manager, "C'mon Brian, the guy came all the way from New York."

Once Epstein agreed, Judy had the difficult job of ordering outfits for the Beatles from their own Saville Row tailors. Saville Row was renowned for dressing heads of state, the elite of the world, and of course, London's leading financiers. But the tailors refused to divulge the wardrobe sizes for the Beatles saying, "That information is absolutely confidential."

It was an absurd moment. Calls from Brian Epstein to the tailors failed to persuade them to disclose any measurements. I concluded the class-conscious tailors were utterly unwilling to assist us in a spoof of their upper-class clients.

After some quick guesswork, Judy ordered the outfits while I scouted locations for a Georgian entrance in London's wealthy Mayfair district. Our wardrobe woman fitted the Beatles, and we secretly brought them to our outdoor location, but within minutes, we were mobbed by screaming teenage girls. How they learned of our confidential shoot remained a mystery.

After we escaped the throng of hysterical adolescents, I hired a set designer to build and reproduce the Georgian entrance in a London studio. As we quickly dressed the Beatles and prepared the shot, Ringo struck me as the most relaxed, while John appeared to be the intellect of the group.

Then we discovered none of the wardrobe really fit: the shoes were too big, bowler hats were too small or too large, and suits had to be taken in with safety pins by our wardrobe woman. But everyone joined the Beatles in their unstoppable laughter—it was a hilarious day.

Lennon tried to calm the group down, so we could work, but the laughter stopped only after I explained,

 I need deadpan expressions. To get in the mood, just think of men whose sole purpose in life is to make money.

Suddenly their grinning faces turned somber, empty, and bored with a touch of sadness. "Great," I said. "That's the cover."

On our next set, we hung a seamless-blue backdrop to create a clear-sky background and placed the Beatles in a rented convertible Mercedes. The boys waved while assistants from above threw pounds of confetti over them like a ticker-tape parade. After the shot, the Beatles grabbed handfuls of colored paper and showered me with confetti to say goodbye.

From London, I headed northwest to Liverpool to photograph the Beatles's working-class neighborhood and the Cavern nightclub, formerly a vegetable warehouse, where the Beatles were discovered.

In the Beatles's hometown, the "Foursome from Liverpool" inspired a phenomenon: one out of every 15 "Liverpudlians" between the ages of 15 and 24 belonged to a rock-and-roll band. In his text, writer Alfred Aronowitz referred to Liverpool as the "slum of England," where he counted 350 groups trying to "make it." Among them were The Blue Jeans, The Mersey Monsters, and The Undertakers, musicians who traveled on scooters to gigs wearing old-fashioned black top hats, dressed like morticians. All performers were striving to rise above meager factory wages or escape unemployment, poor diets, and often malnutrition, dreaming and hoping to emulate the Beatles's success.

Eventually, I'd cover success stories of popular American musicians like Bob Dylan, Joan Baez, and Judy Collins. In one picture, I captured Dylan speeding on his motorcycle, not long before a serious accident on his bike nearly ended his legendary career.

While I was working with the Beatles in London, Yukiko and five-month-old Chris traveled to Japan. At Sakuragaoka, or "Cherry Blossom Hill," near Osaka, our son was introduced to his grandparents and great-grandmother on Yukiko's mother's side.

After a month in Japan, Yukiko and Chris, according to plan, would meet me in Paris where we'd stay at the fabulous mansion of our old friend, Curt Prendergast, the Time-Life bureau chief in Paris. From there we'd visit Marly-le -Roi and introduce Christopher to my large family. Once again however, I had to cancel our plans in order to cover the royal premiere of the Beatles's first movie, *A Hard Day's Night*, in London.

As I broke the news over the phone, I could tell Yukiko was hurt and profoundly disappointed, but as always, she hid her feelings. "Well, since the Prendergasts are leaving on an unexpected journey," she said, "Christopher and I will spend a month in Milan with Anne Marie and Fernando." Fernando Casablancas had just been named Time-Life's advertising manager for Italy.

As I tried to justify the need for covering the premiere, Yukiko was getting angrier by the minute. She obviously didn't want to hear about my problems and why it was so important for me to shoot an encounter of the Beatles with royalty. To express her outrage, she retreated into absolute silence: for me, that inflicted more punishment than harsh words. I promised to come to Milan, but from the silence on the line, I was no longer sure if she cared.

Unwilling to compromise an unfinished project, I again placed the importance of work above family. Because there wasn't enough light for the evening premiere, we rented every huge strobe light we could find in London and set them up the day before the event. In tuxedos and evening dresses, the "cream of English society" arrived in Rolls-Royces for the film's opening. As I photographed the Beatles, Princess Margaret, and thousands of screaming fans, the scene resembled a Hollywood gala event.

Though the assignment put a great strain on my marriage, it was a pleasure to work with the "four mates from Liverpool." The Beatles were good actors, and the idea of Liverpool's working class spoofing London's financial class appealed immensely to their irreverent nature, while reflecting their good-humored contempt for the British establishment. As much as they loved it, so did our American readers—the Post's August 8–15, 1964, double issue sold out.

Finally in July, I was able to spend one day with Yukiko, Chris, and the Casablancas. On the shore of Lake Como, I played with Chris who had just turned six months old. He seemed to remember me, but I may have been fooling myself.

Because Japanese culture traditionally emphasized the importance of absolute racial purity, I was apprehensive about how Yukiko's parents had reacted upon meeting their French-Japanese American grandson. But apparently Chris won the hearts of Yukiko's mother as well as her grandmother, who was a patron of the arts and an avid supporter of classical musicians: as our son's great-grandmother carefully studied Chris's hands, she said, "*Kuri-chan h*as large hands and long fingers just like Chopin." In Japan, Christopher was nicknamed, *Kuri-chan* or "little chestnut."

Yukiko's father, who was reserved even with his own daughter, seemed to have been won over by *Kuri-chan* as well. One night while Yukiko pretended to be asleep, Chris's grandfather quietly knelt on the tatami near his face, and in the glow of the night lamp watched his grandson sleeping peacefully "for what seemed like hours" to Yukiko. At last he gently pulled the futon blanket up to Chris's chin, making sure his grandson was fully covered before tiptoeing out of the room.

During my short visit in Milan, I promised Yukiko we'd introduce Chris to my parents at Christmas, and in the meantime, spend a day together on our way back to New York, but she said, "I don't want to go home." Since she had enough traveler's checks to last months, I didn't insist. After kissing Chris and saying, "À bientôt" to the Casablancas, I waved goodbye to Yukiko: our marriage seemed beyond repair as I flew back to Paris and on to New York alone.

When I arrived at our apartment, I paced around, looked at Christopher's empty crib, and felt Yukiko's presence in all things. Sensing our love had perhaps ended in Milan, I was overcome by a deep loneliness. With regret, I felt I finally understood what Yukiko must have endured during my absence when we could no longer travel together on assignments. Chris was still too young to feel or understand the effects of my absence, but he would in time.

In Milan, Yukiko was hurt but not lost. She could not be the traditional Japanese *Oku-sama* wife, or "person at the rear of the house."

At the end of July, I was away again when Yukiko returned from Milan, but fortunately, the ever-gracious Kurt Kornfeld went to greet her at the airport. When I returned in August, I talked to Yukiko about possibly separating for a while, saying, "I don't mean a legal separation, just a physical one, so we can think things over. You and Chris can continue to have the lifestyle you're accustomed to." Yukiko simply responded, "Maybe."

If I had a better understanding of the stoic qualities of Japanese culture, I would have realized that Yukiko's "maybe" was actually a pained rejection of my suggestion. Though sensing her disapproval of separating, I took her answer at face value, and we would separate for a few months.

Under deadline pressures, I had little time to dwell on Yukiko's hurt feelings or the regret I felt after our hasty decision to separate. It was August 12, and I needed a visa to go to Egypt. The *Post* had purchased exclusive rights to publish excerpts from the *Autobiography of Malcolm X*, written with Alex Haley, and on August 14, I had a midnight appointment in Cairo to meet the man known as a "black American revolutionary."

MALCOLM X

THE INTERVIEW

CAIRO 1964

I had never heard of Malcolm X and sensed from Hank Walker's briefing that his knowledge of the man was sketchy as well. As he handed me copies of the book excerpts that the *Post* would publish, Hank explained, "After talking with his agent, all I know is Malcolm X might meet you around midnight at the Hilton Hotel in Cairo or leave instructions for you to meet him in Alexandria. He's presently in Egypt to establish his movement among African leaders to indict the United States for racial crimes before the United Nations. He hasn't agreed to being photographed, as he told his agent that pictures of him are already available in the States. But we want photographs of him in Egypt, not here."

Hank continued, "Now you have to understand that Malcolm X, whose real name is Malcolm Little, is a black American, a Muslim revolutionary, a rebel. He says he hates the 'white man' and doesn't understand why we're sending you to Egypt, so if you actually meet him, be prepared for a hostile encounter. At best, you'll have just one day of shooting time, but if you succeed, we'll hold the presses for a cover and double-page lead. It's imperative you cable me on August 15, as I'll need to know, one way or the other. Good luck."

After an overnight, 18-hour TWA flight with stops in Paris and Rome, I checked in at the Cairo Hilton late in the afternoon on August 14. From excerpts of his autobiography, I learned that Malcolm X's life had been scarred by racism, violence, and degradation, which eventually led him to the Muslim faith. From his writing, it was obvious why and how racism and life in America's ghettos triggered his rebellion against the establishment. I was appalled I had never seen or known about the conditions he described, and that there was such a dark side of America of which I was completely ignorant.

" In the sacred setting, he thoughtfully looked directly into my lens, as I captured the *Post*'s cover of him… "

Unfamiliar with Egypt, I bought a book from the hotel newsstand and looked for pictures of the Great Mosque of Mohammed Ali in Cairo. Using pyramids for a background seemed a little obvious for a photo; since Malcolm X was a black American Muslim, the mosque would be an ideal location.

With still enough light in Cairo's summer sky, I rushed to the mosque, removed my shoes, and entered the great prayer hall to study the light. By dusk, I knew exactly where I'd photograph Malcolm X if he showed up; finally satisfied with my plan, I let my driver take me back to the Hilton.

To pass the time until midnight, I had dinner, tried an undrinkable Egyptian wine, and switched to Coke. In my room, I mentally prepared myself for a long wait and opened William Shirer's *The Rise and Fall of the Third Reich*. Because of its 1,143-page length, it had remained unread on my bookshelf for years but seemed perfect for the 36-hour trip and the wait for Malcolm X.

Unable to concentrate, I jumped ahead to a chapter on "The Collapse of France" and read the first paragraph several times till I settled on a line, "The French were doomed." I simply couldn't focus and put the book down on a coffee table, paced around, and looked out the window at the Nile flowing northward to the Mediterranean Sea. The recurring question was, "How do I approach a black man with explosive ideas who has overwhelming reasons to hate me?"

I constantly looked at my watch as the minute hand ticked past midnight. Finally, not long after 1:30 A.M., a receptionist informed me, "The visitor you expected is on his way to your room." A few moments later, I opened the door for Malcolm X, and we said, "Hello." I extended my hand, but he didn't take it.

I felt more magnetism than anger in him as I said, "I thought I might have to go to Alexandria to meet you. I'm glad you came." He just stood there as I added, "After reading excerpts from your autobiography, I understand why my editor told me to expect a hostile man." "Do you?" was all he replied.

I answered him by quoting something he had written about Barry Goldwater, the Republican nominee for the 1964 presidential election. "You said you respect him as a man because he speaks his convictions. 'He isn't another liberal just trying to please both racists and integrationists, smiling at one and whispering to the other.'"

Malcolm X sat down for the first time and spoke. "That's right. I respect Goldwater because with him, I know exactly where he stands, while with liberals, I don't know."

I asked, "Do I call you Mr. X or Malcolm?" He responded, "Call me Malcolm." I said, "My father encourages the humanist ideal. In his mind, there's absolutely no excuse for racism or oppression. I hope I inherited his values."

Since he knew nothing about me and my accent was too faint to betray my French background, he responded, "So, you're a typical New York liberal, claiming compassion and understanding of racism and its oppression. But you don't know the first thing about oppression, nor can you begin to understand oppression."

I wasn't sure what a New York liberal was, but perhaps my reading Shirer's chapter on "The Collapse of France" several times had unconsciously prepared me to respond. "Malcolm, it's true I don't know the first thing about racism in your country, which I've adopted as my own. It's also true I don't know the first thing about the oppression of your people in America. In fact, I know more about Japanese racism against Koreans than American racism against its...black citizens." I had hesitated to use the word "black" because Negro was commonly used in the media in 1964, but I remembered the *Post* intended to call Malcolm X a "black Muslim."

I continued, "But I don't have to be black to have known oppression. I was 11 when the Nazis invaded France and the Vichy Government enthusiastically collaborated. For the next four years we suffered oppression both from German Nazis and French police. We endured four long years of hunger, anger, and humiliation."

Malcolm X sensed I was still angry at the memory. I made an impassioned speech and knew I had reached him when he said, "Four years is a long time, but just imagine a lifetime." After relaxing the stern expression on his face, he actually smiled and asked, "John, what would you like to do?" After outlining my plans, I added, "If we have time, we can travel to the pyramids."

I immediately knew the idea of being photographed in the Great Mosque appealed to him, but I pointed out, "I'll need your help with the authorities." It was past 4:00 A.M. when our discussion ended, but a few hours later, we met again and rushed to the mosque to obtain permission to photograph.

I spent the afternoon of August 15, 1964, photographing Malcolm X in the Great Mosque of Mohammed Ali. In the sacred setting, he thoughtfully looked directly into my lens, as I captured the *Post*'s cover of him with his fist against his chin and the ring of a crescent moon and star on his finger, symbolizing Malcolm's connection to the faith of Islam. Then, with just enough daylight remaining, we rushed to the pyramids, as all tourists did, and finished our shoot as the sun set on ancient Egyptian tombs.

In a cable, I informed Hank Walker it was safe to hold the presses. I described to him the contents of what I shot on two different sets of film for two different labs—in case one made any mistakes—and asked Hank to have someone meet my plane on arrival at JFK.

Before my New York flight, Malcolm and I had a convivial dinner at the Hilton Hotel where we had an easy and honest conversation about the paradoxes in our lives. Malcolm X was inquisitive about my early youth in France during the war years, so I explained why, during Hitler's occupation of France, America for me became an idealistic symbol of freedom. I described how after the war, I left France, locked in its class struggles, and made my way to America in search of a more egalitarian society with greater opportunity. I told him, "America for me lived up to its promise."

> **His American story was radically opposed to mine: all he had ever known in the U.S. was "racism, segregation, oppression, and little opportunity.**

I knew more of India's caste system and "untouchables" than I knew of America's segregation of black citizens, especially in the South—segregation made no sense to me.

I asked Malcolm X, "How could America liberate Western Europe, yet simultaneously oppress you and your people?" I wanted to know. "That's a very long and complex story," he said, as he intelligently and articulately gave me a short course on black history in America.

I realized his account might be prejudiced by anger or his own suffering, but his story underscored my ignorance of "his people"—I could have listened to him all night. I had many questions to ask, but he had to write a letter that he wanted me to personally deliver to his wife Betty Shabazz in Queens, New York.

We met for the last time the next morning. He gave me his letter fully addressed and again asked me to deliver it in person, saying, "Don't mail it. I don't trust the mail, but I trust you." I promised and personally delivered his letter to Betty Shabazz, soon after returning to New York.

Malcolm X and I shook hands just before I left for the airport, and our eyes met and held. We had spent 16 hours together, and it seemed we mutually understood

our personal rebellions and had empathized briefly with one another. His struggle for the rights of "his people" made my own search for a more egalitarian society seem insignificant, the privilege of a free white man. As my driver pulled away, we waved goodbye. Little did I know I would never see Malcolm X again: he was assassinated just a few months later in the Audubon Ballroom in Manhattan on February 25, 1965.

Nothing in my American experience had prepared me for meeting that remarkable man whose personal history stood for the history of African Americans. He had shaken my idealistic vision of America, but I found some solace in the fact that John F. Kennedy had initiated the Civil Rights Bill and that President Lyndon Johnson made sure it was enacted by Congress. In time, I'd expand my knowledge of "America's dilemma" during an assignment to photograph one of the ghettoes Malcolm X described.

My portrait of the fiery black leader made the cover of the September 12, 1964, issue of *The Saturday Evening Post*. Excerpts from his autobiography ran 14 pages with a five-column lead photograph of him praying in Cairo's Great Mosque and a near full page of him speaking with the mosque's Grand Mufti. Quoting his own words, the cover was headlined; "Malcolm X: 'More riots will erupt.'" It was subtitled: "His own story of crime, conversion, and black Muslims in action."

Hank was full of praise for my work in Egypt when I met him at our new offices in the *Post* building at 641 Lexington Avenue. After he showed me the dummies and cover of the layout, I was pleased to hear Hank's compliments. At Toots Shor's restaurant, one of Hank's regular watering holes, I felt elated.

Raising his glass, Hank said, "Let's toast your fifth cover this year. Keep this up and soon you'll beat Norman Rockwell." We laughed at the idea—no one could match Rockwell's 322 covers for the *Post*. For nearly half a century, he painted covers for the magazine, depicting a sentimentalized and idealized America, but the Rockwell era at the *Post* had ended in 1962 when Clay Blair's regime took command.

Malcolm X's wife Betty Shabazz and their children.

A GOOD FIGHT

THE CHANGING OF THE GUARD

NEW YORK 1964

After hearing more praise from Hank, I ordered a second martini to build up the nerve to tell him that Yukiko and I were about to separate. He had first met her in Tokyo and had gotten to know her at several dinners she hosted at Two Tudor Place. The last time he saw her, he told me, "Yukiko is remarkable."

Since Hank had been a mentor, I sensed my separation from Yukiko would meet with disapproval, so instead of confessing, I asked, "What's coming up?" Once again he had an assignment "tailor-made" for me. He explained, "Our writer W.C. Heinz—Bill Heinz to you—covered the Battle of the Bulge in World War II, and the *Post* has assigned him to retrace his footsteps 20 years later. Since you must've been a teenager in France during that last great battle in Europe, I thought you'd be interested in joining Heinz on his pilgrimage."

I was certainly interested. I vividly recalled the days of uncertainty in Paris around Christmas 1944 when hysterical rumors spread that the American front would collapse in southern Belgium's Ardenne Forest, and my own fear that the German infantry's 17-division "Wehrmacht Monster" might again invade Paris. The rumors setting off panic were not totally unfounded. For six weeks, the outcome of the fighting remained uncertain. After 158,000 casualties on both sides, the "Battle of the Bulge" concluded, marking "the beginning of the end of Hitler's Thousand-Year Reich," as it was later described by the *Post*.

Hank and I agreed that I'd join Heinz in Belgium early in September after finishing a job photographing Alexander Calder and his mobiles at the Guggenheim Museum. Curious about the *Post*'s financial health, I asked Hank if the copper recently found on Curtis Publishing Company landholdings would help the magazine. He simply said, "Wait for the annual report."

Remnants of war in the Hürtgen Forest, Germany.

His answer was unusually reticent, because normally he gave me glowing accounts of the magazine's condition under Clay Blair and scathing reports of incompetence by the men running Curtis Publishing.

What Hank didn't tell me about at Toots Shor's was his role as a key player in a rebellion organized by Blair and Marvin Kantor, chairman of the magazine division. Their aim was to oust Matthew Joseph Culligan, president of Curtis Publishing.

Blair and Kantor had recruited the top editors and advertising executives at Curtis magazines to draft and sign a manifesto attacking Culligan whose "inefficiency and incompetence would mean the bankruptcy of the Curtis Publishing Company, and if he were not removed from power at the next board meeting, all signers would resign."

I never knew the content of their explosive manifesto until much later when I read Otto Friedrich's definitive book, *Decline and Fall: The Struggle for Power at a Great Magazine*, published in 1969, some five years after the fact.

The rebels' final meeting began in September at a restaurant in Greenwich, Connecticut, and ended at Hank Walker's residence, according to Friedrich. From Hank, my friend and mentor, I learned absolutely nothing at the time.

For my assignment in Europe, it was visually difficult symbolizing a passage of time and evoking the horror of a bloody battle that took place two decades earlier. For a writer with notes and memories, it would be an easier task than for a photographer. Yet I found powerful remnants of the war like an American GI's bullet-pierced helmet rusting in a shallow stream; since the area was still littered with live mines from the battle 20 years ago, I hired a technician with a mine detector to gingerly clear a path, so I could safely set up a tripod a few feet away from the forlorn helmet.

Using a very slow shutter speed, I captured the red and yellow leaves of autumn carried by a gentle current, blurring their motion as they passed the still, anonymous helmet resting in a shallow stream of the Hürtgen Forest in Western Germany.

In the church cemetery of Strauch, I found rows of graves of the German infantry's dead, buried under birchwood crosses capped with distinctive, fear-inspiring steel helmets of the German army. From a distance, with helmets perfectly lined up on the crosses, one almost imagined the soldiers back in marching order again.

While I was busy searching for signs of a battle from the winter of 1944, Yukiko split our belongings and instructed movers to take our possessions to separate apartments. She and Chris moved to a Manhattan ground floor apartment at 310 East 70th Street with a patio garden, while my effects were taken to my studio apartment at 220 East 60th Street.

On October 9, a day before our seventh wedding anniversary, I flew from Paris back to New York, but I wasn't going home to celebrate—I wasn't going home at all. I sat down on my brown sofa by the southern windows, and, resting my feet on an equipment case, wondered how I had let things go so far.

I stared at the packed boxes in disbelief: the studio looked like a warehouse. With the refrigerator off and empty, there was no ice, whiskey, food, and no telephone. But self-pity was a trap: to escape, I rushed 10 blocks north to visit Yukiko and Chris, who was then nine months and two days old.

Babbling on a toy telephone, Chris seemed pleased to see me, but Yukiko was reserved. I had intended to ask, "Don't you think our decision to separate was pride driven and irrational?" But when I noticed she had already decorated their cheerful apartment, I remained silent. Meanwhile, Chris had the run of the place, crawling in and out of the patio, enjoying a New York Indian summer.

Yukiko and I made small talk about old battlefields I covered in Europe, but she didn't seem interested. I watched the bond between mother and son as Chris indicated his wish to be picked up, and I understood why I wasn't missed—I had been away for most of his young life.

As I left Yukiko's apartment, her doorman, a fatherly old gentleman, politely inquired if I was Chris's father. When I said, "Yes," he responded, "Bright little boy, Chris, with a very nice, pretty mother." I thought, "Only in New York would the doorman know my son's name eight days after his arrival."

Giving a cab driver my studio address, I glanced at the *New York Times* that Yukiko had given me. In disbelief, I saw the headline: "Curtis Editors Accuse Chief of Mismanagement" and redirected my driver to *The Saturday Evening Post*. It was late Friday night, and Hank Walker was not in the building: the few assistant editors still there knew nothing.

I could only speculate. Long before the editors' rebellion made the *Times*, I knew from Hank that Clay Blair's ambition was to create a new dynamic, to shake up and modernize the anachronistic management of the Curtis Publishing Company.

Reasoning Blair's moment of triumph had arrived, I imagined he'd soon be named president of Curtis, but I generally wasn't interested in corporate matters. I just wanted the *Saturday Evening Post* to be the best magazine in America. If all editors, writers, and photographers strove for excellence, I was sure we'd succeed. I wasn't alone in my idealism: the creative energy was high at the *Post*, manic at times.

It was impossible to find out any new details, so I informed the lab I wanted my films processed by Monday and left the *Post* for my apartment, promising myself to set up bookshelves. The next day's headline read: "Curtis Aides Vow to Press Growth." Unable to reach Hank, I drilled walls and anchored shelves, filling them with books, and the studio finally acquired some warmth as yesterday's loneliness eased.

When anguish and anger prevailed during the Nazi oppression of France, I had found solace in reading and writing poems: at an early age, writing poetry had helped me face solitude and adversity. Later, in southern California's sunny land without seasons, I discovered Walt Whitman's *Leaves of Grass*. In Whitman, I found another rebel and free man, conveying the essence of the American experiment, its rebellion, humanity, boundless energy, manic pace, and continental optimism. When fear and doubt crept into my soul, I often turned to his imagery for reassurance.

At dusk in Manhattan, I turned on the only light and opened my timeworn copy of Whitman's *Song of Myself*. Though hardly in a mood of personal celebration, I read on, cheered by Whitman's imagery. I read over and again, "I am he that walks with the tender and growing night; I call to the earth and sea, half held by the night, please close, bare-bosom'd night....mad, naked, summer night."

On October 11, I was shocked to read the front page of the *Times*: "Curtis Suspends Two Culligan Critics....Blair and Kantor Relieved of Duties in Policy Rift." Because Marvin Kantor operated on the business side of the *Post*, I hardly knew him, but Blair's dismissal as editor-in-chief by the board of directors struck a personal blow.

I could only guess that Hank Walker's career at the *Post* was endangered as well, and I couldn't imagine the photographic department without him. Hank had brought high-quality photojournalism to the *Post* for the first time in its long history, but because most *Post* editors were text-oriented, Hank needed Clay Blair's full support to make photography a significant and integral part of the revitalized magazine.

It was Sunday, and I couldn't reach a soul on the phone. The following week, when I finally saw Hank Walker, he had no time for a briefing. He simply asked me to help pack Blair's personal files and "take them out of here before the Pinkerton guys seal the place." After several hours, we carried boxes of files to a hotel on Lexington. As he left for his home in Connecticut, all Hank would say was, "It ain't over yet."

He was wrong. Blair was gone and Hank was so stripped of power, he resigned instead of waiting to be fired. On the day he left, we had drinks at Toots Shor's. He seemed philosophical, saying, "We fought a good fight and lost." Hank was not the type to dwell on events, so after a few drinks, he rose to leave, and we embraced and wished each other good luck. It was the last time I saw him.

Managing Director William A. "Bill" Emerson assumed the role of *Post* editor but without title. Rumors of who'd be assigned Clay Blair's old job were endless. Names mentioned included Emerson, Otto Friedrich, Ed Thompson, and President Kennedy's former press secretary, Pierre Salinger.

I shuddered hearing Friedrich's name mentioned. Though he was a highly cultured man, music lover, and good writer, he seemed to have little appreciation for photography or understanding of the role it had come to play at the *Post*.

Emerson understood and appreciated good photography, and he attracted support among editors and writers by sincerely treating them as individuals, massaging their egos, and charming them with southern eloquence; he called his coworkers "Tiger"—both colleagues as well as staff whose names he couldn't remember. I liked him, and we had an easy-going relationship.

I thought of Emerson as a leader who'd stand by you. Naturally, I liked the idea of him taking charge. The photographic department was currently leaderless since Picture Editor Marshall Lumsden, recruited by Hank Walker, had left for California to become editor of the weekly supplement, *West Magazine*, published by the *Los Angeles Times*.

With dark times at the *Post*, the mood in the offices was somber. Things were so bad, a decision was made in January 1965 to turn the old weekly magazine into a bi-weekly. At the same time, we all felt a need to remind the public of the magazine's greatness.

In the December 12, 1964, issue, Assistant Managing Editor Otto Friedrich spoke of the *Post* as an ever-changing yet "uniquely traditional magazine" that "is completing a year of extraordinary excellence" and is prepared "to match our 1964 record against that of any magazine anywhere."

Friedrich continued: "We'd like to cite Roger Kahn's dramatic report on Harlem, "White Man Walk Easy," and Edward R.F. Scheehan's penetrating survey of the Catholic Church in America, "Not Peace but the Sword." The *Post*'s fiction too had been unique. Saul Bellow's *Herzog* was first excerpted in the *Post*; Arthur Miller's controversial play *After the Fall* appeared in its entirety in the magazine; and stories have come from such distinguished writers as James Gould Cozzens, John Updike, Graham Greene, Louis Auchincloss, and John O'Hara."

Bill Emerson added a few words to Friedrich's editorial, perhaps to acknowledge the visual quality of the magazine, stating, "We will produce a more important, more lustrous magazine than ever before." Friedrich ignored photography's contribution to the *Post* in his editorial and got away with it because Walker was gone and no one spoke for photographers.

As the year ended, Curtis's board of directors had yet to name an editor. Emerson continued as "acting editor," while the photographic department operated in a vacuum, leaving photographers in limbo. Rumor had it that Walker's position as assistant managing editor would be eliminated along with other cuts. Losses at Curtis were expected to surpass the 1963 figure of $3.5 million: in the end, the loss for 1964 reached $14 million.

Moving in to fill the void, Art Director Asger Jerrild assigned me to research a project on Russian women. Cooperating with the Soviet Press Agency Novosti helped me obtain a visa for the Soviet Union. Scheduled to leave for Moscow on January 5, 1965, I decided to put off questions about the *Post*'s future until completing my assignment.

A month before departure, Yukiko and I celebrated Chris's 11th month in the world. At that time, aware Yukiko was an aesthete with a refined visual appreciation, I encouraged her to take on a part-time job at Black Star, and Kurt Kornfeld assured her that she'd be an asset. Working at Black Star's picture library for three half days a week, she'd only earn $15 a day, about the same we paid the kind, very religious Polish grandmother who worked as our babysitter, but money was never the issue for Yukiko. For her, it was important to meet other people, especially other women, beyond the few friends she knew in Manhattan, so on December 8, she began her own long career in photojournalism at Black Star.

That Christmas season, I felt strangely vulnerable. Yukiko would celebrate Christmas dinner at Kurt's family house in Huntington, Long Island, but I was not invited for "obvious reasons." I'd join Yukiko and Chris at her place on Christmas Eve, but it was just an occasion for exchanging gifts. My plan was to make a plea to Yukiko for a reunion on New Year's Day, a few days before leaving for Moscow.

Weighed down by troubled thoughts, I went Christmas shopping. I had never known Christmas in New York. Manhattan was in a festive mood with New Yorkers rushing about, loaded with shopping bags, windows cheerfully decorated, Christmas carols resounding in stores, and bright lights everywhere. Strings of tiny white brilliant lights glowed like distant stars. Midtown Manhattan seemed merry, fully soused in the spirit of Christmas. But I hated shopping.

Taking the easy way out, I perused Saks Fifth Avenue and found one of Yukiko's favorite perfumes, Chasse Gardée, (Private Hunting) by Carven. At FAO Schwartz, I bought a beautifully crafted red and yellow dump truck for Chris, big enough for him to climb into.

Chris, now nearly a year old, could walk, even dash around, and I hoped he'd have fun pushing the toy truck around his living room. Giftwrapped, it was a huge bundle, almost too big for my arms, and the salesman wished me, "Merry Christmas!" He urged, "Look for a Checker cab, you'll need one."

But at 4:00 P.M., New York's cabbies changed shifts and disappeared with their "off duty" lights shining. It seemed I was out of luck, so I awkwardly walked the half a mile to my East 60th Street apartment, cradling Chris's first Christmas gift.

On Christmas Eve, Yukiko's doorman announced, "Chris's father is on his way." His words brought home the reality of our separation, which during travel had remained abstract. I planned to appeal to Yukiko's idealism and reason, so our very young son and his parents might live under a single roof.

Yukiko and Chris greeted me warmly at the door, and with an expression of wonderment, he gazed at my big red bundle. "Chris, this is from Santa." He just babbled a few words. Yukiko said, "Chris met one Santa for each day we went shopping, but he was only mildly interested. What really fascinated him were the uniformed men and women of the Salvation Army singing carols in the streets. You should have seen the joy in his face."

Yukiko decorated a Christmas tree on one end of the dining table, "out of Chris's reach." Its star nearly reached the ceiling. Underneath were exquisitely wrapped presents—giftwrapping was an art form in Japan. The rest of the table was arrayed with canapés, plum wine, a bucket of ice cubes, and a bottle of Chivas Regal.

Chris sat on the floor, gleefully unwrapping his toys as Yukiko and I toasted each other with a formal "Merry Christmas." Exchanging gifts, the perfume wasn't a surprise, nor was my silver Dunhill cigarette lighter. I savored another paté de foie gras canapé. The beautifully set table with my favorite whiskey and hors d'oeuvres gave me a sense of belonging, and for an instant I thought I had a family again.

In my enthusiasm, I suggested we take our first ski vacation in France after my Russian journey. Yukiko responded somewhat coldly and resented the fact I had planned it alone. In previous years, I had made most major decisions in our lives, largely dictated by my work. But by Christmas of 1964, Yukiko had been on her own for more than two months: she held a job and seemed to have easily learned to manage her life with Chris.

I didn't know it at the time, but she had written in her diary, "I believed you wanted us to be reunited out of a sense of duty, not out of love, and I didn't want that. So I was cool to the idea and wasn't sure a ski vacation at Megève could overcome the divide that had grown between us."

The rest of the evening was spent wheeling Chris around in his toy truck. His laughter filled the apartment, and we shared it joyfully, but as I watched Yukiko discreetly, subtly seeking approval, I realized my wish for a reunion would take more than a child's laughter on Christmas Eve.

Her culture didn't permit me to be confrontational. In Japan, I had learned to read her heart if not her mind. Our differences had never been solved by head-on discussions; instead I communicated through letters appealing to her sensitivity about the pain of our shared crisis, rather than discussing the crisis itself.

At first I found it difficult to express myself in a roundabout way, exploring the effects of our problems rather than the causes. But I had lived in Japan long enough to appreciate the subtle nature of Japanese culture. Such a discerning approach had worked for me in journalism when covering delicate subjects in her country.

Heated words were brutal to her and would only elicit absolute silence, which was painful. So in our first five years together, I had used letter writing as an art form to investigate and face our problems. Yukiko in turn would respond in the same poetic manner.

But by the end of 1964, we had lived in New York for two years, and I no longer had the patience to communicate under such constraints, as I reverted to my inherent nature, both consciously and unconsciously. My American culture dominated my thinking, because I loved its openness, informality, and simplicity, in many ways the opposite of Yukiko's culture.

Despite two years in Manhattan, Yukiko's cultural thinking and behavior remained profoundly Japanese. On Christmas Eve, I again understood that to discuss a possible reunion, I'd have to write a letter. I'd write of the frailty of human relations, and if I could make my appeal poetic, all the better. In no case would I speak again of a ski trip to Megève.

Soon Chris was sleepy, and Yukiko tucked him in as I kissed him goodnight. Then I kissed Yukiko on both cheeks as I would a sister and left, wishing her "Merry Christmas with Kurt's family."

For Christmas and the following days, I checked equipment and emulsions of color films, which was critical in 1964, because the fastest films were not always reliable. Afterwards, I was confident and felt prepared for any emergencies. But I didn't like the fact that I'd shoot 4,000 images and never see a single frame on assignment. The problem was that American film could not be processed in Russia or shipped safely to New York for appraisal.

In the last hour before midnight on New Year's Eve, I was overwhelmed by the silence of my apartment. I had yet to install a television or hi-fi, so I stepped out and took a cab to as close to Times Square as possible. Dropped at the corner of Fifth Avenue, I walked west and joined the outskirts of a noisy, unruly crowd. I was unable to see the crystal ball dropping at midnight but heard it fall, in cheers, squeaky noisemakers, and whistles in a multitude of revelers wearing funny hats.

Shaking hands with total strangers, we wished each other "Happy New Year." In that first instant of 1965, surrounded by thousands of people celebrating or pretending to be happy, I could not recall ever feeling so desperately alone.

Later in the day, I wished Chris and Yukiko a "Happy New Year" and spent a few hours with them. After I handed Yukiko the letter I had written shortly after the Times Square experience, we said goodbye. I promised to send a cable or call if the phone lines in Russia weren't too primitive.

On the evening of January 5, I took off on a Pan American 707 for Paris. Enjoying the luxury of first class, I sipped champagne and reread three pages of notes written by the *Post*'s Women's Editor, Jeanette Sarkisian. She provided a broad outline of Russian women I might want to cover, in every imaginable situation or job. Sarkisian noted that she covered all possible categories, "so you can make your own script in Russia."

Interest in Russian women was sparked by 26-year-old Valentina Tereshkova, the first woman to circle the earth in a Russian Vostok spaceship in June 1963. Her successful orbit was another blow to the pride of the American space program but a huge boost to Russian women. The Soviet Union's propaganda machine exploited the space shot to glorify merits of Marxist-Leninist ideology, and the superiority of the Soviet social system, its people, and its women.

In a subsequent trip to the United States, Soviet deputy minister for health Mrs. Gregory Sirotkina raised further interest in Russian women when she said, "It's no longer in fashion in the U.S.S.R. for a woman to be without an occupation or profession. A husband appreciates his wife more if she keeps growing intellectually instead of just being a wife and mother. American women were the first suffragettes in the world, yet today American women do not become active until they have reached the sunset of their lives."

The text of *Post* writer Olga Carlisle and my photographic essay were to address two principal questions. Had women of the Soviet Union achieved full emancipation? Had Russian women reached a true level of equality with Russian men?

With a strong tailwind, we crossed the Atlantic in just over six hours. It was 7:30 A.M. when we landed at Orly Airport. Since I never slept on planes and my Aeroflot to Moscow wasn't scheduled for departure till the afternoon, I checked into the Orly Hilton and slept poorly.

Arriving at Le Bourget airfield, the departure screen displayed that my Aeroflot Tupolev 104 flight to Moscow was "delayed." We were originally scheduled for takeoff at 16:30, or 4:30 P.M., but there was no indication of how long we'd be delayed. There was no one to ask: the Aeroflot counter was not staffed. Eventually it was announced our flight would be delayed for one, two, three, then four hours.

After liftoff, the captain, speaking French with a heavy Russian accent, explained that their original departure from Moscow to Paris had been delayed by a snowstorm. With a two-hour time zone difference we'd land at Moscow's Sheremetyevo International around 2:30 A.M.

Approaching Moscow's airport, we were violently buffeted by a snowstorm. Visibility outside the window was zero except for snow in the reflected glow of the Tupolev landing lights. I couldn't see lights on the runway. Though Russians were by all accounts ahead of us in space exploration, I shared no confidence in Soviet civilian technology. I remembered how it had taken nearly 20 minutes with several unscheduled stops in the elevators of the Ukraine Hotel in Moscow to reach the lobby from the 17th floor. In fact, every mechanical thing I saw in the civilian sector during my 1961 Siberian journey seemed to belong to the 1940s.

Our plane descended, then hit the runway hard several times, settled, and rolled. It was a relief to hear engines smoothly roar into reverse thrust as the Tupolev slowed. It took a long time to reach a barely visible terminal. When the ground crew rolled stairs to the plane and the stewardess opened the hatch, a great wind blew into the first-class cabin, blasting snow into the passengers' faces.

I'd flown many photographic missions and learned firsthand some basic facts about aviation safety, so it was beyond me how the tower granted permission to land in such a storm. I wondered why the captain didn't request to land at an alternate airport, which was his right.

As I descended the stairs, blinded by snow and struggling not to fall with my camera case, I thought to myself, "These Russians are crazy when it comes to safety. Perhaps that's one of the reasons they lead us in the space race." Decades later, in the 1990s, when secrets were revealed about Russia's rush to the stars, the world uncovered their high accident rate, much higher than Western intelligence suspected.

In New York, I had received confirmation from the Novosti Press Agency that my flight would be met by an English-speaking researcher from Novosti, an automobile from Intourist, and an interpreter. Novosti's message specifically assured, "Our man will be in the customs area to speed you through."

At customs, I saw no one looking for me. Waived through with a personal suitcase and five cases of equipment, I stood around and waited, wondering how I'd find a taxi in a late-night blizzard.

Finally I saw a burly man in a parka and muskrat hat gesticulating in the waiting area on the other side of customs. When he waved a slate with my name written in chalk, I identified myself and pointed to my baggage. After he negotiated with a militiaman, he joined me, and we shook hands. I didn't speak Russian, and he didn't speak English. With his hands, he mimed steering a wheel and imitated sounds of an engine: he was my driver from Intourist.

He then mimed a female figure, cupped his hands a few inches from his chest and waved toward the terminal: I deducted my interpreter was a woman who had left. When I asked about "my Novosti man," he responded, "Novosti," and waved in the distance. He too had left.

What didn't fit in the trunk, we stacked by the driver's seat, and I took my seat behind the driver. It was now close to 4:00 A.M. Moscow time and snowing lightly—the blizzard had passed. We drove through what seemed to be a forest of birch trees in our headlights. All was white, the road freshly covered, not a single tire track to be seen. My driver was apparently using tree lines as visual markers to guess the center of the road. It was a beautiful scene, magical, virginal, befitting the Russian winters of my imagination.

Great white silence was broken by the hum of our engine, which suddenly began to sputter. The car jerked, and the engine quit along with the heater. As we came to a stop, my driver threw his hands up, got out, and lifted the hood. Opening the radiator, steam shot up hissing. The radiator was empty.

Reaching for the drain valve, my driver turned it shut. He saw my bewildered expression, and in pantomime worthy of Roman times, managed to convey that he had emptied the radiator at the airport to prevent freezing. Hilariously, he made it understood there was no vodka for radiators in Russia, only for men. It dawned on me that by "vodka for radiators," he meant antifreeze. We both laughed, splintering the hush of the wilderness.

After calming down from laughter, he began squeezing handfuls of snow into the radiator. Each attempt created a few drops of water. Forcing snow into the narrow opening was hopeless, so I came up with an obvious solution. Climbing on the bumper, my driver held my back while I unzipped my pants, aimed carefully, and emptied my bladder into the radiator.

My newly made friend was elated, repeatedly exclaiming, "Ochen karasho!" ("Very good!") In turn, he climbed on the bumper to empty his own bladder. I was sure we had produced a powerful new antifreeze—mine was champagne-based while his was vodka, mixed from his flask at the airport. Between us, we produced enough fluid for the engine to start and drive a few miles to a housing project, where my driver woke a family for some water to top his radiator.

AN ARMY OF WOMEN

BALLERINA, POET, SOVIET IDEALIST

RUSSIA 1965

I t was 5:30 in the morning and snowing heavily when we reached the National Hotel in Moscow. In the streets, I saw what looked like an army of women bundled in heavy clothing, shoveling snow into a long line of trucks driven by men who'd later dump the snow into the Moscow River. The regiment of women swept and shoveled the snow as fast as it fell. The surrealistic scene of a myriad of black figures against the white background would've made a good picture for my essay on women's manual labor, but the streetlamp lighting was too weak for even my fastest film.

Finding hotel doors locked, my driver knocked loudly and woke a grumpy guard who helped carry my gear inside. As my driver motioned goodbye, we exchanged bear hugs like old friends. I never saw him again.

It seemed as though I'd just fallen asleep when the phone rang. On the line, a sweetly accented Russian voice said, "My name is Oksana Mikhalova, your Intourist interpreter. I'm to take you to the Novosti Press Agency for a ten o'clock editorial conference."

In a sleepy voice, I asked her to give me one hour. After a quick shower and shave, I found the dining room and was handed a menu. I asked for an omelet but was told "nyet" ("no") by a surly waitress standing with arms crossed against her ample bosom, as she stared at me for a full five minutes in the empty dining hall.

It was "nyet" again for borscht soup with sour cream. Annoyed, I pointed to the menu for black bread, tea, and fresh Beluga caviar. Since my order required no preparation, I got it in minutes, but without a smile. It was my first fresh caviar and so delicious, I ordered another 30-gram jar. At $10, it was a bargain and an upbeat way to start an assignment, though it went against my principle that pleasure and luxury was deserved only after completion of a successful assignment.

On the sidewalk, I met my interpreter, Oksana. Shaking hands, she apologized for not meeting me at the airport, explaining she and Novosti's reporter had waited till their last train home was leaving. When she asked about the driver, I said he was "a great guy with a wonderful sense of humor" but didn't mention the story of the empty radiator, reasoning it might get him in trouble.

Twenty-four-year-old Oksana was pretty with high cheekbones, blond hair, and hazel eyes. She wore no makeup and seemed unsophisticated. When she smiled, she glowed with the freshness of a country girl: her cheeks were red from the cold, the color of poppy in a meadow. I was charmed. In the freezing bleakness of Moscow, she immediately cheered me up and helped me forget the unfriendly woman at the hotel.

Delighted with Oksana, I knew I'd put her in my essay. I suspected from our discussions that she had been carefully selected for my project: because of her upbringing in the Komsomol Youth and the ideals she expressed about becoming a Communist Party member, she was the party's model "Soviet woman." I'd learn much about her during the two weeks we worked together.

There was so much conviction in her "faith in party," it was impossible to dismiss her thoughts as purely brainwashed. Oksana's sincerity was palpable. Communism was her religion, so I couldn't contradict her, nor did I try. By 1965, propagandists persuaded the majority of people that their Soviet system was the superior experiment in government. In Oksana, it had created a believer.

At Novosti, I was introduced to an editor and four research reporters, all men. Sitting down at a huge round table, I immediately noticed my two 1961 "Trans-Siberian Express" essays placed in the center. When I discussed my needs with Novosti prior to arrival, I hadn't mentioned my previous work in the Soviet Union. The agency appraised my credentials solely on my previous coverage of their country.

The Novosti editor remarked, "Before agreeing to collaborate with you, we had to see your work." I responded, "To you, my work is only what I've photographed in the Soviet Union!" Slightly embarrassed, the editor laughed and said, "Of course, we had to be certain your coverage was fair, balanced, and not full of negative pictures of our country, too often exploited by your colleagues in the West."

Passing the test of "Soviet objectivity," I wanted to know, "So what is a negative picture?" The editor responded, "Your full-page photograph in *Time* magazine of two old ladies in a house built before the revolution." I had to laugh. The picture was of two peasant women gazing out the window of a traditional Siberian log cabin on Lake Baikal. It was true their flowers on the windowsill were in beaten tin cans and the house needed a paint job, but it was a delightful scene, highlighting the innocent curiosity of two peasant women.

Closing the discussion, I said, "Look, I am not a propagandist. I'm here to study the emancipation of your women, their equality with men in the workplace and elsewhere, in brief, their lives." As the editor relaxed, I displayed my outline listing 35 possible subjects in politics, all professions, sciences, arts, factories, farms, and manual labor. I had refined my presentation on the flight from New York to Paris.

Listed were names of three specific women I wanted to interview and photograph: Valentina Tereshkova, the first woman to orbit the earth; Maya Plisetskaya, one of the greatest ballerinas in the world; and Anna Akhmatova, the "dean of Russian poets," persecuted for her daring writings during the Stalin years. Anna was expelled from the Writer's Union in 1946; after this date, publishing her work was forbidden. By 1965, Stalin had been dead for 12 years, so I hoped to meet 77-year-old Anna Akhmatova.

I requested geographical diversity. I didn't want my coverage limited to Moscow and the 40-mile radius around the capital that was imposed on all Western correspondents without specific Foreign Ministry authorization. Authorization was a time-consuming hassle, and permission to travel was usually denied.

I speculated and hoped a "Soviet Women" subject was innocent and nonpolitical enough to gain greater freedom of movement than that allowed to permanent correspondents. I wanted to give readers more insight into the lives of the Soviet Union's people than the superficial, restricted coverage I'd seen in the West.

Of the 12 locations I had requested, I received permission to work only in and around Moscow, Leningrad (St. Petersburg), Kiev in the Ukraine, Tbilisi, Batumi in Georgia, and Tashkent in Uzbekistan. I'd been in Siberia's Irkutsk nearly four years earlier, but even that area was off limits. I was told Irkutsk was "too cold in January."

For the next 47 days, I photographed and interviewed Russian or "Soviet women" who achieved power in all fields of the workplace, but none had achieved real political power. In the Soviet government, the highest position held by a woman was the Minister of Culture, Mrs. Ekaterina Furtseva.

Lenin (Vladimir Ilyich Ulyanov) had said in the early years after the 1917 revolution, "It's impossible to win the masses for politics unless we include the women. We must win the millions of women in city and village for our cause, and in particular for the Communist transformation of our society."

The college-educated women I covered agreed that Lenin, who died in 1924, had opened Russian society to the emancipation of their women despite the brevity of his leadership. They said that when the Germans invaded Russia in 1941, it marked an "absolute turning point." Leningrad's Deputy Mayor Anna Boikova told me, "The war was a school of life for Soviet women. When men went to war, women took over nearly all jobs and never went back to simply being mothers and housewives. Today we have nurseries for babies when couples decide to have babies, and only when they decide."

Mrs. Boikova didn't mention that at the time, abortion was the only form of contraception for women, free and readily performed in clinics all over the country. Nurseries were accessible in cities I visited but scarce in rural areas—there, "babushka" grandmothers cared for children. In cities, young couples regularly lived with in-laws due to massive housing shortages. So there too, babushkas often replaced nurseries.

Because of cramped living space, most Soviet couples limited themselves to two children at most, yet government policy encouraged women to have large families. Each child entitled a mother to six months maternity leave with two-months pay. To women who gave birth to 10 children, the government gave a medal and bestowed the ultimate honor of being a "Heroine of the Soviet Union," which included a gift of $275 and a small monthly allowance of $16.50 for each child.

None of the women I met wanted to be a "Soviet Heroine." They agreed, "It's hard enough to deliver children to the nursery before going to the factory or office, pick them up at the end of the day, and then, since husbands are useless in the kitchen, cook dinner."

Regardless, it was necessary for most husbands after work or during frequent sick leave to stand on inevitably long lines to buy food. In the Soviet Union, standing in line was a way of life. With most couples living with in-laws, babushkas were also enlisted to wait in lines since feeding a family of any size required standing in several lines, several times a week. I spoke to a babushka with two grandchildren, who stood in line simply because it was there: she had no idea what she was on line for. "Whatever I get, I will need," she said. Hers was not an isolated case.

Soviet application of Marxist-Leninist ideology produced a society where all its women received equal pay and equal higher education, and all citizens were entitled to free medical care and low-cost housing. They also endured shortages of just about everything needed for everyday survival. Equality for Soviet women created an economy where a family needed two salaries to survive. I asked several mothers I photographed, "Would you rather stay home to raise your children?" All agreed, "That's an academic question. We don't have a choice."

Nearing completion of my essay, I concluded Soviet women worked longer hours than men, did more manual work at home, and had little political power at the summit. According to government statistics, 86% of health service positions were held by women, and 75% of doctors were women. Women accounted for 71% of public catering, 70% of education, 65% of communications, 44% of scientific institutions, 46% of industry, 43% of agriculture, 29% of construction, 26% of transportation, and 50% of menial jobs like street cleaning. Official statistics were not available for Soviet women in certain professions like architecture, politics, or the arts.

In 1965 Deputy Minister of Health Mrs. Gregory Sirotkina could rightly and easily argue, "Russian women have achieved greater equality, if not full equality, compared to their American or Western sisters." But she conceded, "American women have generally greater material comfort."

All the women I photographed yearned for material comfort, if only for a small refrigerator to save them hours of standing in food lines. None had dishwashers or washing machines. After I was invited to see their living quarters, all women confessed hating to share communal kitchens and toilets. All dreamed of having their own space, free of in-laws, and complained of the lack of intimacy in their married lives.

Expectant mothers often said, "Four out of six months of maternity leave without pay mean years of savings for a motorcycle or car sacrificed for a new baby." In Leningrad, a pregnant mathematician told me, "Each new child will push our dream of owning a car to a distant future."

Even with enough savings, buying a simple automobile took years of waiting, but not for the few members of the Soviet elite like Valentina Tereshkova. As the first woman cosmonaut, she completed her space flight at the age of 26. In Soviet ideology, Tereshkova became a symbol of the revolution, living proof of the superiority of communism over capitalism. As a perfect tool for Soviet propaganda, Tereshkova still had a schedule heavily loaded with national and international functions, even a year and a half after her voyage into space. When I first encountered her, she was cutting a ribbon at the Moscow Museum displaying "The Arts of India." She was then whisked away to the Lenin Museum, where I photographed her by a mural depicting an idealized image of the 1917 October Revolution.

Tereshkova had no time for an interview, but I did get a few party line platitudes. Curious to know how well she had been briefed for a meeting with an American journalist, I led her on by asking, "What in your society made your achievement possible?" I wasn't disappointed. She answered, "Any woman will tell you, emancipation of our women was made possible by the revolution. Lenin and the men who made the revolution created laws that gave our women total equality. We women today take it for granted that we can work the same jobs and govern as well as men."

My time was up as my Novosti escort said, "Just one more question." I asked Tereshkova about her ambitions. "I dream of a group flight in space, perhaps with

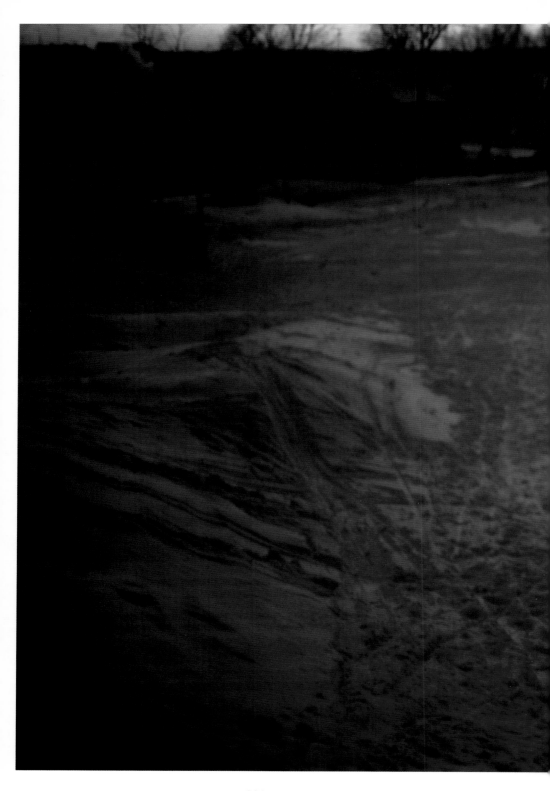

293

my husband," she said. "I also look forward to meeting American cosmonaut women in space. Goodbye."

Her answers were well rehearsed. She even managed to take a crack at the American space program, which in 1965 had no plan to send American women into space.

I was tempted to ask why, despite her country's remarkable achievements in space, many villages I had seen, even Troparyovo a few miles west of Moscow with its 800 families, were still without running water. And why was it the women's burden to carry heavy buckets of water from the village's only well to their homes at least twice a day?

Even the world's first woman in space could not have explained the glaring contradictions in the spending priorities of her government. But submitting such provocative questions would have prompted an immediate end of Novosti's collaboration with me.

My escort had already cringed when I photographed an old woman lumbering under the weight of two heavy water buckets, as she headed down her village's slippery, snow-covered road at nightfall. He complained, "You will make her look like a beast of labor." I argued, walking a tight diplomatic rope, "The children laughing on their sleds within the composition captures the essence of a classical Russian village in winter." My escort relaxed but insisted, "John, that's still a negative picture!" I replied, "Not with the magical blue of a Russian dusk."

Enjoying the aristocratic privileges of the Soviet elite was Maya Plisetskaya, one of the greatest ballerinas of her time. She belonged to that tiny fraction of Soviet citizens that never stood in line for food, was allocated spacious apartments and dachas in the country, and never waited years to buy a car. They had access to the country's "hard currency" stores, stocked with food, fashionable clothing, and "all luxuries of the West." She earned hard currency, a scarce commodity forbidden to the majority of people in the Soviet Union. Plisetskaya was a member of the Bolshoi Ballet, which toured capitals of the West, even the U.S., in 1959. A star ballerina, she shared in the Bolshoi's foreign earnings and privileges.

At the time of my visit, she was at the Bolshoi Theater rehearsing the role of Odette for Tchaikovsky's *Swan Lake*. Her very short leotard complimented the beauty of her long legs, tiny waist, elegant long neck, and classical face. Watching her dance, pirouette, and leap in the air, I understood the acclaim she received from critics in all major capitals of the world. Mesmerized by her grace and seemingly effortless movement, I wasn't sure a still photograph could convey the beauty of her dancing. She suggested, "Try to photograph the absolute summit of the movement, the fraction of a second that is ephemeral in each movement. Any time before or after that magical moment is seldom graceful in a photograph." She was right of course. Photographing for several hours, I understood precisely what she meant as I learned to anticipate her "absolute summits."

Plisetskaya was the freest artist I met in Russia. Soviet ideology could not influence her art, which took her abroad and exposed her to other truths. Triumphant wherever she performed, Plisetskaya could have danced in another time for Catherine the Great, the eighteenth-century empress who introduced ballet to Tsarist Russia. Plisetskaya's art was above the dictates of emperors or Soviet dictators, unlike that of other women artists I photographed, such as Bella Akhmadulina.

Bella was a 28-year-old poet, a creamy-skinned exotic beauty and idol to young women. A prodigy in her late teens, she was courted by Yevgeny Yevtushenko whose love poems were a sensation in the 1950s. The glamour girl of Soviet literature, Bella had intellectual appeal and was in good standing with the Writer's Union.

The Writer's Union approved her debut and nurtured her to fame, yet could destroy and expel her if her writing was critical of Soviet ideology. Like all writers in the Soviet Union, she had to tow the party line to be officially published, but in our conversations at her dacha in a suburb of Moscow, Bella seemed to be a fervent believer and willing servant of the state. If dissent was in her soul, I didn't suspect it and assumed she'd remain in the state's favor for an unforeseeable time.

All published and publicly exposed artists I encountered claimed to be believers. Some were given extraordinary financial support by the state. This was evident on the set of film director Sergei Bonderschuk whose production of Tolstoy's *War and Peace* was underway, starring the lovely Lucia Saveljeva as Natasha, whom I photographed for several days. With thousands of extras costumed in Russian and French military uniforms of that period, the director apparently had an unlimited budget. *War and Peace* took Tolstoy seven years to write—it would undoubtedly take several years for Bonderschuk to finish his film.

The scale of his production reminded me of Sergei Eisenstein's 1928 film *October.* His depiction of the storming of St. Petersburg's Winter Palace during the 1917 revolution was an early example of cinematic art dedicated to Soviet ideology and the state. Facts were irrelevant in Eisenstein's film: *October* celebrated fearless workers overpowering the tsar's guards when in fact, palace defenses offered little resistance. Yet *October* was considered a masterpiece by the Soviets as well as the "realistic school" of Western filmmakers who seldom questioned its authenticity.

It wasn't difficult to appreciate that men, women, idealists, humanists, and revolutionaries in 1917 believed in a new social order. Harder to fathom was that after nearly half a century of totalitarianism, almost all women I encountered still believed in the system despite the hardships of their lives and failure of the state to live up to the communist dream. I wondered, "Where are the women dissenters?"

Knowing Novosti would not lead me to dissenters, I patiently and diplomatically insisted on photographing and interviewing Anna Akhmatova, born in 1888, one of the finest Russian poets of the first half of the twentieth century. Widely translated and admired in the West, her poetry spoke of love during the terror of the Stalin years. She was published until 1945 but attacked in 1946 by the Central Committee as "empty and Bourgeois." Expelled from the Writer's Union, she was denied access to all publishers, could give no public readings, and was deprived of income from her poetry.

After Stalin's death in 1953, state disapproval of her work waned, but not until February 1956, after Nikita Khrushchev's public denunciation of Stalin's war crimes, could Anna Akhmatova's name be spoken again in Russian literary circles.

After much cajoling, Novosti agreed to let me interview and photograph her. Before meeting Akhmatova in the village of Komarovo, north of Leningrad, I surveyed the frozen Gulf of Finland, a few miles from her modest dacha. At the shore where the tide's icy waves were frozen in motion, silenced for the long winter, I realized I had found the perfect background to photograph the poet whose voice had been silenced two decades earlier.

Akhmatova greeted me warmly: "Welcome, welcome, I seldom get visitors nowadays," she said. I was honored to meet her, but not until gently shaking her hand did I recognize how frail she had become at age 77. From research, I knew she was beautiful in her prime and known for her profoundly personal love poems. Studying her face now, I could see how time and sorrow had taken their toll, exaggerating her already advanced age. As I watched her walk, it was obvious that taking her to the shore of the Gulf of Finland would be out of the question.

Improvising, I suggested photographing her by the white birch trees and immaculate snow surrounding her dacha. After her housekeeper helped her into a heavy black overcoat and wrapped her head, neck, and shoulders in a shawl, we stepped into the deep snow. I photographed the "dean of Russian poets" as a fragile black figure framed by vast untainted white snow, with her arms crossed, defying her age and sorrows. After a few minutes, it was too cold for her, so I gave her my arm, and we walked the few steps together into the warmth of her small salon.

Though I took a few photos of her writing at her desk, I was angry at myself for taking ordinary pictures of the grand old lady of Russian poetry, the woman who dared accuse Stalin of murder. As we sat sipping tea, I was anxious to ask about the late 1930s and years of terror during the Stalin trials, but it was obvious she wasn't comfortable speaking in front of my Novosti escort who arranged our meeting. Then with a twinkle in her eye, she said, "John Launois, that's a French name. Parlez-vous français?" Our conversation continued in French.

Translating from English to French, I read aloud a prologue she had written in the mid-1930s for *Requiem*, which claimed, "That was the time when only the dead could smile." I translated the last line of her 1940 epilogue: "Here, where I endured 300 hours in line before the implacable iron bars." I asked, "Was it your lover and other loved ones behind the iron bars?" She nodded, smiled sweetly, and sadly said, "Monsieur, vous êtes indiscret" ("Sir, you are indiscreet"), then smiled again.

Our intimate exchange disturbed and enraged my Novosti escort. He kept on interrupting, "What are you talking about? Why are you speaking in French?" We ignored him as I simply said, "Sorrowful times in your history." When I asked more about the terror under Stalin inspiring her tragic poems, she said, "You were born in France. Didn't you read *Russia in 1839* by Le Marquis Astolphe de Custine?"

Embarrassed to admit I'd never heard of him, she enlightened me, "Custine, during his three-month journey from St. Petersburg to Moscow in 1839, witnessed and documented the tyranny and bestial reign of Tsar Nicholas the First, when men, women, children, and animals endured sheer brutality and were reduced to absolute silence. Custine depicted Russia as a penal colony, a vast Siberia. Prophetically he foresaw Stalin's years of tyranny. Monsieur, please find his book and read it. What Custine wrote in 1839 is a mirror of Stalin's terror a century later."

I wanted to hear more of her personal years, but she was tired. Strangely, she had not spoken a word of her own writing, only of another writer's work from a century earlier. She looked exhausted—I didn't know she was in the last year of her life. As we parted, I whispered to her, "But only you, Madame Akhmatova could have written, 'That was a time when only the dead could smile.'"

It was a moving encounter, not to be forgotten. Later that year, I was happy to hear that she was honored at Oxford University with an Honorary Doctorate of Literature. When I learned of her death on March 5, 1966, a little more than a year after our meeting, I felt guilty for not having read Le Marquis de Custine's *Russia in 1839*.

Of the 35 women I photographed and interviewed, only one belonged to Anna Akhmatova's generation. She was Tatyana Strelets, a 65-year-old illiterate Ukrainian peasant who lived with her son, daughter-in-law, and three grandchildren in Kiev. In 1937, when she was a mother of four children and married to an illiterate farm worker, Stalin's security police arrested her husband and shipped him to a prison camp. Twenty-eight years later, she still didn't know where he was taken nor why. Though her son Pavel was only six years old in 1937, he remembered vividly the night four armed civilians with armbands barged into their house. "It was cold winter when we all slept in the only heated room, when they yanked father out of bed and ordered him to dress. We were terrified, clustered around mother. He waved to us, told us not to worry, that he'd be back soon. That was 28 years ago. It had to be a mistake. Mother still believes he'll return, because he was innocent. All he ever did was to work 16 hours a day. But I stopped hoping a long time ago."

As Pavel spoke, his mother listened silently, tears streaming down her face, as her three grandchildren gathered around her. Composing herself, she waved to her family and said, "Things are easier today, but I am too old to enjoy them."

Subway executive Zinaida Troitskaya in a Moscow station.

All the younger women featured in my essay had been children during Stalin's rule, so to them, the years of terror remained abstract. Worshipping Stalin as the father and savior of the nation, they had all grieved his death in 1953: millions wept, and the empire mourned their loss. They heard Khrushchev's 1956 denunciations of Stalin's crimes in disbelief.

In 1956, nearly half a century after the 1917 revolution, the majority of college-educated women I encountered believed the Soviet Union was headed for greatness. Soon Russia would be a land of plenty, and shortages would end—the litany went on and on. Information came from the media of a totalitarian state. A free press had never existed in Russia: the tsars shot or exiled critics, then, repeating history, Soviet commissars exiled or silenced dissenters.

Those women were believers, proud to tell me, "We are first in space. We have the most powerful military force and a far-reaching nuclear arsenal for defense. Peoples of the world will eventually espouse our ideals." It was commonly said, "We are better off than our mothers were."

Those typical convictions were expressed by my lovely interpreter, Oksana Mikhalova. Born in 1941 when Hitler invaded Russia, Oksana was indoctrinated from a tender age, as were millions. As a member of Komsomol, the Communist Youth, and an officer arranging cultural events for her local party cell, Oksana had the immediate ambition to become a member of the Communist Party. She told me, "When I become a member, I'll have two tasks: to help establish the material basis of communism so no one in the country is in need, and to bring up a new man in society with a near-absolute communist morality. We still have in our society too many people who exclusively follow their individualistic interests, ignoring the greater interest of the community."

For six demanding weeks, Oksana traveled, worked with me, and seemed deeply ashamed whenever I photographed women engaged in heavy labor. Embarrassed to see several families cramped on a single floor of an apartment building sharing a communal kitchen, she was grateful I didn't take any pictures. I diplomatically told her, "I don't need that scene." She knew I wanted it, but I was still building up good will, saving my chance to later capture "negative scenes" of Russian life.

In 47 days together, we developed a close working relationship. Once she trusted me, she was more forthcoming about her ideals. Daylight hours in a Russian winter were short for outdoor photography, so when I insisted my team work on weekends, Novosti complied and Oksana gracefully agreed, arranging much of our travels on Sundays without a complaint. Though she was professional at all times, she was shaken when I lost my eyesight in the middle of the night in Leningrad.

Accustomed to working in photographic darkrooms, I counted the dial holes on my rotary phone and woke her: "Oksana, I am blind." At a factory the day before, I photographed a woman welder's flame with my eyes unprotected.

Twelve hours later, I felt a sting in my eyes. Getting up, fumbling for the light, I turned it on, but the room remained dark: I was nearly blind. Terrified, I made my way to the window, pulling curtains aside, but couldn't see the streetlights outside my room at the Europa Hotel. Oksana already had an ambulance waiting outside when she came to my room to guide me. In her voice, I heard fear and compassion as she helped me climb into the ambulance.

At the hospital, Oksana held my arm as she rushed me through a blur I guessed to be the emergency ward. A woman doctor examined me, confirmed my suspicion, and told Oksana that the intensity of the welder's flame slightly damaged my irises, pupils, corneas, and particularly the right eye, my camera eye. "We will treat his eyes with drops for the next few hours and slowly he'll regain his full sight." Oksana translated as the doctor gently released drops in my eyes. Half a day later, I could see normally again.

After that incident, Oksana and I grew closer. As she described how frightened and worried she had been, I saw such purity in her expression, I knew I'd photograph her as a "cover-try" before departure: there was a good chance her pretty country look could compete with ballerina Maya Plisetskaya's refined classical look.

With February ending, I'd taken nearly 5,000 photographs, including more than a hundred of Oksana by the Kremlin, yet I hadn't seen a single picture developed. Oksana and my Novosti escort took me to Sheremetyevo International Airport early so we could have some time to ourselves.

Sitting in Air France's first-class lounge, I ordered fresh Beluga caviar, iced vodka for my Novosti escort, and orange juice for Oksana. She always frowned as we drank vodka. We had become a close team, shared a wealth of experience, and eaten three daily meals together for 47 days. We kept our clashing ideologies in check and our relationships on a human level. With hugs all around, it was a warm, emotional goodbye—I would genuinely miss them both.

Landing in Paris, I called my younger sister Lucette to tell her I wasn't sure if we'd come soon for a ski vacation in Megève—I didn't mention that Yukiko and I had separated. Back in New York the next afternoon, I rushed my hand-carried films to two different labs. When I called on Yukiko and Chris in the evening, both seemed delighted to see me. Chris had celebrated his first birthday on the seventh of January, while I had been in Moscow discussing my outline with Novosti.

The next few days were spent editing down thousands of pictures to 160 "first choice" photographs for projection to the editors and art director. The remainder was stored at Black Star for distribution to European agents.

Though I felt confident, I became anxious when the lights went out and I began narrating my slides. No one at the magazine had seen a single frame, and the project's assistant director who normally followed my progress in the field had received only laconic messages from Russia. My communiqués to her were cautious and deliberately vague, because I assumed every cable sent from Russia was monitored.

I was too close to my essay to be objective. Not having read a Western newspaper in nearly two months, I felt a sense of isolation. Our Moscow correspondent and "old Russian hand," Edmund Stevens, would say, "'Russian Women' as a subject gave you an open passport to document the lives of the Russian people. Be assured you got further than I ever could have." But I still didn't know exactly what I had.

At the projection were top editors Bill Emerson, Otto Friedrich, Jeanette Sarkisian, Asger Jerrild, and the project's assistant editor. I wasn't on trial but my work was. Without comment, I displayed my three cover candidates: ballerina Maya Plisetskaya, a Komsomol Youth teenager, and my interpreter, Oksana Mikhalova.

When the lights came back on, I heard enough praise to ease my anxiety at last. Since the editors were incapable of faking admiration, I knew their enthusiasm was genuine, but I couldn't fully appreciate it—feeling depressed and down now that my assignment had finished, I had to decompress.

As editors selected the woman for the cover, I felt revived when it became clear Oksana was the overwhelming choice. The space allocated for the project jumped from 10 to 14 pages with a double-page "opener" on Oksana. With three pages of text by Olga Carlisle, the story closed with 11 pages of photographs plus the cover in the June 19, 1965, issue.

I was glad Oksana, "my communist idealist," was so prominently featured. Marxist-Leninist ideology had shaped her idealism and "the Party" was her gospel. With her good looks matching her ideology, she was a perfect product of the system, convinced she'd "help bring up a new man with a selfless communist morality for the good of the greater community."

When the Soviet Union collapsed in 1991, I thought of her. She was 50 then, a patriotic Russian and witness to her country's painful and stumbling beginnings in democracy and capitalism. Instead of her idealistic "selfless man," she must have seen the birth of "robber barons" worthy of America's nineteenth-century oligarchy, a new plutocracy she could not have imagined.

The following year, I felt sad for her and wondered if the idealist in her had survived the new revolution, the plunder of her country's wealth, which she believed belonged to the workers. I hoped she could adjust to the vagaries of

Left: Kindergarten girl in Moscow electric plant. Right: Moscow's "Rainbow Girls" performing in Tashkent.

Russian capitalism and the fragility of Russian democracy. I sincerely hoped she wasn't brokenhearted.

Invariably after a long, difficult assignment, I felt drained. In the palpable absence of my work's familiar rush, I'd return home to a kind of melancholy. When Yukiko and I were living together, she'd anticipate my apprehensive mood and cheerfully surprise me by decorating the apartment with beautiful flower arrangements and preparing exquisite gourmet meals. But Yukiko and I had separated.

When the final layout of "Russian Women" was shown to me, I realized how lonely my home life had become. Dreading to return to my near-empty apartment, I called Yukiko to discuss the pain I had discovered in the lives of Russian women I met. "John," she said, "you've always understood the pain of people you've met around the whole world, but you've always failed to understand the pain you've inflicted here at home."

While Yukiko complained that I was an egoist, memories of the Nazi-German occupation of France returned. I remembered my mother serving a meager meal and saying, "Here I am struggling to find food for six children, and your father brings to dinner two of his Algerian workers because they haven't eaten for two days. Your father's like that. He'll give his shirt away before he understands his children's shirts are worn out beyond repair."

Yukiko and my mother both had a point, which I conceded when I joined Yukiko and Chris that evening. In the eight years of our relationship, it was the first time Yukiko openly expressed the anger and pain she had suppressed for so long. Yet there was no bitterness in her words: it was more an observation of my personality, which she reluctantly tolerated.

Gracefully, she changed the subject of our conversation to Russian women. Since college-educated Japanese women in 1965 were still largely reduced to serving tea in offices, Yukiko was interested in the state of Russian women's emancipation.

For dinner, I was delighted that Yukiko had prepared a Japanese gourmet dinner with sushi, tempura, and bowls of sticky rice as only the Japanese can. Chris sat in a high chair, preferring to eat rice with fingers instead of chopsticks. The convivial feeling of eating at the table as a family made me again regret our separation.

After dinner, as I was about to leave, Yukiko asked, "Do you still think we should learn to ski in France?" It was an opening I hadn't expected. I immediately said, "Yes."

KISS ON THE CHEEKS

HIGH HOPES FOR A SKI HOLIDAY

MEGÈVE, FRANCE 1965

In early March, we took off for France. Arriving a few miles west of Paris at La Celle St. Cloud, we met the family of my youngest sister Lucette. Chris was amused and puzzled by the French custom of greeting one another with four kisses. After Chris was kissed twice on each cheek by Lucette and her children, Pascal and Valerie, Yukiko and I laughed as we counted the number of kisses Chris would receive from all his French relatives. With 21 relatives, there'd be 84 kisses on arrival. While Chris stayed with Lucette's family, there'd be 12 kisses good morning and 12 good night.

Chris seemed to like the ritual of kissing, but as a child, I never liked the custom and eventually reduced my kisses to one on each cheek and only with women. Visiting my father, we recalled how my family and teenage circle of friends had called me "*l'Américain,*" while father vehemently insisted his son's name was Jean. After I explained that "Jean" in the English language was a woman's name, my father reluctantly accepted the fact I had changed my name to John. Nevertheless, during our visit, father insisted, "Only my grandson is a genuine American. John is a French idealist whose roots were transplanted on American soil." He then placed 14-month-old Chris on his lap and said affectionately, "Mon petit Américain."

Fluent in French, Yukiko described her life with Chris in Manhattan and how I was often away on assignment. We agreed not to mention our separation as it would have spoiled my family's first meeting with Chris.

At the end of the day, mother gave us a box of pastries as Chris held his grandfather's hand in the vegetable garden leading to the driveway. Many kisses later, we waved goodbye.

The next morning, Yukiko and I left Chris with Lucette and headed for Megève. Chris had rarely been away from his mother, yet, as we drove off, he waved to us happily, while holding the hand of his very pretty three-year-old cousin Valerie, who immediately treated him as her young brother.

After 11 hours of driving through mountain roads, we checked into the Park des Loges Hôtel in the old village of Megève, some 300 miles southeast of Paris.

The bedroom in our suite appeared small though it really was not. I suspected Yukiko and I both shared a fear of intimacy after nearly six months of separation. High off the ground, the double bed with its twin pillows and heavy eiderdown looked narrow and oppressive. Yukiko and I exchanged glances, and I saw anxiety in her eyes.

Uneasy with each other, we went downstairs for dinner, limited conversation to our long drive, and agreed it would have been wiser to fly to nearby Geneva. We delayed returning to our bedroom, lingering at the dinner table in silence. Settling into our suite, Yukiko disappeared into the bathroom. As she had during our entire married life, Yukiko reappeared in her nightgown, turned off her bedside light, and climbed into bed. Following the same ritual, I slipped into my side. Claiming exhaustion, I said good night and fell asleep.

Through our married years, Yukiko and I, out of sheer ignorance, naiveté, and simple puritanism, never discovered the full delights of intimacy shared by lovers. We had never bathed together nor seen each other naked in the light. Years of ritual would not be changed by our first night in Megève.

Ironically, when we checked into ski school, Yukiko and I were advised to learn from separate instructors, so after sharing nervous laughs on the slopes and ski lift, we were separated. During lunch, we discussed our progress on the slopes, remaining estranged and awkward, like newlyweds in an arranged marriage.

Silence punctuated evening meals. We talked about the beauty and majesty of Mont Blanc's mountain range but not of the mountain dividing us. Because of Japan's culture of suppressing passionate displays of affection, our marriage lacked basic expressions of physical love. Even though Yukiko's father loved her dearly, he never so much as kissed her on the cheek to show affection.

In France, as I watched young lovers kissing passionately while riding the ski lifts, I was reminded of the freedom missing in our relationship. We came to Megève with high hopes and an unwritten promise of rediscovering and rekindling our love, but to no avail. We shared the same bed for nine nights without either of us offering a single gesture of intimacy. Why? I don't think we knew. In her diary, Yukiko wrote, "It was a disaster."

Returning to Lucette's, we found Chris in an ebullient mood. Lucette said that during Chris' stay, there was "laughter all the way," more than we could say about Megève, though we pretended otherwise.

On our flight back to New York, Chris spoke some French phrases to the Pan Am stewardess, and we laughed at his American accent. We looked like a happy family. From Kennedy Airport we took a limousine back to Manhattan, and after dropping off Yukiko and Chris at their apartment, I returned to mine: it looked even emptier than when I had left it.

GOOD PICTURES

EXPOSING NUCLEAR WAR, ANIMAL CRUELTY, AND RACIAL INJUSTICE

HIROSHIMA, QUEBEC, HARLEM 1965–1966

I called on Bill Emerson to congratulate him as he had been appointed new editor of *The Saturday Evening Post*. Because I wasn't sure photography would continue to play a major role at the magazine, and the photographic department was leaderless, I seriously thought of resigning my contract. Emerson anticipated my thoughts.

"Tiger," he said, "don't even entertain the thought of leaving us. You simply can't. I need you. The *Post* needs you. Why? Because you bring great intelligence to your work." Emerson appreciated good pictures and was convinced photography was an integral part of the magazine. He promised that he'd find the best director of photography in New York and made me feel leaving the *Post* would be like jumping ship. With Emerson at the helm, I felt reassured I could appeal to him directly in a crisis.

In April, Kurt Kornfeld informed Yukiko that the penthouse at Two Tudor Place was available if we still wanted it. He knew the penthouse with its huge terrace and views of the Chrysler and Empire State Building was Yukiko's dream apartment and saw it as a chance to reunite us.

We agreed such a move could give us a chance to discover each other again. Determined to give our marriage another chance, we felt optimistic at the idea of our family reunited under one roof.

Again Black Star's Phil Rosen helped Yukiko with movers while I was on assignment in Japan, completing an essay on Hiroshima and the consequences of the atomic bomb that killed over 70,000 on August 6, 1945. The greater part of the city had vanished instantly, so 20 years later, there was no way to photographically convey the full horror of the city's obliteration.

A photo of the atomic cloud double exposed with one of Hiroshima 20 years later.

The steel skeleton of Hiroshima's domed industrial exhibition hall became "the symbol of the world's first atomic bomb." While I studied the dome at dusk, I remembered survivors telling me, "First came the flash, the blast, then the cloud hung there above us." The ghost of the mushroom cloud still loomed above the dome when they closed their eyes in the fading evening light.

Since I couldn't photograph ghosts or haunted memories, I obtained the U.S. Air Force's official photograph of the mushroom cloud rising over Hiroshima and double exposed it with my photo of the dome as I found it two decades later. In the picture, instead of burnt suffering survivors crying for water, there were lovers strolling through the Park of Peace.

After devoting the rest of my essay to eyewitness accounts of the bombing as well as peaceful scenes around the newly built city, I photographed survivors and mourners lighting thousands of paper lanterns, releasing them onto currents of the Ota River. A grieving survivor explained, "Each flickering light is a living soul traveling to the Inland Sea and beyond to eternity."

The story's eight pages of text and pictures in the August 14, 1965, issue of the *Post* was headlined: "Hiroshima: In a flash it was gone." The subtitle read; "The vanished city has been rebuilt, but the mushroom cloud haunts it still."

After 40 days on assignment, I returned to Yukiko and Chris who warmly greeted me at the door of our new apartment. Yukiko proudly led me to the terrace that she had furnished with garden tables, multicolored parasols, and chaise longues, one of which was reserved for Kurt Kornfeld who had personal access to the terrace for his afternoon naps.

Delighted, I congratulated Yukiko on her tasteful choices. We'd never known the luxury of a penthouse in the heart of Manhattan. In good weather, the terrace became a second living room as mounted stereo speakers under an awning filled the atmosphere with music. With the sounds of traffic distant and muted, our new home was idyllic. Our "dream apartment" helped bring us together again and made it easier for Yukiko to contend with my absences.

She enjoyed seeing Chris playing and running around the terrace, while our next-door neighbor Kurt became Chris's regular afternoon grandfather. In our new home, we entertained writers, photographers, editors, and United Nations diplomats. These were happy, carefree days. While I enjoyed extraordinary freedom at the *Post*, Yukiko learned to edit photographs as she began her path to becoming Black Star's chief picture editor.

At the *Post*, Emerson lured Joe Sapinsky from *New York Magazine* to become our director of photography by the end of June. A reserve Navy-fighter pilot who flew in World War II, Joe was handsome, individualistic, cool, and not at all bureaucratic. He loved and appreciated photography's power to communicate. We immediately hit it off.

While Sapinsky's innate understanding of professional photojournalism lifted the photo department's morale and ushered in renewed creativity and enthusiasm, rumors of the *Post*'s dire financial straits were circulating.

Howard Chapnick, who had become Black Star's president in 1964, suggested at lunch, "A freelancer shouldn't put all his eggs in one basket. Maybe once in a while you should take a *National Geographic* assignment." Howard contacted *Geographic*'s director of photography, Robert Gilka, from whom I received an assignment to cover Canada's province of Quebec and the St. Lawrence River.

Before I left for Quebec City in early 1966, it snowed in Manhattan. In our penthouse, I photographed Chris in a magical moment as he spread his fingers and rested his nose on the terrace window, fascinated by the sight of snow for the very first time. He stood in wonderment as the snow blanketed the terrace with a foot of white powder.

On my arrival in Quebec City, I recruited a Laval University student named André to assist me. André's ancestors were settlers of the original French territories in North America before the fortress of Quebec was conquered in 1759 and all territories once known as New France were ceded to Great Britain in the 1763 Treaty of Paris. Quebec's struggle for independence had been fought by separatists for over two centuries. In 1966, the struggle was still very much alive in Quebec

and in my new colleague. So at dinner in the Labrador Mining Company's executive dining room, when the company's engineers and managers rose to sing, "God Save the Queen," André rose to his feet and defiantly said, "*Jamais!* Never! Over my dead body!" He stormed out, leaving me embarrassed and everyone around us stunned. Sulking and angry, André refused to come back in.

After dinner, I humored him by saying, "I promise from now on to keep you away from anyone praising the Queen of England. Just remember, here in Labrador City, we're 53 degrees latitude north of nowhere. There are no roads out of town, so we'll need the company plane to get out of here." He laughed and agreed to keep his nationalism in check.

For one project on hunters of baby harp seals, I had to leave a disappointed André on shore because helicopter cargo space was reserved for seal furs. I had to pay a stiff premium just to secure a copilot seat.

Each year in March, thousands of harp seal pups were born on ice floes on the Gulf of St. Lawrence and massacred for white furs. In their first three weeks, pups were unable to swim and were helpless on the ice, when the sealers came.

While photographing, I was sickened to see the sealers clubbing and skinning helpless baby seals, leaving carcasses in pools of blood. My project editor at *Geographic*, Robert Patton, argued, "We can't show all that blood to our readers. Instead show us the beauty of innocent pups while they're still white and defenseless on the ice." The Post also claimed the pictures were "too cruel and bloody for our readers."

Black Star, however, released the controversial pictures to European magazines. After publication in Europe, there was an immediate and furious public outcry against the slaughter. What had started out as a local story on the income-producing tradition for the island's sealers and inhabitants of l'Île de la Madeleine, (Magdelene Island), suddenly became a story that inspired international outrage. In following years, international organizations against cruelty to animals descended on the island demanding a ban on the killing.

To produce beautiful pictures of baby seals requested by *Geographic*, André was happy to join me in a large helicopter with taggers from the Fishery Ministry. André was fascinated by the thought of landing on ice floes. Visibility was unlimited, and we could see thousands of pups on the ice despite the quota of 50,000 seals that had been killed and skinned a few days earlier, their carcasses still on the ice.

After we touched down, André's face beamed with child-like joy at the irresistible appearance of the baby seals who seemed to enjoy being rolled on the ice. While I lay prone in shooting position, concentrating on a close-up of the big black watery eyes, black snouts, and whiskers of three pups, I heard a loud, thundering crack: suddenly André disappeared into the icy water through a two-foot-wide crevice, which broke along hundreds of yards of ice. Thanks to the buoyancy of his parka, André bobbed up to the surface. In a single movement, our pilot yanked a wet and shaken André by his collar, put him on firm ice, and led him to the chopper where he turned on a huge heater. He laughingly explained, "We came prepared for such an eventuality."

In a few minutes, a warmed and blown-dry André rejoined me but the excitement in his face was gone. By the end of March, as our 10-week assignment neared completion, we were convinced we had covered more subjects on the St. Lawrence River than Jacques Cartier had in 1525 when he discovered "the greatest river in North America." The Quebec and St. Lawrence essay with Howard La Fay's text was published in 46 pages of the May 1967 issue of *National Geographic*.

After the icy St. Lawrence River, Manhattan's weather felt tropical—so much so I suggested to Yukiko that we have dinner on the terrace. She refused, saying, "I am not an Eskimo." When Chris joined me as I rested in a chaise longue with a drink, I was once again painfully reminded of how little time I had spent with him. The fact that he was already more than two years old underscored the guilt I felt for having sacrificed my time with my son for my career in photojournalism.

The summer of 1966 would again keep me from spending time with my family. In June, *Newsweek*'s special editor Robert Engle asked me to produce a color essay on Harlem, America's most famous black community. Engle explained, "Up till now, mostly small black-and-white photos have illustrated stories in *Newsweek*. Your essay will be the magazine's first color essay. We'll need a color photograph for the cover as well."

Malcolm X had described the squalor of black ghettoes in America when we met in Cairo. In disbelief, I had listened to Malcolm X's descriptions, which remained abstractions in my mind. The assignment was my chance to see reality for myself.

From press reports, I knew despair and anger had provoked explosive riots in Harlem in 1964, Watts in 1965, and Chicago's westside ghetto in 1966. More violence was predicted. Walking alone as a white man with cameras around my neck through volatile streets of Harlem seemed like folly: my mere presence would invite hostility if not violence.

To build trust in the community, I needed a black friend to assist. Black Star's Howard Chapnick said, "I know just the man for you: Bob Clark. He's a beginner—

he needs work, and he's anxious to work with experienced photographers. Bob's bright, fast on his feet, a winning personality."

The next day, I met Bob in a coffee shop. He was tall, lean, and athletic, and his handsome face inspired trust. I liked him right away. He'd be a valuable asset on a sensitive assignment requiring immediate trust based on first impressions. Leveling with Bob, I admitted I'd never been to Harlem, and my only knowledge of a black ghetto came from what I heard from Malcolm X. Bob said he knew Harlem but never lived there.

The following morning, we rented a car and drove north to Harlem to get an initial sense of the atmosphere and see what happened in the streets during long summer days and nights. We'd eventually conduct interviews and make contacts to lead us beyond the stoops where people sat listlessly in heat just to escape the unbearable, stifling temperatures inside the tenements.

In seven years of covering Asia, I had witnessed and photographed misery, suffering, and destitution, but even that had not prepared me for the poverty, despair, and hopelessness I discovered in Harlem's summer of '66.

We met and photographed families, many fatherless, living in sullen tenements. Walls and ceilings had collapsed onto floors; scattered, rusty pans anticipated leaks of the next rainfall; and gas and electricity were often cut off.

We met a young mother, Addie J., and her five children. All were afflicted by parasitosis like children I'd seen suffering in Korea and Laos in the 1950s. Addie J.'s face expressed chronic hopelessness as she explained how she received a welfare check of $35 every other week to feed her children.

To clothe her children, she depended on charity. Her youngest went barefoot in summer. Her eight- and nine-year-old sons wore men's shoes, four sizes too big, with newspaper stuffed in the toes, and adult-sized pants, rolled up at the bottom with waistbands pinched several inches in the back.

As Addie J. and her children in their dilapidated kitchen stared blankly at the camera, I studied her face and thought she must have been very pretty not long ago. But in the shot, she was expressionless as if drained of all emotion, resigned to despair. She was 28.

On assignment, I felt stunned and shocked. I wondered how we Americans with such great wealth and ideals could close our eyes and let so many of our people live in such inhuman conditions.

For days, we interviewed and photographed militants preaching defiance and beautiful black women nationalists resurrecting history in wild hunting dances,

rekindling pride in the old African heritage. We also befriended an angry preacher, Walter R., and photographed him as he delivered a sermon about salvation—he became our cover subject for *Newsweek*. Being on the cover of a national magazine brought him instant fame in his neighborhood as well as a larger following. After the story was published, Walter R. visited us in billowing African robes, prompting our doorman to announce that a diplomat from the United Nations had arrived. Walter R. had found new pride in his African roots.

It was 104 degrees in Harlem on July 4, 1966. Defying police, children opened caps on fire hydrants, releasing exploding water to seek relief from relentless heat. Even the engine of our car boiled over and quit.

America was celebrating its independence, that "all men are created equal, endowed by their creator with inalienable rights." That day the promised equality for the black people of Harlem seemed as remote as it was the day the Declaration of Independence was signed in 1776.

Harlem didn't conform to my vision of the generous, egalitarian America I admired and loved. It was un-American. But Harlem was an American reality I had to face and photograph to enlighten my own ignorance of my idealized country.

As night fell on the Fourth of July, fireworks exploded in southern skies of Manhattan while up north, bleak-faced Harlem youngsters gathered on street corners to await grim, empty hours, random violence, and desperate night. They had nothing to celebrate.

Bob Clark and I finally made our way back to Two Tudor Place. It was impossible to settle into the luxury of our penthouse after the abject poverty we witnessed in Harlem. Yukiko served us drinks on the terrace, but we were in no mood to celebrate anything. As we toasted each other, we burst into tears.

For another two weeks, we covered Harlem. My last photo was of a man in despair as he attempted suicide by jumping from his third-floor window. He landed on the concrete sidewalk at 235 West 131st Street, and, bleeding profusely, was rushed to Harlem Hospital where he was diagnosed "in critical condition." When I checked on him later, doctors told me he'd survive.

Our eight-page color essay, "The Black Ghetto," closed in the August 22, 1966, issue of *Newsweek*. It was the magazine's first photographic essay and part of 39 pages of remarkable exposure of the nation's racial crisis. One page was titled: "Black Ghetto Landscape: Sudden Tragedy and Chronic Hopelessness." The text told of "The longest, hottest summer" and "The *Newsweek* poll distills an overriding message: The Negro revolt will go on. Its militant leaders will cry out for black power, or separation of the races, or even open warfare."

My American idealism was deeply shaken by Harlem, but I found some solace in that a national magazine devoted so much space to a major moral and social issue, which was dividing the nation again. A divided House of Representatives had just passed the third civil rights bill in three years: the march for greater equality was on, and I believed its direction irreversible. I found reason to rekindle guarded optimism.

As life moved on, my idealism receded, but I couldn't emotionally afford the luxury of dwelling on assignments. Such were the demands of journalism.

The summer of 1966 was the hottest summer we had known in Manhattan. Yukiko even thought our shaded terrace was too hot for Chris to play on, so she kept him inside our air-conditioned apartment.

By the end of July, I called on the *Post*'s art director, Asger Jerrild, who suggested, "John, on these hot days, your son ought to be on the beach in Darien." He and *Life*'s John Dominis constantly praised Darien, Connecticut, as "the ideal place to raise a family." In Manhattan's sweltering heat, the thought of living near the beach seemed rational and seductive. The next day, Yukiko and I drove to Darien.

Through a recommendation from Jerrild, we met with a pleasant real estate agent named Marjorie who wasn't pushy or aggressive. Yukiko and I fell in love immediately with a beautiful split-level home with four bedrooms, a dining room by a large screened-in porch, a large den, huge basement, attic, spacious living room with bay windows, fireplace, and two-car garage opening onto a driveway along a stream, leading to a quiet residential road.

Built on one and a quarter acres of land, the house was surrounded by a huge lawn shaded by old trees that lined a beautiful stream. The railroad line to the city was less than a mile away, not far from the sandy beach of Long Island Sound.

Over coffee, the couple selling the house for $80,000 praised Darien's quality of life and said they'd miss it. That afternoon, I wrote a check for the deposit.

Marjorie introduced us to a lawyer to conduct a title search for the house and a banker who set up, at 6¼ percent, our $60,000 twenty-year mortgage. It was amusing how friendly our banker became after I showed him my credit references, and he understood that the price of the house was approximately what I grossed a year. "Impeccable," he said as he congratulated us, welcoming us to Darien.

We had gone to Darien only to look around, but in one afternoon we bought a house, the first house in my family. My parents never dreamt of becoming property owners. Buying the house in a day's time was impulsive but turned out to be an emotionally and financially sound move. Payments were only slightly higher than rent on our penthouse, and Connecticut in 1966 had no income tax, so our purchase made great financial sense. In that house, we'd spend the five happiest years of our lives.

From Darien, it took only 50 minutes to drive back to Manhattan. We couldn't wait to tell dear old Kurt Kornfeld the good news and that one of two guest rooms would be reserved for him. But when we told him we were moving to Darien, he seemed shocked and unhappy. Later he privately said in a troubled voice, "John, how can a well-informed man like yourself not know Darien is a stronghold of anti-Semitism in America. You should read *Gentleman's Agreement*. When I eventually read the book by Laura Z. Hobson, made into a praised film starring Gregory Peck, I came across a scene where a main character said of Darien, "I loathe it, but New Canaan is worse. Nobody can sell or rent to a Jew there. But Darien is...Well, it's a sort of gentleman's agreement when you buy." Kurt felt betrayed and hurt even after I pointed out that Hobson's book had been published in 1947, almost 20 years in the past.

Though sorry we had displeased Kurt, we made plans to move. Meanwhile, I completed another *Post* assignment on nationwide air pollution, inspired by Rachel Carson's best-selling book, *Silent Spring*. Just like my earlier water pollution project, "Our Dying Waters," which shocked me at how foul and degraded our once beautiful waters had become, the air pollution story was another foray into "crusading journalism." In the editor's words, subtitled in our essay, the *Post*'s duty was to create a "new public determination to save our natural heritage from recklessness and greed."

For the cover of our nationwide assignment, I chose Manhattan's huge Con Edison plant just south of United Nations headquarters. I instructed my chopper pilot to fly as low as possible along the East River so our approach wouldn't be detected by power plant managers. Just as we reached the plant, the pilot immediately brought our chopper up so I could capture the giant smoke stacks spewing air pollution.

The *Post* was the first major magazine to expose the danger and devastation of man-made pollution, making it a public issue. The magazine's example was followed by reports on television and the rest of the news media. Eventually, the subject became a national issue, and Congress reacted by passing legislation to cut down and control man-made pollution.

By August's end, our furniture had been moved into our new suburban home with lots of room to spare. With Yukiko's first driver's license, I bought her a four-year-old black Chevrolet. For myself I purchased a new white hardtop Buick Riviera, the first new car I had ever owned.

Since Yukiko wanted to continue her two-day-a-week job at Black Star, we were lucky to find a lovely babysitter in Darien. White-haired Mrs. Grant was like a perfect grandmother for Chris, teaching him how to look at nature and appreciate creatures in and around the stream. Chris found a playmate in her grandson. With the Jerrild and Dominis families living nearby, we soon had as many friends as we had in Manhattan.

Seeing Chris on his tricycle racing along our driveway to greet my car gave me a sense of happiness I had never known. Returning to Darien became a pleasure. As Chris waded in our clear shallow stream and rushed barefoot to see me, I became overwhelmed by the feeling of having a real home at last, a place to grow roots. Darien changed Yukiko as well: she looked more cheerful than I had seen her in years, and she embraced the responsibility of taking care of our new home.

Despite Yukiko's repeated invitations, Kurt Kornfeld visited only once, claiming in his old age that the nearest bathroom was too far from the living room. But he had no intention of spending time in a town identified with anti-Semitism. Like his closest business partners, he had escaped Nazi Germany in 1935, and the trauma of that dark time never eased in their minds.

Kurt soon forgave me but not before reminding me, "Ignorance is never innocent." He died a year later in 1967 at the age of 80. By that time I'd known him for 20 years. We loved him dearly and truly missed him.

At *The Saturday Evening Post*, photographic essays were only assigned after a finished manuscript was approved by managing editor, Otto Friedrich. To bypass Otto, I directly approached Bill Emerson and insisted, "I cannot wait for an assigned writer if I'm to meet the photographic needs of an essay on 50 years of Communism."

Though the 50th anniversary of the Bolshevik revolution was more than a year away, I'd have to begin the assignment a full year early to cover the 49th anniversary on November 7, 1966. I needed to photograph the annual display of Russia's military might in Moscow's Red Square, so pictures of marching troops, missiles, tanks, and weapons could be part of a major story about the 50th anniversary aimed for release on November 7, 1967. Emerson and Friedrich, agreeing it was a story of powerful significance, gave me a "green light" to work immediately on my own in Russia and coordinate with a writer the following year.

Yukiko, Chris, and I enjoyed an Indian summer and New England fall, watching leaves turn yellow and red. In mid-October, I regretfully left for JFK as Chris ran after my car, waving goodbye. The next day I was in Moscow in the National Hotel overlooking Red Square. From my fourth-floor window, looking at the Kremlin's brightly lit red star shining on its spire, I saw the symbol of a ruthless, brutal ideology, orchestrated to control thoughts and actions of millions of believers.

In an editorial meeting the following morning, I was greeted warmly by the Novosti Press Agency's team. The editor-in-chief said my essay on Russian women was "fair and beautifully photographed but your photo of the old woman carrying buckets of water in her village a few miles from Moscow revealed a very primitive Russia that we think was misleading."

The point of the photo was to show how the Soviet Union neglected its people's immediate needs, such as running water in suburbs of Moscow, while prioritizing its space program, missile building, and military might. But I simply said, "Look at the entire photograph. At the edge of the composition, there are children on sleds illustrating an eternal Russia and its magical winters." As I had done before with my escort, I again disarmed my critics by being lyrical about Russia.

That settled, I explained, "I'll need your full cooperation and a reporter-researcher for two weeks, now and for eight weeks in 1967. Also, to photograph Soviet leadership on top of the Lenin mausoleum as they watch displays of intercontinental missiles during the November 7th parade, I'll need a few things immediately. Though I know it's closed to the public and takes place in the middle of night, I need permission to study the parade's rehearsal. And I need a good position in the VIP section of the bleachers."

Fortunately, Novosti was cooperative. Standing in bleachers as Moscow slept, I watched the rehearsal parade of Soviet weapons rolling through a deserted Red Square. The secrecy and blackness of night, lit by the headlights of missile carriers, had the quality of something sinister and awesome. As I aimed my camera to study angles for the parade, I felt a chill under my skin, realizing other missiles not on parade were aimed at American cities.

On November 7, I got my pictures of the Soviet Union's aging civilian and military leaders saluting at the parade of Russia's military arsenal. The ceremony made a powerful statement: Russia of 1917 with its millions of illiterate and superstitious peasants had become the world's second superpower within half a century.

In a prelude to the forthcoming 50th anniversary, I photographed the extravaganza of fireworks over the Kremlin. A year later, it made the cover of *The Saturday Evening Post*.

The next few weeks I spent in Leningrad photographing and interviewing veterans of the "storming" of the tsar's winter palace in November 1917. Soviet propaganda had shaped their collective memory as they recalled heroic tales of the historic event. The *Post*'s writer Richard Armstrong nonetheless noted, "Vladimir Ilyich Lenin and his fellow Bolsheviks seized control of Russia in an almost bloodless coup that changed the course of history."

The veterans, now in their seventies, lived through childhood plagued by illiteracy, ignorance, and dire poverty under the tyranny of Tsar Nicholas II. It wasn't surprising that to them the revolution had taken on mythical and heroic proportions.

By 1966, their children received basic education if not higher education, and some of their contemporaries had risen to positions of power. Veterans enjoyed a pension and were entitled to cheap housing and free medical care.

What little veterans knew of the mass killings under Stalin's regime had receded in their memories, so for them as it was for millions of other citizens, there had been "a great revolution."

By mid-November, daylight hours were too short for photographic needs. After leaving a carbon-copy list of subjects to be covered in June 1967 with my Novosti escort, I took an overnight train to Moscow. My contact at Novosti had six months to secure "photographic permission" from authorities.

The following afternoon, I was back in Darien and happy to see Chris and Yukiko again. Though our house had developed a warm, lived-in feeling, I felt restless as always after an assignment. As night fell, the three of us sat around the fireplace, while I nursed a drink, watching flames dancing in the hearth. Though I was home, I was far away, still scripting imaginary pictures for the coming essay on Russia.

Early Christmas morning, we watched Chris unwrapping gifts near our tall, brightly decorated Christmas tree. In following years, away on assignment, I often thought of that particular morning as the symbolic start of our happy years in Darien.

New Year's Eve was spent at a champagne-toasting party at the nearby home of Asger Jerrild and his beautiful wife Esther. Through early 1967, for several months, I read dozens of books on the Soviet Union, learning of chronic agricultural shortages reported in Maurice Hindus's *The Kremlin's Human Dilemma* and the collectivization of Russian farms described in Mikhail Sholokhov novels.

I discovered that as early as 1928, Stalin's collective-farm policy resulted in the slaughter of the peasantry and well-to-do Kulaks. One of the greatest massacres took place on the Kuban steppe where Cossack peasantry fought to hold onto their land against a sea of Red Armies, only to be slain, herded onto collective farms, or shipped to labor camps with millions of peasants.

Some 800 miles south of Moscow, the Kuban steppe was the Soviet Union's largest wheat bowl. Its tragic, historic past made it an essential location for coverage of collective farmers, but it probably was off limits to Western journalists.

While I prepared for Russia between assignments, snow fell in Darien, and I helped Chris build his first snowman. Unlike snow that turned gray in Manhattan, snow in Darien remained pristine most of the winter. Our frozen stream was covered with a white mantle, and when it melted, the stream swelled, announcing the arrival of spring.

In May we threw an afternoon housewarming party. After chartering a bus to pick up Black Star's staff in New York, we hired a bartender, waiter, and an off-duty policeman to direct traffic.

With two assistants, Yukiko insisted on doing all the cooking, treating us to paté de foie gras, marinated shrimp hors d'oeuvres, fried chicken, filet mignon, and ice cream and chocolate cake for dessert. My role was to entertain the guests.

Another time, we threw a party for neighbors in Darien. A vice president of Tiffany's lived across the road, while other new acquaintances included corporate CEOs in the financial world. Again we hired an off-duty policeman to direct parking and a young man to tend the bar. Yukiko with our cleaning woman devoted a week to preparations.

The neighborhood party was a success, but it also increased our awareness of just how white and Wasp-like Darien was: Jews were unseen; African Americans worked as daytime servants; Italians were excluded from the country club. Except for the proprietor of the Chinese laundry, Yukiko appeared to be the only Asian in sight—years earlier, she would not have been so quietly accepted. Even then, when she went to the post office with little Chris one day, an elderly postal worker asked if she was the babysitter.

In contrast, the mixture at Black Star included Jews, Hispanics, and Bob Clark, my black assistant on the Harlem story. Though he had become a successful fashion photographer, Bob told us, he and his white girlfriend were subjected to prejudiced insults "even in liberal Manhattan."

During our party in Darien for Black Star's staff, Bob and I talked about "whites," "blacks," and racism. Little Chris absorbed more of the conversation than we realized. Climbing up on Bob's lap, he declared, "I'm going to be sky color!"

But I had no time to dwell on America's race-related shortcomings. Foremost on my mind was "Fifty Years of Communism." At the end of June, I left for Moscow, well prepared after months of research. As a photojournalist, I knew that any knowledge I obtained on a subject would sharpen my way of seeing. All the books I read could only enhance my intellectual perception and help me see pictures I couldn't have visualized otherwise.

During my absence, Novosti worked hard on securing permission to cover all the subjects I had outlined in my original script. But what they had not seen were my notes to myself on sensitive subjects: "Tiny plots of land that were not collectivized furnish half of Russia's produce. Such plots are denounced as 'creeping capitalism' by authorities. Yet in nearly all city markets, peasants are selling privately grown produce. Note: Must also contact dissident artists, painters, and writers."

FIFTY YEARS OF THUNDER

THE SOVIET UNION'S 50TH ANNIVERSARY

MOSCOW 1967

To avoid conflicts with the Soviet government, I wouldn't cover sensitive subjects until close to the end of my trip. My original script was broad, so we didn't waste any time setting off on our 20-thousand-mile, seven-week journey into the Soviet empire.

I began by covering subjects on schools, industry, agriculture, the Black Sea beaches, Stalin's birthplace in Georgia, Communist youth organizations, the space program, and Leningrad's Winter Palace where the 1917 revolution had begun. I met with Ilya Ehrenburg, the officially approved novelist, journalist, poet, and one of the most important, controversial Russian cultural icons of the twentieth century.

Though Ehrenburg originally referred to the Bolsheviks as "rapists and conquerors," he later enthusiastically served in Stalin's propaganda machine as an Izvestia newspaper correspondent in France. He was one of the few writers to have survived Stalin's dictatorial purges in the 1930s.

Ehrenburg lived a privileged life. He served French cognac to visitors. Among his friends were Picasso, André Malraux, Diego Rivera, Isaac Babel, and Ernest Hemingway. When I photographed him in July 1967, he seemed ill but became animated when he described in fluent French his early days in Paris where he met Lenin in exile. I later discovered Ehrenburg was suffering from bladder and prostate cancer—he died just a few weeks later on August 31, 1967.

In the Kuban steppe, I captured images of collective-farm workers removing chaff from grain by shoveling tons of combine-harvested wheat, just as predecessors had done 40 years earlier, before being massacred or shipped to labor camps during Stalin's collectivization of private land.

Lying down in wheat, aiming my wide-angle lens upward, I photographed falling wheat grains in the air, creating a pointillist image. It was a beautiful picture and proof that Soviet combine harvesters failed to thresh and clean the grain. I was elated by that picture but my Novosti escort, whom I'll call Dimitri, was silent and moody as we traveled back to the city of Krasnodar.

We had dinner in the city. On a multipaged menu, only a few dishes were available. Mineral water tasted like chlorine. Like many cities closed to tourists and Westerners, Krasnodar was "off limits" and suffered from chronic food shortages.

Dimitri seemed depressed, fearful, and deeply worried. Barely touching his food, he began drinking vodka, always available even in the most remote regions of the Soviet Union. I wasn't sure if he realized my last photograph conveyed a profoundly negative statement about modern Soviet agriculture. With great reluctance, he had escorted me to the Kuban steppe and only after overcoming objections of the regional party leader.

The more vodka Dimitri drank, the more sorrowful he became. I asked, "Dimitri, please tell me what is making you so sad. Did you make a mistake in bringing me here?" "No," he said simply.

By 11:00 P.M., we were the only guests as the hotel's restaurant closed. After sharing the last glasses of vodka with Dimitri, I accompanied him to his room.

There he sat down, tore out the front page of the Pravda, and wrote a message I couldn't decipher. After pulling out some wheat grains lodged in the cuffs of his pants and spreading grains on top of the paper, he took out from his pocket the John F. Kennedy half dollar I had given him and placed it on top of his note.

With tears running down his cheek, he left the room without a word. Heading for the street, I followed him and asked, "Dimitri, where are you going?" "To the river," he answered. "Why?" I asked. He confessed, "My wife and two children have left me. I don't have any reason to live anymore." As he headed for the Kuban River, determined to drown himself, I pleaded, "Dimitri, the river is in the opposite direction."

He suspected I was misleading him. But he wasn't sober. Managing to seed some doubt in his mind, I put my arms around his shoulders and led him away from the river. While we walked for hours, Dimitri would argue every few minutes, "John, the river is the other way!" But I insisted, "No it isn't," and walked him further away from the river.

Our little game went on all night. By daybreak, I brought a somewhat sobered and embarrassed Dimitri back to the hotel. Apparently, the hotel director found Dimitri's farewell note, woke our interpreter and notified Novosti. Our interpreter had been up all night waiting for news from police patrols. Dimitri was immediately recalled to Moscow. We had no chance to say goodbye. Novosti assigned me a new man whom I met in Volgograd. After inquiries, I was told Dimitri was fine.

Toward the end of my assignment, I wanted to photograph the plots of land not collectivized, the plots where peasants defied Soviet law by engaging in "creeping capitalism."

Though I had seen private plots in the countryside outside Irkutsk during my Trans-Siberian journey, my Novosti escort steered me away from them. My 25-year-old interpreter, whom I'll call Svetlana, bravely took a different position. She was an attractive woman who openly flirted with me. Most important, she had not been hired to be my "watchdog" and readily agreed to help. Referring to my Novosti escort, she said, "We'll just leave before he wakes up."

Before sunrise, Svetlana and I left for Siberia's countryside. Our driver obeyed Svetlana's instructions. Though peasants were reluctant and even afraid to be photographed, Svetlana reassured them, "Don't worry, he's just a tourist."

Upon our return to the hotel, we found my angry Novosti escort waiting in the lobby. I calmed him a little by insisting, "I didn't want to wake up two people so early just to shoot sunrise scenes." He said no more. I knew I had trespassed into a sensitive area that the Soviets wanted hidden from Western cameras.

After we flew back to Moscow and arrived at the National Hotel, I claimed I needed to work on captions and suggested that my Novosti escort might as well take three days off. In reality, I wanted to work alone with Svetlana and photograph dissident artists.

In the evening, Svetlana called and asked me to meet her downstairs to plan our day. Instead of settling in the lobby as usual, she led me outside to Red Square. Unsure and anxious, she said, "John do not repeat what I'm about to tell you. Starting tomorrow, you'll be under surveillance by the KGB."

I was astonished by her news and courageous audacity. "Your regular Volga will be replaced by a Zil limousine with listening equipment," she continued. "They will hear what you say and record everything. You'll be followed by agents not only while you work but wherever you go."

"But why?" I asked. "Novosti or you were with me at all times." "I don't know," she answered, "but I suspect our driver in Irkutsk informed authorities that you were photographing Siberian peasants working on private plots. That could be considered subversive anti-Soviet propaganda. For your safety, don't photograph any sensitive subjects alone."

Stunned Svetlana not only helped me in Siberia but also took a serious risk informing me of the KGB, I held both her hands in mine and thanked her discreetly. Between us, we shared a fleeting flash of tenderness, a moment of silence, a secret understanding, appreciated only between two people under the watch of a totalitarian society.

Still surprised, I asked, "Why are you telling me this?" Svetlana looked as if I betrayed her. The sad truth was, I didn't entirely trust her nor understand why she knew about the operation by the dreaded security police.

The thought of being shadowed by the KGB was as disturbing as the idea of being locked up in Moscow's notorious Lefertovo prison on trumped-up charges.

At the "Dollar or Western Currencies Only Bar" in the National Hotel, I sat at the far end of the room with my back against the wall and ordered a double Scotch. I needed a plan of action. At stake were weeks of work, an intellectual, financial, emotional investment, and 90% of my essay completed in more than 4,000 undeveloped photographs. At all costs, my pictures had to be safeguarded. But how?

While sipping my whiskey, I thought of a solution. I kept the lights off in my hotel bedroom, feeling a touch of paranoia in the shadowy, lingering glow of Moscow's summer night as I looked over my equipment and captions with a penlight.

From my five big strobe units, I removed the 440-volt batteries and hid 93 rolls of film in the battery compartments. In my camera bag, I put the remaining 31 rolls, carefully selected from minor subjects that could be sacrificed if confiscated by the secret police. My reassembled strobes looked perfectly normal. In the hotel's dining room, I relaxed a little and ordered caviar, chicken à la Kiev, and a hundred grams of vodka.

To avoid creating more suspicion, I decided not to leave Moscow immediately. I dropped plans to interview dissident artists and decided to limit coverage to innocent summer scenes in public places.

At eight in the morning, Svetlana greeted me at the entrance of the National Hotel. She bowed her head toward the large black limousine parked a few feet away, courtesy of KGB. Her story was checking out. I felt chills running through me as we entered the limo. I instructed Svetlana, "I need some leisure scenes in the capital, like the parks of Moscow."

As we pulled out, a man and a woman agent in a gray Volga followed some 200 feet behind. When we walked into parks, one of the KGB agents, usually the woman, trailed our every move. Sitting on a bench, she pretended to read whenever I looked in her direction. As I focused on her with a 300-millimeter lens, she raised her book to hide her face.

I couldn't concentrate. Since I had covered beaches of the Black Sea, I didn't need any more pictures of Russian leisure time. I was only pretending to work.

By early afternoon, tired of putting on an act, I whispered in Svetlana's ear, "Tell that KGB driver of ours to take me to the American Embassy." She whispered, "Okay, but you should know he speaks English."

At the gates of the embassy, I told Svetlana, "I'll see you again tomorrow morning," and happily dismissed the limousine driver. While saying goodbye, I noticed the KGB agents in the gray Volga parked in the distance.

The embassy's American flag fluttering in the Moscow summer breeze eased my anxiety: I was on American soil. After I requested an emergency meeting for an off-the-record conversation with a political officer, I was taken upstairs to a soundproof room where I disclosed the license plate number of the KGB Volga and explained my situation in detail. The officer scribbled notes, remained silent for a long time, and finally said, "John, this is very serious. God only knows what the KGB are up to."

I listened intently as he insisted, "From now on, you must never be alone. Don't walk the streets of Moscow alone or even eat alone outside your hotel unless you're with a colleague from the American press corps. Continue to shoot a few more days as planned, then get out of Russia. Call me every day but make your conversation casual. I'm sure your phone is bugged."

We shook hands as he said, "I'll secure a staff car to take you back to your hotel." I thanked him and half jokingly said, "I hope in a few days I can set foot on American soil again."

The American Embassy briefing was not reassuring. It was clearly suggested that I could be subject to arrest or abduction. Even so, there was some comfort in the fact that the police knew I had contacted American diplomats, and my disappearance, if it occurred, would be noticed.

I returned to my hotel room to check my strobe units. My single strands of hair carefully glued to each unit were still in place. They were untouched and I relaxed for a moment.

For the next few days, chauffeured by the KGB and followed by the same agents in their gray Volga, I photographed Moscow's parks and public swimming pools. The two agents lost track of us in a huge crowd at, of all places, Karl Marx Avenue. I appreciated the irony for an instant, but they found us again at the premiere display of the Vostok spaceship.

After Air France informed me of an unexpected cancellation and offered me a first-class seat to Paris leaving August 10, I notified my embassy contact.

On my day of departure, Svetlana and our Novosti escort drove me to Sheremetyevo Airport in a standard Volga. Though it was a relief not to ride in the police limousine, the two agents in their gray Volga were still tailing us.

At the airport, the weight limit for carry-on luggage was 40 kilograms in first class. As I stacked my 95 kilograms of equipment on an old-fashioned scale, my Novosti escort surprised me by wedging his foot under the scale to prevent it from going over the limit. He astonished me even more by instructing customs officers to rush me through. I had a total of nine pieces but not a single one was checked. My strobe units concealing 93 invaluable rolls of film were loaded in the first-class cabin with me.

In the departure lounge, I asked my escort, "Why did you block the scale?" He answered, "John, I know what you've been going through for the last few days, and this morning you looked so tired and worried. I simply had to do something for you." Then he hugged me. "Yes, it was an exhausting trip," I said as I embraced Svetlana. Each of them knew how sincere my thanks were as I bid them goodbye.

As I flew away to "the free world," I thought of Svetlana who seemed so sad as I was leaving. I was puzzled at how she and my Novosti escort both defied the Soviet system—by informing me of the KGB operation, she had risked being accused of engaging in subversive acts against the Soviet state and possibly treason.

However, their defiance was more an act of friendship than rebellion. In truth, they were no more a threat to the Soviet system than the peasants growing half the empire's produce on privately owned plots, filling needs created by the failure of "collective farming."

I'd seen a Soviet Union proud of its achievements and world status as a military power yet brimming with contradictions. Luxury imports from the West were becoming available, while major cities had been refurbished.

Months before the Soviet Union's 50th anniversary, the empire was celebrating. People in streets of the capital looked happy and without being asked were eager to inform visitors that their revolution was the "world's greatest revolution."

After managing my last days in Moscow in a state of controlled fear, I promised myself that for a long time to come I wouldn't accept another assignment in the Soviet Union. Touching down at Paris's Orly airport, I was in a tired, depressed mood and remained convinced the totalitarian empire of the Soviet Union on the edge of its 50th anniversary was there to stay. Nothing I had seen hinted otherwise.

On August 12, 1967, I was back on American soil. My regular Darien driver and limousine met me at the airport, Yukiko and Chris welcomed me home, and it was my turn to celebrate.

The November 4, 1967, issue of *The Saturday Evening Post's* "Soviet Russia 1917–1967...50 Years of Thunder" essay, at 16 pages and a cover, with Richard Armstrong's text, was released with the subtitle: "Out of the revolution that shook the world came a Communist colossus that controls the destiny of half mankind."

END OF AN ERA

THE FOLDING OF AN HISTORIC MAGAZINE

NEW YORK 1967–1969

I closed the year of 1967 in *The Saturday Evening Post* with double-page portraits of two American millionaires. The "old money" millionaire lived on the east coast. In his New York Fifth Avenue apartment, I photographed him, surrounded by eighteenth-century French furniture, and even a gilded doghouse for his wife's poodle.

The "new money" millionaire was an oilman from New Mexico. I photographed him standing against a stuffed polarbear that he had shot in Alaska. At six foot two with bulging muscles, the oilman was the image of virility.

When my coverage was published in the December 30 issue of the *Post*, the "old money" millionaire who looked refined but much smaller than the oilman sued the *Post*, claiming my picture made him look "effete." Our lawyers eventually had the case dismissed in court in 1968.

The magazine by 1968 was in desperate need of millions of dollars, old or new. Curtis Publishing posted a loss of five million for 1967, and the company's president, Martin Ackerman, estimated a loss of another five million in the coming year. It was grim news. Though no one knew how long the *Post* could survive, I naively believed editorial excellence would overcome financial difficulties plaguing the magazine.

Dramatic events were unfolding in Vietnam. During Tet, the Lunar New Year, the Viet Cong launched coordinated attacks against major South Vietnamese cities and struck the American Embassy in Saigon.

Though I supported JFK's policy in 1961 to train the South Vietnamese Army to defend the country from a communist takeover, by 1968 I had serious doubts about the wisdom of escalating the war in Vietnam. It became clear that our intervention was doomed to fail.

Mr. and Mrs. Robert Gardiner in their Fifth Avenue apartment.

As early as 1965, *The Saturday Evening Post* had been a lonely dissenter, sharply criticizing involvement in the war. In 1967, Otto Friedrich said in a scathing editorial: "We can claim that we have a right to veto who will govern South Vietnam or anywhere else. We can claim that we have a right to kill anyone who stands in our way. But patriotism is not a justification for everything, nor was the world designed to suit our convenience, and in due time we all learn to judge our leaders by the wisdom and justice of their causes, and not by the amount of blood they shed in their quest for shining victories."

A year later in '68, shortly before I was scheduled to spend a week at the White House to photograph Lady Bird and Lyndon Johnson, the president responded to the mounting criticism of his conduct in the war by announcing in a television and radio address, "I shall not seek and I will not accept the nomination of my party as president."

As I began my assignment, I hoped that the president had forgotten the *Post*'s editorial. It was a bad time all around. Momentous events raged across the country. In the aftermath of Dr. Martin Luther King's assassination on April 4 in Memphis, major cities were engulfed in riots.

At the White House, as the president was preparing to host a state dinner for King Olav of Norway, I was adjusting lights in the state dining room when Johnson appeared unannounced. He took me by surprise. Before I could utter my rehearsed, "It is an honor to meet you, Mr. President," he slapped my back

New Mexico oil tycoon Tom Borack.

and said, "It's nice to see you again young man." I had never met him before, but I adjusted my greeting, "It's an honor to see you, Mr. President."

Though I was given limited access to the president, I had enough coverage to satisfy my editors. Even so, I regretted my pictures were not intimate enough to catch the inner despair, the emotional turmoil, which events at home and abroad inflicted on Lyndon Johnson in the last year of his presidency.

The First Lady was hard at work on her celebrated "Beautification of the American Highway" program. She did most of her writing in a bedroom large enough to accommodate an office. When I suggested, "A picture of you at work in your bedroom would be more important than all the photos I have of you at official functions," she understood and gave me all the time I needed.

Lady Bird was one of the most graceful of all the American women I had met. Her good manners came so naturally, she made me feel it was her pleasure to meet my demands and impositions. If her husband could be criticized for his coarse behavior, she could only be praised for her refinement.

"A Week at the White House" was published in the June 29, 1968, issue of *The Saturday Evening Post*. Earlier in the month, Senator Robert Kennedy was fatally gunned down in Los Angeles, and James Earl Ray, wanted by the FBI for the murder of Dr. King, was arrested in London. Like millions around the world, I was stunned by the assassinations.

The *Post*'s financial straits seemed insignificant when compared to events occurring in America and Europe that year. Russian tanks had put an end to the "Spring of Prague" when students dared to demand democratic freedom. The event saddened me, but the brutality of the Soviets was no surprise.

More disturbing and shocking was what was happening to America, the world's first democracy, under siege in Chicago in August during the Democratic Convention. Antiwar and antiestablishment protesters were crushed and beaten by Chicago police under orders from Mayor Richard J. Daley. Members of the press were not spared from police violence: 21 were hurt filming, photographing, and recording the chaos.

Television in full color brought nightly images of the brutality and upheaval in Chicago to every living room in America. Despite their quick closing time, weekly magazines like *Life, Time,* and *Newsweek* couldn't compete with the TV networks. It was true enough that powerful pictures could satisfy the public's desire for lasting memories of extraordinary events like the death and funeral of John F. Kennedy, but I began to fear that those publications, *Life* especially, were in danger of becoming irrelevant in the age of television.

I felt a deep wave of pessimism as a citizen, photojournalist, and idealist. No one in my generation seemed optimistic. Many wondered out loud, "Where will it all end?" Student uprisings spread to over a hundred college campuses. No one knew if the coming presidential election would set the nation on a more rational course. The nation appeared headed for anarchy, which I feared might invite a reactionary course.

Each successive issue of *The Saturday Evening Post* was getting thinner, and at 68 pages per issue, the *Post* was losing money. Many advertisers defected to the three television networks. In a nutshell, television was killing us. Photojournalism as I had known it was on its way out.

I tried to remain enthusiastic while on assignment in the U.S. where the *Post*'s woes were public knowledge. Readers asked me anxiously if the *Post* would disappear: one woman said, "My family has been reading the *Post* for four generations. We don't want anything to happen to it." I tried to reassure her.

Though I couldn't see how it would survive, I too wanted the *Post* to go on for generations. Millions of readers would genuinely miss the magazine but perhaps no more than filmgoers missed silent films in 1928 when the "talkies" were introduced.

My last cover for the *Post* was published on October 19. The story on modern dancer Merce Cunningham included a six-page layout with Cunningham perfectly sharp in a shot while dancers blurred around him. My last story, "The American Highway Threatens to Despoil Landscapes, Cities," appeared on December 14. The year was ending and with it *The Saturday Evening Post*.

Between my last cover and my last story, Richard Nixon was elected the 37th President of the United States. To quote a chapter title in William Manchester's *The Glory and the Dream*, 1968 was "The Year Everything Went Wrong."

January 10, 1969, was the last day for the magazine, now 242 years old, that had become an American institution. Management of Curtis Publishing closed the doors and stopped the presses. "I watched *The Saturday Evening Post* being put to death," Otto Friedrich wrote in *Decline and Fall*, his account of the publication's struggle to stay alive.

The magazine was originally delivered by horse-and-buggy as far back as 1821. Edgar Allan Poe's, "The Blue Cat," was published in the *Post*, along with other works by famous writers. Circulation at the start was 2,000: when I signed on as a photojournalist in 1963, its circulation was 6.5 million with some 27 million readers.

It was all over. The last day was somber as editorial staff gathered in Bill Emerson's office. Usually a witty, brilliant speaker who'd amuse the most recalcitrant audience and make stony faces break into laughter, Bill was at a loss to fully express his sorrow. "It was a great voyage," he said, "and a commendable attempt to save a great magazine that deserved better from its owners."

Emotions ran high as New York papers, *Life*, and the three networks filmed and photographed the sadness in the faces of people who tried to save the *Post*. In *Decline and Fall*, Friedrich observed: "I do not mean, of course, that all traditional institutions must be preserved as fossils....on the contrary, it is the constant process of internal renewal that keeps these old institutions alive and valuable. The *Post* was, I think, such an institution, genuinely renewed, and it deserved to live. When it was killed, therefore, we lost not only an independent voice in American society but an irreplaceable part of our national past."

The death of the *Post* meant the end of the freest time I had ever known in photojournalism. Along with a substantial loss of income, close friends drifted away, some never to be seen again.

When the *Post* folded in January 1969, I was 40. It was emotionally painful, and my principal source of income was gone. *Post* editors had given me extraordinary freedom, access to the best assignments, and invitations to Manhattan's best restaurants at the end of each job. Though I didn't lose sleep over the loss of expensive three-martini lunches, I did miss the struggle to prove the magazine was worth saving. Editorial excellence was our weapon of choice, and like naive missionaries, we believed we'd overcome all threats to the *Post*.

Black Star President Howard Chapnick would say in his 1994 book, *Truth Needs No Ally*, that "John Launois...and other photojournalists who had done so well in the star system created by the magazines...found it difficult to suddenly stop chronicling world issues."

Chapnick was correct. I'd never again do politically significant projects like "Fifty Years of Communism." Even so, I continued to take on fascinating subjects for *National Geographic* on several continents.

By 1970, I had secured enough work to ease financial worries, so much so that I accepted an offer to direct a short-fiction film from Fernando Casablancas in Paris. Casablancas was a ladies' man and a handsome, cosmopolitan Spaniard educated in Swiss schools, the Sorbonne, and Wharton business school. *Time* magazine had assigned him to Asian advertising sales in Tokyo in 1960 while I was living in Japan. Though we hit it off immediately, we often disagreed about France, where he had lived a privileged life. His France wasn't my France.

One of Fernando's ambitions was to become a film producer, so in the spring of 1970, we agreed to shoot his concept for a short film entitled *La Fête à Jojo* or "Jojo's Birthday."

THE BELLY OF PARIS

"JOJO" AND FRANCE DE L'ÎLE

PARIS 1970

Yukiko and Chris wanted a vacation, and I needed a creative adventure. Directing my first short-fiction film for theater release seemed like an exciting way to leave behind my morose mood after the death of the *Post*.

Fernando and I decided to write our script on the Greek island of Corfu. His wife Anne Marie and Yukiko were happy to join us, and six-year-old Chris was fascinated by the idea of traveling to sandy beaches of a faraway island.

"Jojo" was the story of a 15-year-old virgin boy whose older friends wanted to give him a special birthday gift by arranging his first sexual experience in one of the prostitution districts in Paris. In his macho manner, Fernando explained, "After Jojo goes off with the woman, there'll be a passage of time. Then he returns triumphant. Because he is no longer a virgin, Jojo brags to his friends that he is now a man." Disagreeing, I insisted, "No, Fernando, it's much stronger if Jojo is afraid, maybe horrified as he goes with the prostitute and is unable to perform.

At the end of July, we returned to Paris but Fernando and I still disagreed about the film's ending. Regardless, we began casting. We found the perfect Jojo in the nephew of our director of photography. At 14 years old, he was a shy, gentle, blue-eyed boy with blond hair and a handsome, innocent face.

For the prostitute, we cast a 35-year-old French belly dancer on leave from her nightclub act in Cairo, Egypt. After casting eight extras to play other women in the district, we were ready. But the night before the shoot, Fernando and I were still passionately arguing about the ending—by two in the morning, our disagreements were getting nastier with each shot of whiskey. As our arguments overheated, it dawned on me that only real prostitutes could help resolve the ending.

Angrily, I said, "Alright Fernando! Let's drive to the red light district on Rue St. Denis and ask three to five prostitutes what happens when a 15-year-old boy goes up for the first time. We'll go with the majority opinion." Convinced he was right, Fernando agreed immediately. In his wife's tiny Fiat 500, we headed to Rue St. Denis.

At three in the morning, business was slow. Instead of standing by respective *hôtel de passe* sidewalks, most women were relaxing at all-night cafés, enjoying a break. Of the first three prostitutes, one said, "Young boys are usually too scared to try the first time. They get pressured by friends, so a boy will go up, pay his money, and freeze. I often suggest they stay for 10 or 15 minutes before they go back to friends downstairs." The two other prostitutes confirmed her story.

Surprised, Fernando reluctantly agreed to my ending, which in part was inspired by my own experience and conviction that his ending had no twist.

Three hours later, I arrived early to meet our crew at 7:00 A.M. at a café near the Châtelet Theater. I made a list of questions for our cinematographer Daniel Henneveux who had a solid reputation as a D.P. Since photography and cinematography were two different disciplines, I needed Henneveux to watch over me in case I began to compose scenes like photographs. A good photographer sees large and small details and unites them into a single aesthetic frame, while a good cinematographer faced with the same elements lets his camera move and discover each detail separately.

Henneveux immediately understood my fears and assured me, "John, don't worry, I'll make sure you see in motion." Alban Labourier playing Jojo and the three friends we cast all arrived on time. The eldest at 21 was street smart and spoke Parisian slang: his tough-guy demeanor was completely natural. Next to him, the virginal Jojo looked like an angel. From research, I knew our Jojo had never been to Paris's prostitution districts, so I deliberately under-briefed Alban and didn't mention that the women on the sidewalk were not actual prostitutes but extras hired for production. I wanted to capture his natural expressions when scantily-dressed extras accosted him in the district where several genuine prostitutes were working.

Jojo's initial reactions were delightfully innocent as our camera caught him shyly casting his eyes downward while extras boldly exposed as much of themselves permissible under French law. Because all of Jojo's encounters were unrehearsed, a spontaneous and natural quality was etched on film.

Though Chris and Yukiko were visiting us on location, they were also sightseeing in inevitable spots like the top of the Eiffel Tower. Paris was delightful in August. Though the production scheduled a seven-day shoot, we took eight. With our highly professional crew, things rolled smoothly until genuine streetwalkers attacked our "prostitute" extras for trespassing on their turf. Two police foot-patrol *flics* plunged into the melee to separate the women. Things immediately quieted down when I pointed out the camera hidden in the doorway and explained that our women were just actors. All the women and Parisian cops exploded into laughter.

For our interior scene in the *hôtel de passe*, Jojo sat on a chair as his *fille de joie* stretched on the bed and called him softly to join her. Because I had not warned him that our actress would fully undress, Jojo froze on his chair, blushed, and quivered as the camera focused on his face, then panned across the woman's naked back, and settled on her whispering lips. Jojo's alarmed innocence could not have been rehearsed.

In the closing scene, Jojo rejoined his friends who slapped his back, congratulated him, and asked, "How was it?" A genuinely shaken Jojo could hardly respond: his reactions were melancholic, not scripted at all. His "friends" were puzzled by his mood but played their roles as they parted and watched Jojo walk away, passing under the small Arc de Triomphe at the end of Rue St. Denis.

I had directed my first motion picture. Editing cut the film to 15 minutes, but I felt as if I had directed *Lawrence of Arabia*. Eventually it was shown across theaters in France, England, Spain, Switzerland, Belgium, Japan, and on Swedish television.

After eight days of shooting, we celebrated Yukiko's 38th birthday. Fernando secretly arranged for a beautiful cake, baked at a Left Bank restaurant, to celebrate her birthday and the end of filming. Fernando and Anne Marie were convinced *La Fête à Jojo* would lead to bigger things. It was a happy evening.

As we all sang "Happy Birthday" and Yukiko blew out candles, I took a long look at her and reflected that she had always been a very pretty girl, but while I hadn't paid attention in America, she had turned into a beautiful woman.

In late August, I took Yukiko and Chris to Orly airport for their return to Connecticut. I felt deeply in love with her again and was delighted with Chris as he ran around the airport. Our 1964 separation was nearly forgotten. We were a happy family again, and I knew I'd miss them during post-production in Paris.

Ten days later at a screening of our rough cut, an unknown and uninvited guest appeared as the lights came on. Our cameraman and editor immediately noticed the mysterious woman's striking beauty: "God, she looks like a young Ava Gardner, only more tragic."

At our editing studio, she stood there as if looking for someone. When I asked, "Can we help you?" she simply answered, "I heard you speaking English. Actually, I'm a translator of English to French film scripts. I have a friend whom I translate for, and I was hoping to find him here."

Her story sounded credible. She explained in an English-French accent that she had studied English at Oxford University. Finally, everyone but she and I had left the studio, and since I didn't feel like eating alone, I invited her to join me. That turned out to be the biggest mistake of my life.

She was a 26-year-old from an aristocratic family with roots in French and European history, going back centuries. Because of a promise I made to her mother, I'll call her "France de l'Île" since her middle name was France and she lived and held court in her studio on l'Île St. Louis, an island on the Seine River.

Together we went to where restaurants remained open all night in the city's wholesale market, Les Halles. Emile Zola described it as "The Belly of Paris." Through the night, France de l'Île did most of the talking, telling a long maudlin tale of suffering. The sentimentality of her story affected me.

I asked, "Who was the dear friend you were looking for at the studio?" She confessed, "He's a big French film producer who threw me out of his apartment in the middle of the night." I asked, "Why?" She answered, "That was his habit." She made it sound as though it happened yesterday. In fact, it was a very old story, but she still haunted him from studio to film studio.

Because she appeared anxious, I asked, "Are you afraid of me?" She said, "No, but I'm afraid because I have an incurable muscle disorder, myasthenia gravis. If it attacks my heart, it will kill me."

As I listened, looking at her beautiful face and purple eyes framed by long black hair, the romantic in me fell for her compelling story. In my travels, I often met total strangers who'd openly confess the story of their lives and then wave goodbye at the end of a trip, but my meeting with France de l'Île was different. Her sheer tragic beauty veiled the largely false and melodramatic essence of her tales. Irrationally, I was captivated.

When my evenings were free, I found myself inviting France de l'Île to the best restaurants in Paris. She toyed with her food, taking only a few small bites. She said she was watching her weight, but she had a perfect figure, so it seemed ridiculous.

I listened in fascination to her tales of childhood suffering in southwestern France. She had been sent to a gloomy convent school ruled by stern nuns who made her kneel on frozen tiles of the chapel at six in the morning to pray before breakfast. She said the washrooms were so cold, ice had to be broken before she and classmates could wash their faces.

Her life in the family castle sounded just as grim with only a few rooms heated and no running water until the 1960s. She made her father, "Le Marquis," sound like a cold tyrant, a distant disciplinarian who insisted on a strict Catholic upbringing for his children before sending them to study at leading international universities.

Her father's purpose, it seemed, was to be sure his daughters were fluent in several languages to make them suitable for marriage to European aristocrats. France de l'Île had class and refinement, but she was ill prepared for modern times. She could not drive a car, type, or even cook for herself.

She could barely pay her rent or survive making English-to-French translations for a few francs a page. Though she had learned aristocratic manners and how to look beautiful to attract a husband in that circle, nothing had prepared her to earn a living.

At aristocratic "rallies" where families of the same standing sent adolescent progeny to social functions in hopes of a suitable match and new alliances, France de l'Île was displayed. Twice a week, from age 15 to 18, she was praised for her delicate beauty, but no relationship lasted, even though in the words of her sister, "She had the world at her feet."

In that late summer of 1970, I didn't know who France de l'Île really was. Completely smitten in a whirlpool of emotion, I began to drown in a passion so powerful and foreign to my experience, it frightened me. If idealism and reason guided me before, those principles were suddenly far out of reach.

When *La Fête à Jojo* was finished, Fernando arranged a private screening on the Champs Elysées. Among selected guests, he invited the Paris-based critic of *Variety*, Gene Moskowitz. Though he didn't review shorts, Moskowitz complimented us for the film's sensitivity and clever ending. His praise was tonic for our egos and encouraged us to celebrate, eat canapés, and drink champagne late into the night. When France de l'Île joined our party, Fernando sensed something stirring, but in Paris, he didn't take it seriously, because in his world, love affairs were common and nothing to be concerned about.

In late September, *Time* magazine asked me to shoot a photographic color essay on "Moscow's New Skyline." But because of my past experience with the KGB, I had serious misgivings.

It was a dilemma: in Paris, I was in an emotional crisis, while in Russia, I might be on the KGB's list of subversive American journalists. But I needed time to reflect on my involvement with France de l'Île. I had to get away from Paris and be on my own. Since *Time*'s subject was not political or controversial, I left for Moscow.

In a departure from Stalinist architecture, the Soviets had built Russia's first modern skyscrapers. Working with my old Novosti team, it was a relatively easy assignment. Captions took little time to draft, so one evening, I wrote at length to Yukiko about Russia's tragic history, closing my letter with, "After this assignment, I'll need time on my own to figure out my life and career." As I would learn, Yukiko sensed something was terribly wrong.

The trip to Moscow had not helped me gain perspective. I reflected on the time Yukiko and I were newlyweds visiting Singapore. An American friend, a best-selling author and *Life*-magazine writer, had asked me, "John, tell me how could I have fallen in love with another woman while I'm so in love with my wife?" Though the question was frightening, I was sure I'd never face that dilemma. I had no answer for him then, and in Moscow, I had no answer for myself.

Returning to Paris, keeping guilt at bay, I became engulfed in a passion for France de l'Île. As a romantic, I believed there remained only a few precious days before our affair would be over.

Aware that I'd soon leave for Connecticut, France de l'Île said she wanted me to meet her uncle, a man whom she claimed adored her. In the past, her uncle introduced her to potential suitors from the top of a grand marble staircase by his castle's majestic entrance.

Her uncle's ancestors ruled parts of Europe for centuries. Aristocratic privileges and titles were supposed to have been abolished ages ago, but in 1970 France, her uncle was still reverently addressed by his original titles of "Prince de Y" and "Marquis de A."

My journalistic curiosity was aroused. During childhood, I rebelled against my country's oppressive class divisions and eventually left for America. Since I had never known people who lived in castles, I unconsciously wanted to breathe that rarefied air and see for myself whether their lifestyle was as lofty as I had imagined long ago.

France de l'Île's uncle was a genial man. *"Enchanté.* Welcome. So you are France's American. She's told me so much about you." Shaking hands I asked, "Should I address you as Prince de Y or Marquis de A?" He laughed and said, "Call me André and I will call you John."

He insisted speaking in his labored English though he knew I was fluent in French. Since I was an American, distinctions of our French "social ranks" were leveled. His huge castle had been spared during the 1789 revolution but over time was badly damaged by the rainstorms of the Rhone Valley: water leaked in most of the 110 rooms except for five suites where the prince, his wife, and two young daughters lived.

André showed me the study where for nearly a decade he had been working on the history of his ancestors. He cheerfully noted, "I've only got six more centuries to go." The grand staircase France de l'Île had described to me was draped with cobwebs, and the chandelier was broken. André's castle was once staffed by 60 servants and 10 chefs who'd serve as many as 200 guests. The kitchen ran the length and width of the castle and seemed the size of a soccer field, but by 1970, the prince's wife cooked meals on hot plates in a kitchenette.

Like many other French aristocrats, the prince was in financial ruin. "A reversal of fortune," France de l'Île explained. As with Versailles and other grand places, André hoped his castle would be classified as a *Patrimoine National*, or "National Heritage," so taxpayers would help pay for restoration.

It was a nostalgic trip for France de l'Île, but it saddened her to see so much of the castle covered with canvas tied to the gutters. France de l'Île asked, "Promise to meet my mother. She's flying in just to see you." Her mother, "La Marquise," was a sweet woman who adored her first-born daughter. Since I had just read Hemingway's *A Moveable Feast*, I took her to Paris's La Closerie des Lilas, one of the author's hangouts. Photographs of "Papa Hemingway" were displayed above what owners claimed was Hemingway's table. On the terrace in the mild October air, La Marquise spoke of her daughter's fragile health and diagnosis of myasthenia gravis. But what her loving mother did not tell me was that since childhood, France de l'Île had serious psychological problems and suicidal tendencies.

Before leaving France, I needed to see my father, a man I always regarded as a model of moral rectitude. He'd been raised with values close to the Protestant puritanical ethic. Because mother often said, "Women were always attracted to your father," I wanted to know if father ever strayed. If he had, my guilt-ridden mind might have found relief.

As father and I walked under poplar trees lining a beautiful stream, I asked point blank, "Did you ever cheat on mother?" I masked my distress on hearing his first words. "Well, during the war years, many of my clients were women whose husbands died or were prisoners in Germany. Some women would unashamedly open their doors in flimsy nightgowns. I have to admit I felt tempted at times but was disgusted that they could even consider being unfaithful to men who fought in the war. So, no, I never cheated."

Then he looked in my eyes and asked, "Did you cheat on Yukiko?" I answered, "Yes." Sadly, he looked at me for what seemed an eternity and said, "Not only have you betrayed Yukiko, you have betrayed yourself."

Driving back to Paris with father's words ringing in my head, I wondered if my financial ability to satisfy France de l'Île's every whim and weeks of exposure to upper-class promiscuity in Paris had corrupted the integrity and idealism my father had passed down to me in the poverty of my youth. It had been a mistake to expect leniency from father.

Departing from Paris in mid-November was manic. France de l'Île was hysterical. She fainted several times on our last night together, and the next morning, she ran after my taxi begging me to stay.

Fernando met me at Orly airport to accompany me to Connecticut. During our flight, he urged, "John, you cannot wreck your marriage just for some crazy love affair in Paris." But I was beyond his rationale, and I could not imagine lying to Yukiko.

Prior to our arrival, Anne Marie had been staying with Yukiko for a few weeks. Yukiko showed Anne Marie my ambiguous letter from Moscow, declaring, "John has fallen for another woman." Anne Marie laughed, "No, not John."

Torn and ashamed, I found it extremely painful to see Yukiko and heartbreaking to see Chris greeting me so cheerfully in all his innocence. As Anne Marie, Fernando, Yukiko, Chris, and I settled around the dining table, Fernando tried to diffuse the tension. As his witty and brilliant remarks failed to reach me, he noticed I was deliberately avoiding eye contact with Yukiko.

Taking me aside, he desperately tried to cheer me up and persuade me to not say a word about France de l'Île. Ironically, Fernando and I had adamantly disagreed 10 years earlier in Japan, when we discussed the moral and proper behavior of a married man. Indiscretions in marriage were not permissible to me, while he saw them as "mostly meaningless."

Prophetically, he had warned me, "John, you're so straight and puritanical. Worse, you don't know much about women. Someday it'll backfire on you. A cunning woman will sweep you off your feet. You'll fall hard before you even understand what's happening, and in the process, you'll wreck your marriage. Of course, I hope it never happens to you and Yukiko, but beware."

In Darien, his words from long ago became all too clear. I had fallen hard for France de l'Île, and before the night was over I'd inflict on Yukiko the kind of pain that a union born in idealistic romanticism could not survive.

After Anne Marie and Fernando went to sleep, Yukiko and I sat at the kitchen table as I poured myself another double Scotch and Yukiko awaited in total silence my shameful confession. Every word I spoke inflicted deep pain, but in her dignity and stoicism, she never acknowledged the cruelty of my testimony. Instead, she silently stared at me in disbelief.

In her diary, which she let me read 30 years later, Yukiko wrote: "I was deeply hurt and just wanted to hurt him back....but I did not cry then....Perhaps my biggest mistake was not to show my anger openly. It might have been easier for us if I had screamed or thrown things at him...Instead I tried to understand, to analyze and endure the pain. In the end, I let my wounds become too deep."

When my one-way conversation ended at dawn in the home where we spent the happiest years of our marriage, something precious and irreplaceable ended. As Yukiko went to our bedroom, I descended downstairs to my books and bar to escape, in her words, "to his turmoil, to drink the dawn away."

On November 23, 1970, Yukiko reached out despite her agony and gave me a new light suitcase for my 42nd birthday. In her diary, she noted, "Life is full of irony, for it was that new suitcase John packed and left home with to join France de l'Île."

Upon my departure, I escaped one bad dream only to enter the next chapter of an all-consuming nightmare. In my foolishness, as if deluded or self-hypnotized, I imagined I could work out a way to live in New York with "France" while remaining close to Yukiko and Chris. So in the winter of early '71, I brought France de l'Île to New York on Pan Am. In midflight, she suffered what seemed to be a panic attack. As I berated her for consuming too many tranquilizers, she burst into tears, washed pills down with champagne, and fell asleep.

Though concerned about her frightening behavior, I assumed it was due to fear of flying. At the time, I was unaware of the depth of her psychological problems. I only knew she was a fragile, beautiful young woman who had completely captivated me.

I first learned of France de l'Île's obsession with her figure and appearance when she became hysterical upon discovering the Greenwich Village apartment that I rented did not have a full-length mirror. The small medicine cabinet mirror in the bathroom didn't console her as she sat crying on the convertible sofa. Unfurnished, our apartment looked desolate, but empty rooms didn't bother her. Sobbing, she said, "It's just that there's no full-length mirror!"

Holding her in my arms, I begged her, "Please don't cry." She immediately stopped crying when I suggested we go buy a new mirror.

In a glass shop, we found a mirror taller than her five-foot-three frame. Since it couldn't fit in a taxi, I carried the huge glass under my arm to University Place. As I entered our apartment, the mirror slipped out and crashed to the floor, breaking into several pieces. France de l'Île became hysterical again as she screamed, "Breaking a mirror will bring *sept ans de malheur*," repeating endlessly, "*sept ans de malheur*" (seven years of misfortune). It was just superstition, but she believed it.

When I realized the shop had failed to tape one end of the box, I repacked the broken pieces as she cried inconsolably. I returned to the shop, and the owner gracefully admitted his mistake and gave me a second mirror without charge. When I carried it back to the apartment, she met me at the door and again wailed, "*Sept ans de malheur.*"

This time I carefully unwrapped the mirror, setting it horizontally against the living room wall and gaffer-taped it down to the parquet floor, not wanting to risk another "seven years of misfortune." Her tears stopped instantly.

After undressing, she spread out on the floor and sensuously rolled herself back and forth in the most erotic and narcissistic act I'd ever seen. As a photographer, I had covered wars, riots, poverty, and wealth; I had experienced sublime emotions inspired by fleeting light touching faces and landscapes before darkness set in.

But the sight of this stunning creature in a trance was beyond anything I had ever witnessed. As horizontal rain slashed across the windows, I wondered how a woman could have been created so perfectly from head to toe.

After loading cameras and setting lights, I photographed her. I was 42 years old and trembling, for I'd never seen France de l'Île fully nude before: to seduce me in Paris, she had only let me glimpse the perfection of her form in candlelit shadows of her bedroom.

She was happy to be "on stage" for me. In the past, the nudes I photographed were like paintings in museums or dancers in nightclubs, but with France de l'Île, I felt I was photographing a living work of art. When I ran out of film, I was overwhelmed by passion and all too quickly forgot about her seizures of hysteria.

By 1971, I was well established at *Fortune* magazine. In February, the picture editor at *Fortune*, Libby Waterson, called me and said, "We have a double assignment for a cover and inside layout on General Motors' robot welders at GM's Lordstown plant in Ohio. Are you interested and available?"

On cover shoots, I knew *Fortune*'s Art Director Walter Allner liked to be on the set. Trained at the Bauhaus School of Design, Walter had a Teutonic approach to his work and "no nonsense" attitude, so I was apprehensive about bringing France de l'Île on assignment.

When I told her to stay behind, she simply fainted. In retrospect, it was a theatrical gesture, but at the time, I was reluctant to leave her alone without a friend in New York. On Central Park South on our first night together in Manhattan, a gust of wind literally lifted her off her feet. Since New York frightened her, I reasoned Allner would understand why I brought her along.

When I introduced her to Allner at La Guardia before our flight to Youngstown, Ohio, I knew he disapproved. Loaded with tranquilizers, France managed to disguise her fear on the plane, but I knew she was terrified.

Lordstown was desolate. After a cordial but second-rate dinner at our motel, we bid goodnight to Allner. The next morning, France de l'Île was dressed in what she called her "working clothes," jeans and a top so tight, it left little to the imagination. Allner took me aside. "John," he said, "you can't take her with you to General Motors. With her looks, she'll stop the assembly line."

Diplomatically, I promised to bring her with me after the cover shoot and Allner's departure. After I photographed Vegas automobiles being vertically loaded onto new "Vert-a-Pac" railroad cars, Allner left for New York with the cover.

I took a chance and brought France de l'Île to the assembly line. The welding robots did not stop working, but the men supervising them certainly did. Whistling, they asked, "Who's the pinup girl?" Sexy compliments poured over her. As robots continued to throw off showers of sparks, their supervisors surrounded France de l'Île. She beamed with joy, and the gloom in her heart lifted—her admirers made her day.

The April 1971 issue of *Fortune* was extraordinary if not unique for offering readers my cover story as well as numerous photographs I'd taken on assignments for three other different subjects: "A quadruple play," *Fortune* called it in a heartwarming 500-word "Editors Desk" description of my career in photojournalism. It was good news.

Managing Editor Richard Lubar wrote, "It is evident from this recent sampling that Launois is a camera artist of uncommon variety and scope, as well as great sensitivity." His tribute ended with a quote from the art director: "Whenever we have anything tricky or difficult to do, I have confidence Launois can bring it off. He is a real no-nonsense guy." There was a certain irony in Walter Allner calling me a "no-nonsense guy." My work was the only rational part of my life—my personal life was a disaster.

Though I continued to see Yukiko and Chris between assignments, she had written in her diary, "I stopped fighting." In her magnanimity, Yukiko never criticized me in front of Chris. Despite her pain, she was always considerate and made certain my relationship with our son remained unspoiled.

At the end of March, France de l'Île's visitor visa would expire. Our immigration lawyer failed to deliver a resident's visa despite his promises and a $1,000 fee. Before her departure for Paris, France de l'Île wanted to learn how to become a photojournalist, but I didn't think she had the stamina. When I tried to tell her it would take years to learn, she angrily yelled, "How will I ever know if I don't start?"

So I bought her two Nikons, four lenses, and a light meter. Because she was fascinated by beautiful black women she had seen in New York, I helped her photograph African American women in city streets during her last two weeks in Manhattan. As I composed her shots, she was happy to simply push the shutter-release button. Her illusion of being a photographer was too pure to spoil. I didn't expect her to learn anything in so short a time, but it was pointless to suggest that she had learned almost nothing.

Taking her back to Paris, I felt emotionally drained and exhausted. Though I felt somewhat manipulated giving in to all her whims, and had come to realize I'd never be able to fulfill her psychological needs, I could not yet fully break off my relationship with her.

Years later, one of her brothers bluntly said, "It's sad to say, but after all those years of tears, excess with alcohol, prescription drugs, and attempted suicides, all our hearts with the exception of mother's were drained of compassion. We had nothing else to give." On our return flight, France de l'Île was again terrified, but she seemed to recover quickly once back in Paris as she held court for her friends and admirers, describing her American experiences and start in photography.

After two weeks in Paris, I had to leave her to prepare for a trip to three continents for a *National Geographic* assignment on longevity. Before departure, her old friend and admirer, the aging "Marquis J. de St. A," explained, "John, you have to understand that France de l'Île's fainting spells, tears, and need to hold court are customs inherited from nineteenth-century France." The old monarchist loved those "qualities" in her. In his nostalgia for an ancient past, he idealized France de l'Île and was always at her side when she didn't feel well, which was often.

I knew my relationship with France de l'Île was doomed, yet I couldn't bear the pain and tears in her eyes in the last days before my departure. Torn between logic and emotion, I reasoned I'd probably see her again in some distant future. When I left for New York in mid-April 1971, after she had gone through a series of fainting spells, the old marquis was there to console her.

Yukiko and I agreed to sell the Connecticut house and move to a lovely three-bedroom Manhattan apartment on Central Park West with a view of the park. Unsaid was the possibility that we might reunite and save what was left of our marriage. Unknown to me, Yukiko was determined to start a career of her own. As she wrote in her diary, her goal was to "stop living in John's shadow."

Howard Chapnick had offered her a full-time picture editor position at Black Star, so for Yukiko, living in Manhattan near the agency made sense. As for my feelings about leaving Darien, I had already destroyed the years of happiness we had known there.

In the summer, we moved to Manhattan but failed to save our marriage. I didn't know how to live with my guilt. Yukiko tried to nurture a sense of normalcy in our daily lives and tried desperately to calm my nerves, but the more she tried, the guiltier I felt.

All the while, through cables and letters addressed to the office, I was hounded by France de l'Île. I knew I could not live with her, yet when apart, I missed her.

Yukiko believed it was not France de l'Île's sheer beauty enchanting me so much as her social rank in France that had always been unattainable to sons and daughters of the working class.

Well-meaning friends offered theories too. Fernando bluntly told me, "You discovered passion for the first time with France de l'Île. I warned you not to underestimate the power of the flesh." That might have been part of the answer, but I simply didn't know. Little calmed the turmoil.

Cover of *Fortune* magazine featuring General Motors.

ON ASSIGNMENT

THE SEARCH FOR LONGEVITY

ECUADOR, PAKISTAN, REPUBLIC OF GEORGIA 1971

Work itself was therapeutic and had immediate effects. As soon as my plane leveled off and I was on assignment, I felt in charge of life again, in control of my mind and emotions.

In September 1971, I had my first encounter with the distinguished professor of clinical medicine and chief of medical services at Massachusetts General Hospital, Alexander Leaf, M.D., who was also a professor of medicine at Harvard Medical School. We met in London to begin a *National Geographic* project on longevity.

The assignment took us to three known "bastions of longevity" located in three of the most remote and mountainous regions on the globe: Ecuador's Andean village of Vilcabamba, the Karakoram range in Hunza in the Pakistani portion of fabled Kashmir, and Abkhazia in the Republic of Georgia in the southern Soviet Union.

Hunza, Kashmir.

For the acclaimed Dr. Leaf, the assignment represented another step in his lifelong quest to fathom mysteries of old age. For me, it was an escape from my personal distress—I'd disappear, at least for a while, into remote and inaccessible places. There I'd photograph centenarians surviving and enjoying extreme old age.

Working in fields, climbing steep hills, riding mules and horses, those old people rarely complained. An exception was a man in Abkhazia, Magul Surmenelia, "108 years young," who grumbled, "My children won't let me do anything anymore." And Miguel Carpio in Vilcabamba, age 123, who sadly said, "I can't see the women too well anymore," then added with a laugh, "but I can feel them!"

In 1971, there were about 3 centenarians per 100,000 in the U.S. but 39 per 100,000 in Hunza and Abkhazia. The village of Vilcabamba with a population of 819 had 9 individuals above the age of 100. Dr. Leaf had no conclusive explanation for those phenomenal statistics.

In Leaf's opinion, as published in *Geographic*, "The old people of all three cultures share a great deal of physical activity. The traditional farming and household practices demand heavy work, and males and females are involved from early childhood to terminal days. Superimposed on the usual labor in farming is the mountainous terrain."

Our cover story, "Search for the Oldest People," was published in the January 1973 *National Geographic*. Decades later, when I discussed longevity with Dr. Leaf, the retired professor emphasized the role played by genetic factors in extreme longevity but informed me, "Subsequent research on our centenarian subjects proved their ages had been exaggerated when we interviewed them in 1972."

Prior to meeting with Dr. Leaf in September of '71, I spent 10 days in the Philippines to join Manuel Elizalde Jr.'s expedition into the wild unbroken rain forest in southern Mindanao to find the hidden home of the Tasaday Stone Age tribe. They had been sighted and contacted a month earlier by Elizalde's Panamin, the Private Association for National Minorities.

But the expedition was delayed indefinitely when Elizalde, in early August, became a senatorial candidate for President Ferdinand Marcos's Nacionalista Party. I became increasingly angry at his failure to answer my request to join his adventure. Finally he told me, "I apologize for having made you wait so long at the Manila Hotel. I know your credentials from Black Star's Manila photographer, Romeo Vitug. So I tell you what. When the expedition goes in, I'll give you a world exclusive. Write down the terms of the agreement and I'll sign it."

In a world-exclusive agreement with Panamin, I stipulated that the expedition's photographer could not release his pictures until mine were published.

Vilcabamba, Ecuador

On my long flight back to New York, I couldn't stop thinking of the Tasadays and the idea of going back to the Stone Age. Years ago I told *The Saturday Evening Post*'s editor, "If NASA ever permits journalists on future flights, please put my name on the list." But the thought of the Tasaday tribe fascinated me more than going to the moon.

Returning to New York, I gave Elizalde's agreement and letter of exclusivity to Howard Chapnick. I was doubtful however that I'd ever get the call to join the expedition, so I soon forgot about it.

About eight months later, in March of 1972, while viewing my "Longevity" pictures with *Geographic* Senior Editor Bill Garrett and Director of Photography Robert Gilka, a secretary interrupted us saying, "Mr. Launois, you have a call from someone named Manda in the Philippines." Manda was Elizalde's given name.

A woman's voice with a Filipino accent came on the line, "Mr. Launois, please hold for Mr. Elizalde." Then I heard, "John, this is Manda. Your New York office told me you were at *Geographic*. The Tasaday expedition is on. When can you come to Manila?" I said, "In three or four days." I asked him for "a moment." Holding the phone, I turned to Gilka and Garrett and said, "I have a world-exclusive agreement for the expedition to the Tasadays. Do you want first crack?" Since the Tasaday sighting had received worldwide coverage the previous year, they immediately said yes. I told Manda, "I just got an assignment from *National Geographic*. It will be the first picture magazine to publish the Tasaday story." Thrilled, Manda shouted, "Great! See you soon."

A few weeks earlier, on March 2, Yukiko and I went to our lawyer's office in a lighthearted mood to legally separate under New York state law. We laughed as we skipped along sidewalks of Park Avenue, not quite comprehending why, after such agony, we felt so happy. It seemed like a great weight had been lifted.

Our lawyer told us, "I can't represent you both." "Fine," I answered. "Just represent Yukiko. I don't need a lawyer." After he explained that alimony and child support had to cover the style of living Yukiko was accustomed to, I cheerfully signed the separation agreement.

Because Public School 6 had an excellent reputation and would be perfect for Chris, we found an apartment for Yukiko and Chris in an Upper East Side doorman building between Park and Lexington in PS6's district. After furniture was arranged, I still hadn't fully realized that it was the end of the family life I'd known for over a decade.

Through cables and letters, France de l'Île said photography had changed her life. By traveling to the Asian continent to photograph famous women like Indira

Gandhi in India, she conquered her fear of flying. In her own words, she had gone through "a full transformation." Though she didn't send me clippings, she told me a Japanese paper in Osaka published her work. I was skeptical but wanted to believe her. Somehow, I still missed her.

By March of 1972, I had not seen France de l'Île for nearly a year. Despite ominous signs of doom, our relationship was still alive. When we again met, it was an emotional reunion, but we stood there, looking at each other as if trying to appraise what was left of our relationship: unsaid was the understanding that something had ended.

On March 15 in Tokyo, we were together again. I arranged for France de l'Île to stay with my old friend Kanda-san while I'd be in the Philippines covering the Tasadays. Kanda-san was my former assistant to whom I taught photography and English. Years ago when Kanda-san found himself homeless after his father died, I gave him full use of my apartment. By 1972, he was so successful as a commercial photographer that he picked us up at Tokyo's Haneda airport in his spanking new Mercedes-Benz.

Kanda-san always addressed me as *sensei*, "teacher" or "master"—he refused to call me John. After introductions and greetings, I told Kanda-san, "I don't know how long my expedition in the Philippines will take." He simply answered, "*Sensei, it's an honor.*" In his culture, I was actually doing him a favor by giving him a chance to repay the debt he felt he owed me. For him, it was a question of *giri*: "duty," "obligation," and "honor." I knew he and his wife would treat France as an "honored guest."

As I boarded a taxi to the airport, France de l'Île watched me silently. I'd given her a thorough briefing on Japanese culture, explaining how it would be in bad taste to express emotions publicly. She behaved respectfully, yet once again I saw sadness in her eyes. As I flew to Manila, I realized how heavy a weight it was to carry someone else's sorrow. I doubted I could bear it for long.

Landing in Manila in late afternoon, I met with *Geographic* staff writer and senior assistant editor, Kenneth MacLeish. A Panamin staffer excitedly told us Elizalde had recently met with Tasaday tribesmen by a clearing at the edge of the jungle and was convinced the Tasadays lived in caves in "a place back inside a mountain." It was an extraordinary piece of information, which later led MacLeish to observe, "The only people I remember from my research who lived in caves in the Philippines were the Palawan Filipinos, but that tribe was from tens of thousands of years ago."

Abkhazia, Georgia.

SHADOWS OF THE JUNGLE

STEPPING INTO THE STONE AGE

THE PHILIPPINES 1972-1973

Taking off for Davao, we flew to Alah Airport, near a Manubo-Blit tribe settlement on the edge of Mindanao Island's great rain forest. The forest stretched over several hundred square miles of tangled vines, bamboo, palms, and acacias, all shaded in a permanent dusk from 200-foot-tall trees. The lush jungle, covering jagged slopes, limestone cliffs, and 5000-foot peaks, extended to the sandy shores of the Celebes Sea.

In the late 1950s, I had been to Mindanao's jungle to photograph changes in the life of a Tboli tribe, just as gun-toting men in bulldozers cleared great oaks and mahogany trees to exploit rich earth for agricultural land. While photographing the clearing, we encountered a boa constrictor so huge, about a foot in diameter and 30 feet long, it could only be captured after it had swallowed a deer. Because the deer's three-foot-wide antlers created a bulge in the snake's upper body, the hunters were able to lasso the boa where the antlers bulged, using half-inch-thick cable and a winch mounted on a bulldozer.

While the cable was connected, there was genuine fear in the lumberjacks' eyes as one of them said, "That monster will kill you with a single snap of its body, lick, and swallow you in an instant. But it'll take him weeks to digest the deer, so it should be harmless for a while."

After workers built a huge bamboo cage, a winch operator released the tension on the cable and the boa gracefully slipped out of its noose into the cage, destined for a zoo.

From above, the rain forest looked dark and mysterious. Somewhere in that inviolable sanctuary dwelled the Stone Age tribe of Mindanao. Since it was impossible for our helicopter to land in the unbroken rain forest, Panamin's chief, Manda, concocted a daring strategy to transport our expedition to where he believed the Tasaday tribe could be found.

The evening of March 18, Manda enthusiastically told us, "Two days ago, I ordered a ground party of 30 Tboli and Ubu tribesmen equipped with ropes, chain saws, bolos, weapons, and supplies to head toward the caves where I believe we'll find the Tasadays. Some in the ground party are expert carpenters and have experience building treehouses for their people. They'll choose a strong tree at least a hundred feet high and build a platform on top, so we can jump onto it from our chopper. A Manubo-Blit tribesman hunter, Dafal, who made the original contact with the Tasadays, will lead them. I've given them a week and six days to trek into the forest, and one day to build the platform. The flying time to our drop will be about 15 minutes."

The morning of March 23, Manda, reporter John Nance, Kenneth MacLeish, and I took off with the Alouette helicopter pilot, Bart Bartello. He was in radio contact with our ground party, but they couldn't tell us exactly where the tree platform was located. Since we didn't have Global Positioning Systems in 1972, Bartello flew under low rain clouds along ridges, skimmed over peaks, and then plunged 200 feet down into valleys framed by huge green walls of lush growth.

Suddenly to our left, two red flares exploded. As Bartello made a sharp turn, we saw almost directly below a flimsy platform built on top of a 75-foot-tall tree. The ground party selected the tree because it was on a ridge top and towered above the jungle canopy. Each side of the ridge dropped sharply for another 300 feet to an unseen valley floor. MacLeish said, "That platform looks about as big as a postage stamp, and maybe as solid as a deck of matchsticks."

Upon approach, as we hovered five feet above its edge, John Nance said, "The platform's grown...now it's the size of a ping-pong table." As I surveyed the tiny saplings used to construct it, I seriously wondered if the platform could hold our collective weight and my 250 pounds of equipment. For an instant, I envisioned my heavy strobes and equipment crashing to the ground, but there was no time to think of my own safety.

As leader of the expedition, Elizalde jumped first and was grabbed by one of the tribesmen on the platform. I jumped next and sprawled, followed by MacLeish. As John Nance was about to jump, the Alouette's rear wheel got caught in the rope fence of the platform, shaking the helicopter violently, but from his seat, pilot Bartello couldn't see his entangled wheel. For a few frightening seconds, Elizalde, MacLeish, and I gestured wildly with hand signals to "peel off right and rise," and he deftly pulled the wheel off the fence. Nance jumped and we grabbed him, then a crewman lowered my four cases of equipment with a rope as the platform buckled from the downdraft. Through a trap door built on one side of the platform, we descended on a ladder made of saplings, tied by vines, while the expedition's gear and my equipment were lowered to the ground with ropes.

Dafal, the hunter, and his advance party cheered as Elizalde climbed down the ladder. Balayem, the only Tasaday tribesman at the jumping site, hugged Elizalde while shielding his face against downdraft of the helicopter that had returned with more members of the expedition, including an anthropologist, doctor, radio operator, interpreters, cooks, and Elizalde's armed bodyguard, Felix.

Balayem called Elizalde "the great bearer of good fortune" as foretold in Tasaday legends. They had met before in the previous sighting. Though the Tasadays did not have an appointed leader, it was Balayem who'd lead us to the caves of his people.

We couldn't keep up with the acrobatic Balayem who dexterously hurled himself toward the valley floor. He seemed to fly across the dense jungle, swinging and sliding on vines and branches.

Other than a leaf covering his groin, Balayem was naked. In contrast, as a visitor from the modern world, I wore heavy combat boots, khaki pants tied at the ankles with rubber bands to keep off insects, a safari jacket with film, notebooks, traveler's checks, passport, and cameras around my neck. Watching Balayem swinging gracefully on vines while I stumbled on the greasy jungle floor, I felt a little ridiculous.

As Nance struggled to stay upright on slippery earth through dense foliage, he exclaimed, "It's like walking through neck-deep water!" We all crashed down the slope, scratching our hands as we grabbed thorny vines for support. After an hour, we reached a flowing stream on a valley floor, where four barefoot Ubo-Blit tribesmen who carried my heavy equipment had been waiting a long time.

Less heavily weighed down than myself, Elizalde and MacLeish managed to stay closer to Balayem, who constantly slackened his pace to wait for his stumbling and awkward visitors.

We heard them a hundred yards ahead but could only see dark shadows of the jungle. My light meter had to be read on its lowest scale, for even though it was noon, in the forest it looked like dusk. The darkness and thickness of the rugged terrain explained why the Tasadays remained unseen by outsiders for perhaps a thousand years or more.

Exhausted, we reached a water-carved ledge in the mountain. We paused to rest, then shouted, "Manda, where are you?" MacLeish and Manda called back, "Here, up here." The voices sounded near, only yards away, but we couldn't see them. On all fours, we crawled over huge ferns, exposed roots, rattan, and slabs of rock until we saw a patch of yellow light illuminating a growth of bamboo. We climbed upward, and suddenly before us were three dark caves gaping from the mountain: we had just crawled into the Stone Age.

As we joined Manda and MacLeish resting at the foot of the cliff, shy and curious faces appeared in the upper caves. All had brown skin and dark eyes framed by long black hair. Cautiously, several of the Tasadays approached us. Other than the leaves covering their genitals, all were naked. Later we counted 24 in the tribe: 10 men, 5 women, and 9 children. Because Balayem had no wife, he begged Manda to bring him one.

I started to take photos immediately. Later there'd be time for reflection at our base camp set up with terracing and platforms large enough to sleep on, perched on a slope some two hundred yards below the caves. After our ground party finished building the base, our camp resembled a giant hundred-foot-high stairway covered with tarpaulins for shelter. Heavy rainfall repeatedly showered down in late afternoon, hitting the canvas stretched over our camp, reverberating like multiple waterfalls.

Other than occasional bird calls and the exchange of our voices, the jungle seemed mysteriously silent, but each new fall of rain signaled millions of creatures and insects to join in a cacophony of jarring and deafening sounds, which I initially interpreted as a staging for an immediate invasion of our camp.

Nothing happened, but I still covered my entire body with a thick coat of insect repellent. The only creatures that made me uneasy before going to sleep fully dressed that night were some huge black-and-striped-legged spiders.

Around eight o'clock in the evening, the deafening noise faded as the rain stopped. From a humid 70 degrees Fahrenheit in the day, the temperature dropped to 50 degrees as we gathered around a fire in the evening. While cooks prepared chicken and rice for dinner, we began to unwind.

Stunned by our discoveries, MacLeish eloquently described the emotions we all felt, seeing the Tasadays sitting at the edge of their caves. In *Geographic*, he told of "what it was like for visitors from the Space Age to see people from the Stone Age...visitors where none had visited before, sat in silence, dazed as travelers in a time machine might be dazed upon arriving at their most distant destination."

John Nance would later write in his thoroughly documented 1975 book, *The Gentle Tasadays*, "We looked inside to a vision of time flung backwards." Nance quoted MacLeish as saying, "That scene was not neolithic, it was paleolithic, from 75,000 years ago." Nance said one of the three Panamin anthropologists, Carlos Fernandez, "felt that few scientists would quarrel that the Tasaday story was the most significant anthropological discovery of the century."

The next six days, we photographed and tried to understand the Tasaday culture. I didn't envy MacLeish's job of questioning the tribe: his English had to be translated into Tboli and then Manubo Blit, which was similar to the Tasaday language. It would take months to begin to understand and record the Tasaday language in its primitive state. At best, MacLeish got imperfect answers.

My assignment seemed relatively simple. All I needed to do was follow and photograph the Tasadays' daily food gathering in the jungle by the stream in the valley below. I'd show how they used stone tools and made fires in caves to cook and eat food they gathered.

It turned out to be an excruciating task. The Tasadays moved like monkeys, swinging on vines from one slope to another. When not swinging, they moved like cats, while I crashed, fell, crawled, and protected my cameras as best I could from the greasy floor of the jungle.

When I caught up to them, the men were using bolos provided by Panamin to cut *ubud* from palm trunks. *Ubud* was a forest delicacy to the Tasadays that tasted like artichoke hearts.

Women nursing infants were easier to follow as their hands deftly grabbed tadpoles, frogs, and freshwater crabs from swift-flowing streams. They wrapped

367

their catch in orchid leaves and placed the handy meals next to coals in the caves for cooking.

The staple of the Tasaday diet seldom changed. On a good day, they gathered a wild yam called *biking* as well as varieties of unidentified fruits and leaves from which only the wild bananas could be recognized. Fat grubs from rotted logs were also a favorite of the tribe. Food gathering was a daily ritual, taking only a few hours; then returning to their caves, the Tasadays made fires, cooked, and slept. They stored nothing.

By March 28, our sixth day in the forest, coverage of the Tasadays became repetitive. But worse, the helicopter pilot, Bart, whom I befriended and whose landing spot had just been cleared, confided that his Alouette chopper was "way overdue for a maintenance check. It should really be grounded immediately."

That evening I took MacLeish aside and repeated the essence of my confidential conversation with Bart. MacLeish reviewed his notes and listened to his tapes, while I made a list of subjects I had photographed. Both of us concluded that we had enough material for 24 pages and a cover for *National Geographic*. Though the expedition was scheduled to remain in the jungle three more days, we doubted we could get anything new in the remaining two.

I looked at MacLeish and said, "If Bart's helicopter breaks down, do you know what our alternative is, seeing that Panamin can't charter another chopper in this part of the world?" "Yes," MacLeish answered, "at least a 10-day trek or more to the edge of the jungle."

Because John Nance's radio reports to the Associated Press had created worldwide interest, requests for coverage were pouring in from television networks, newspapers, and magazines from all over the world. An NBC crew was already in Manila, clamoring to get in. I feared our exclusive might be compromised. MacLeish concurred—we had to get out. Just before dinner, we asked Elizalde for permission to leave in the morning. He readily agreed.

At nightfall, we climbed to the caves for the last time with two interpreters to bid goodbye to our Stone Age friends. The men embraced us, and we embraced everyone in return. The women and children sat and stood in the glow of fires. Some of the men murmured, "Kakai Ken, Kakai Tasaday" ("Friend Ken, Friend of the Tasaday"). My name was "Jambangan," and I was given the same farewell ritual.

I spent some of our last night in the jungle talking with the helicopter pilot. Bart had built his sleeping platform on stilts, five feet above everyone else. I wanted to know why. "Simple," he explained, "this forest is full of snakes and there's one kind out there that belongs to the cobra family, only it's more deadly. Because these snakes are blind, they seek body heat to guide themselves to strike prey, animal or human. In fact, this particular snake inspired the scientists who designed the 'sidewinder,' one of the first heat-seeking missiles built back in the 1950s. So anyway, at five feet above the ground, I figure I'm above its sensors."

I slept uneasily that last night in the forest, trying to comprehend my journey to the Stone Age, only to fall asleep in fits, waking and scanning my area with a flashlight for blind cobras.

I had good reason to be fearful. Just before our arrival, one of the barefoot tribesmen from our ground party had been bitten on the ankle by a snake. His whole leg swelled to twice its size in a matter of minutes. Because a landing area had not yet been cleared for our helicopter, he had to be carried out of the jungle on foot on an improvised stretcher. His friends doubted that he could survive the one-week trek to the edge of the forest where he'd be rushed to a hospital. Upon departure, we still didn't know if the man had made it out alive.

On the seventh day of our expedition, March 29, 1972, we thanked Elizalde for taking us on an incredible adventure with his team and made our way to Bart's idling helicopter.

As we ascended, rising above the jungle, I asked Bart to level off at 500 feet and circle the hidden valley so I could photograph our jumping tree in the unbroken rainforest and perhaps shoot the caves and cliffs from the air. But I saw nothing: the wilderness below seemed primeval, dark, and virginal. In his text, MacLeish quoted me as having said, "It's hard to believe we were ever there."

After landing in Surallah, Bart immediately grounded the Alouette. The leading edge of the rotor blade had come loose. Glad to have escaped with our lives, we caught a flight to Manila.

Later we learned from AP bulletins that Elizalde and his party were stranded in the jungle. They were eventually rescued by a U.S. Air Force Chinook helicopter from Clark Air Base, north of Manila.

Our *Geographic* team arrived in Manila just as darkness set in. Riding a cab from the airport to the city, we found ourselves looking at the modern world as if we had never before seen a metropolis. We'd known the lights and skylines of the city for decades yet felt we were discovering it for the first time. The experience prompted MacLeish to remark, "Look at all those crazy people. Listen to all those drivers honking, revving their engines at traffic lights. Look at all that neon. God! What an insane world."

The shock of reentry into modern civilization soon faded after we took our first showers in 11 days and treated ourselves to a luxurious dinner. Champagne toasts to "the gentle Tasadays" inspired MacLeish to quote Jean Jacques Rousseau: "Nothing is more gentle than man in his primitive state."

The next day, we parted, and Kanda-san and France de l'Île met me at Tokyo's Haneda Airport. When I saw how genuinely happy she was to see me, I guiltily realized that in the jungle, I had not missed her a single instant.

As Kanda-san and I loaded my gear into the trunk of his Mercedes, he whispered, "*Sensei*, your friend must be a very sad lady. We heard her cry in her room every night. We didn't know what to do." All I could say was, "Thank you for looking after her." With no explanation for her tears, I simply asked him to take us to the Hilton Hotel.

Settling into our room, France de l'Île appeared deeply depressed. Although she attempted to smile bravely, she resisted being cheered. Once again she was in her melancholic realm, which always made me feel helpless. The intimacy we once shared belonged to an ancient past. Refusing dinner, she fell into a deep sleep and didn't wake even when I started typing my captions, which had to be shipped with film the next day to Washington.

There were only 38 rolls of film from the expedition, an extremely low number for a major *National Geographic* project, which normally took hundreds of rolls. But photographing the Tasadays was extraordinary and unique, since it was their actions alone that controlled the content. Coverage of breaking news events could be anticipated, but all the Tasaday scenes had been captured in fleeting instants on a single frame or two. Other than a strobe-lit group picture in the main cave, planning had been out of the question.

When my 38 rolls arrived at *Geographic*, the picture editor looked at my small packet in disbelief and surely thought, "This has to be Launois's first shipment." But anxiety turned to enthusiasm when the pictures were projected. MacLeish and I calculated we had enough for 24 pages, but, "The Tasadays, Stone Age Cavemen of Mindanao" closed with a cover and 32 pages in the August 1972 issue of *National Geographic*. It was the first time in my career that such a small number of pictures shot in so few days had produced so many pages.

My mud-caked cameras took a beating in the jungle. The climate and heavy rainfall had taken a toll on all my equipment as did my numerous falls on the steep greasy slopes of the forest.

After spending an extra day in Tokyo to buy new equipment, I flew to Washington for the layouts. Arriving at *Geographic*, I wasn't prepared for the enthusiastic welcome from Bob Gilka, Bill Garrett, and other staff. Congratulations poured in and Garrett, who was normally fair but gave sparse praise, led the cheers. Quickly and deftly he had the layouts approved by *Geographic's* editor, Gilbert M. Grosvenor.

Garrett took me to a round of cocktail parties in Washington where he announced to anyone willing to listen that "John Launois has just returned from the Stone Age." His announcement received attention even from some of the more blasé drinkers who were full of questions.

France de l'Île was staying with Bill and Lucy Garrett in Great Falls, Virginia. She had been sick, refused most meals, and slept most of the time. Bill gently whispered, "France de l'Île is a beautiful young woman, but she is too fragile for you and your work." He had been more diplomatic than my dear old friend and mathematician, Bob Laupheimer, who upon meeting her for the first time at our Greenwich Village apartment said, "You poor son of a bitch," as I escorted him out of the building.

Returning to Manhattan, France de l'Île was profoundly depressed, even though in a rare, lucid moment, she was realistic enough to acknowledge there was no hope for our relationship. The passion we shared had slowly burned out, and while my work and constant traveling had been painful for Yukiko, who was strong, stoic, and self-sufficient, it had become unbearable for a person as neurotic, dependent, and fragile as France de l'Île.

In June 1972, we separated once again for what I believed would be the last time. Determined to continue her project on Asian women, she received financial help from her mother, but it wasn't enough. After I promised to help her for one year, she responded, "On my honor, I swear to pay you back."

It was a disturbing feeling that I perhaps was buying my freedom at a bargain price. But my conscience felt clear when in our last days together, she claimed her "aristocratic honor" was on a level that could never be understood by commoners: her words reminded me of why I had left France's class-ridden society in the first place. Outraged, I sarcastically responded, "I have just photographed our ancestors in caves. Believe me, they came from a better stock than you and your titled friends!"

It was possible we exchanged insults to veil the pain of another breakup. On the way to JFK, France de l'Île was subdued, proud, and dignified. The next time I heard from her, she was writing about and photographing women of Cambodia. In her letters, she wrote of the risks she took for her work. She sounded rational enough, but I still wondered about her mental state as I recalled her violent and fearful refusal to see a psychiatrist when I suggested it back in Manhattan.

Decades later, in 2000, when I set out to write about that painful part of my life, I realized I knew almost nothing of the woman for whom I destroyed my marriage. In that search for her past, I began to understand why France de l'Île was "so tragic in life and even in death."

Her brother told me that a friend and psychiatrist "helped her live the last 10 tormented years of her life." I called the doctor to learn more. "She was a profoundly disturbed woman," he said, "suffering from anorexia nervosa, deep anxiety, panic attacks, and suicidal tendencies. Obsessed with her physical beauty, she remained beautiful in an anorexic way into middle age, and to a lesser extent, the end of her life. Strangely and cruelly for her family, she became horribly disfigured on her deathbed. I could not explain why. It had nothing to do with lymphoma and uremia, which were the causes of her death."

In 1970, during our brief days in Paris, Normandy, and the Rhone Valley, she seldom betrayed the fragility of her mental health with the exception of her permanent fear of dying from myasthenia gravis.

The doctor continued, "I knew if she actually had myasthenia gravis, her addiction to tranquilizers and the amounts she ingested would have killed her." In 1984, her test results came up negative, proving her former doctors had misdiagnosed her "incurable disease."

Her doctor said, "In fact, she never had myasthenia gravis! But she didn't find any relief in that knowledge. Till the end of her life she claimed she was still afflicted by it. Such was her need for attention, love, and sympathy." She died at age 50 in June 1994.

After France de l'Île's departure in 1972, my work again helped stabilize my emotional state. I expected regret and sadness to set in but instead felt a peace I had not known for nearly two years.

Soon before my 44th birthday that November, *Geographic* asked me to shoot an essay on Thailand's capital, Bangkok. I considered it a birthday present.

Before leaving for Bangkok, I spent some time with Chris. He had refused to see me with France de l'Île: after his first awkward encounter with her, he quickly left to comfort his mother. Though only eight years old at the time, he blamed France de l'Île for our marital problems. In his young mind, she was the villain. Apparently, it hadn't occurred to him that I was equally guilty—or perhaps it had.

On December 2, I joined one of *Geographic*'s senior writers, Bill Graves, at the Erawan Hotel's pool bar in Bangkok to discuss our assignment. Other than on rare occasions, such as our meeting with the King of Thailand, we'd work separately, because our needs were different. We agreed to coordinate our work over cocktails at the end of each day.

On the night of December 8, 1972, a somber Bill Graves said, "John, I just received some sad news from my brother." His brother, Ralph Graves, was *Life's* managing editor. Bill read from a note he held in his hand: "*Life* magazine will suspend publication at the end of the month with its December 29, 1972, issue. It will be announced to the staff in a few hours around 10:45 A.M., New York time."

I was shocked. It was as though someone had told me the sun would not rise the next morning. *Life* had inspired me to become a photojournalist. In the Far East, *Life* had been my guide in search for excellence and uncompromising professionalism. It had given me the first major breaks of my career. Time Inc.'s management killed it. For me, the end of *Life* meant the death of something purely American—it had been part of my American dream long before I became a citizen.

Life was the last of four famous mass-circulation publications to implode, and I had worked and depended on all four for assignments: *Colliers* folded in 1956; *The Saturday Evening Post* collapsed in 1969; *Look* died in 1971; and now *Life* was gone as well.

Bill Graves and I mourned the death of a great American institution that night in Bangkok, drowning our sorrows at the Erawan Bar. When the bar closed, we went to Bill's room to finish his bottle of Remy Martin V.S.O.P. cognac.

As for Bangkok, our coverage would end on February 7, 1973. Reverence for the monarchy and Buddhism had always been placed above any respect for Thailand's military rulers and disorganized civilian parliamentarians. So my lead photograph featured a 16-foot-tall statue of Buddha on a flatbed truck, inching through the city's choked, heavily polluted traffic to a temple in the suburbs. It symbolized a constant and stable element in Bangkok's chaotic life. The essay was published in the July 1973 issue of *National Geographic* as "Bangkok, City of Angels."

Returning to Washington, the death of *Life* was being discussed in the halls of *Geographic*. "John, you worry me," Bill Garrett joked. "You worked for all four of the big magazines that have collapsed. Please, spare *Geographic*."

Until 1973, the University of Missouri School of Journalism's highest award was "Magazine Photographer of the Year." That year, the university went a step beyond by creating a "World Understanding" award to be given to a magazine photojournalist for his full body of work. It was presented to me in April.

On a two-foot sculpture of a father, mother, and child dancing in a circle, the plaque stated the award was presented to John Launois: "In recognition of superb creative ability to use the medium of photography to instill a deeper measure of understanding among the peoples of the world."

I had received various first and second place plaques over the years but the "World Understanding" award was the ultimate recognition of my work. Black Star's Howard Chapnick beamed with pride during the presentation.

Flying from St. Louis back to New York, I reflected, "I am at the summit of achievement in photojournalism, a medium that now has an uncertain future. In the meantime, I've destroyed my marriage. And though my love for France de l'Île lingers on, in all practicality, it's over." I felt a certain irony at being praised for "understanding the peoples of the world" while failing to understand my own life. Landing at La Guardia, I felt empty.

France de l'Île still wrote to me regularly. In a moving letter, she described harsh conditions for women in Bangladesh. She seemed at last to be considering other people's problems rather than her own. Often she ended her letters with, "When we meet again, I know you'll be proud of me."

Back in March of 1972, I introduced France de l'Île to a European freelance writer based in Tokyo, who was immediately smitten with her and wanted to help her if he could. Around May of 1973, he began calling me daily in New York to tell me of France de l'Île's "extraordinary work on Asian women," while subtly suggesting it was a mistake not to give her another chance. Before hanging up, he'd put her on the line. She'd say, "Asian women have taught me to be strong," insisting she was no longer the fragile person I had known.

Eventually, I reluctantly agreed to see her again in New York. When we met, I instantly knew it was a mistake. I could tell she had been starving herself to keep her precious figure: she looked emaciated and more fragile than ever.

Regardless, I invited her to accompany me to Martinique where I was working on a story for *Geographic*. Martinique island, one of the largest in the volcanic chain of the West Indies, had been colonized by France in 1635. Because French occupiers drove out the indigenous people, slaves would eventually account for most of the population. Martinique's fame, other than being the birthplace of Napoleon's wife Josephine, rested mainly on the wonder of the May 8, 1902, volcano blast when the town of St. Pierre was destroyed, 30,000 people died, and a single survivor crawled out of his thickly walled prison cell.

In 1973, with a population of 340,000 divided on the issue of independence from French colonialism, the island was marked by strikes and occasional violence, and its future was uncertain. As things turned out, Martinique remained so attached to France that it maintained its status as an "overseas department" with full representation in the National Assembly and Senate.

The assignment required visits over a number of months. With text by Ken MacLeish, the story was published in the January 1975 *Geographic* as "Martinique: *Liberté, Egalité,* and Uncertainty in the Caribbean."

Immediately after our flight to Martinique, France de l'Île went to sleep. She slept for most of our two weeks on the island, though I saw her at lunch and dinner often. By the end of our stay, she recovered enough to entertain thoughts of marriage, but I had no such thoughts. I knew marrying her was pure folly.

Working hard on the story, I left our hotel each day before sunrise and didn't notice that she consumed a lot of vodka. It was not until we returned to Manhattan that I discovered she needed a drink early in the morning.

In late August, I flew with her to France. In a friend's apartment in Paris, she attempted suicide by slashing her wrists. At a psychiatric hospital unit, she was treated by a doctor who wanted to keep her under observation, but she escaped as soon as her wounds were treated. When I opened the apartment door in Paris and saw her with her wrists bandaged and her beautiful eyes looking at me, confused, I could only wonder why fate had been so cruel to her.

I called her mother for advice, and she begged me to put her daughter on the next flight to a city in southwestern France, near the family castle. It was then she admitted for the first time that France de l'Île had been plagued with "psychological problems since childhood."

The next morning, I put France de l'Île on a plane. On arrival, she was met by her gentle mother who assured me "France" would get immediate care. So ended my relationship with a beautiful and tragic young woman: it was an affair that overwhelmed common sense.

On October 18, 1973, Yukiko and I were divorced in a court in New York, almost exactly 16 years after we were married in church on October 10, 1957.

SURVIVAL'S PATH

JOSIANE B., ERIK BYE, AND CARNEGIE HALL

PARIS, NEW YORK 1974–1975

When I betrayed and eventually divorced Yukiko, I lost myself. By Christmas 1973, I missed the stability she had brought to my nomadic life. Consumed by guilt and loneliness, sleep seemed impossible, even with pills, except with the aid of Chivas Regal.

Watching me during visits with Chris, Yukiko realized I had taken "a turn down a destructive path." She begged me, "Accept your mistake. You are human after all." From my perspective, my mistakes were unforgivable. I could not understand how passion could have driven me to the summit of my profession while leading me down a road of self-destruction.

Yukiko invited me to Christmas dinner with some old family friends who rightly sided with her during the divorce. When we sat at what had been our family table to enjoy the turkey she had lovingly prepared, conversation was difficult. Our old friends who disapproved of my behavior were kind not to express any hostility on Christmas Day. Uneasy, I left the table early, played with some of Chris's new toys and promised to see him on his 10th birthday in January.

In late April 1974, Howard Chapnick invited me to his favorite Italian restaurant to discuss story ideas. He thought he could bring me out of my mood by expressing outrage at the news that France was retiring the *France*. The great and beautiful ocean liner, pride of the French nation, was due to go out of service within months. "Can you imagine?"

I responded, "So what? Who cares? It's the end of an era." He seemed annoyed I didn't share his nostalgia, but at that point, my marriage was over, photojournalism as I knew it had ended, and I wasn't about to mourn the passing of the *France*.

Regardless, our conversation awakened my memory. I remembered an oath I made to myself in 1950 while sailing across the Atlantic in a shared third-class cabin above the roaring engine of the French liner, *Liberté*.

Back then, I wondered how I'd survive in America with $50. Though constantly haunted by a distant sadness, I was afraid of inaction. If I stopped climbing in difficult times, I would not survive. I believed always in action: it was my oxygen, my path to survival.

On the *Liberté*, confined by strict regulations to a third-class deck, I had cunningly fooled the crew and slipped up to the luxurious first-class deck. There I met and photographed Ray Milland, the movie star celebrated for his stunning portrayal of an alcoholic writer in *The Lost Weekend*. A steward who appeared and seemed ready to haul me away was dismissed by Milland. "Can't you see the young man is working?"

After examining Milland's large, luxurious cabin, I swore I too would one day cross the Atlantic as a first-class passenger, if only to quell the disapproving voices of my family and friends. With the exception of my pal Claude, they all insisted my decision to go to America was a terrible mistake.

By 1974, I had nothing to prove to anyone in France: I was successful in my profession beyond my own imaginings. Yet the gleeful disapproval of family and friends decades ago still hurt. My anger was suppressed, but it would resurface like a drifting wound, stirring and mixing itself with recent sorrows.

The prospect of a final Atlantic crossing on the legendary *France* coincided with an open invitation from Fernando Casablancas to "come spend a few months in Paris." Though while he had a love affair with the city, I never romanticized Paris. I didn't believe a trip to France would heal any wounds, but I liked the idea of fulfilling my vow to cross the Atlantic in first class. At a minimum, the ocean voyage might well calm the soul.

My office reserved luxury accommodations for the June 28, 1974, sailing to Le Havre. The day before departure, I bid Chris and Yukiko goodbye—I did not want anyone to see me off. As a steward briefed me on my cabin's spacious and impressive facilities, I felt neither joy nor solace. Immediately I realized that sailing across the Atlantic in first class wouldn't ease any troubles.

As tug boats pulled us away from the docks of Manhattan, I looked at the Statue of Liberty without emotion but remembered how inspiring its first sight had been in 1950. The tug boats blew their horns to wish us "bon voyage" and then left us as we headed for the open Atlantic. New York and then land disappeared as engines kicked into cruising speed. Leaning over the stern, I looked at the water shaped by the ship's huge propellers in the vast ocean. Watching wakes from ships had always been soothing, especially when the future was uncertain.

I explored the liner's opulent first-class interior and scanned the grand staircase to the main dining room. Adorned with huge chandeliers, it did look like a "floating palace," but I was indifferent. I needed to find a bar—I needed a drink.

I found a bar near my cabin. Walking in, I saw it was empty except for a solitary drinker. He didn't look up from his glass as I settled into the third stool to his right and ordered a "Double Chivas on the rocks." The barman said, "A double used to be the size of a single in the good old days of the *France*." As my eyes adjusted to the dimly lit bar, I recognized the other drinker: he was Richard Burton, a great actor, one of the most famous personalities on earth, and man of a million headlines. He and Elizabeth Taylor had recently broken up their stormy affair once again. I felt a certain bond with him, but I said nothing and kept to myself.

As I finished my second Scotch, my name was paged: "Mr. Launois, we have a cable for you. Please tell us where you are." I identified myself to the bartender. He had the cable delivered to the bar.

It was from Black Star's Phil Rosen and in part read: "Dear John. Have just received several-thousand-dollar offer from national tabloid if you can realize interview and pictures of Richard Burton who is apparently a fellow first-class passenger on the *France*. Their correspondent will meet you at Southampton where your ship docks for several hours. If you succeed, guarantee might reach five-figure number. Good luck. Please answer soonest. Thanks and best, Phil Rosen."

As I sat a few feet from Burton, it was strange reading the lengthy cable's suggestions on how to photograph the actor to show "the agony he was in." Glancing up, I saw Burton brooding and looking at his drink. I thought, "If you only knew what I'm reading." Then I got angry at my old friend Phil and returned to my cabin to answer his cable.

Furious, I composed several drafts wondering how dear Phil Rosen, one of the kindest men I'd ever known, could think I'd work for a tabloid, even for a large sum. But after I recalled Phil's extraordinary kindness to me over the years, I calmed down. Phil was simply a salesman—before Black Star, he successfully sold furs on Seventh Avenue. For him, I realized, a tabloid sale was just another sale, not a morality play.

Convinced that Phil saw nothing wrong with photographing Burton since he was a public figure, I toned down my reply: "Dear Phil. Shame on you. You have known me for a long time and should have known I'd never work for a tabloid at any price. F.Y.I., when I read your cable, Richard Burton was a few feet away and the only other drinker in a small bar on the upper deck. But we didn't speak, and I have no intention to start a conversation. I am angry at you Phil. Best wishes, John Launois." A few hours later, a cable returned, "Dear John. I am sorry I hurt your feelings. Forgive me. Phil."

At the same bar over the next few afternoons, Richard Burton and I were still the only two drinkers. Like two strangers acknowledging each other's sorrow, we once clinked our glasses, toasting each other with, "Cheers." It was the only word we exchanged.

At Southampton on the southern coast of England, the national tabloid's correspondent buttonholed me with questions about Burton. Annoyed I answered, "I never saw him at the captain's table during meals, and I didn't see him on deck. End of interview." That was a truthful answer.

A few hours later, docking at Le Havre, I was met by my younger sister Lucette and younger brother Jacquot whom I affectionately called, "the Bourgeoise and the Communist."

Ironically, Lucette acquired some typical bourgeois mannerisms from her husband's family who were financially at ease, while Jacquot joined the far-left Labor Union Party and would rail passionately against the ruling bourgeois' exploitation of workers. Regardless, my younger siblings remained emotionally close.

My relationship with Jacquot was paradoxical. While admiring his idealistic fight for the rights of French workers, I was angry he let the French Communist Party so thoroughly indoctrinate him. Because he trusted me completely, I was able to seed over time serious doubts about the convictions that the Communist Party had planted in his mind.

As Lucette and Jacquot knew it was one of the last journeys for the *France*, they wanted to see the luxury liner's interior. While my steward arranged to unload my luggage, I took them both on a grand tour of the first-class deck. Hugging me, Jacquot jokingly exclaimed, "You became an American capitalist!" I responded, "No little brother, just an American photojournalist."

On the drive to Paris, Lucette who was nine when I left France wanted to know, "Have you returned to France for good? We've only seen you a few times in the last 24 years. It'd be nice if you became a member of the family again instead of a stranger." I said, "I doubt I've returned for good, because I'll miss my son and my life in New York."

I didn't mention that I was overwhelmed by guilt and searching for answers. What I didn't know was that the state of my mental health would lead me over the next few months into my first real depression, to the heaviest drinking of my life, and to a lonely five-year journey, relieved at irregular intervals by two romantic encounters and challenging assignments.

I thanked my brother and sister for helping unload my equipment at Fernando's Paris office. As we hugged, I promised to attend a family reunion, but it was a filial duty I wasn't sure I'd keep. As Lucette rightly said, I was "a stranger in the family" and in my mind, I wanted my roots to be buried for eternity.

I'd simply be an American in France for a while. To eliminate doubts, I exaggerated my American accent while speaking French to bury my childhood and perhaps exorcize the outrage I remembered from the shameful years of Vichy France and Nazi occupation.

When I found Fernando, he was surrounded by a bevy of beautiful models working for his Agency Elysées 3. Most were from Western Europe and America, all chattering in English. As Fernando introduced me warmly, praising my work as a photojournalist, I thought it a befitting picture for him, beautiful women galore hanging on to his every word, seduced by his natural, charming manners. Surely that job was more exciting than selling advertising for *Time* magazine.

Later that evening, Anne Marie greeted me like a long-lost brother in their comfortably large fourth-floor walk-up on the Left Bank. After drinks, the three of us had dinner in the kitchen, but I failed to be drawn into Fernando's witty conversation. Both knew me for nearly a quarter century and immediately sensed something was wrong. They had never known me so deeply withdrawn.

Retiring to the living room, Fernando tried to humor me by loudly playing Frank Sinatra's, "I did It My Way," on his hi-fi. He had a point of course, but I didn't think it was very funny. It was a performance he repeated over and over for the next few weeks whenever he saw me in a gloomy mood at dinner or cocktail parties that he gave to cheer me up. Only later did I fully appreciate his efforts to lift my spirits.

My guestroom doubled as Anne Marie's ballet-dancing studio where she taught a few Parisian women, so there was no privacy when I needed it most. I found myself not wanting to see anyone, sleeping badly, and postponing a shave for eight to ten hours, shaving only minutes before my friends came home for dinner. I had read enough about depression to vaguely understand its insidious and paralyzing effects, which hit me for the first time at the age of 45.

I began to feel ashamed for sitting silently at dinner without any appetite, so I soon made excuses to go out. Instead of sharing dinner with my dear friends, I'd walk two blocks to Café de Flore to order a sandwich and several whiskies. There on the terrace, I could watch in total anonymity the flow of pedestrians for hours as I thought about nothing and everything.

Most of my life I feared inaction, but there I was, incapable of creating the simplest plan of action for myself and too paralyzed to even feel fear or any other emotion. I just drifted from thought to thought, anchoring to none. When my need for solitude overwhelmed me, I decided to look for an apartment of my own. It was my first decision in weeks.

It could've taken months to find a reasonably priced apartment on the Left Bank, but with luck, I met a woman leaving with her lover for Denmark indefinitely, looking for the right person to rent their apartment. "We'd rather leave our pied-à-terre empty," she said, "unless we can be sure we rent it to someone responsible." While saying this, I knew she was appraising me. After answering a few discreet questions about my lifestyle, she seemed to approve but I'd also need the approval of her lover.

Over drinks, we met, and her boyfriend, a banker, approved. When I was shown their "love nest" on Rue de Verneuil in Paris's 7th District, I was delighted with its high ceilings, nineteenth-century wooden beams, and windows overlooking a beautifully stylized French garden. After I agreed to a three-month deposit and to pay advance rent before going on long journeys, I moved into their partially furnished flat in early 1975. I had become deeply embarrassed that my depression was noticed daily by my genuinely concerned friends, so it was a relief to finally have a room of my own.

During my last weeks with Fernando and Anne Marie, I met by chance a renowned, award-winning French sculptor whom I'll call "Josiane B." She lifted my spirits by inviting me to her house and atelier. Josiane provided a salon for her friends in the artistic community where I met poets, writers, painters, musicians, filmmakers, and architects. Very few were recognized artists; most were struggling, others practically starving.

When not working on monumental sculptures, Josiane cooked enormous meals for her community of artists. Those financially at ease brought excellent wines; others brought cheap bottles of *vin de table* (table wine).

The atmosphere at Josiane's was congenial. Conversations were stimulating and sometimes animated. Food was plentiful and drinking was often heavy. When not on assignment, I appeared as a regular at Josiane's open house. She presided over our evenings like a benevolent queen or proverbial "Italian mama" even though she was a well-endowed Jewish woman of 38 with long legs, ample hips, large breasts, long brown hair, chiseled face, hazel eyes, and high cheekbones. At five foot nine, she was taller than the average French woman.

Everyone at her parties worshipped her. She seemed to know all their personal stories and shared each one's joy and sorrow. The men with culinary talent came early to help with cooking, while others like me drifted in around nine. Curiously, most of her guests were men who came alone, while Josiane was often the only woman. The men seemingly needed to bathe in her warmth and compassion, and I suspected she also needed to fill the emptiness that came after completing a major sculpture. Her parties provided an escape from solitude, which invariably followed intensive creative acts.

Eventually Josiane cajoled me into telling her my story. She responded in a motherly way. With tender gentleness, she kissed my forehead repeatedly as though I were a wounded child.

On assignment, I traveled to the U.S. to photograph a couple of essays and covers for *Fortune*. One was a March 1975 cover photo of a Japanese chief executive being taught to use a lasso in Texas. During my absence, Josiane wrote me long poems about nature, light, and love, which I read upon my return.

In her poetry, I felt a yearning to love and be loved again. Day by day in her company, my depression evaporated. There was no longer the need to take the pills a Paris doctor had prescribed. In fact, I refused to take them regularly for fear that antidepressive medicine might destroy my creativity.

One night as Josiane's guests were leaving, she whispered, "Stay a while longer. Let's talk." It was the start of a passionate but brief love affair. Her regular guests discreetly stayed away for a few weeks, and it was a blissful "honeymoon." When she won a major contract to create a sculpture, which in early sketches looked like a huge chunk of the Great Wall of China, we went to lunch for what I thought was a celebration. Instead Josiane simply said, "John, I know the creative man in you will understand I cannot divide myself between you and my work. As of today, I belong only to my work. No more parties at home, but let us stay friends." Stunned, I took her to her car and waved goodbye. I tore up her love poems. Later, I understood how we helped each other in a time of transition.

Her departure had been so sudden, I felt numb and irrational. Fortunately there was no time to dwell on feelings. My friend Neil Schwartz called from New York in March 1975 and said, "John, listen. A famous Norwegian television producer hired me as executive producer to coordinate a sesquicentennial program for Carnegie Hall on the 150th anniversary of Norwegian immigration to America. It's a huge production with film, photographs, a choir, and Norway's broadcasting orchestra. Erik Bye is looking for a director, and I suggested you. I think you have an excellent chance. When can you come to New York for an interview with Erik?"

I had no idea how to direct a multimedia stage show. Regardless, Neil booked me a room at the St. Moritz on Manhattan's Central Park South. When Neil introduced me to Erik Bye in the St. Moritz restaurant for my interview, his powerful handshake and charming demeanor immediately appealed to me.

The writer, Lillian Ross, in her "Letter from Oslo" in the October 6, 1975, issue of the *New Yorker*, would say, "Erik Bye, a poet, composer, singer, and television producer...tall (six foot five), handsome, charming, sailing type, is as well known here as the King of Norway or the Norwegian actress Liv Ullman."

That was the gentle giant I met at lunch that spring day. To a toast of dry martinis, Erik immediately asked about my experiences as an immigrant arriving in America. After a brief résumé of my early years, I gave a less humble account of my success in photojournalism. Erik shook my hand and said, "John you are the perfect man to direct our production."

He elaborated, "The program will commemorate the first arrival of Norwegian immigrants in America. There were 46 on board a sloop named Restauration, including a baby born en route. Their journey took three months, and on October 9, 1825, they reached New York. Our Carnegie Hall show will be based on their dramatic letters from 1825. Text will be read on stage by Celeste Holm and Peter Graves, actors of Norwegian origin. What appears on a huge screen behind them is for you to decide with Karl Erik Harr, one of Norway's greatest illustrators. You'll synchronize all visuals with Oivind Bergh and his 65-member Norwegian Broadcasting Orchestra and direct Liv Ullman's reading of my poem: 'Our Neighbors are Indians.'" As Erik spoke, I knew I'd shoot Liv Ullman reading the poem while walking in a forest.

Erik Bye concluded by speaking of Eric Sevareid, one of America's most-admired news broadcasters and commentators. "To finish the program, Sevareid will read on stage his letter to his unknown grandfather who emigrated from the tiny farming community, Sevareid, on the west coast of Akra Fjord, and in 1854 settled as a homesteader in Minnesota."

At the end of the meeting, Bye gave me a list of contacts for production. It was a challenging, ambitious assignment, which immediately threw me into a healthy state of anxiety.

"To make sure you have the best people working with you at Norway's National Television Network, NRK," Bye said, "I'll spend a few days with you in Oslo." Through him, I met my film crews, editors, two assistant producers, and orchestra conductor, Oivind Bergh, who had long dreamt of conducting in Carnegie Hall. On my own, after Erik returned to America, it took me five months to piece together illustrations from Oslo and complete filming in Norway.

For the opening scene at Carnegie Hall on October 7, 1975, I arranged for Erik as the master of ceremonies to arrive on screen sailing down Norway's Oslo Fjord at dusk on his old fishing boat, greeting his audience from the "old country." As the screen faded to black, I wanted him live on stage with all spotlights on him. It worked. Applause erupted for Erik and the illusion of him stepping from the movie screen onto the stage.

The show was off to a good start. It ran close to fours hours. Since it was risky synchronizing film and photographs to live performances, I was a nervous wreck during the entire program, pacing quietly in the back of the auditorium.

But everything went according to plan. The commemoration closed to long, sustained applause in a full house of nearly 3,000. I was exhausted. Erik brought me on stage and whispered in my ear, "First bow your head in the direction of the King and then to everyone else."

The next evening, King Olav V invited our entire crew of artists to a sumptuous dinner at the Waldorf Astoria Hotel. Erik suggested I invite Yukiko, whom he had met with Chris during intermission.

Yukiko arrived at the Waldorf in a designer dress, lovelier than ever. I was certain the romantic in her delighted in the idea of being invited to dine with a monarch. King Olav V warmly congratulated Bye and me before dinner. Though I had been introduced to the king in the last year of President Johnson's term, I learned more about him by accompanying Erik as he briefed the king in Oslo in 1975 during lunch on his yacht.

From history books, I couldn't recall reading of a truly democratic royal ruler, but I met one in Olav V. When Olav took walks through Norway, he behaved like a common man, and people greeted him with the same reserve displayed to all fellow Norwegians.

Directing Erik Bye's "A Salute to Norway and the Heritage We Share" at Carnegie Hall was exciting. But it was a relief to return to assignments that wouldn't require collaborating with so many people. I longed to be alone again and depend only on myself.

From Paris publisher Jean Pierre Mahain whose love for photojournalism was legendary, I received a contract to create a photographic book on Egypt. Though I knew little about the country apart from my time with Malcolm X, I was sure the combination of the Nile, modern cities, and an ancient civilization would amount to a photographer's dream.

I wasn't disappointed, and in Egypt I found my spirit renewed. My search for beauty led me to the simplicity of daily gestures in tiny villages, which remained practically unchanged for thousands of years on both sides of the Nile.

Working mostly winter months, the quality of light in Egypt was extraordinary, especially at sunrise. After I roamed the desert at night to photograph an oasis at first light, all my senses were overwhelmed by the beauty of the desert landscape. It was an inspiring assignment, published in a photographic book in France in 1977.

In late June 1976, an assignment brought me to a famous and glittering oasis in another desert. But this time, I wouldn't find any nomads with camels stopping for water beneath the shades of palms: I was headed to Las Vegas, Nevada, where luxury hotels and casinos were lit by billions of watts of neon. In the 1970s, over nine million visited Las Vegas annually to be entertained, to drink, gamble, celebrate sexual freedom, and for some, get married. I discovered poetry in the beauty of Egypt's deserts, but I'd find something else in the dry heat of Nevada.

OASIS

ILLUSTRATING *MARIO PUZO INSIDE LAS VEGAS*

LAS VEGAS 1976–1979

When editors of Grosset and Dunlap commissioned the celebrated author of *The Godfather,* Mario Puzo, to write an "insider" book on Las Vegas, they decided to publish it with more than 150 pages of color and black-and-white photographs. Through Black Star's Howard Chapnick, I won the publisher's bid for the lucrative color photo assignment.

As a veteran of Las Vegas gaming tables, Puzo knew everything about the city and could consequently write his book on the east coast. But he promised to spend a full day with me in Vegas so I could script my assignment.

On an early afternoon in June when Puzo arrived at the Tropical Hotel, we shook hands as he said, "John, I came just to tell you as much as possible before I return to New York tomorrow morning."

I was curious to hear how he had researched his famous book on the Mafia, but time was short, and I never had the chance to ask. But when I asked if he was commissioned to write the book on Vegas because of his knowledge of organized crime, he answered, "No, despite rumors, I've reluctantly concluded casino gambling is honest in Vegas. It has to be. I think I was chosen to write this book because I have a reputation of being a degenerate gambler." He'd reiterate that in the opening chapter of *Mario Puzo Inside Las Vegas.*

Through the entire afternoon, dinner, and late into the night, he answered my questions. I mostly listened as he spoke of the history of the desert city, from its dusty, small town days of honky-tonk gambling joints to its gambling city of luxury hotels, which in 1976 generated close to two billion dollars in winnings. It was mostly built on losers' money.

Puzo knew about losing. If he won $10,000 in a single evening, he'd lose as much as $30,000 another time. But he said, "I can't afford to gamble anymore. I'm too rich now to take that risk."

His personal advice was, "If you run out of money gambling, do not ever sign a marker or IOU. Just quit!" Puzo had a lot of experience signing markers. Laughing, I reassured him, "I've gambled on ideas all my life but not in casinos. I know the odds against winning. In Vegas, I need three months for the assignment, and I've put aside $200 to play a few games of Black Jack. When that's gone, I'll stop. I won't sign any markers."

"John, that's a rational attitude. So I don't have to worry about you." Puzo briefed me on the history of gambling kings and told me what he liked about the city. Vegas offered the most democratic form of gambling in the world. Widowed old ladies with nickels and dimes could play in casinos just like millionaires flying on private jets. Puzo also believed there were more beautiful women in Vegas than in any other city in the world: "They come here from all over the United States and the globe."

I could have listened to him all night, but he had to catch his plane. His last words were, "One should never spend more than three days in Vegas. Don't let it get you down. Good luck."

I ended up spending 14 weeks in Vegas. Despite prominently displayed signs of "No Cameras Permitted" in every hotel casino, I photographed gambling men and women, glamorous shows, strippers, and gaudy neon illuminating the strip in all its fascinating vulgarity.

Permission to photograph was negotiated with the management of each hotel. At a luxurious casino where teamsters were holding a convention, I convinced nervous hotel management that teamsters would not be recognized at gaming tables because I'd blur all faces.

On the evening of the shoot, my assistant Kirk Payne and I set up two cameras with tripods. One camera was loaded with high-speed color and the other with Polaroid film, which immediately proved we could blur all faces.

Satisfied, the manager allowed us to shoot with our regular camera. At a two-second exposure, I shot about 10 frames. We had worked five minutes when suddenly a burly teamster bodyguard shoved the manager aside and violently knocked over our equipment. We caught the cameras and tripods as the teamster said, "Give me your film or I'll break your heads."

As I gave him the already exposed Polaroids, the manager meekly tried to explain how all faces would be blurred; it would have been easier to reason with an ape.

He tore the Polaroids into many pieces while unnoticed I slipped the camera with the good pictures into a camera bag. The huge bodyguard then pushed us toward the entrance of the underground garage where our car was parked.

Riding the escalator down, we realized we were being followed. I remembered that a week before, an investigative journalist digging into labor union corruption in Phoenix, Arizona, was blown up starting his car. As the newspaper headline flashed in my mind, I exclaimed to Kirk, "What are we doing? Where do we get a taxi?"

At the bottom of the garage, we took the escalator up with the bodyguard on our back. He followed us to the exit and watched us get into a cab. Reasoning that the cab driver might be a member of the teamsters too, I told him to take us to Caesar's Palace instead of our hotel. At a bar in Caesar's Palace, Kirk and I were still shaking as we downed a couple of stiff drinks.

The next morning, Kirk received a call from the manager begging us not to return for our car until the teamsters left town—we took his advice seriously. In the end, one of the pictures the bodyguard failed to confiscate became a double page in Puzo's "Inside Las Vegas." As promised, all faces were blurred beyond recognition.

"No one should ever spend more than three days in Vegas." Though Puzo's advice was meant for gamblers, it hit me in my sixth week. Overwhelmed by loneliness, I roamed the sleepless city of windowless casinos where clocks were conspicuously absent. It felt like being caught in a time warp of permanent night.

When I consciously searched for daylight, the intense desert heat of July, often above 110 degrees Fahrenheit, drove me back inside the air-conditioned casinos where gamblers in their frenzy didn't know or care if it was dusk or dawn.

In six weeks, I saw it all. In Vegas, there were characters worthy of F. Scott Fitzgerald's *Great Gatsby*. I noticed a few delirious winners tipping cocktail waitresses hundred dollar bills, but mostly I saw losers. I photographed stunning half-naked showgirls. In interviews, gorgeous, high-class call girls from Europe claimed to make more money in one month in Vegas than six months in Hamburg or Stockholm. I saw a few beautiful people, many freaks, and a lot of ordinary people. In the end I reluctantly agreed with Puzo. "Las Vegas is the most democratic gambling Mecca on earth."

Of course I realized there was nothing democratic about a city where millionaires could lose $50,000 in a single evening and take off on a private jet the next morning, while newlyweds would ruin their honeymoon after selling their car to recoup losses, leaving with just enough to take a Greyhound bus home.

To me, Las Vegas was an illusion. Nothing was real. The more I thought about it, the more depressing the artificiality of Las Vegas became. I simply didn't understand the greed, lust, or whatever it was that motivated the gamblers of Las Vegas.

My spirits were low when I met a waitress whom I'll call Alice at a restaurant where I sometimes ate. Alice was unlike any woman I'd seen in Vegas. She seemed like a wholesome, sweet, and innocent girl who could've been a high school cheerleader.

One evening while I brooded and toyed with my food, she came over with my check and said, "I've noticed you always seem so sad. Have you been losing badly?" Seeing an expression of concern on her pretty face, I answered, "No, I don't even play." Since her shift was ending, I nonchalantly invited her to join me. With a curious look in her smile, she said, "OK, let me just change."

She returned wearing a light loose summer dress, conservative by Vegas standards but light enough for me to guess she had a beautiful figure. She asked, "If you're not here to gamble, what are you doing in Las Vegas?" I explained I was on assignment. Puzo's name gave me instant credibility.

As I'd noticed she wore no makeup and seemed like a genuine all-American girl, I asked, "What's a sweet girl like you doing in Las Vegas?" "I was born here, lived here all my life," she answered. "Right now I'm working here, but I'm taking night courses in management."

Listening, I looked at her innocent demeanor and lovely face, and found myself deeply attracted. But when she told me she was 23, I laughed and said, "At 47, I could be your father. But I'd be proud to have a daughter like you." She laughed and surprised me by saying, "Actually I prefer older men. They're usually kinder and more interesting than men my age."

I didn't know if she was daring me, but I asked, "Would you go out with me?" She immediately answered, "I'd love to." It seemed too simple, but she made my invitation seem natural.

That night we went out. She confided, "I wanted to go to college but my family couldn't afford it. I always regretted that. That's why I'm going to night school." She said, "There were hard times," but she cheerfully refused to dwell upon them. She seemed so optimistic, I couldn't help comparing her with my neurotic, sad French aristocrat.

Watching Alice's smiling face, I felt my gloom lifting. By the end of an enchanting evening, she had seduced me with her natural charm. I drove her home, off the strip, where she had a small rented apartment. I expected no more than a goodnight kiss but she invited me in for a nightcap. We became lovers that first night. At dawn, when I left her apartment, I forgot my inhibitions about being twice her age.

The next few weeks, we saw each other daily. Eventually, she confessed she had fallen in love with me. I couldn't say the same but I was smitten. Though Vegas was depressing, I felt creative again.

My assignment would soon be over, and the thought saddened us both. We didn't want our affair to end. One evening, seeing her pretty face so sad moved me to say, "You're unattached. I'm free. Why can't you come with me to New York and Europe where I have assignments waiting?" Her face beamed with joy. "Yes, yes, yes," she said. "I've always wanted to see New York."

I hadn't thought out my invitation, but I had lived alone for too long. I enjoyed her company and was sure she'd cheer me up and ease the emptiness between assignments.

On our last evening in Vegas, Alice seemed pensive. I feared she was having second thoughts and said, "Alice, you can still change your mind." She answered, "No, I'm afraid you might change your mind." After falling silent for a long time, she said, "I tried to tell you but I couldn't." Then she blurted out in a confessional hush, "Several years ago I was a call girl in Vegas until I got arrested by an undercover cop. Now I have a record. I was 18 years old. It was a terrible mistake."

I was stunned. I wondered how I could have thought she was so pure and innocent when in fact, her story made sense in that gambling city's culture of greed and lust. I felt profoundly naive as a man and more so as a journalist. But when she said, "John, that was a long time ago," I remembered this was a woman who just canceled her lease, sold her car, quit her job, and applied for the first passport in her life to go away with me. All I could say without much conviction was, "Let's give our lives a little fun."

After 14 weeks in Las Vegas, we took off for New York. It was early September 1976. Alice, Yukiko, and Chris got along well on their first meeting. Yukiko had the impression Alice was a sweet girl and felt comfortable enough to invite us to dinner the next day.

At the office, Jeanette Chapnick was truly happy for me. When we visited Neil Schwartz and his wife Mare in Pawling, New York, Neil took me aside and said, "She's an all-American girl, just like a cheerleader." It was funny Neil had the same impression of Alice as I did upon our first meeting in Vegas. Mare whispered, "Alice is so sweet. She's like an angel."

The enthusiastic reception Alice received eased the sadness I originally felt when she confessed her past. I began to think of her as a victim of Vegas's environment. Perhaps I was fooling myself, but I wanted to forget.

Showing her New York's wonders for the first time, I took her to the observation deck of the Empire State Building. She seemed bored visiting the Museum of Modern Art and Metropolitan Museum, but was excited to see Broadway at night: a world of neon light was closer to her than the old masters and modern artists.

In mid-September, we flew to Paris. On our overnight TWA flight, we spoke of finding her a measure of financial independence and agreed she'd work for me as an assistant on a monthly salary. I could afford to take her on most assignments in Europe and couldn't imagine her waiting for my return, alone in Paris without knowing the language.

When we entered my Paris apartment, Alice jumped with joy, repeating over and over, "It's so romantic." When she discovered I never cooked for myself but had a fully equipped kitchen, she wanted to cook our first supper together in Paris. It was a wonderful dinner and my first home-cooked meal in a long time.

The next two months were fun as we traveled through France and Norway. Alice was a fast learner, and soon I could rely on her to take notes and dictation. She quickly learned enough French to shop and travel on her own. Our adventure had overtones of a Pygmalion story as I spent hours making her repeat French words she had difficulty pronouncing, like *raccrocher*, "hang up," and *rappeler*, "call back." Together, we were like two ex-sinners: I betrayed Yukiko, and she had sold herself.

At dinner on the second floor of the Eiffel Tower with its magnificent views of "the city of light," I explained the difference between New York and Paris. Unsure whether she was interested, I summarized, "Essentially, Paris glorifies and restores its past while Manhattan constantly builds its present and its future."

In a way, I assumed the role of teacher, while Alice seemed like an eager student, anxious to please and always in a cheerful mood, even when I was deep in thought about a future project. Nothing spoiled our idyllic days together except the nagging memory of her confession, recurring every time I thought of making love.

I tried hard to forget, but her businesslike approach to sex always reminded me. It was ironic—before I knew her past, I admired her total lack of sexual inhibition and found it extraordinarily natural. In time, I desired her less and less and was sorry she had felt a "compelling need" to confess.

In May 1978, Alice and I bid goodbye to family and friends in France. We headed "home" to New York on a Pan American flight and settled in the Gramercy Park Hotel. Howard Chapnick greeted me like a dear brother who'd been truly missed.

In Manhattan, fruitlessly searching for an apartment with a view, I became intrigued by an ad for a highrise in Fort Lee, New Jersey, at 1590 Anderson Avenue, where an extra-large apartment on the 18th floor with a panoramic view was available. It was so huge, our Paris apartment could have fit in the living room. From the balcony and all its windows, we could see the George Washington Bridge with traffic passing silently in the distance. Below was the building's swimming pool. To the east was the Hudson River flowing south toward a shimmering Manhattan, its skyscrapers beautifully lit at sunset.

I immediately signed a two-year lease. Alice and I were excited to move, but we knew something had ended in Paris. We had become bored with each other, and I doubted an apartment with a panoramic view of the Hudson would make a difference.

Fort Lee seemed dull after returning from a thought-provoking assignment in Chile. There I had celebrated my 50th birthday alone on a mountaintop in the Chilean desert watching the awesome, indescribable beauty of the Magellan clouds and canopy of stars. The overwhelming sight led me to wonder what we amounted to, we human creatures, and to ponder the significance of our place in that chaotic, fiery, and extraordinarily beautiful spectacle above.

During the month-long assignment for the German magazine, *Geo*, which was originally inspired by *National Geographic*, I'd travel that soul-searching experience every night in the Southern European observatory, La Silla, some 300 miles north of Santiago and 8,000 feet high in the Chilean desert mountains bordering the Pacific.

It was an inspiring assignment. I found it intellectually stimulating to have countless conversations with Europe's brightest astronomers after their nightly observations of the galaxies. With a text by well-known German science writer, Hoimar V. Ditfurth, the story was published with 19 pages in the July 1979 issue of *Geo*.

Home again in Fort Lee, I was forced to contemplate my tattered life and relationship with Alice instead of the stars. I could sense our affair was nearly over. Though I enjoyed the deep solitude I felt in the Chilean desert, I again feared the loneliness of an empty apartment.

I missed my old life. As holidays approached, I called Yukiko and dropped some hints about her traditional Christmas dinner. Generous as always, she said of course Alice and I could join her for what turned out to be a memorable day.

I had given Chris a Super-8 Beaulieu movie camera a few years earlier, and he showed me his latest films. I was relieved he was fascinated with filmmaking instead of photojournalism, which I believed had reached the end of its glory years.

On that Christmas day I marveled at how easily Yukiko and Alice got along. The atmosphere was festive and full of laughter as we exchanged gifts before settling around a table adorned with tasty dishes and a golden turkey.

The dinner had the feel of a family reunion, but it was the last meal Alice would share with Yukiko and Chris. Within months, our doomed relationship simply ended. She met someone else who wanted to marry her, and I too had met someone else. It was pointless to go on, and in the summer of 1979, we went our separate ways.

THE PROMISE

SIGRID AND A SHANGRI-LA STORY

LIECHTENSTEIN 1979–1994

Near the end of the 1970s, I presented to *National Geographic*'s Bill Garrett a well-researched suggestion for an essay on the "Golden Triangle" of Burma, Laos, and Thailand. Garrett was impressed but said, "John, your idea has to wait. After all the flak we got from our readers following reports we did on Harlem and the apartheid in South Africa, what we need now is a Shangri-La story to calm our readers and lift their spirits."

I didn't know exactly what a Shangri-La story was but imagined the Principality of Liechtenstein qualified. Located in a valley and sandwiched between mountainous Austria and Switzerland, Liechtenstein stretched only 20 miles end to end. It had one of the highest per-capita incomes in the world, and there was no unemployment. The police force enlisted only 25 officers, and jails were seldom occupied. A criminal lucky enough to be behind bars in the picture-postcard capital city of Vaduz was served meals catered by one of the finest restaurants.

The last time Liechtenstein went to war was during the Austro-Prussian conflict in the nineteenth century when the ruling prince dispatched soldiers to help Austria. In their six-week expedition, they never saw combat or reached the front. They returned home to Vaduz with an Austrian who joined their contingent in Feldkirch: 80 fighters had left for war and 81 returned.

Years earlier, as *Geographic*'s Robert Gilka reminded me in April 1979, I had written a story suggestion about Liechtenstein. It was the smallest and least ambitious subject proposed in 20 years but the idea struck me as a pleasant diversion.

Two months of photography in Liechtenstein led to a rendezvous with destiny. There I met Sigrid Mayer, a tall, elegant, and beautiful Viennese woman. A 38-year-old lawyer practicing at a leading firm in the capital, she had never

married and enjoyed her independence. We began a relationship that evolved into a lasting commitment.

In September, Sigrid made her first American journey and joined me in New Jersey at my apartment overlooking the George Washington Bridge. Before she left for a tour of New England, she met Chris, who had composed a song for her based on my descriptions of what she was like. Yukiko invited us to dinner and eventually the two women became friends.

Despite several trips, our transatlantic romance was not easy to sustain. By 1981, fearing our relationship might fade away and knowing I'd miss her, I realized I had to give up my home base in America.

My agents Howard Chapnick in New York and Barbara Grosset in Paris were convinced I'd get plenty of assignments based in Europe, so in May 1981, I took off for Paris. Chris was hurt and refused to help me pack.

My younger brother Jacquot met me at the airport with a trailer to carry my 14 cases of equipment. At my family reunion, it was clear I had become a complete stranger to everyone. As a point of honor, I insisted, "I'm not returning to France. Paris will just be one base. The other will be Liechtenstein." No one in my family cared one way or the other, since by then I had merely become an abstract figure in their lives.

In August 1981, my father died in his sleep: he was 81. My mother's death at 76 in February 1975 had not filled me with sorrow at her funeral, though I had forgiven her long ago. With my father, my feelings were something else. For a year, I had tried to pry open the story of his life, but in vain, so in the end he took with him the account of hard times he considered of "no importance." He'd always say, "The past is the past."

The rest of 1981 Sigrid and I spent renovating a loft with nineteenth-century wooden beams that we had bought in Paris. Together we designed the interior, working with various craftsmen. Then came the most disturbing occurence of my life: from May through July 1982, I found myself in a total manic state.

While writing and photographing a concept for an international bank's luxurious 24-page color brochure, I demanded 14-hour days from my team, and we finished the project in three weeks. At the final projection, the art director, my Paris agent, and the bank's president thought it was brilliant, but I knew it could have been better.

It became difficult to sleep. My imagination raced at such speed, I couldn't articulate it. Ideas overflowed. I'd drink countless bottles of mineral water and stand under a cold shower for hours to cool my mind.

Flooded with grandiose thoughts, I concocted a master plan for peace in the Middle East. To carry it out, I spontaneously recruited a staff of peacemakers at the Harris Bar in Paris. I hired a trilingual driver who was fluent in Arabic, Hebrew, and French, and kept him and his Mercedes on call 24 hours a day. It seemed that he believed in my peace plan—only the people closest to me realized I was breaking down. In short, I was losing my mind.

Not even my dentist questioned me when I told him the reason I was having so many problems with my bridge. I informed him that he "failed to calculate the rotation of the earth." At that point, Sigrid consulted a psychiatrist in Austria and another in Paris. She then met with my dear friend Barbara Grosset—after they slipped a powerful tranquilizer in my orange juice, they convinced me I needed to rest.

Barbara suggested I go to a château clinic for VIPs near Paris, and I agreed to go for a week if the clinic accepted my American Blue Cross Blue Shield insurance. I was told they'd accept the coverage, though later I learned they had never heard of it.

I was diagnosed as suffering from "hypomania." The American Heritage Dictionary defined it as "a mild state of mania involving slightly abnormal elation and overactivity." In my case, I was in a state of euphoria.

At the luxurious clinic, I accepted medication orally but absolutely refused injections. Consequently, two burly male nurses tied me up and injected me with

massive doses of haloperidol for about a week. I fell into a deep coma and was rushed to the intensive care unit of the American Hospital in Neuilly, France.

When I woke up two days later, I had no idea where I was or what had happened. The cardiologist, Dr. Pierre Groussin, simply said, "You came back from afar. You must have a strong heart." All my brothers and sisters had been summoned in anticipation of my death—I didn't realize I had come so close to the edge. My full recovery closed a strange and frightening chapter of my life.

In 1983, during a time of depression and deep anxiety, I was terribly afraid hypomania would strike again and checked for all the symptoms. An Austrian psychiatrist, Dr. Radmeyer, assured, "Hypomania usually strikes at a much younger age. Since you are now 54 and have no prior history of it, I'm convinced it will not strike you again in your lifetime."

In the spring of the following year, I began a project in Switzerland, only 120 miles from Sigrid's home. It was about a 77-year-old man who fought for 35 years to save the storks in Switzerland. I was still depressed, so the idea of one man fighting alone appealed to me.

Dr. Max Bloesch was a short, wiry, former schoolmaster from the Swiss region of Solothurn, commonly known by children as "Mr. Stork." Selfless and dedicated, he was profoundly disturbed by "man's idiotic destruction" of nature. "People used to take great pride in their storks and believed their presence brought good luck," Bloesch told me. Across Western Europe, farmers had constructed round platforms on their barn roofs for storks to build their nests, but after World War II, storks began to disappear.

Surveying Switzerland in the summer of 1949, Bloesch was horrified that only one nest remained in the country. "In postwar industrial recovery," he said, "the stork's source of food was depleted as countless feeding grounds in Western Europe were drained or taken over by industry, ushering in a permanent exodus of white storks. By 1970, most storks never returned from their migration to the Nile Valley and Africa. They all but vanished from Western Europe."

In the early 1950s, experts suggested that the only way to keep storks in Switzerland was to cut their wingtips. Still angry, Bloesch recalled, "I told those doctors I did not want another zoo with crippled storks in a cage. I've seen pelicans with cut limbs in zoos, and it's a sad sight children should never see. I want children to see storks in flight like I did."

Bloesch embarked on an acclimatization project to bring storks back to Switzerland. With his personal savings and a few donations from academic friends, he began his mission.

After years of research and consultations with prominent European ornithologists, Bloesch went to France and Algeria to bring back young storks to mate in the Swiss village of Altreu. In a sense, Bloesch bet on love, knowing that when storks unite, it was usually for life.

Over two decades, "Mr. Stork" created 22 acclimatization stations for the storks of Switzerland. The principal Altreu station provided stork couples free of charge to West Germany, France, Sweden, and the Netherlands so long as they followed the "Bloesch Method."

By 1985, Switzerland's stork population reached 400. In West Germany, Max-Planck Institute ornithologist, Dr. Gerhard Thielcke, insisted, "Without Bloesch, the white storks would have vanished completely from Western Europe."

I stayed with the project through spring, summer, and winter, and slowly I overcame my anxiety. My last photograph was of three storks that missed their summer flight to North Africa. Their wing tips froze in 26 degrees below zero weather as they landed awkwardly on upper branches of black trees lining a frozen stream. I watched them flapping their wings violently to remove ice from their feathers as they landed in the mist hovering above the stream. They settled on their high perch after a last pathetic effort to take off.

The three storks missed their summer flight south. They reminded me that in my depression, I missed many journeys as well. But as I focused a long lens on ice covering their frozen wings, I understood my mind was no longer frozen. I could function again—I could take off again. My depression ended. When I showed a projection of the storks to Sigrid, she too understood. Pictures of the storks were widely published in Europe and America. It was the last project in my career, ending more than 30 years of photojournalism.

For the next eight years, I worked on highly paid corporate assignments until official retirement in 1993. Those assignments required exceptional photography, color filters, and special effects. It was satisfying to make beautiful photographs, but for me, photography without journalism was not interesting. Trying to make a pharmaceutical corporation's ordinary assembly line look glamorous or exciting struck me as the antithesis of my life with a camera.

In 1997, as I was writing with my son, I sold all my cameras and photographic gear. I realized I didn't miss photography even though I often saw pictures in my head, traveling or watching scenes unfold from my seat in a café.

At that time, uppermost in my mind was a meeting I had years earlier, in November 1979, with Don Schanche. Formerly an editor at *Life, The Saturday Evening Post,* and *Holiday* magazine, Don was then a Middle East correspondent

for the *Los Angeles Times*. The big news was about Iran and fanatics who had abducted the staff of the American embassy.

After narrowly escaping Teheran, Don met with me in his Cairo apartment. We spent the whole night discussing our lives and times. When we parted, he made me promise to write my memoirs. "I'll be your editor," he said, but it was not to be.

Shortly before Don died in Florida on November 17, 1994, he made me promise again. I am keeping my promise.

L'AMÉRICAIN

John Launois

NOVEMBER 23, 1928 - MAY 5, 2002

EPILOGUE

CHRIS PAN LAUNOIS

On a Sunday afternoon in the spring of 2002, my father, John Launois, "*l'Américain*," died in his sleep from heart failure at the home he shared for 23 years with his wife, Sigrid, in Liechtenstein. He was 73.

That day, May 5, Sigrid called my mother, Yukiko, in Manhattan, to tell her the sad news. My mother called me at my bandmate Cassandre's apartment. Shaken and upset, Cassandre mumured, "Your father," and handed me the phone.

"Daddy's dead," my mother said, crying and pausing on the phone. "Now you're the man in the family." I couldn't respond as she said, "You have to go on." I listened quietly, unable to speak, as tears were silently falling from my cheek.

My father had called me a few days earlier from Liechtenstein to say he had just returned from the hospital after being treated for heart and breathing problems. It was difficult for him to speak clearly. When we hung up, I cried inexplicably. Though Sigrid was confident he'd be fine once his medication took effect, the doctors hadn't told her how serious his condition was. Somehow, intuitively, I knew immediately after that phone call that it might be his last.

As Sigrid made arrangements for the funeral, I booked a flight to Vienna to meet her in Austria. My father was to be buried in Baden's cemetery. I asked my mother if she wanted to come with me to the funeral. "It's probably better if you go alone and take care of Sigrid," she said. "This is her ceremony and her time to mourn."

My mother mourned in her own way. For the week following my father's death, she was very ill. "When you lose your husband," she'd say in a letter, "at least you have the memories to cherish, but not if he betrayed you. Though I think I forgave John a long time ago; when he died, it felt as if he had come back to me."

The Pan, my rock and roll band, had a show scheduled at the Continental the day before my departure. I dedicated it to my father. My guitarist, who lost his own father years earlier, thought I should cancel. I wanted the show to go on as a tribute. I was sure it was what my father would have counseled. He was with me in every word and every step on the stage. The next day, I took my flight.

When I arrived in Baden, I could see Sigrid was suffering terribly but was amazed at how brave she remained. Though seemingly strong on the surface, we both were in shock.

On a Friday afternoon in May, ceremonies were held in a church by the Baden cemetery. I glanced up to see Sigrid's glistening eyes, knowing she had lost her closest friend and only beloved. My father always had a flair for the dramatic, yet not even he could have foreseen such a sudden demise. Though he was often an impossible man, he had a beautiful heart. Mellowing with age, finally settled into the creative life of a writer in a comfortable home in a beautiful corner of the world, he was ironically forbidden from enjoying the fruits of his last endeavor.

Prior to May 5, we were certain my father and I would finish *L'Américain* together and we'd all celebrate. But we ran out of time. Working together on the book for seven years, he and I became closer. As creative allies, we reached a higher ground of camaraderie. Then destiny twisted the ending.

My mother, Sigrid, and I agreed *L'Américain* should end with an epilogue I'd write, drawing on his notes, files, and our collective memories to complete the arc of my father's life story. In Baden, in a house she shared with her sister, I recorded interviews with Sigrid about her years with my father. Sigrid had always encouraged him to tell his story.

To fill some gaps in his life's account, I'll refer to him as John. For his Liechtenstein assignment, John flew first to Switzerland where *Geographic* booked him a room in the Dolder, the most prestigious hotel in Zürich.

Geographic's writer, Robert Booth, phoned to say, "John, everything is great in Liechtenstein. It's beautiful." It was beautiful but not exciting. As John saw it, there were picture-postcard images everywhere but little for a photojournalist.

On May 23, 1979, while John was seated at an outdoor café with Walter Wohlwend, his Liechtenstein press contact and guide, an attorney named Dr. Sigrid Mayer strolled by, heading home from work. Vaduz was a small town where "everybody knows everyone," so Walter called out to Sigrid and made an introduction.

Over dinner, John obviously liked Sigrid, and she found him interesting as well. As weeks went by, John relentlessly tried to impress her. At first, Sigrid found his stories about exotic places hard to believe but eventually realized they were true.

Since John was denied access to photograph the country's small prison, Sigrid called a judge, a good friend, who granted John permission to photograph the jail cells, which were empty at the time. His Liechtenstein story was published in the February 1981 issue of *National Geographic*.

After the story was completed, John returned to America. During Sigrid's visit in the fall of 1979, my mother and I found her to be a very engaging, beautiful, and charming woman who might bring stability to my father's turbulent life.

John was still plagued by the anxiety of waiting for assignments in an ever-narrowing field, and continued to feel guilt about destroying his marriage with Yukiko. So when John was apart from Sigrid, he'd drink heavily. He expressed his longing for her in a tape recording made at the end of a visit to Liechtenstein.

"All my life," he recorded, "I have searched, and I have searched, and then I met you here in this small country, and you give me so much that I do not believe I can live without you. Please overlook what might appear a melodramatic aspect of what I'm saying and think about a man, or rather a boy, who believed in an idealistic, kind world, and then learned the hard way that this world, or his world, does not exist, yet he still searches for some kind of rationality. It is obvious today that it was a dream, but I refuse not to dream, and perhaps I'm right in a sense, because dreams do come true. They do come true—I met you, and you changed my life. You taught me to laugh again, just to laugh, and you have given me great moments of happiness."

By 1982, he relocated to Paris, and though able to see Sigrid more often, John all too often felt the sting of a career in decline. When he presented photos of Egyptian children to Bill Garrett at *Geographic*, Garrett remembered it as "a sad day." He had to tell John, "There just isn't anything here we can use."

Noting the excessive drinking and depression, Garrett worried John might spin out of control. Because of John's drinking, Sigrid began to worry too. They argued as she noticed all the bottles in her bar disappearing. As a wave of insecurity peaked from an intangible source, a breakdown was surfacing.

In the summer of 1982, vacationing with Sigrid in Skiathos, Greece, John, no longer drinking heavily, began to act strangely. From Greece, he'd send telexes to *National Geographic* about world peace. He said he needed a genius sent to him urgently to work on his "Middle East peace plan." Bob Gilka responded, "We have no genius."

While in Paris, John sent his newly hired chauffeur to deliver a note to the president of France. The note read: "Dear President Mitterand, On behalf of the American people, we wish you a Happy Fourth of July." Black Star's Ben Chapnick had the impression John was nervous about taking on new assignments and found it increasingly difficult to understand their conversations.

At first, Black Star's Jeanette Chapnick thought John was having some brilliant brainstorm but quickly realized something was terribly amiss. His ego was inflating while plagued by self-doubt.

John began to demonstrate extreme pathological behavior—delusions of grandeur, rash spending, outpourings of scientific gibberish—in short, suffering a terrible bout of hypomania he thankfully overcame with haloperidol medication. During a long recovery, John searched for story ideas. But as his manic euphoria faded, he found it difficult to find enthusiasm to create an assignment.

Beginning in the summer of 1983, he stayed when he could in Sigrid's home in Liechtenstein overlooking the serene mountain peaks of Switzerland by the Rhine. Though it was a tranquil place, he was still insecure about his mental state. His recovery began with his discovery of Dr. Max Bloesch and the struggle of "Mr. Stork" to preserve the beautiful white storks of Switzerland. Seeing the assignment as a way out of his depression, he worked through three seasons to get his pictures.

It was clear to Sigrid and his colleagues at Black Star and Rapho that John had reclaimed his faculties. His photography was again elegant and first-rate, and his spirits lifted in a surge of optimism. Though *National Geographic* turned it down, the stork story appeared in European and American magazines, most notably in the February 1985 issue of *Bunte* in Germany. Yukiko and Howard Chapnick entered the work in competition. In 1986, "The Storks" won second prize for best single picture in the nature category at the prestigious Press Photo World Awards in Amsterdam.

John's last venture in photojournalism coincided with a happy event. He had asked Sigrid to be his wife in the early 1980s. At the time, Sigrid did not feel marriage was necessary even though John saw it as symbolically important. After his hypomanic episode, John never brought up the subject again, but in 1985, Sigrid asked if he still wanted to marry. He joyfully said "Yes." They were wed at last in Vienna on May 2, 1985 and celebrated with a honeymoon in Spain.

Based in Liechtenstein and Paris, John left photojournalism behind after the stork project and worked on high-pay corporate photography assignments. But corporate jobs were meaningless to him. When Sigrid realized how terribly unhappy he was, she suggested he just stop. He had worked long enough to retire comfortably.

As might have been predicted, my father was too restless to enjoy retirement. He needed to feel engaged in world events and voraciously read the *International Herald Tribune, Harper's,* and other periodicals.

In the late 1980s as the Berlin Wall came down and Chinese tanks crushed a people's movement in Beijing, John looked to America to lead the world by example but was troubled by domestic and international policies of the Reagan-Bush administration. He welcomed the Clinton presidency in 1992 yet he was content neither with America's behavior as a global leader or his own inaction. Writing his autobiography was always in his mind, but he seemed unable to start.

His retirement was final in 1997 when he sold all his photographic equipment. Visiting him in Liechtenstein in 1996, I felt I had to do something to get his memories on paper, so I asked him to just start telling me his story and I'd write it down.

There were arguments and tense rewrites, but we had begun. Eventually, he handwrote and then typed his drafts for me to refine. Sigrid was delighted he was in a better mood, doing something creative. I returned several times to Liechtenstein to work with my father on the manuscript, little realizing he might not live to see it published.

But his vision began to fail. In August 2001, John learned that he had macular degeneration in both eyes. It was the ultimate irony for a photojournalist. He wrote: "What do you say to someone whose whole life has been dedicated to seeing and understanding, when he can no longer see? You say nothing, for without seeing, he will no longer hear you, for he cannot see you."

As the world in his eyes became hazier, there was still hope that treatment might save his vision, but his anxiety of going blind was relentless.

Then on September 11, New York's World Trade Center Towers were destroyed in the al Qaeda terrorist attack on America. For me, it was a personal loss when a dear and courageous friend, Vinnie Kane, perished as a firefighter in the heroic 9/11 rescue effort; for my father, it was a tragedy that inflicted a forlorn sadness as if hope for a more peaceful world was an impossible dream.

For months after 9/11, he read and watched news compulsively, and was unable to write another word of the book. While I was angry at our government's foreign policies and dependence on oil from undemocratic nations, which I believed had plunged us into the new century's political nightmare, he'd tell me we were faced with "a clash of civilizations."

Yukiko wrote to him: "It's interesting that you and I and those who came to America from outside seem to be more patriotic than those born in America." She went on to say how happy she had been to read about America's generosity at a time when the country was so widely criticized as a bullying superpower. At the bottom of my mother's letter, my father wrote, "Yukiko became an American patriot. This is the genius of the American human experiment."

In 2002 it appeared that John's vision might not deteriorate any further, so Sigrid bought him expensive, high-powered lamps for his diminished eyesight so he could finish his book. Just as plans were finalized to install an elaborate lighting system, John had to be rushed to a hospital in Switzerland to treat severe heart problems and water in the lungs.

My father called to say he was scheduled for another hospital visit in a few days, but his voice was not the same. Saturday night, he stayed up late, smoking and drinking until he fell asleep. Sunday afternoon, while sleeping, he stopped breathing. He seemed to be at peace.

Sigrid said, "It is still difficult to believe John is gone and nothing will bring him back. He was so much a part of my life, and I miss him awfully. The doctor only told me afterward how serious his condition was and must have been for at least a year. His book was nearly finished but not quite—it was John's greatest wish to have the book published."

As my father was writing his story, he was never sure how it would end. For a while, he wanted to travel across America with me to trace his American roots, but we never had time. A long time ago, when there was a kind of distance between us, I recorded a song called, "Son," based on his words to me: "Son, come, sit by me. I have not had the chance to speak to you. You must now find your own way. I am afraid you may not see the truth. Do you? All I'm trying to say is I care. Do you see? All I've done, I've fought and now, you must take over my son."

Over the last decade of my father's life, searching for a way to tell his story, he'd repeatedly ask me, "Who am I to you?" It was never an easy question to answer. After his death, I dreamt my father was still alive as I was showing him notes for this epilogue. Looking over the pages, he said, "What's the point? I won't even be able to read it when it's done."

On Memorial Day, a few weeks after his death, I dreamt of a Japanese symbol with projected images of castles flickering on the wall. Describing the dream to my mother, she told me the Japanese typography signified the river of mankind. In the dream, as I was packing my suitcase and guitar, John's last remaining camera fell to the floor as Sigrid waited for me by the door. In the hall, my father and I hugged as we simultaneously said, "I love you so much." As he walked down the hall with my mother dressed in black, I asked, "Aren't we going the same way?" He answered, "We'll hold the elevator for you." But I knew in the dream that Sigrid and I would have to join them later as the elevator door closed.

After his funeral, I noticed my mother, who since their divorce never displayed a photograph of John in her apartment, was suddenly framing pictures of their wedding and of John when he was young. It was as if he had returned to her after 30 years.

John telephoned Yukiko a few weeks before his death. As usual, it was late at night, a time when he'd be at his sentimental best. He told her that she was a remarkable person and that he was grateful for her being so good to him: she could have stepped on him when he was down and broken, but she never did. He said that he loved her and always would. They both cried and said goodnight. He died a few weeks later.

In that unhappy month of May, Yukiko wrote Sigrid, "Now that John is gone, I'm bewildered by the size of the void he has left behind. When you met, he was a broken man, lonely and tormented. You took him in, cared for him, and nursed him back to life. I have nothing but gratitude and admiration for you. I always felt somehow responsible for John's well being, so it was a comfort to know that he found happiness and peace in his life with you."

Before I left to attend my father's funeral, Jeanette Chapnick wrote a note, which meant the world to me: "Your dad was very grateful for the help and encouragement you always gave him. I hope your trip will not be too sad. You have been a good son." Of all the words on earth, those were what I needed to hear most.

What I often remember about my father was his belief in me, his support of my aspirations, and his relentlessly telling me, "I love you, son." He inspired me to understand that "courage is freedom." Despite his romantic nature and innocent idealism, he was realistic enough to know you are bound for trouble if you care for the world. Nonetheless, you do your best, to fight the good fight.

I'm thankful for inheriting my father's rebellious character, guided by his belief that "the first duty of a free man is to be well informed." His story urges me to appreciate freedom and the food on the table, and reminds me to rebel amid the feeble signposts of oppression and shadowy banality of inhumanity. And though riding the storm in pursuit of "life, liberty, and happiness" may not reconcile the challenges of "the new frontier," such daring might set the stage to turn the tide.

"L'Américain" was a boy who fell in love with America, grateful for her generosity. Though he was as unfinished and imperfect as the idea of America, he was as well loved.

To his unfading question, "Who am I to you?" my answer remains, "You are the voice I will always hear in darkness and in light, the true friend forever gone and forever by my side."

John Launois was a man who took pictures. If he were with us, he would have seen a picture speaking a thousand words: On a chilly autumn day in Manhattan, I watched as Yukiko and Sigrid walked together down a windy street. Yukiko shivered. Sigrid wrapped her coat around her and embraced her. Then they walked on through the icy breeze and fallen leaves. ●

-FIN-

ACKNOWLEDGMENTS

CHRIS PAN LAUNOIS

For the publication of *L'Américain*, I must first thank my father for telling the story of his life in the seven years before he died. Without him, there'd be no story.

Equal thanks go to his wife and widow, Sigrid, whose unyielding support and love enabled my father to live, to tell his tale. She encouraged him to write his story, even when he found it emotionally hard to do so. Without Sigrid, this book, *L'Américain*, would not have been written or published.

And thanks go to my mother, Yukiko, for cataloging and editing the vast expanse of my father's photographic work for this manuscript, a task that only she, being close to my father's photojournalistic work, could have realized.

Thanks also to my father's good friends who urged him to leave behind his story, particularly his colleague, Don Connery, who on late night phone calls supported my father's ambition to tell his tale, and helped me navigate the terrain of cowriting a book with my father.

Thanks go to editor Abigail Wilentz and book designer Timothy Hsu, for respectively bringing greater clarity and an engaging rhythm to the text, and creating a beautiful design for the book.

Thanks for the digital imaging by graphic artist Claudia Miranda (graphicartist25@gmail.com), who also designed our site: www.LAmericain.com.

We are grateful to Regina Ryan, book producer and literary agent, who believed in *L'Américain* from the start. She not only brought together the extraordinarily talented team that created the finished work but went over virtually every detail of its editing and production to ensure the book was of the highest quality.

And finally, thanks to America itself for making my father's dreams possible, and to all our generous friends who've given us encouragement to tell the rebellious and adventurous story of *L'Américain*. ●

INDEX

> **Immense bonheur—tristesse infinie. Je t'aime pour la vie.** -Jean

TOKYO AUGUST 12, 1957